Western Portraiture,

AND

EMIGRANTS' GUIDE:

A DESCRIPTION OF

WISCONSIN, ILLINOIS, AND IOWA;

WITH REMARKS ON

MINNESOTA, AND OTHER TERRITORIES.

BY DANIEL S. CURTISS.

NEW YORK:
PUBLISHED BY J. H. COLTON,
86 CEDAR STREET.
1852.

STEREOTYPED AND PRINTED BY PUDNEY & RUSSELL, 79 JOHN-ST.

Dedication:

TO HENRY O'RIELLY, ESQ.:

Whose vast Enterprise has been eminently advantageous to The West; who extended a generous confidence to me at an early age and when a stranger—Confidence, the noblest principle in Human Nature, as Faith is the sublimest in Christianity—and whose manly friendship I have subsequently enjoyed, this Book is cordially Dedicated as a Token of Grateful Remembrance

By the

AUTHOR.

CONTENTS.

PREFACE.

Most persons who design emigrating to The West—whether Americans or Foreigners—have but a limited, and often incorrect, knowledge of that region—its lands, resources, facilities, and business—of the distinguishing features of different sections; hence, they cannot easily determine which way to direct their course; so that they are anxious to make inquiries, and elicit facts, from those who are acquainted with that country; which, at most, is a limited means of information. It would be convenient and advantageous to emigrants, to have, before starting, some general and reliable statements, respecting the distinct characteristics of the various Western States, or of the different portions of each of those states; it might save them much travel and expense.

There have been published several very useful and interesting Guides and Gazetteers of the West—*for times past*—but the transformations, the improvements, are so rapid and extensive, that those books give only slight and imperfect knowledge of that progressive region, as the *present* finds it. So quick and numerous are the changes in the West, that the traveler of the spring, returning by the same route in autumn, scarcely knows his whereabouts; and the pioneer who makes a summer's visit to his old home-place, is equally surprised, on his return, at the changes which have taken place, the advancement made there, and he hardly recognizes the locality of his new home, after the short absence of one season. Immigrants have "located," new shantees have been stuck up, and they even succeeded by new houses, new fences have been made, new roads laid, and new ditches dug.

The enchanting power of industry, in a genial clime, on a fertile soil, has done this; but it is not illusory enchantment.

Thus, the descriptive book of the earlier days, is but a dim volume now; and another is wanted nearly as much as if the first were not written.

To try to supply this want, to that enterprising class, is the object of the writer in preparing this little volume—in a plain and faithful narrative of facts, in regard to appearances, prospects, and statistics, of the Great West.

While traveling several years, on business connected with newspapers and telegraph lines, through the states of WISCONSIN, ILLINOIS, and IOWA, spending some time in nearly all of the principal towns and cities, the writer made examinations of the soil, and collected facts of business and progress, which enable him to give generally correct and familiar descriptions of the great and various resources of those states—their lands, mines, improvements, conveyances, markets, etc., the peculiarities of the different tracts of land—from personal inspection; and all contrasted with the facts and condition a few years previous.

Some general remarks are also given upon the character and prospects of *Minnesota*, though but briefly, as the writer is less acquainted with that territory than with the three states named.

It is not pretended, in this little Emigrant Manual, to furnish extended and detailed accounts of the discovery and early trials and settlement of the West, as that is more the sphere of the historian, than of the traveling delineator, whose aim is to portray present scenes and aspects, yet some brief items of history are given.

Still, the more fully and forcibly to convey some adequate knowledge of the rich resources and proud progress of the New Country, the writings of several interesting Tourists, in 1833, 1837, and 1846, have been freely examined, and extended extracts copied from them, that the present may be more clearly appreciated, as viewed in contrast with the past.

The extensive system of Railroads and other Improvements which the Western States have recently projected—and are engaged in, soon to be completed—have excited at the East a lively and increased interest in the destiny of the New States, eliciting more earnest attention to them, and inducing more numerous emigration from among the wealthy and business classes of the older states.

Besides, millions of the surplus means of Eastern capitalists have, within a short period, been invested in the Internal Improvements of the New states, which also tends to enlist curiosity and attention toward the West, creating greater earnestness for knowledge in regard to that region, as to its operations and natural resources.

It is hoped and intended that this work shall, to some satisfactory degree, gratify that desire, and thus secure for it a ready sale among those interested.

Those great and popular national enterprises—a line of Telegraph, with stockades of armed and mounted mail-carriers, and a Railroad to the Pacific—are becoming earnestly-talked-of projects, demanding the special attention of the General Government, having enlisted the lively exertions of many Senators and Representatives in Congress.

Under these circumstances, the great Mississippi Valley country becomes invested with a more vast importance than any other equal section of our nation, and must be so regarded by the people generally; hence, every source of information in regard to it will be useful and sought after by the whole community, and even by large capitalists beyond the Atlantic.

Most of my facts and descriptions are given from personal observation and inspection; but where not, the best authorities have been consulted, such as accredited Gazetteers, Books of Travel, Surveyors' Reports, Correspondence, Colton's late maps, and others; so that it is believed the statements are reliable, at least in all essential matters.

It is believed, too, that the information contained in this book is made so plain, complete, and explicit, that it may be serviceable to Emigrants and Emigration Companies in Europe; so as to enable them to set out for the new lands in America more intelligently than they otherwise could do.

As matter which will be interesting to readers generally, for the facts which they contain, and for the graphic descriptions which they present, of some features and locations in the West, I have inserted several letters written by Rev. J. P. THOMPSON, of New York, who made a tour through some of the Western States, during the past summer, which may be relied upon. Of the necessity of reliable portraitures and statistics of the West, Mr. Thompson says:

"One of the most necessary accouterments for a journey Westward is a good set of maps and guide-books. These enable you to keep your whereabouts while shifting from place to place. I have found Dinsmore's *Railway Guide* for the United States entirely reliable, so far as railroads are concerned; but in a journey of thousands of miles in a new country this of course answers only for part of the way. The *Western Tourist* and *Emigrant's Guide*, by J. H. COLTON, together with his new series of pocket maps of

2

the Western States, has been of much service to me in fixing localities."

"The *Tourist*, though published last year and therefore somewhat imperfect as regards the newer routes and also as to statistics of population—being based upon the census of 1840—nevertheless contains much information important to the traveler, and expressed in a clear and concise manner. Its tabular view of distances on the main routes of travel is especially valuable."

By the many questions which have been addressed to him, together with the requests of many good friends, he is induced to hurry out this work at this time; as a guide to the emigrant westward, whether farmer, mechanic, merchant, or professional man.

It is also believed that such a book would oftentimes be an advantage and convenience to merchants and other business men in the Atlantic cities, as a matter of reference, respecting the business and prospects of Western towns; as much care is taken that the statement of facts shall be correct.

Our Great West is a fertile, healthy, and beautiful country, whose bountiful products reward toil and enterprise more liberally than any other part of the world; and already begins to number its millions of industrious and intelligent population, with millions more turning their thoughts and faces thitherward.

The schemes of Internal Improvements there are liberal and extensive; and many routes, in various sections, are being prosecuted with great activity and progress; being works of such palpable utility as to have secured large and sufficient amounts of the surplus capital of the Eastern States and England, for their construction, without embarrassing the New States with onerous debts.

Our Canals are dug and doing a large business; portions of our Railroads are built and in operation; and the whole are under safe and speedy advance toward completion; so we have no grounds to fear the suspensions and confusions which took place a few years ago—for want of funds to proceed with; they are provided for from the rich coffers of the millionaires in the older settled countries. So that there never was a more auspicious season for purchasing and settling in the West, than the present; and if this little volume shall prove beneficial to any—either those who wish to buy, or those who want to sell—my efforts will not have been in vain, in this undertaking.

The writer's home is in The West, a country with which he has been more and more pleased, as he became better acquainted with it; and to all for whose happiness he feels interested, he could scarcely give them more kindly counsel, than to advise them fairly to consider the claims and prospects of the West, then remove there and enjoy them.

The work will be accompanied by a superb Map of the three states, Illinois, Wisconsin, Iowa, and the territory of Minnesota, prepared in accordance with the latest authorities.

D. S. C.

CHICAGO, *November*, 1851.

INTRODUCTION.

For many years, particularly after the late war with Great Britain (1812–15), emigration has been considerable from the older to the New States; and until recently, much the larger portion of that emigration settled in Ohio, Michigan and Indiana; not many venturing beyond the Great Lakes; the States and Territories in that region, along the large rivers, were slowly but steadily, in early times, receiving settlers from some of the Southern States, which for many years constituted the largest portion of their accessions of population.

But now, the case is different: Wisconsin, Illinois, and Iowa, are receiving a large majority of the throngs of industrious and enterprising people that are seeking New Homes in the New Country; while the Territory of *Minnesota*, a rising star in the north, is also receiving considerable acquisitions to her population, by the flood of immigration.

Perhaps, right here, a few passing remarks will not be out of place, explanatory of the words so much in use, now-a-days, viz: *migrate, emigrant, immigration.* To migrate or migrating, I understand to mean, simply, to change location periodically or temporarily; as, in the hot seasons Southerners come north to spend the summer, and Northerners go south to pass the cold season, both designing soon to return; but not locating or settling permanently in a new place. Emigrating is leaving a country; and immigrating is coming into a country; as an Englishman or Irishman is an emigrant with respect to his own country upon leaving it; and, coming into this country, he is an immigrant with respect to it. This definition may serve, in some degree, to prevent that confounding of these terms, so common with many.

Texas, Oregon, California, Deseret, Nabraska, and all of the really "Far West," attract a share of the swarms of flying population to their borders; but it consists more of adventurers than of such as are seeking permanent homes for steady business, though not wholly so.

Of these latter it is not my intention to speak further; Illinois, Wisconsin, and Iowa being the region with which the writer is more conversant, and to which it is designed especially to devote these pages.

It is well known to most of the country, east and west, that the *snags, bars, sawyers,* and other *obstructions* in the large rivers; and *rocks, reefs, lack of harbors, light-houses, dredge-work,* etc., along the great lakes, had become crying and disastrous evils, causing innumerable frightful and destructive calamities, to both persons and shipping, navigating these waters. And good men began to realize seriously that some efficient measures must be speedily adopted by the nation and government for safety and relief.

Accordingly, in the years 1846 and 1847, a movement was started for bringing together a large *Mass Meeting* of the nation, at some point, to deliberate upon some measures, and disseminate intelligence in regard to these affairs, which resulted in the assembling of an immense *National Convention* at CHICAGO, Illinois, in the first week of July, 1847; the business of which was to collect and present facts and arguments, and prepare matter and petitions for Congress; and otherwise to procure the speedy improvements required along these important waters to give greater safety and facilities to the extensive commerce that floated upon them.

That call was triumphantly responded to in one of the most numerous, intelligent, and enthusiastic gatherings that ever convened in the West, or any part of our country, popularly known as the great *Harbor and River Convention;* where were met many of the most profound statesmen and eloquent orators of our nation.

That convention is an important era in the destiny of the West; an event beneficial both for the general earnest interest which it excited, and the arguments that it promulgated in favor of a liberal policy of Improvements by the Government, and for bringing together thousands of enterprising witnesses, from the East and South, to behold the fresh and blooming WEST, to examine its resources—persons who, but for this occasion, would scarcely have ventured to its borders, where they might admiringly look upon its rich prospects and boundless beauty. The writer, then for the first time visited the states of *Wisconsin* and *Illinois;* and notwithstanding all that he had learned of this fine country, from enthusiastic travelers, he felt really that the half had not been told him. And he has since met many now residents in those states, who, like himself, first came here as delegates to the Harbor and River Convention, and upon seeing, at once resolved to locate permanently. And in *Iowa*, too, many have settled in the same manner.

To adventurers in different departments of business, it presents advantageous openings; to the rich capitalist, secure and profitable sources of investment; to the poor, easy opportunities of procuring pleasant and independent homes, with comfortable competence; and to all industrious, honest classes, a clear field and a fair strife; and in very few instances have those who were even moderately prudent and industrious, been disappointed in accomplishing their aims and expectations, or to do much better than they would have done, with the same means and effort, at the place from which they moved.

Hence, those who originated and carried out the scheme of the great Harbor and River Convention have done good service to the country, which will long be joyfully remembered, as well by the early pioneer as the more recent settlers.

In a communication to the *N. Y. Tribune*, HORACE GREELEY, after speaking of the crowded state of the hotels on this occasion at Chicago, says:

"But the citizens threw open their dwellings, welcoming strangers in thousands to their cordial and bounteous hospitality." "The people of Chicago have earned a noble reputation for hospitality and public spirit." "I never witnessed any thing so superb as the appearance of their fire companies, with their engines drawn by led horses, tastefully caparisoned. Our New York firemen must try again; they have certainly been outdone."

On the close of the Convention he thus writes:

"Thus has met, deliberated, harmonized, acted, and separted, one of the most important and interesting conventions ever held in this or any country. It was truly characterized as a Congress of Freemen, destitute, indeed, of pay and mileage, but in all else inferior to no deliberative body which has assembled in twenty years. Can we doubt that its effects will be most beneficial and enduring?"

In calculating the growth of New York and Chicago, he writes, July 19, 1847:

"Rapid as the growth of Chicago has been, large as it now is, whoever proceeds westward and southward across the prairies, and notes the unequaled capacities of the soil, its universal fertility, its susceptibility of easy culture, and the rapidity of its transformation, from a waste to a garden, can hardly doubt that New York in 1800 will be surpassed in business and population by Chicago of 1900. There is not a century's difference between the two in aught but origin. The spacious Illinois Canal will soon add immensely to the trade of this Northern Emporium; but a railroad to Galena must soon follow, and will prove even more beneficial and remunerating."

The Canal *is* in full operation, and also between fifty and sixty miles of the Galena Railroad.

From this period, particularly, then, is to be dated the commencement of that rush of immigration which has so rapidly peopled the states west of the Lakes; and which still continues, and long must continue, to pour a tide of population into that vigorous, progressing region. For the convenience of such, is this little book thrown out upon the public for its approbation; and while the writer is well acquainted and well satisfied with the West, he confidently recommends all who are not satisfied with their situation in the Old States, to remove and settle in the New Ones; where every thing is fresh and improving, not sinking under moss-covered dilapidation, but where the very appearances of all around are luxuriant and beautiful, affording new hopes, new energy, and new successes.

Here are peculiarly promising inducements to thousands of those ingenious, energetic, and laborious young mechanics, who overthrong Eastern cities, to drive their trades, or engage in farming, or both, as may best suit their inclinations and circumstances. Thus, all will be benefited—those who go, by finding new and enlarged fields for operation, and those who stay, by having steady work and less competition.

New towns are springing up on every hand, and rapidly growing; farmers are numerously settling down in snug and sociable neighborhoods; and they must have various kinds of mechanic work, for which they will make sure pay at fair prices. Then in the young villages printers are wanted, with their world-moving implements—Press and Types—to bring them the news and advertise their operations. Then let a portion of you, in the several branches, "pack your kits," and with resolute hearts and active hands, remove to the large and new scenes of enterprise, and be sure success and happiness will reward your efforts.

Even though you are mechanics, it is well to buy a small farm, as soon as you conveniently can, that you may have a sure and independent footing on *terra firma ;* which will afford you a profitable opportunity to devote your labor, should you not be fully employed all the time in your trade. In this way the *toiler* may receive a just share of the products and profits of his labor; and *capital* will not swallow up the "lion's half," as is too often the case in large cities and densely populated districts, where most of the property is owned by a few, and the many labor for them.

Capital and labor should be real friends, and each receive its just share of honors and profits and rights; they are natural brothers, designed to be of eminent service to each other, and should exist and strive together, hand in hand—then both will be safer, happier, and nobler.

Much more than formerly, the great resources of the West, its rapid increase in population, wealth, and political influence, have now become subjects of lively interest and daily discussion, throughout the country; and the Great West like brilliant visitors in the rich boudoirs of the fashionable and elegant, is now the general object of remark and admiration. Its location, as will be seen by reference to the map of the United States, asserts its important position, and indicates with clear certainty, that the voting majorities, and the direction of our government, will soon be with the West; the "Old Thirteen" possessing only about one fifth the area of territory that the New States and Territories embrace.

In this connection, the following remarks of Judge DOUGLAS, in his address before the late Agricultural Fair at Rochester, N. Y., are appropriate:

"Those regions are particularly adapted to grazing. They are for the most part elevated, dry, and healthy, abounding in rich grasses and pure water. The extent of country to which I refer, embraces an era more than twice that of the original thirteen States of the Union, and is destined to be occupied by an intelligent, industrious, and energetic race of men, not inferior in any respect to those who inhabit the old states. Nature has designed it for the habitation of an agricultural people."

"The farms of Western New York demanded the construction of the Erie Canal, and the farmers of the Western States now call for its enlargement. As the Western States and Territories become settled, and agricultural products accumulate, new railroads and canals become necessary to furnish means of transportation to the seaboard. The West is desirous of securing every avenue to the sea. It requires the navigation of the Mississippi and of the St. Lawrence, the canals of New York, Pennsylvania, Ohio, Indiana, and Illinois, and all the railroads now constructed or in process of construction, from the sea-coast to the Mississippi valley. And all these facilities will yet prove insufficient to form adequate outlets for the constantly accumulating products of the Western farmers. New lines of communication will be called into existence, and it is doubtful whether the capital and enterprise of the country will keep pace with the increased demands for internal improvements."

From New York and other Atlantic cities, as well as the interior country, there are numerous quick and cheap lines of travel and transportation westward; and astonishingly so, when viewed in comparison with the difficulties that had to be encountered by the natives of New England when they early began to settle portions of New York and Ohio.

In those early days, to undertake such an enterprise was, in fact, taking their lives in their hands, as it were, to part with friends at the dear old homes, with blessings and sadness, in trembling apprehension whether they should ever again meet in time—to set off on the long and perilous journey, to Central or Western New York, in quest of new homes and fortunes; considered then a brave, adventurous undertaking; and by the more staid and cautious ones, it was pronounced a fool-hardy project; a tour, which at that period did, indeed, require more time, hardships, and deprivation, than is now suffered in a trip to the Missouri river.

Some, even, with extra undaunted enterprise, ventured far away to Ohio, Michigan, and Indiana, then equal to a trip now to Oregon or California, and was entered upon with as much deliberate preparations as are the long journeys at the present time to the Pacific.

Those expeditions were performed at the slow, tedious movements of pack-horses and tardy team-wagons, through Indian trails, or half-cut roads. Even migration from Eastern to Western New York, at that period, was considered by many, as a wild and doubtful undertaking.

Upon the completion of the Hudson River Railroad, from New York to Albany, in the first week of October, 1851, the *New York Daily Times* publishes the following bit of steamboat history, which is not inappropriate here, and will be interesting to many:

"The opening of the Hudson River Railroad, and the transit from New York to Albany in the short space of four hours, present a new era in the annals of travel. The steamboats have reigned supreme over the noble waters of the Hudson for *forty-four years.* It was on September 28, 1807, that FULTON's boat first undertook the arduous task of statedly ascending the river to the capital, for the transmission of passengers. The following advertisement was discovered yesterday in a stray copy of '*The American Citizen*,' a weekly paper published in this city, and dated October 5, 1807. The coincidence of the times and seasons for the commencement of steam navigation and of steam travel by rail on the river is striking. And the contrast of the time and fare table with that now used on the railroad is quite as remarkable :

"'The Steamboat.—Being thoroughly repaired and arranged for passengers, with a private dressing-room for ladies, it is intended to run her as a packet between New York and Albany, for the remainder of the season. She will leave New York exactly at 9 o'clock in the morning of the following days, and always perform her voyage in from 30 to 36 hours.

Monday	Sep. 28	Monday	Oct. 12
Friday	Oct. 2	Friday	Oct. 16
Wednesday	Oct. 7		

The charge to each passenger is as follows :

	DOLLARS.	TIME.
To Newburgh	$3	14 hours.
To Poughkeepsie	4	17 hours.
To Esopus	4½	20 hours.
To Hudson	5	30 hours.
To Albany	7	36 hours.

For places apply to Mr. VANDERVOORT, No. 48 Cortland-street, at the corner of Greenwich-street.'

"It was then *the* steamboat. No other floated on the waters of the world; and profoundly did the good folk admire at the courage of those who ventured to trust themselves to the perilous enterprise. Think of the prodigious advance upon previous modes of conveyance, when the trip from one town to the other was actually accomplished in '30 to 36 hours,' instead of four or five days, as the old lumbering stage-coach or tub-like sloop was wont to have it. There were who had great faith in the invention, and foresaw dimly its grand results. Witness the following communication, which appeared in *The Evening Post* of October 4, 1807 :

"'Among thousands who viewed the scene, permit a spectator to express his gratification at the sight this morning of the steamboat proceeding on her trip to Albany on a wind and swell of tide which appeared to bid defiance to every attempt to perform the voyage. The steamboat appeared to glide as easy and rapidly as though it were calm, and the machinery was not in the least impeded by the waves of the Hudson, the wheels moving with their usual velocity and effect.

"'The experiment of this day removes every doubt hitherto entertained of the practicability of the steamboat being able to work in rough weather. Without being over-sanguine, we may safely assert that the principles of this important discovery will be applied to the improvement of packets and passage-boats, which for certainty, safety, expedition, and accommodation, will far surpass any thing hitherto attempted. The invention is highly honorable to Mr. Fulton, and reflects infinite credit on the genius of our country. NEW YORK.'

"Time has justified the vision of this seer, and gone infinitely further than the promise. Could the veil of the 'to come' have been lifted before the eyes of the prophet, and the log-book of the *Baltic* or the time-table of a railway train been presented to him, how inconceivable must have been his astonishment. How short the time it takes now-a-days to work wonders!"

But the original stock, from which sprang these various adventurers, was of the right stamp: The PURITAN was that noble tree, hardy and vigorous, which had thus spread, and still is spreading, its roots and branches far and wide; knowing no narrower bounds to their achievements than, that the project is RIGHT and DESIRABLE; this fairly settled, it must be accomplished; danger, obstacles, privations, enter not into the account, until the enterprise is commenced; and then only to calculate how they may be best removed or surmounted. This was the original Puritan in his transit and settlement to this continent, and afterward to many states of the Union. And in those original architects of this great nation, whom the "May Flower" bore to *Plymouth Rock*, we have an example of glorious daring and marvelous accomplishment—in principle and project—surpassing any the world ever saw, or soon again will witness—worthy fathers of an enterprising progeny who have commenced peopling the West.

"Know ye the land where a royal oppressor
Bade the burghers and husbandmen bow to his will;
But they fought the good fight, under God, the Redressor,
And the heart of Humanity beats to it still!

Where lakes, plains, and mountains, inspiring or solemn,
Keep their tales of that strife, and its monuments be
The Statue, the Tablet, the Hall, and the Column,
But, best and most lasting, the souls of the free !"—WHITTIER.

After the *Erie Canal* was built—the glorious father of transit improvements in our country—the great financier that has paid and made the internal improvements of the Empire State—a different state of things exists; by even that line alone—connecting the Hudson, the Ocean, with the Lakes, and before the advent of railroads—transportation of persons and property was comparatively easy, cheap, and quick; the speed and cheapness with which flour, pork, and other articles were carried from Buffalo and Rochester to Albany and New York, and merchandize brought back, were matter of delighted marvel to thousands, even those who had been most sanguinely anticipating the completion and operations of that extraordinary work—an artificial water-passage, three hundred and sixty miles, from Ocean to Lake!

And well may the people of the Empire State, of the Western States, feel lively respect for the great minds who projected and stuck by it to the day of its completion. They are held in honor as public benefactors, not only for its beneficial effects immediately on the line and in the state, but for the general spirit of *enterprise*, and far-reaching *confidence* in magnificent *improvements* which it has excited and fostered; *this* is *the* great benefit of the construction of the Erie Canal—the will and confidence which it has inspired throughout the nation in such enterprises.

Soon, however, the universal Yankee nation began to feel that the five-mile-an-hour gait of canal was too slow, they should not be able to get on in the world at such a pace; they must be shot ahead with steam; they must have *Railroads*.

And Railroads we have; the cars are found dashing and smoking through the country in every direction; so that we now have railroad, steamboat, and canal packets between the Atlantic and Great Lakes. Emigrants and travelers will make their own choice among these several conveyances from the Eastern cities to Dunkirk and Buffalo; where again they can take safe and pleasant boats for the Western States.

There is steamboat communication all of the way, and railroad part of it, from Lake Erie to Wisconsin, Illinois, Iowa, and Minnesota. Passenger and freight carriage is done very cheap and with very little delay; affording speedy returns and receipts for the sale of their produce.

And this fact shows that the rich, fertile lands of the West, are nearly if not quite as valuable, in truth, as those east of the Lakes—the present facilities for transport and conveyance to the seaboard markets being so favorable that the Western farmer will realize about the same profit, one year with another, from his land per acre, as is obtained at the East; even estimating the lands of both regions at the same price; but when we consider that the price of the lands East is five, ten, or fifteen times higher than at the West, the ratio of profits is far greater in the New States; because there, the same amount of gain is derived from much less capital. This consideration is worth looking at a moment.

Similar was the effect produced on the relative value of lands in Eastern and Western New York, by the opening of transportation through the Erie Canal; those West being of comparatively small value until the market facilities were opened; but since that time, they have risen to nearly or quite equal price, acre for acre; those on the Genesee and Tonawanda, with those on the Hudson and Mohawk rivers.

To give a more distinct idea of the growth of Western New York, and the favorable effects of increased market facilities, incident upon great internal improvements, I copy some brief extracts from a valuable work, entitled "Rochester, and Western New York"—highly useful as a book of reference—published in 1838, by HENRY O'RIELLY, Esq.; than whom, no one could well be found better qualified for the task; who, to a largely observing and enterprising mind, added long familiar acquaintance with the locations of which he wrote. Mr. O'Rielly became a resident of Rochester when it was but an embryo village—he early commenced the publication of a weekly newspaper there; and soon after started, in that place, the first daily paper printed west of the Hudson river. He continued in the editorial chair, at that city, some eighteen or twenty years; and held, at different times, important city offices, and several appointments under the General Government. He was also among the first to suggest and ablest to advocate several important measures of state policy; as the enlargement of the Erie Canal; the formation of the new Constitution; and the construction of railroads and telegraphs; while of the latter, his enterprise has extended lines through the Western and Southern States, far more extensively than has been done by any other person. In his book, Mr. O'Rielly says:

"The suddenness of its rise, the energy of its population, the excellence of its institutions, the whole character of its prosperity, render ROCHESTER prominent among the cities that have recently sprung into existence throughout a land notable for extraordinary intellectual and physical advancement."

"In expressing astonishment at the career of Rochester, DE WITT CLINTON remarked shortly before his death, that when he passed the Genesee river on a tour with other commissioners for exploring the route of the Erie Canal, in 1810, there was not a house where Rochester now stands! In 1812 there were but two frame dwellings here, small and rude enough—one of which yet [1838] remaining to remind us of the change since the period when the occupants of those shanties had to contend against wild beasts for the scanty crop of corn first raised on a tract now in the heart of the city."

"It was not till the year 1812 that the '*Hundred Acre Tract*' was planned as the nucleus of a settlement under the name of Rochester, after the senior proprietor. This tract was a 'mill lot,' bestowed by Phelps and Gorham on a semi-savage, called 'Indian Allen,' as a bonus for building mills to grind corn and saw boards for the new settlers in this region at that time. The mills decayed as the business of the country was insufficient to support them. Allen sold the property to Sir William Pultney, whose estate then included a large section of the 'Genesee country.' It is but thirty-six years since the tract was thus owned by a British baronet. The sale to Rochester, Fitzhugh, and Carroll, took place in 1802, at the rate of $17.50 per acre, or $1,750 for the lot [hundred acre tracts] with all its *betterments*."

Some of the land on the east side of the Genessee river in Rochester (the hundred acre tract being on the west side) was sold to Phelps and Gorham, in 1790, for eighteen pence per acre."

Now (1851) Rochester is an important city of over 40,000 population, and many of its lots are worth from $100 to $500 per foot. Mr. O'Rielly further remarks:

"The immense facilities for trade and intercourse furnished to Rochester [and Western New York] by canals and railroads, and the benefits flowing from the Genesee river and Lake Ontario may be estimated by any one who is capable of comprehending the range of improvements now in progress, as well as that already completed."

Speaking of New Englanders, he pays the following well-merited tribute to their noble character:

"Those who properly appreciate the New England character, as exemplified by the Pilgrim Champions of Human Rights, and by their lineage from the first settlement down to the present period, may view with interest the living monument of intelligent enterprise which has sprung into existence through the transforming influence of Yankee colonists in the Western Wilderness. 'New England!—rich in intellect, though rude in soil—the intelligence and enterprise of her sons in a fertile land have largely aided in rendering the Genesee country the garden of this state.' Such were among the sentiments with which a statesman of Eastern origin was greeted by the people of Rochester. The city itself is a worthy monument of the glorious truth—a truth applicable to the social condition, perhaps, as well as the physical improvements of this region."

Upon the growth of Rochester Mr. O'Rielly very justly exults, and challenges comparison, in this wise:

"With all the rage for speculation Westward—with all the new villages and cities that have been laid out through the 'Far West' during the last twenty years, where, in what place, through all that broad and fertile region, can there be shown any town which has surpassed ROCHESTER in the permanent increase of population, wealth, and business."

The writer of this little book was born in the "Genesee country," passed his childhood there; then lived years in Rochester to "serve his 'prenticeship;" and afterward settled in the West; so that he will not yield to Mr. O'Rielly, even, in feelings of pride and partiality for Western New York. But at this date, he can truthfully record the statistics of a city which has proudly outstripped Rochester in the growth of its business and population.

CHICAGO has vastly surpassed that city. In 1833, when Chicago *commenced*—as the small nucleus of an immense city—with half a hundred buildings and less than three hundred population, Rochester was already a city of some 12,000, the former thus only about one thirty-sixth the size of the latter; and *now*, in some eighteen years growth, Chicago has advanced with such unequaled strides, that the "Garden City" contains above 30,000, or over three fourths as much population as the "Flour City."

And further: Mr. LAPHAM, in his useful book on Wisconsin, replies to Mr. O'Rielly, in favor of MILWAUKEE, as follows:

"We may answer the question by making a little comparison.

"Rochester was laid out in 1812, and in 1816, or four years, the population was three hundred and thirty-one. In 1820, or eight years, the population was fifteen hundred.

"Milwaukee was laid out in 1835, and in 1839, or four years, the population was fifteen hundred—or as much increase in *four* years, as Rochester had in *eight*. But in 1843, or eight years, the population of Milwaukee was over six thousand, or four times as much as Rochester during the same period."

And both Chicago and Milwaukee are beautifully lighted with gas, whose manufactories are neat and permanent.

Thus the West most clearly and triumphantly bears away the palm for rapid growth; but she had a proud example, to be sure, in the progress of Western and Central New York.

Many counties in the Western States have already established Agricultural and Horticultural Societies, annually holding their Fairs and Cattle Shows. Wisconsin has also instituted a State Agricultural Society, which holds its first regular Meeting and Fair this Autumn.

And here, before entering upon the general matter of this volume, several hints, of great importance to emigrants, suggest themselves to me. Persons moving West, who can do so, will find it much to their advantage to take with them a good supply of the necessary Materials and Stocks for raising fine fruits; such as seedlings, choice grafts, scions, buds, etc., of all kinds, from grapes, raspberries, gooseberries, and apricots, up to peaches, apples, pears, etc. They will find it not only a pleasure, but also profitable; as all such things once started in the West, are in constant demand at good prices; while all varieties of fruit always command ready sale.

Seedling chestnut trees, filberts, and some other kinds, not indigenous to the States of Illinois, Wisconsin, and Iowa, are much wanted, and will find ready sale, in case you should take with you more than should be needed on your own premises. Locust seed is also useful and much needed there; as that specie of tree (the thorn locust is preferable) grows very rapidly and makes excellent fencing stuffs; besides being highly ornamental and comfortable, both to residences and to stock, on wide prairie farms. I have seen it grow to trees of four to six inches in diameter, in from three to five years, from the time of planting the seed, on those rank prairie-soils. Various thorn trees, or seeds, will be found useful where the emigrant can take them with him; the buck and the branching white varieties being generally preferred. The Osage orange is much used, and generally to advantage, but that is procured from an opposite direction of country—west of the Mississippi, and can be bought at Cincinnati, St. Louis, or Chicago.

And particularly will those moving West find it desirable and profitable to take with them as much improved blood stock, sheep, hogs, and poultry as they can; for no region will more richly remunerate all expense and pains expended in such matters, than will the Prairie Country; where those things have been too much neglected.

Far better is it for farmers and business men, going West, to take with them these articles, than to take so much furniture as many do, and so many farming utensils; these latter are useful, to be sure, but then, better ones can be procured at the factories in Western towns than are generally taken there from the East; for it is true that better plows, and harvesting and thrashing machines, are made there than in any other portion of our country, and better adapted to that section; therefore, it is decidedly better to transport stock and fruit than farming utensils.

With a soil and pasturage unsurpassed on this continent; and a climate of great variety and highly favorable, the Western States ought to surpass their older neighbors, at the East, in stock-raising; and they can do it with proper effort—care in selecting good breeds—and by judicious crossing, and the high feeding so attainable on the prairies.

Whether we consider stock-raising, grain-growing, or fruit-culture, there is nowhere combined more favorable circumstances, than in the region we are speaking of, for the agriculturist to "cause two blades of grass to grow, where but one grew before;" and thereby become the best "benefactor of mankind;" and this will science and industry accomplish.

WESTERN PORTRAITURE.

TRIP TO THE UPPER LAKES.

"KNOW ye the land where the Forest and Prairie
 Spread broadest away by the Cataract's fall!
Where the harvests of earth the most plenteously vary,
 And the children that reap them are happiest of all;
Where the long rolling rivers go mightily trending,
 With wealth on their billows, thro' many a clime:
Where the lakes, 'mid their woodlands, like seas are extending,
 And the mountains rise lone in the center sublime!"—WHITTIER.

AT BUFFALO, on Lake Erie, in the State of New York, we will take cabin or steerage passage—just as we feel able or inclined—both are comfortable, from the manner steamboats are now constructed and arranged; the price of the former is $6 to $8, and the latter $2 to $4, to any of the towns on Lake Michigan, in Wisconsin and Illinois.

However, if they desire, and wish to save one or two days' time, persons can take steamboat to Monroe, Toledo, or Detroit; then the railroad across the State of Michigan, to Michigan City, in Indiana, then steamboat again to Chicago, and other towns on the western shore of Lake Michigan. Though performed in quicker time, the fare is higher. But for a view of the fine scenery, we now will take steamboat for the trip round the Upper Lakes, particularly as we are not in a great hurry.

Soon our splendid steamer is on a start for a trip of some ten to twelve hundred miles through the Great Lakes, which is performed in from three to five days, the weather more favorable at some times than others; while some of the boats make better speed than others.

After passing through Lake Erie, touching on our way the beautiful and flourishing towns of Erie, Cleveland, and Detroit, besides many other smaller ones, we run up Detroit river, St. Clair lake, and a deep narrow river of the same name, on whose banks are several small towns, engaged principally in the lumber and fish trade; and soon we reach the foot of Lake Huron, with shores here, of a dry sandy soil, which present two handsome tables, one rising a few feet above the other, on which is situated the delightful little town of Port Huron, with the elegant evergreens sprinkled all through it, and nearly covering the ground, with a thick grove in the rear. A little farther on is the U. S. Station called Fort Gratiot, which, with its white buildings and pickets shining in the midst of the straight green pines, presents any thing but the grim-visaged appearance of war.

On the opposite or northern side of the narrow river is the Canada shore; and it is a fact very generally noticeable, that almost the entire distance from the head of Lake Erie to the foot of Lake Huron, the Canada shore is the most beautiful, and presents a more favorable appearance for agriculture and business generally than the other side; and yet the tillage, the towns, the business, every thing on the States' side is incomparably ahead of that displayed upon the other. For the reason, every one can exercise his own philosophy or judgment—we simply give the fact.

We make but a short stop here, and our steamer is off again to dash her way through that broad, deep, bold sheet, Lake Huron, whose shores, if the weather be favorable, and allow us to be outside, will present to our view some surpassingly wild and romantic scenery, in the mingled features which compose its borders—huge pine forests skirting and fringing the rugged, sand-drifted banks, in many instances the bald hills rearing their yellow summits high among the tall trees, blending their forms and colors in fantastic beauty, presenting to fancy's eye the dreamy outlines of birds, animals, and ships—as the "mystic ship," the "sleeping bear," the "flapping eagle," and various others as curious and suggestive of mysterious legendary, as the grotesque formations along the Hudson.

But if Old Boreas happen to be blowing some of his rude blasts of shivering breath, piping all hands above, there'll be cold comfort to sight-seers, and lively times throughout the vessel, until we reach MACKINAW, and under the lee of its lofty rock towers and wooded shores obtain secure and tranquil moorings.

But before reaching the harbor, and upon entering the celebrated Straits, we shall pass two large and picturesque islands, of wild and rugged aspect—timbered and rocky; the largest is *Bois Blanc*, and the other *Drummond* island.

Then we soon reach *Mackinaw* island, on which is situated the town and old fort of the same name. Here was established one of the earliest posts of French Jesuits, in their adventurous explorations about the middle of the 17th century; some ambitious for discovery, and others in quest of fortunes by trading with Indians for their furs.

About the close of the last war, Lieut. DANIEL CURTISS, with a company of soldiers, was stationed at this fort, where, some years after, his wife was killed by a flash of lightning, while sitting at her window engaged on a piece of embroidery. He afterward died at Fort Howard, near Green Bay.

Here is the deep, narrow channel through which the waters pass from Lake Michigan to Huron; and here is seen the most rugged yet picturesque scenery to be met in our whole route, and surpassed by but few locations in any part of our country. Here are towering ledges of pillared and strata rocks, summit-crowned with everlasting pines, and surrounded with deep, clear waters, where are taken in great quantities the noted Mackinaw white fish and trout, which constitute an important article in Western commerce.

Mackinaw is becoming every year more and more a place of summer resort, principally by Southerners, for health and pleasure; as the opportunities for hunting and fishing are considerable. With pure water and air, and exciting incentives to healthful exercise, it cannot well fail to meet the expectations of visitors, and effect the end for which they go to that place.

The permanent population is composed of French, Indians, and half-breeds, with a few business men; besides the officers and soldiers stationed in the U. S. Garrison on the hill above. The articles of export consist almost entirely of lumber, fish, peltries, and Indian fabrics; the latter being much purchased by visitors and passengers, while the boats make their short stops for wood, fish, etc.

What, with the neat white buildings, bastions, fences, and other fixtures of the fort, as they stand along on elevated terraces, and the winding walks ranged around, one above another, up the towering banks of green turf and gray rock; the waving forests and beetling observatory still rising in the back ground; with the busy little village under the bluffs along the water's edge, and the Indian canoes scattered about upturned on the pebbly beach, while numerous schooner masts and steam pipes stretch up from the harbor—altogether, Mackinaw exhibits some of the most charmingly diversified and unique views that can well be imagined, particularly as seen from the boat on a bright day when riding through the Straits. On the other side the shores and peaks present more of a bald sandy appearance, studded with scattering clumps of pine trees, and small shrubs of other varieties.

Yet, above all, the gorgeous spectacle of *sun-setting*, as

seen at this place, exceeds every thing of the kind that I have ever beheld. The glorious sun, as he swings down from the circling, curving strata of deep red and blue clouds in the west—piled up in series closer and darker along the lake's horizon, but becoming more mellow and dispersed as the sight stretches farther up the soft ethereal vault above—emblazons the rippled surface with crimson and molten gold, as it were chased in brilliant metals, while the small broken ridges of serf curl along with a whiter glow, like flowing robes studded with sparkling gems; investing the whole scene with the most enchanting splendor. And at such times may be seen, through the mellow radiance, vessels standing away upon this glittering mirror beneath the blood-red clouds, stretched one over another in fervid folds, their canvas taking the hues of the surrounding elements throw back their reflected duplicates into the swelling bosom of the deep; and, with more or less sail set, as the breeze will permit, are wafted gracefully along, resembling so many giant birds with their glittering wings all spread, and plumage of varied hues—fabled phenixes—just risen from the flaming depths, as if, with their own fiery wings fanned into existence, so little do they resemble cumbrous earth-forms. And at these times, too, when the lakes are on fire with the gleaming sunbeams, to see the mighty steamer like a thing of life plowing through this sheet of waving crystals, emitting clouds of smoke, sparks and vapor, gives to fancy the impression that it is the legitimate voyager of these promethean elements.

To the enthusiastic student of nature—be he pencil-artist, poet, or philosopher—a visit here is above pecuniary price. Once witnessing these scenes will furnish the mind with more matter for delighted and elevated reflection, than scores of horse-races, prize-fights, and circus-routs. And any one who can spare time and money for a trip to Mackinaw, in summer or autumn, ànd stay long enough at least, to see the sun rise and set, should do so; he will be amply, delightedly compensated for all his pains. Kings love royal robes of magnificence; but all others dwindle into tame insignificance, when the King of Day here displays the splendid vestments of his morning and evening wardrobe. Go then, and see, for I can but faintly portray, the brilliance of this picture gallery of nature; unsurpassed even by Oriental dreams of mystic enchantment in fairy isles.

Then visit, ye lovers of pleasure and sight-seeing, Lakes Huron and Michigan—bathe in their waters, hunt among their island forests, read in their grottos, where fragrant boughs are wildly interlaced above you, and you may drink deep of the fullest cup of rural life and romance.

"The silver light, with quivering glance,
Play'd on the water's clear expanse;
Each purple peak, each flinty spire,
Was bathed in floods of living fire.
* * * * * * * *
It is a wild and strange retreat,
As ever was trod by outlaw's feet."

The following lines by WILLIS G. CLARK, though descriptive of a different location, express enough in common with this place to render them an appropriate quotation here, while their high-toned genius make them acceptable everywhere:

"Who that hath stood, where summer brightly lay,
On some broad city, by a spreading bay,
And from a rural hight the scene surveyed,
While on the distant strand the billows play'd,
But felt the vital spirit of the scene,
What time the south-wind stray'd through foliage green,
And freshened from the dancing waves, went on,
By the gay groves, and fields, and gardens won?
* * * * * * * * * *
When the tired sea-bird dips his wings in foam,
And hies him to his beetling, eyry home;

When sun-gilt ships are parting from the strand,
And glittering streamers by the breeze are fanned;
When the wide city's domes and piles aspire,
And rivers broad seemed touch'd with golden fire;
Save where some gliding boat their luster breaks,
And volumed smoke its murky tower forsakes,
And surging in dark masses, soars to lie,
And stain the glory of the up-lifted sky;
Oh, who at such a scene unmoved hath stood,
And gazed on town, and plain, and field, and flood,
Nor felt that life's keen spirit lingered there,
Through earth, and ocean, and the genial air?"

Upon passing out of the Straits, on the left, are *Beaver* islands, the largest of which has become somewhat noted as the location of a *Mormon* town or colony, who are building considerable, making other improvements, and doing a fair amount of business; though evil-disposed persons, it appears, have been inclined to harrass them, for some reason or other. The soil is good, the timber excellent, and the general appearance of the island is delightful. They are situated at the mouth of Traverse Bay. Other small timbered tracts called the *Fox* islands are located near by them.

Somewhat farther up the lake, to the left of the usual steamboat course, are the *Manitou* islands, two romantic and healthful resorts, where fishing and hunting may be enjoyed to the highest zest of those rural sports; the shores and forests are beautiful, the water clear and cold, and the air bracing; there is some resort to these bright pastoral retreats for health, pleasure, and business; and steamers land here for wood, fish, etc. The pleasure of a few days' rambles here will richly compensate the pleasure-seeker for his expense and pains.

In the opposite direction, near the entrance of Green Bay, are the *Grand Traverse* islands, which possess many of the characteristics of the other islands in Lake Michigan; any of which, in their wild and picturesque features, present charms that well reward the trouble of a visit.

These islands passed, we soon reach the State of *Wisconsin.* After running along off the coast of that long, narrow strip or promontory, jutting up between the lake and Green Bay, called *Door County*, the first town we reach is—

MANITOWOC, county-seat of *Manitowov* county. It is a thriving town of some 1,500 population, having a fair harbor at the mouth of the river, with a pier and lighthouse; considerable business is done here, and numbers of emigrants land every year.

The county contains a population of about 4,000. The land is heavily timbered, generally, with pine, oak, maple, and other varieties; and some places considerably broken by the water-courses, which furnish good water-powers. The soil is rich and deep, mostly a heavy clay, with frequent strips of sandy loam. The lumber trade from this region is extensive, and a source of gain to the inhabitants. Much good government land is yet for sale here at $1.25 per acre; and on the whole, the county presents fair inducements to the farmer and mechanic to settle in it.

SHEBOYGAN is the next town, as we proceed south, or up the lake, some thirty miles; it is somewhat ahead of the last named town in population and business, but much the same in general characteristics, with a similar kind of business—lumber and fish; having good piers and other harbor facilities, which must enable it to attain considerable importance in commercial operations.

Sheboygan county contains some 8,400 population, and in the general description of its soil, timber, streams, etc., resembles the last named county, though in improvements it is more advanced. Emigration to this county is considerable; but still there is plenty of land to be bought at government prices. Like most of the lake counties, this one has *Plankroads* passing through it toward the interior of the state. In various parts of these counties there are settlements of industrious Dutch and Norwegian immigrants, who are making worthy progress in felling the forests and tilling the soil.

It was off this port that, a few years ago, the terrible and melancholy catastrophe of the burning of the propeller *Phœnix* happened; in which over one hundred and thirty human lives were destroyed, swept away by the flames and flood; and among them those two interesting girls, the *Hazletines*, perished, and even in sight of home, as they were returning after a year's absence, at school in Ohio—in sight of their father's dwelling, suddenly and frightfully cut off without reaching and greeting that anxious, loved home-circle; the family even expecting them, and on the look-out, were compelled to witness the vessel and its inmates go down with the flames to the deep.

Ozaukee (formerly Port Washington) lies still south some thirty miles; it is the county-seat of *Washington* county, and contains a population of near 2,000; with convenient harbor facilities; and sustained by a country much the same in soil, timber, inhabitants, and business pursuits, as that north of it; and which is being rapidly settled up by the tide of emigration, and by them industriously cultivated.

Washington county contains about 20,000 inhabitants, and presents many fine farms, with ample room for many more. Water-power and timber are abundant here; and much government land yet for sale. In this, as in the other counties north of it, good *quarries of stone* are found, both for building and lime.

Milwaukee is the next place reached; it is the largest city in Wisconsin—being the Emporium market-town of that state, and the most important town on Lake Michigan, except Chicago, which is ninety miles farther south.

Milwaukee is a city of some twenty years' growth, and now contains 20,000 population. It is the county-seat of *Milwaukee* county, which contains near 35,000 inhabitants, a large number of whom are Dutch, Swiss, Norwegians, and Irish, and who are, for the most part, quiet, industrious people.

Milwaukee is destined to become an important city in point of business and population. It is noted for its splendid blocks of buildings, and its superior *brick*, which probably surpass those made in any other part of our nation. They have become a valuable article of export to many towns on the Great Lakes, and are an object of admiration with all who see them, being hard, smooth, and of a beautiful straw color.

The *Milwaukee and Misissippi Railroad* is already in operation to Waukesha, a distance of about sixteen miles; and designed to be continued, as fast as possible, through Madison, the state capital, and thence to the Mississippi river. There are also several *Plankroads* leading from the city to different points in the interior, affording valuable convenience for hauling the country produce to the lake for Eastern shipment, and taking merchandise back.

A better idea of the progress and character of this fine young city and county may be formed from reading some extracts from Lapham's book, published in 1846, in contrast with its present size and business. He says:

"In 1842, the population of the county of Milwaukee was 9,565; and such has been the rapid increase, since June of that year, that the population may now (1846) be safely estimated at twenty-five thousand." * * * "The county is twenty-four miles square; with a soil, generally speaking, abundantly rich, adapted to the growth of the usual crops in this climate and latitude, and mostly covered with a heavy growth of fine timber." * * * "The shore of Lake Michigan, in this county, consists of a bank of clay from twenty to one hundred feet high, and as nearly perpendicular as the nature of the material will admit.

From this, the country gradually rises, as we pass Westward, until we attain the summit between the Lake and Rock river, which is three hundred and sixteen feet above the level of Lake Michigan."

"The surface of the country is broken by the valleys of several streams, mostly running toward the south; but these valleys are usually not much depressed below the general level." "Some of the highest points in the western part of the county are probably five hundred feet above the lake." "The whole county is based upon limestone, mostly of a light-bluish gray color, disposed in thin nearly horizontal layers or strata; and is an excellent building material, and affords good lime."

"Milwaukee is now incorporated as a city; it is situated on the river of the same name, near its mouth or entrance into Milwaukee bay, of Lake Michigan, ninety miles north of Chicago, one hundred and four southeast from Green Bay, and about eighty due east from Madison. It was laid out as a village in 1835." "Such was the rapidity with which its population increased that in June of the succeeding year the number of its inhabitants was one thousand two hundred and six." "Within ten years from the time when the first inhabitant arrived here, with a view to permanent residence, we see a city with a population of at least ten thousand."

"Milwaukee bay is a semicircular indentation of Lake Michigan, about six miles across, and three miles deep. The north and south points or capes protect the shipping from the effects of all storms and gales of wind, except those from the east, which seldom occur. The bottom is clay, affording good anchorage ground."

Though Mr. L. was a resident, and an earnest well-wisher of Milwaukee, he scarcely anticipated what that city has already become, while its growth must still be rapidly onward. The location is healthy and beautiful; and has attracted many settlers from various parts of Western New York, with their capital to invest.

As an instance of the value of property in Milwaukee, the *Daily Wisconsin* publishes the following notice of sales of lots in that city, a short time since, for cash, and remarks:

"This shows that there is some money here in spite of the

'hard times,' and also that there is a confidence in the rising value of real estate in this city:

Lot		Block			Lot		Block		
Lot	5	Block	7	$195 00	Lot	16	Block	117	$105 00
"	4	"	7	127 50	"	15	"	117	75 00
"	1	"	7	90 00	"	17	"	119	250 00
"	4	"	20	25 00	"	1	"	112	250 00
"	4	"	88	135 00	"	14	"	121	37 50
"	5	"	88	140 00	"	10	"	129	195 00
"	11	"	105	77 50	"	6	"	59	505 60
"	19	"	114	87 50					

The same paper gives the following account of a hunting and *ducking* excursion in that vicinity:

"One of our prominent citizens, receiving a visit from an eastern friend, thought it incumbent upon himself to 'show the lions' of the city, and the adjacent country. Among other things, a *gunning excursion* up the *Menomonee* river was planned, and, to a certain extent, executed. In order to give the visitor a vivid impression of these 'western wilds,' and to shoot Teal after the fashion of 'wild injuns,' a *dug-out* was chosen, in preference to a more modern specimen of naval architecture. With considerable internal trepidation, but with much external confidence, our 'old settler' succeeded in paddling the *log* up to the shooting-ground. On arriving there, he spied a duck among the reeds, and as is natural for a mind occupied with an absorbing idea, in his eagerness for the *duck* he forgot the dug-out, and started up to fire. There was a report of a gun, two individual shouts, and two heavy simultaneous splashes; and 'there might have been seen,' for a few seconds, nothing but a dug-out floating bottom up on the surface of the water. Our friends had made an involuntary disappearance in the cool waters of the stream. A few minutes later, and two dismal-looking figures 'might also have been seen' astride of the log, casting rueful glances at each other, and relieving their over-filled mouths and nostrils of a very dubious-looking fluid. One still retained his gun with a convulsive grasp. The other, doubtless, considering his as an incumbrance under water, had left it there. After collecting their scattered faculties, they made a straight wake for shore, and thence to their residence, wiser if not sadder men. One has had enough of 'primitive' gunning, and the other has ever since had implicit faith in modern improvements."

From the large amount of excellent flour that is manufactured at Rochester, N. Y., that place is called the "Flour City;" and from the same principle, the thriving, queenly city of Milwaukee should be designated the "Orange Brick City," from the vast numbers of superior yellow brick which are made there.

RACINE is the next city, some twenty-five miles south of the latter city; and contains about 5,000 population. It has a fine harbor and piers; is a place of extensive business; and is county-seat of *Racine* county. Mr. Lapham says of it:

"The population of Racine was ascertained in October, 1845, to be two thousand five hundred and nine. The amount of trade has very considerably increased since 1842, especially in the exportation of wheat, flour, beef, pork, and recently, wool is among its exports."

Since then the business and population has greatly increased.

Racine county is a very small one, with about 15,000 population, and composed mostly of beautiful, gently rolling prairies, of the most fertile kind, with occasional oak and hickory groves, and strips of timber along the rivers; though timber is rather scarce, yet the cheap price of lumber and coal, by lake, in a degree compensates for the want of timber. Some quarries of limestone are found in the banks of the rivers.

KENOSHA (formerly Southport), is a city lying ten miles south of the latter place, containing nearly the same number of population, and doing about the same amount and kind of business. It is the county-seat of *Kenosha* county, and has a fine harbor.

Kenosha county is also a small county, which was recently part of and set off from Racine county. It contains about 11,000 population. The soil, timber, streams, etc., are similar to those of that county—and presents some of the most fertile, well-cultivated farms, in all the West —with much excellent stock. The prairies which are found in these counties, five to ten and fifteen miles from the lake, are among the most beautiful in any part of the prairie world. This is the southern lake town in Wisconsin, and though we are now to leave the state, we hope soon to return and describe the interior portions.

We have now passed the last county in Wisconsin, lying on the lake, and fifteen miles south, we reach—

WAUKEGAN (formerly Littlefort) in Illinois, county-seat of *Lake* county. It is a thriving city of about 4,000 population. With its green sloping shores, its deep dusky ravines, and rounded swelling hill in the center, on which stands the court house; this is probably the most attractive location on the western shore of Lake Michigan. It is a place of much business, and must have a rapid growth for years, backed-up as it is, in three directions, by a rich and extensive farming country, and a good harbor and piers in front. It is about forty miles north of Chicago. For a few miles immediately next around it, there is considerable timber, and beyond that fine prairies. Lake county is well watered by the head-fountains of Fox and O'Plain rivers, which run south, and empty into the Illinois.

All the towns which we have thus visited and described, have at least one Newspaper published in their midst; some of them two; while at Milwaukee there are about a dozen, some daily, others weekly and monthly; at Chicago there are over twenty, some daily, weekly, and monthly. There are also, passing through all the towns, from Milwaukee to Chicago, two Telegraph lines—O'Rielly's and Col. Speed's; and both doing an active business, which evinces great amount and activity in the commercial transactions of the towns.

CHICAGO is the next place we reach, although there are

one or two little embryo villages starting up along the lake between this city and Waukegan, where are short piers, wood-yards, and a few tenements.

Chicago, the county seat of Cook county, is much the largest city on the lakes west of Buffalo; and is the great shipping point for northern, western, central, and even portions of southern Illinois. The *Illinois and Michigan Canal* brings immense amounts of produce from the south and southwest, while the *Galena and Chicago Railroad* brings large quantities from the west and northwest, all of which is shipped at Chicago, for the Atlantic seaboard; and in return these conveyances carry back to those several interior regions the vast vessel loads of merchandise which come up the lakes, and are required by this western and southern population.

The city is situated at the mouth of a river of the same name, the main body of which sets back near two miles into the town, then divides into two branches, both of which have a uniform depth of from 12 to 15 feet water, all furnishing a commodious and almost unlimited harbor for an immense amount of shipping, of every description, from the graceful yacht to the huge bark and magnificent steamer; which continually throng the many miles of wharfing, and crowd the channels with their exits and entrances, daily and hourly.

The leading articles of export from this city are wheat, flour, pork, beef, cattle, horses, wool, lard, etc., eastward by steamboat and sail vessels; lumber, merchandise, ironware, wood and iron machinery, farming utensils, etc., southward by canal, and westward by railroad. But the *lumber trade*, more than any other, distinguishes Chicago. It has hitherto been claimed that *Bangor*, Me., did the most extensive lumber business of any city in our nation; but by reference to commercial tables in the newspapers of that city, a short time since, it will be seen that, for the last year, the lumber trade of Chicago exceeded that of Bangor by nearly two hundred thousand feet, and each place overgoing 175 millions feet. The following, from the *Chicago Tribune*, shows the lumber business of that city:

"For the benefit of our cotemporaries, we copy from our 'Annual Review of the Trade and Commerce of Chicago, for the year 1850,' the amount, respectively, of the different descriptions of lumber received by Lake for that year:

Lumber (boards),	feet,	100,367,797
Shingles,	no.,	55,423,750
Lath,	pieces,	19,890,700
Pickets,	"	100,393
Staves and Headings,	"	3,000,000
Shingle Bolts,	cords,	3,132
Square Timber,	cubic feet,	63,579
Cedar Posts,	no.,	64,564

"The lumber trade has become one of the great features of the commerce of Chicago. The following table exhibits very briefly the operations in this department for the present year, contrasted with that of 1849:

Receipts.	1849.	1850.
Lumber, ft.,	73,259,533	100,364,797
Shingles,	50,579,750	77,347,750
Lath,	19,281,733	19,890,700"

Chicago, being located on the shore of Lake Michigan, embracing both sides of the river, on the borders of a wide, rich, and beautiful prairie, extending in different directions for many miles, handsomely diversified by small groves and strips of timber, which spring up at commodious intervals along the banks of the river, and in some places on the lake shore; all forming a very delightful and diversified picture, as it is viewed from some of the elevated observatories of the city; and particularly, when taken in combination with the long, broad, and shaded avenues of green which lead away into the expanded prairies, or terminate in the glittering lake, passing many beautiful gardens and elegant villas, does the scene become one of enchanting loveliness.

The lands all about Chicago, with few exceptions, for twenty to thirty miles distant, are valuable and held at high prices; but the character of the soil is such, that it is better adapted to grazing and growing of corn, oats, barley, and root crops, than to wheat; it being an exceedingly rich, deep, rank soil, upon which garden vegetables, strawberries, and fruits flourish in great luxuriance. For the most part, the soil is peaty loam, containing small portions of marl and sand, with a stiff clay subsoil, and occasional sand ridges, running through the meadows, parallel to the lake, which leads many to the conclusion that the lake has, from time to time, been receding from its original bounds, leaving these ridges as its beach at various periods.

There is no marsh or impassably wet land about Chicago, as strangers often imagine from a casual glance, though the surface is very level, at a hight of from three to five feet above the lake and river. And the winds, off and onto the lake, create fluctuations in the water of the river from twelve to twenty inches, much like tides in seaboard rivers, and have a fine effect in promoting health, by keeping the waters active and fresh.

In regard to the direction of transportation and trade, as touching the West and North West, the *Chicago Daily Tribune* has the following:

"We have repeatedly called attention to the fact that the opening of the *Illinois and Michigan Canal* had changed the course of trade of a very large portion of the productions of the *Illinois River Valley*. Previous to that event, that region of country found its only outlet to market by following the downward course of the rivers to the Gulf of Mexico. The amount of corn, wheat, pork, lard, beef, and tallow, and many other articles, that have taken the Northern route the present season, is immense.

"Not only is it in the productions above referred to, that we find a remarkable change in the course of trade, but merchandise of almost every description, passing from the East to the Illinois, Mississippi, or Missouri rivers, are now forwarded by way of the Lakes and the Illinois and Michigan Canal. Within a short time past, we have noticed large consignments coming up the Lakes, *en route* for the St. Louis market. Not only dry goods, boots and shoes, but heavier articles, such as sugars, molasses, iron, and machinery, are now taken by this route from the Seaboard into the heart of the Great West.

"A late number of the *St. Louis Intelligencer* notices the arrival at that place of a canal-boat load of Porto Rico sugars, which had been brought through from New York for 65c. per 100lbs., and insurance one per cent. Large quantities of fruits, teas, wines, etc., are received in that city also by the same route.

"Furs, peltries, wool, etc., from the River Region, south of us, are also being shipped North and East by the Illinois and Michigan Canal and the Lakes. Cotton is also seeking a Northern market by the Lake route. A late number of the *Albany Evening Journal* says:

"'A canal-boat is now in the basin, consigned to MONTEATH & Co., laden with cotton—being the fourth which has brought this staple from the West this season. The experiment bids fair to prove successful.' Large quantities of tobacco have also been shipped East the present season, by the same route, and we understand contracts have been made for future heavy shipments.

"In addition to the above, the shipment of beef cattle, by Lake and Railroad, to the New York and Boston markets, has become quite an important business. The *New York Express*, noticing this fact, says: 'Beef is now sold in this city from cattle that were grazing on the plains of Illinois a fortnight before. Cattle are brought from Chicago to New York, all the way by steam, arriving, of course, in much better flesh and in a more healthy condition than if they had been driven.'

"These are movements in which the people of the North West cannot fail to feel the most lively interest. They indicate important results, and should be carefully studied by all who are in any way connected with the commercial affairs of the country. Henceforth, is our region of country, not only to sustain highly important commercial relations with both South and North, by reason of its abundant productions, but also, as a medium through which the commercial exchanges of those remote districts will be effected. We have only seen 'the beginning of the end.'"

The following tables, from the Commercial Reports in that paper, will be interesting, as showing the amount of tolls received from the Canal business, the dates of opening and closing its navigation, together with similar information in regard to the Lake operations:

"The following table shows the amount of tolls collected at all the offices of the *Canal* for three years:

	1848.	1849.	1850.
March	..	..	4,986 26
April	..	4,694 69	17,114 06
May	6,227 84	13,112 87	15,986 15
June	10,889 10	19,263 42	14,521 86
July	11,258 37	11,954 68	11,938 02
August	10,480 21	14,913 76	8,446 76
September	21,150 49	18,177 67	14,055 57
October	16,961 26	18,480 41	22,235 56
November	9,597 21	16,546 58	15,267 63
December	109 42	1,643 24	370 34
Total	$86,673 80	118,787 32	124,974 21

"NOTE—Of the tolls for 1850, $87,856, $65,000 were received at the Chicago Office."

"Date of	first clearance for Lower Lakes,		April 4th
"	last "	"	Nov. 27th
"	first arrival from	"	April 6th
"	last "	"	Dec. 17th."

"The whole number of registered clearances for 1850 is 1066
" " " Arrivals " 1668."

Below are farther tables, which show the state of markets, with the amount of receipts and shipments by the various mediums, at Chicago:

"The market for *wheat* opened here on March 16th, at 50a62½ for spring, and 70a85 for winter. By the first of April large lots of spring were changing hands at 73a78 cents. Prices continued advancing, with now and then slight fluctuations. On the 13th May, spring wheat was firm at 90 cents, and winter at $1.10. At the same time *flour* ranged at $3.75 to $6.00, from inferior country to extra city brands. In June the culminating point was reached at $1.00a$1.05 for spring wheat, and $1.15a$1.20 for winter, and $4,50a$7.00 for *flour*. At this period the crops at the South gave indications both of an early and abundant harvest.

"The first *wheat* of the new crop reached our market on the 20th of July. At that date spring was worth 54a60, and winter 62a70. Since then prices have fluctuated from 38a45 for spring, and 50a65 for winter, to 60a65 for spring, and 70a83 for winter—choice lots for milling going higher. At the present time 47a60 for spring wheat, and 65a78 for winter, are ruling rates.

"Corn, in the early part of the season, came forward freely by Canal, during which time prices ranged in this market at 40a50c."

"The following figures will show the entire receipts and shipments of Grain and Flour from Dec. 1st, 1849, to Dec. 1st, 1850:

	Receipts.	Shipments.
Wheat, bu	1,165,481	873,644
Corn	254,314	242,285
Oats	162,536	158,054
Barley	24,868	22,872
Rye	2,000	2,000
Flour, bbls	70,099	100,872

"The above figures are accurate, with the exception of so much of them as comprise receipts by teams. We have made an earnest and continued effort through the whole year to keep an account of the quantity reaching the city by this means. Unquestionably, however, we have, now and then, failed to get an account of every wagon load, and this will account for any seeming discrepancy between receipts and shipments, when the consumption of the city is taken into account.

"The shipments of *wool* by Lake in 1849 amounted to 520,202 lbs,—in 1850 to 913,862—being an increase of 393,660 lbs."

"During the present year there had been received by railroad up to

Sept. 1st	195,200	lbs
By canal to Oct. 1st	482,299	"
Other sources (estimated)	200,000	"
Total	877,499	"

Cincinnati has been long noted as the greatest pork and hog market in the country; but Chicago is as undoubtedly the most extensive cattle and beef market in our country.

The Slaughtering business has been more extensively carried on during the present year than ever before in Chicago. There is perhaps no other Western city that slaughters the number of cattle which Chicago does. The whole number of cattle slaughtered, during the season, was 27,500; and the amount of capital invested, about three fourths of a million of dollars. In addition, about 10,000 sheep have been slaughtered within two months.

The Commerce and Monetary matters of Chicago are carried on by some eight or ten brokers and bankers; thirty to forty forwarding and commission houses and produce buyers; as many lumber dealers; beside a large number of wholesale merchants, in all branches of mercantile operations, as dry goods, grocers, iron, hardware, and all kinds of wearing apparel from head to foot; together with a host of retail dealers, in every description of mechanical work.

Here may be seen Hotels which, in size and accommodation, are surpassed but by three or four in our nation. Some of the Church edifices, too, are splendid specimens of architecture, with many magnificent dwellings.

The three principal avenues of Transportation abroad, are those before noticed—the Lakes, Railroads, and Canal. Though these extracts and remarks give but a birds-eye view of the Trade and Commerce of the "Garden City," still it will afford some idea of the vast amount of business there transacted.

Upon the Wholesale business of that city the *Chicago Democrat* makes the following remarks:

"We have heretofore spoken of the additions made to our wholesaling firms within the past year or two. We still notice that the increase of wholesale houses continues; and this year in a more marked degree than for any year previous. In fact, Water Street is being built up, along its entire length, both on the river and on the south side, with large buildings, fitted up in the best manner for wholesale warehouses. These buildings are now, for the most part, filled with large and varied stocks in the dry goods, grocery, drug, boot and shoe, oil, paint, and hardware lines.

"The completion of the Canal, and still more the extension of the Railroads, have operated rather to the injury of our Retail establishments, which, in many instances were transferred to the country villages; those that remained were compelled in a great measure to confine their business to a merely city demand, which, in the meantime, has been springing up in a most unprecedented manner, and which has now more than made up for the loss caused by the transfer of the country trade.

"The completion of the Canal and the Railroads, has, however, created another trade—the Wholesale one, which has now taken a fair start; one, indeed, that promises well for its future extent and prosperity. Our Wholesale establishments are now the pride of our city, and are fully able to meet all the demands of the trade scattered in the flourishing towns and villages around us.

"We have no doubt at all that it is for the interest of country merchants to at least look in upon Chicago and see what we can do for them. A fair trial is all that our merchants ask. If they cannot sell them at as cheap rates as goods can be obtained for in the East, they are satisfied to allow them continue on their way. If goods can be obtained here, even a little above New York prices, there is still the item of expense of traveling to be counted, to say nothing of time, which, in these days of steam and lightning is more than even money.

"There are other reasons which give Chicago the advantage. A country merchant can here make a more careful selection of his goods without being compelled to make large purchases of articles which remain upon his shelves to be afterward sold at less than cost. He can also run in upon the Railroad, make a selection of a few articles required by him, sell them readily, and thus turn his money quickly, realizing two per cent. where he formerly made but one. In the meantime we would call the attention of our country merchants to our wholesale establishments, to give them a trial, in the full confidence that they will save money, time, and trouble, by trading in Chicago, instead of going East, as many of them have heretofore done."

Another improvement, which is largely characteristic of the Western States, that greatly facilitates the business between Chicago and the country, is the many *Plankroads* which lead, in different directions, out of the city to the various farming districts.

These roads are substantially built of heavy plank, at an expense of from $1,100 to $1,500 per mile; and at toll rates of 1½ to 2 cents per mile, they pay a revenue, on the capital invested, varying from 15, 25 to 40 per cent.

Most of the large towns situated along the Lake, the Railroads, the Canal, and the Rivers, have Plankroads running back into the country, by which the hauling of produce in, and merchandise out, is greatly facilitated. The States west of the Lakes have more of this kind of roads, in proportion to the number of the population, than the older States have.

There are two excellent Agricultural Monthlies published in these States; the *Prairie Farmer*, at Chicago; and the *Wisconsin Farmer*, in that State.

Of that phenomenon, *Aurora Borealis*, which is usually so brilliant in that latitude, a recent number of the *Chicago Journal* gives the following vivid description, under the title of "ærial rehearsal:"

"On Monday evening, the sky presented a succession of the most beautiful appearances we have seen in many a night. The moon with a new coat of silver, rode high in the west, while in the north and northeast, pure, pearly-white overlaid the blue—then deepened to an orange—then turned to a crimson, till it looked like the pillar of fire in the wilderness, or a Daguerreotype of sunset. Anon it changed—the crimson was pink—the blue a blush, and the pearl a delicate green.

"What they were doing up aloft, is more than we know—whether rehearsing sunset or sunrise, 'shifting scenes,' for the never-before performed drama of 'To-morrow,' or spreading out rainbows on the upper decks, to dry, is to us a mystery. Now and then, we saw white, silvery-looking spars extending from the northern horizon, and converging in the zenith; and it occurred to us that may be they were repairing this great blue tent we live under, and that we saw the bare spars, and the red linings of the curtains that were thrown up to keep them out of the way of the aerial craftsmen. And then again, as it crimsoned and pearled, and clouded so exquisitely, we fancied it might be Heaven's grand pattern for sea-shells to tint by, that we had discovered at last. And once more, ere we had quite made up our mind on this conjecture, such a beam, nay *cloud* of red light streamed out into the night, and over the stars, that we were sure it must come from Heaven's painted window, and that somebody—*perhaps*, somebody we once knew and loved, and love still—was passing to and fro, giving us, without the walls, a glimpse or two of the glory within. As we kept looking, we kept fancying, and who knew, but it might not be the evening of some forgotten and long-past yesterday, thus 'revisiting the glimpses of the moon'—one that you and we loved, and have sighed for, more than we would care to tell, and would give a dozen to-morrows to see again.

"As we looked, it changed, and the whole heaven from far below the Dipper to the Zenith, was a *flutter*. Through the silvery lace-work shone the stars and the blue, and the galaxy itself. What *could* it be, but the dim scarfs of the loved and lost, thus waved in token of remembrance to the earth beneath? And why not? How beautiful and how calm lay that earth, beneath the great argus sky. The eyes of hundreds were turned toward Heaven, that during the broad and glaring day, forgot there *was* a Heaven, or a treasure in it. They remembered it then, and were remembered in turn! Ah! if our fancies were only *half* true!

"The books call it Aurora Borealis—what do we care for the books? and the philosophers declare it is electrical in its origin; a fig for the philosophers!—the book of memory and the human heart was printed and collated before that conceited old German, they tell of, ever cut a type, and as for philosophy, there is more wisdom in a thought thus tinted with a ray shining through last night from yesterday, than Seneca, or any body this side of Solomon ever thought of.

"But while we gazed, the vision vanished, the window was curtained, the rehearsal over, the sea-shells taught their lesson, the tent 'as good as new,' the old yesterday faded out, the last scene shifted, and this paragraph ended."

It is generally recollected, no doubt, that in August, 1812, a most cruel and terrible *massacre* was perpetrated upon the whites by the Indians, at this city, minute accounts of which have been often published, both in the books of the late war with Great Britain, and more recently in pamphlets and newspapers. There were few more distressing or destructive scenes enacted during that war, or which developed more daring heroism, than was shown by some of the females, as well as males, then in the garrison at old Fort Dearborn.

As the progress of a city or country will be more fully appreciated by viewing its present condition in contrast with earlier periods, I copy a description of Chicago, and other parts of the West, from a work by LATROBE, written in the autumn of 1833, an intelligent tourist, who visited the Great Lakes and the Mississippi at that time.

After describing a rough and tedious overland journey from Detroit westward—such as many before and since have experienced and can well appreciate—he says:

> "When within five miles of Chicago, we came to the first Indian encampment. Five thousand Indians—Pottawattomees—were said to be collected around this upstart village, for the prosecution of the treaty, by which they were to cede their lands, in Illinois and Michigan, to the whites."
>
> "I have been in many odd assemblages of my species, but in few, if any, of an equally singular character, as that in the midst of which we were surrounded, at Chicago, This little mushroom town is situated on the verge of a level tract of country, for the greater part consisting of open prairie lands, at a point where a small river, whose sources interlock—in the wet season—with those of the Illinois [O'Plain] river, enters Lake Michigan. It, however, forms no harbor; and vessels must anchor in the open lake, which spreads to the horizon on the North and East in a sheet of uniform extent."

And Chicago river "forms no harbor!" This will be news to the thousands of extensive commercial men, whose numerous vessels and steamers now lie safely and commodiously along the many miles of wharfs on the main trunk and branches of that deep and busy river. And it would be astonishing, beyond measure, to this same tourist who, eighteen years ago, wrote that sentence—and in all candor, no doubt—were he now to visit this "mushroom" town, and sail up that same river in one of our magnificent steamers, to witness the fleets of every description of shipping, which, in size and numbers, would make a respectable show, even in his favorite Thames; to look at the mountains of lumber, the hundreds of massive five and six story buildings, count the steeples of twenty to thirty towering churches, and the shining cupolas of splendid school-houses and colleges; with the many tall smoke-chimneys of prosperous factories; and then watch the snorting, dashing steam-horses hauling their long trains, that make the prairies tremble again; and see the more than thirty-one thousand population which occupy this city, and enjoy its advantages and prosperity. But he continues:

"The river, after approaching near at right angles to within a few hundred yards of the lake, makes a short turn and runs to the southward, parallel with the beach. Fort Dearborn and the light-house are placed at the angle thus formed. The former is a small stockaded inclosure with several block-houses, and is garrisoned by two companies of infantry. It had been nearly abandoned until the late Indian war on the frontier made its occupation necessary. The upstart village lies chiefly on the right bank of the river, above the fort. When the proposed steamboat communication between Chicago and the St. Joseph river, which lies some miles across the lake, is put into operation, the journey to Detroit may be effected in three days; whereas, we had been upward of six days on the road."

Should that traveler pass over this route now, he would find himself only a faint prophet of coming events; for, instead of being *three days*, he would perform the trip from Detroit to Chicago in about *fifteen hours*, or less. He continues:

"We found the village, on our arrival, crowded to excess, and we procured, with great difficulty, a small apartment, comfortless and noisy from its close proximity to others, but quite as good as we could have hoped for. The Pottawattomees were encamped on all sides—on the wide and level prairies beyond the scattered village, beneath the shelter of the low woods which chequered them, along the banks of the small river, or on the leeward of the sand-hills, near the beach of the lake."

"A preliminary council had been held with the chiefs some days before our arrival."

"Such was the state of affairs on our arrival; companies of old warriors might be seen sitting and smoking under every bush, arguing, palavering or *pow-owing*, with great earnestness; but there seemed no probability of bringing them to another council in a hurry."

"But I was going to give you an inventory of the contents of Chicago, when the recollection of the warm-hearted intercourse which we had enjoyed with many fine fellows, whom probably we shall neither see nor hear of again, drew me aside."

"Next in rank to the Officers and Commissioners, may be noticed certain store-keepers and grocers, resident here, looking for their custom and profit either to the influx of new settlers establishing themselves in the neighborhood, or to those passing farther westward—not to forget the chance of extraordinary occasions like the present. Add to these a doctor or two, two or three lawyers, a land agent, and five or six hotel-keepers; these may be considered the stationary occupants and proprietors of the score of clap-board houses around you. Then for the birds of passage—exclusive of the Pottawattomees—you have emigrants and speculators as numerous as the sand; horse-dealers, and horse-stealers, rogues of every description—white, black, and red—half-breeds, quarter-breeds, and men of no breed at all; dealers in pigs, poultry, and potatoes; creditors of the Indians, sharpers, peddlers, grog-sellers, Indian agents, traders, and contractors to supply the Pottawattomees."

"All was bustle and tumult, especially at the hour set apart for the distribution of the rations to the tribes. Many were the scenes which here presented themselves, exhibiting the habits of both the red men and the semi-civilized beings around them."

"But how sped the treaty? you will ask. Day after day passed; it was in vain that the signal-gun from the fort gave notice of an assembling of chiefs at the council-fire. Reasons were (by the Indians) always found for delay; one day an influential chief was out of the way; another, the sky looked cloudy, and the Indian never performs any important business, except the sky be clear.

"At length, on the 21st of September, 1833, the Pottawattomees resolved to meet the Commissioners. We were politely invited to be present. The council-fire was lighted under a spacious shed in the green meadow, on the opposite side of the river from that on which the Fort stood. From the difficulty of getting all together, it was late in the afternoon when they assembled."

"Three days later, before we quitted Chicago on the 25th, the Treaty with the Indians was concluded; the Commissioners putting their hands, and the Chiefs their paws, to the same. By it, an apparently advantageous *swop* was made for both parties; the main conditions of which, if we were correctly informed, were—that the Indians should remove from the territory which they now occupied, within three years time, being conveyed, at Government expense, beyond the Mississippi, and over the State of Missouri to the western boundary of the latter, where 5,000,000 acres of rich, fine land were to be set apart for them; and that they were to be supported for one year after their arrival in their new possessions; moreover, the Government bound itself to pay them, over and above, a million of dollars; part of which sum being set apart for the payment of the debts of the tribe, part for a permanent school fund, and part for agricultural purposes, presents, and so forth."

Now, in 1851, this location, of scenes so graphically described, is occupied by a gay, wealthy, and flourishing city, of over 31,000 population; and most of the Indian tract is converted into a fruitful, highly cultivated agricultural district; presenting numerous cheerful dwellings, fine fences, luxuriant crops, tasty gardens, and thrifty stock; the fields inclosed variously, with rail, board, wire, sod, and hedge fences; in all, exhibiting a charming and prosperous picture, to excite admiration and gladness in every observer.

Some idea of the labor and productiveness of the farming region which seeks Chicago as its transportation depot, may be formed from the fact, that in a single year the value of exports from that place has been between two and three millions of dollars; beside its vast lumber trade, of nearly two hundred million feet, distributed in all directions, to supply the wants of a vast country, so rapidly being settled and ornamented with fine buildings fences, etc.

The greatest ornament of Chicago is its Primary Schools —its common or free school edifices are the best buildings, for that purpose, that I have ever seen in any city; while the tuition and management of the schools within are of as high and proficient grade, as those to be found anywhere else.

The School Fund of the city, derived from its school lands, is large and ample, which warrants the payment of good salaries; and, consequently, secures teachers of the highest order of competency. The same may be said, to a certain extent, of the schools of most of the cities and towns in the Western States; the donation or appropriation of the public lands, by Congress, for this purpose, being large and liberal. Beside the amount of lands set apart specifically for educational purposes—both primary and university—being every section sixteen, besides other tracts—a certain per centage, also, of the moneys derived from the sale of all public lands, by the General Government, within the State, is to be appropriated to the school fund: so that there is no part of the Union so richly supplied with school funds, in proportion to its population, as some of these New States—and no section where a liberal education can be obtained at so small expense, as here.

The school houses in Chicago, Milwaukee, Dubuque, and some other places in the West, are really elegant palaces, and ornaments both in size and style; and their operations within are truly fountains of knowledge.

The higher institutions of learning are proportionably useful and creditable; and would even do honor to older cities.

In several directions from the city, at the distance of three to five miles, great abundance of limestone, of the very best quality for lime and building purposes, is quarried; and which proves to be of great convenience and advantage.

Some eleven miles southwestward from Chicago is a pleasant location called SUMMIT; it is situated on the west bank of the Canal. At the commencement of that work, when it was designed for a ship canal, this point was laid out and designed for a large town. It is a beautiful sand and gravel ridge, covered with a fine grove of oak and hickory trees, some two miles long by half a mile wide, bordered in two directions by the best of prairie lands, and skirted on the other sides by the river timber; it lies some 20 or 30 feet higher than the Canal, and nearly 50 feet higher than Chicago; it is the highest point of land for many miles from the city; and presents excellent and healthful sites for farms.

Near by, on the north side of Canal and river, located where the Plankroad crosses the O'Plain river, is the little town of LYONS, a place of note for the great quantities of good lime quarried and burned there—large portions of which are carried into the city, over the Plankroad, and has become a profitable business.

Some 12 or 14 miles south of Chicago, at the mouth of *Calumet* river, there is a new town being built, of the name of the river. It is laid out in lots, many have been sold, and the place is principally owned by men in Chicago. A light-house and some other improvements have been made; the mouth of the river, with some piering and dredge-work, will afford a tolerable harbor and business facilities; and CALUMET may yet become a considerable city.

We have thus taken a hasty look at the Lake Towns of Wisconsin and Illinois, in a short call upon them; and though we have seen very much to delight us, we shall be none the less pleased with the interior towns and resources of the Western States, which we shall examine carefully, on a tour through them, after returning from a flying trip of observation down the Illinois and Mississippi rivers to

St. Louis, in Missouri; and then, up the latter river, to *Minnesota*, of which Territory I will endeavor to give a faithful general description; in regard to its topography, resources, business, curiosities, and prospects.

But here, as in all parts of the West, we shall realize the truth of the following remark: "In describing American scenery, if we would make our picture a true one, we must—

"'Catch, ere she change, the Cynthia of a minute.'"

TRIP SECOND—MINNESOTA.

At Chicago we take Canal Packets, or Railroad and Stages, for La Salle and Peru, southwestward from the city, at the junction of the Canal and Illinois river, and head of steamboat navigation on that stream; though, in seasons of high water, steamers run up sixteen miles farther to Ottawa, where Fox river empties into the Illinois.

The length of this Canal is about one hundred miles; which distance is usually run, by the Packets, in twenty to twenty-four hours; and except when too much crowded affords a very pleasant passage, as they are comfortable and managed by gentlemanly Officers; fare $4; but there is a line of freight and emigrant Packets, which run through in a little longer time, carrying passengers with a fair amount of luggage for from $2 to $3; and for a little additional charge this latter class of boats will carry furniture and light merchandise.

There are also a large number of substantial freight and line boats, which carry families much cheaper, though with less comfort, than the Packets, where it is desired, and where they are in less hurry to get through.

These Packets leave Chicago and La Salle regularly at morning, noon, and evening of each day. The Canal is now in operation its fourth year; and the convenience of travel caused by it, with daily lines of good steamers on the Illinois river, has diverted much of the travel this way, which, before its opening, sought the Ohio river route, to Eastern Summer Resorts; though it is now thought less pleasant than the Illinois and Lake route.

The Canal lies along the fertile and picturesque valley

of the O'Plain and Illinois rivers; crossing, in its way by aqueducts, Aux Sauble, Fox, and Vermillion rivers; and, running along under the Kankakee Bluffs, presents a fine view of the beautiful valley of that river, as it stretches away to the northeast, through good prairie lands, into Indiana, its shores skirted with strips of valuable timber. At the junction of this river with the O'Plain, under the bluffs (some fifty miles southwest of Chicago) is what is commonly called the commencement of the Illinois river, these waters being known by those names only above the rapids at this junction, and as the Illinois below them.

The combination of these singular and varied features of nature and art, at this point—rugged bluffs, gentle slopes, shady vales, fertile cultivated prairies, and dashing streams, with the smooth, regular, and walled Canal—altogether render this one of the most delightful locations for healthy atmosphere and beautiful prospects on the whole route, from Chicago to St. Louis.

There are many thriving and handsome towns, along the Canal, containing from one to four thousand population; and which have almost entirely sprung up since the digging of the Canal, which has been but a few years. The principal ones are Lockport, Joliet, Morris, Ottowa, La Salle, and Peru.

The lands along the Canal, for the most part, are of the very best quality—deep, sandy loam, and alluvion, with occasional ridges of white and yellow gravel, spurs of lime and sand rock, valuable for building and lime; and frequent strips or tracts of marl and clay; beside numerous extensive beds of good coal. The combination of these elements of wealth, with the great facilities which the Canal furnishes for markets, south and east, to the Great Lakes and the Mississippi, render it a highly favored region of country, and one richly deserving the attention of the emigrant, whether farmer, mechanic, or other business man. The Rock Island, La Salle, and Chicago Railroad, is also to run through this section; and the Engineers are already in the field, making explorations.

I believe this project of opening a Canal navigation between the waters of Lake Michigan and the Mississippi, was conceived in 1823, not long after the commencement of the Erie Canal. For this work Congress made a grant to the State of Illinois of each alternate section of government land, within a space of five miles each side of the line of the Canal. In 1823 a Board of Commissioners, with Engineers, explored the route and made an estimate of cost required to construct the work. In 1829 a new Board of Commissioners was appointed, who made a new survey and estimate, and several towns along the line were laid off, and lots sold. In the winter of 1835–6, the Illinois Legislature passed an act for the construction of this Canal, under the title of the "Illinois and Michigan Canal." The following are the dimensions of the work, viz.: seventy feet wide at the top, thirty-six at the bottom, and six feet deep.

The expense of the construction of this stupendous enterprise is to be met from the proceeds of the sales of this vast tract of land, ten miles wide, granted by Congress for that purpose.

It was a truly vast undertaking, for a young state, but it is now completed, and doing an immense business; and beside its inestimable advantages to the State, it possesses great national importance, being greatly beneficial to East, West, and South. A traveler through Illinois, in 1837, writes as follows:

"PERU is situated on the Illinois river, at the head of river navigation, and is the point of termination of the Illinois and Michigan Canal. This Canal, when completed, will be one of the most splendid projects of internal improvements in the Union. It unites the Mississippi with our Inland Seas, and the Gulf of St. Lawrence with the Gulf of Mexico."

Of these Canal Lands, mostly a fine quality of prairie, with occasional groves of timber—considerable quantities have been sold since the completion of the Canal, but large portions yet remain in market; which are offered for sale, at Auction, in May of each year, the appraised value—ranging from $2.50 to $10, and upward, per acre—being in all cases the minimum or first bid. The sales now take place at Chicago, though formerly they were held at different places along the route. The Canal Company also have some fine lands in the "Rock River country," which are subject to the same manner of sales.

The whole amount of land granted for this Canal, and which came into the hands of the Trustees, was 230,000 acres; amount sold up to the spring of 1851, 70,000; remaining to be sold, 160,000.

The whole amount of Tolls received on this Canal for the present year, up to November 1st, was $149,562, being a considerable increase upon any previous year.

Of this Company, Captain Swift, of Springfield, is President; and Hon. Davit Leavitt, of New York, Treasurer.

The whole amount of Produce shipped at Chicago during the same period—much of it received by Canal—was, of wheat, 226,060 bushels; of flour, 33,245 barrels; corn, 2,237,975 bushels; oats, 551,483 bushels. This is also a large increase upon the amount shipped previous years, during the same months. In addition to this, there have been large quantities of beef, pork, lard, and tallow shipped; together with many hundred heads of live cattle, which has not been the case in previous seasons.

In passing over this route the traveler will see many finely cultivated farms, much well-bred and fed stock, and some good orchards, though in this latter luxury, I regret to see far too little attention paid by settlers, generally, though there are pleasant exceptions in some regions.

Here, as in the West generally, the industrious, judicious, down-east farmer, can derive twice as much produce and profit for his economy and toil, as is the usual reward received for the same effort in the old states.

The several counties through which the Canal passes, are—

Cook, of which CHICAGO is the county-seat. Though the land in this county is what is often denominated prairie, still most of it differs from the true prairies of the West; it is more flat and level, and should properly be called *savannahs*, partaking more of the characteristics of that description of surface—nearly resembling the savannahs along the ocean and gulfs—than the Western prairies. They are, however, excellent lands for tillage, gardens, fruits, etc., and afford the finest of meadows. The soil is mostly a sandy loam, alluvial, with traces of marl, and of one to three feet depth, supported on a heavy clay sub-soil. Population of Cook county, 43,385; dwellings, 7,674; farms, 1,857; manufactories, 227.

Dupage county comes next, of which NAPERVILLE is the county-seat, a fine flourishing village, of near 2,000 population, situated on the Dupage river, which furnishes a good water-power, and sixteen miles from the Canal. This is a new county, containing much excellent land, similar to that of the Fox River country. Population, 9,290; dwellings, 1,568; farms, 1,175; manufactories, 38.

Will county is unsurpassed by any in this range, for the good quality of its lands, or the perfection of its improvements, elegant farms, and fine stock, fruits, etc. There is a farming community in one portion of this county, near Lockport, known as the "Yankee Settlement;" which, for well-cultivated, productive farms, and as good livers, will compare favorably with many settlements in the land from which their cognomen is derived. Population, 16,703; dwellings, 2,796; farms, 1,200; manufac. 94.

The county-seat of Will is Joliet, a vigorous, prospering, and beautiful village, of some 3,000 population. The O'Plain and Canal run through this village, and afford valuable water-power, which is considerably occupied with cloth factories, mills, etc. Superior building stone is quarried here in abundance.

The next most important village in this county is Lockport, five miles from the county-seat. It is equal in beauty of location and improvement with any town on the route, and contains about 2,000 population. It possesses extensive water-power, and good stone quarries. Here is located the General Office of business for the Canal Company and its Lands.

Grundy comes next, and is one of the new counties. It is equal to Will in the natural excellence of its lands, though not, as yet, so extensively cultivated; still, it presents some well-improved farms, with a fair show of good stock. In some places good building stone is quarried, and numerous coal beds have been opened. The Illinois and Aux Sable rivers run through this county. Population, 3,023; dwellings, 543; farms, 327; manufac. 7.

Morris, is the county-seat, and has enjoyed as rapid growth, since the completion of the Canal, as any town through which it passes; while its delightful location is unsurpassed by any village on the line, having a smooth and gently inclining surface toward the Canal and river; with pleasant groves on two sides, and rich prairies spreading away to considerable distance in the two other directions. Although of but few years age, its population is now nearly 1,000. As in the other towns named, there is at Morris a Newspaper, and a Telegraph office. Joliet and Ottowa have two newspapers each, and Lockport, La Salle, and Peru one each.

The last county, through which the Canal passes, is *La Salle*. For its good lands and farms, its coal, stone, timber, and water-powers this is a rich and important county. It is watered by the Illinois, Fox, and Vermillion rivers. Pop. 17,815; dwellings, 3,075; farms, 1,336; manuf. 46.

OTTOWA, the county-seat, is a beautiful and flourishing village of some 3,500 population; it is situated on the Canal at the junction of the Fox and Illinois rivers, which cut deep channels through the sand rock, Fox river having perpendicular banks from 15 to 25 feet high. This rock is easily crushed, and is composed of pure white or crystal sand, which is an admirable material for making the finest *glass;* and if as skillfully wrought, no doubt would equal the splendid Bohemian glass. Here is also a fine water-power.

The surface of the land and the scenery, at this point, are very singular; there being two platteaus to the bluffs or banks of the river; one, a rounded smooth slope or small hill lying from half to three quarters of a mile from the river, leaving a level plain or interval of that width between, some 20 to 25 feet above the river, with parts gradually descending, and others perpendicular. On this plain is built the village and runs the Canal. Ottowa is laid out and built with considerable taste and beauty. The Bluff on the south side of Illinois river is a grand position, and overlooks a picturesque and lovely prospect for many miles.

The route of 16 miles from here to the village of La Salle is marked with much romantic scenery, and remembered for strange Indian legendary connected with the high, rough, rocky bluffs of the Illinois, among which are, *Lover's Leap, Starved Rock, Buffalo Rock*, etc., which afford thrilling stories and fruitful themes for the romancer and poet. There are also, near by, some valuable *mineral springs*, which might be improved to advantage, and become favorite resorts.

PERU and LA SALLE, are two growing villages, located

at the junction of the Canal with Illinois river; and lie about one mile apart, but their rapid growth is such, and the land being so favorable, the intermediate space will undoubtedly soon be all built over, and the whole become one large city. This being the point of union between Canal and River navigation, and the eastern terminus of the newly projected Railroad from the Mississippi river at Rock Island, must speedily become a place of great commercial importance; and in the opinion of the writer, will ere long, rank and continue to be not less than the fifth city, for wealth and population, in the state, following in grade the cities of Chicago, Alton, Rock Island, and Galena.

Peru and La Salle are pleasantly situated—the business portions being mostly down by the water, and the residences on the high and airy bluffs above, which overlook a rich varied stretch of country, in different directions, along the river and prairies.

In the river, fronting Peru, is a rich alluvial island, which is highly cultivated, producing large crops and heavy grass; but in times of high freshets, much of the island is inundated. On the side beyond the town, but a narrow channel or slew divides the island from the mainland, the navigable channel being next to the town, where the largest steamers can float or lie with convenience; between Canal and River, is a channel cut, of requisite dimensions for Steamboats to pass.

The prairies, back of these towns, on the route toward Rock river, are exceedingly rich and delightful; and from in June till September and into October, present a great variety of fragrant and many-tinted flowers, which load the breezes with their odors. This is, in fact, true of all prairies and groves in the West—

> "Boon nature scattered free and wild,
> Each plant or flower, the mountain's child;

Here eglantine embalmed the air,
The hawthorne and hazle mingled there;
The primrose pale and violet flower,
Found in each glen a bower."

The O'Rielly *Telegraph* line, from Chicago to St. Louis, passes through the towns along the Canal; thence down the Illinois river, branching off to several interior towns, as SPRINGFIELD, the State capital, Beardstown, Jacksonville, Rushville, and some other towns; and then through Alton, spanning the Mississippi from Illinoistown into St. Louis.

From Peru there is a branch of this Telegraph line, running through Dixon, to Galena, thence to Dubuque, in Iowa; and here it branches off into Wisconsin, through Grant and Iowa counties.

Thus, we see the West is strung in all directions with these communicative lightning wires, which have converted the whole canopy above us into one universal whispering gallery of news and gossip, from all quarters of the continent; while Mr. O'Rielly and others, have a project in agitation, for continuing these lines to Texas and California.

It is not very extravagant, when contemplated in the light of what has been accomplished, with steam and electricity during the last quarter of a century, to predict that before the expiration of ten years—perhaps in five—we shall see a Railroad and Telegraph in successful operation from the Atlantic to the Pacific; either through the instrumentality of our own nation or by the British government.

Should our Government commence building such a Telegraph and Railroad, and make a proposition to laborers that they would give them even small wages in money, say ten dollars per month, more or less, beside board; and in addition give to each man who should work a year 160 acres, or *a quarter section*, of land; to those who should work half a year, half that amount; and in the same proportion for any time; the land to be selected from any government lands on the line and not nearer than one mile of the road; should the Government take this course, or some similar one, they undoubtedly could build the whole line in five years with very little difficulty; and there is very little doubt, that as soon as any part of the Road was built, beyond the Missouri river, either at Council Bluffs, or Weston, or some other suitable point, it would begin to pay for itself, in the lands it would cause to be sold, together with the business it should create in carrying emigrants and their merchandise out, and bringing back the produce they should raise.

There is another very comfortable medium of conveyance from Chicago to the Illinois river, which travelers can take, if they wish; which requires about the same length of time, with the same price of fare as the Canal-route. At the former place, you take the cars of the Chicago and Galena Railroad, to Aurora, some forty miles; thence, stages to Ottowa, where you again take the Packets to the river.

This Railroad and Stage route passes over a varied, beautiful, and fertile tract of country, consisting of rolling prairies and scattered groves; with numerous well-tilled farms, good buildings, fences, etc. That portion traveled by Railroad crosses the O'Plain, Dupage, and Fox rivers, with many smaller streams; which drain a section of prairies and timbered lands, not surpassed by any in the state. And that portion traveled by the Stages, mostly lies along the valley of the Fox river, so famous for its rich lands, fine stone quarries, coal beds, timber, and useful water-powers, already very extensively occupied by mills, factories, and machinery generally; surrounded and sustained by communities of industrious, forehanded, and intelligent farmers.

The Fox River Country, as it is called, is noted as being one of the best agricultural districts in the state; and as well advanced in improvement as any. This river takes its rise in the State of Wisconsin, and runs nearly a southern direction, till it empties into Illinois river at Ottowa. In several of the towns on this river there are good paper mills.

That distinguishing characteristic of the States of Illinois, Iowa, and Wisconsin—prairie, or timberless land—may be seen in its fullest or most perfect aspect, by a journey along this river. I transcribe the following remarks, upon Prairies, from an intelligent writer who traversed the Western States in 1837, as being a more happy description than I can write:

"*Prairie* is a French word, signifying *meadow*, and is applied to any land that is destitute of timber and brush, and clothed with grass; wet, dry, level, and rolling are terms of description merely, and apply to prairies in the same sense as they do to forest lands. Of those prairies these lines of the poet are truly descriptive:

"'Travelers, ent'ring here, behold around
The large and spacious plain on every side,
Strewed with beauty, whose fair, grassy ground,
Mantled with green and richly beautified!'

"Their soil is deep, friable, and of exhaustless fertility; excellent, in apposite latitudes, for wheat, maize, etc.; grapes, hitherto, have not been much cultivated; yet, as wild ones grow luxuriantly, it can hardly be doubted that a *hybridous* species, formed from a union of one of these natives and the exotic vine, would prove prolific of estimable fruit. From May to October, the prairies are covered with rank grass and flowering weeds. In June and July, they seem like an ocean of flowers of various hues, waving to the breezes that sweep over them. The numerous tall towering vegetables which grow luxuriantly over these plains, present a striking and delightful appearance."

In the Rock River Country, which lies parallel to and west of Fox river, the prairies are very similar in all their characteristics, in fact of the same excellence, while they are generally larger, extending often at much greater distance without the interruption of timber.

But the various Railroads already under way, and speedily to penetrate these immense fields—carrying to them all the facilities of business, as lumber and machinery, with the necessary merchandise, and bringing back their rich and abundant products—will place them at once before the gates of the great Seaboard Markets, where they will be welcomed as the granaries and bountiful larders for the millions of mechanical and commercial operatives whom they will feed.

And there are yet thousands of acres of these luxuriant lands, now for sale, in favorable and pleasant locations, at the low price of one dollar and a quarter per acre. Nothing can be more true than the following lines from one of nature's noblest adorers:

> "These are the Gardens of the desert—these
> The unshorn fields—boundless and beautiful,
> And fresh as the young earth ere man had sinned.
> The Prairies! I behold them the first time,
> And my heart swells, while the dilated sight
> Takes in the encircling vastness."—BRYANT.

We say, then, to the mechanic, pent up in dense, suffocating city or crowded town, who can scarcely breathe free and pure breaths, for want of room, or toil freely, and pleasantly, and profitably, from the austere and selfish dictation of many arrogant employers, and who derive at least three fourths of the profits of your labor; to such I say, come to the fresh and fruitful West, where you may easily have an independent and pleasant home.

To the young farmer, who toils the long, hot days, for the paltry sum of ten or a dozen dollars per month; or to him who rents land, returning to others the "lion's share" of all the products of his industry—to all, who would better their condition, rejuvenate their lives, and regain new energies under brightened incentives—to such I say, con-

7

fidently and in a lively friendship, come and appropriate to yourselves any necessary and proper amount of "these Gardens, boundless and beautiful," which you can, so many of you, easily do.

They will return you a greater yield of crops, for less labor, and then you can obtain prices but little under Eastern markets, transportation is now so cheap and speedy; which, as I have said elsewhere, in fact renders these Western lands as valuable as those of the East.

Although the same thorough and careful system of farming will succeed in different locations, to a reasonably fair extent; as for instance, the same general practice that works well in the Genesee Country, will result the same in Connecticut; and the same management of soils and crops which produces well in the Eastern States will also produce tolerably well on the Western Prairies, as a general thing; but yet, a still different and peculiar system or science is required in the management of the Prairies to make them yield their greatest constant profit; there are some characteristics about their soils, and the principles of cropping upon them, which are different and distinct from any other in our country, and which require different treatment than is practiced by farmers of any other region; these facts it would be well for farmers at the West, or going there, to understand.

The writer of this is preparing a work—which will be shortly published—upon Scientific Farming; the application of Chemistry, Geology, and Meteorology to Agriculture, generally; but the work is particularly devoted to the best mode of tilling the Prairie Soils, and securing crops from them—the application of these sciences to *their* peculiarities.

In cases where the ordinary crops produced on plowlands should fail, as they often do, in the Eastern as in the Western country, the growing of *Flax* and *Hemp* is a fortunate and profitable expedient to prevent the cultivator of the soil from realizing that uncomfortable exclamation that "all is lost;" as these are very sure crops, that very rarely ever fail.

The Prairies have been proved to be peculiarly favorable to the growth of Flax; and particularly, since the important and useful discoveries and inventions by Doctor Leavitt, and others—of the science and art of converting it into rich and beautiful fabrics, at small cost—does this article become highly interesting to the agriculturist, and the public generally. The culture of this crop is now eliciting a lively attention which it has never before obtained in this country. It is probably second only to the wheat crop in importance to the farmers of our country, and especially of the West.

A good article of Flax Seed, of approved varieties, is much wanted in the Prairie Country; and should emigrants take quantities with them, they will not find it come amiss. This seed always commands a good price at St. Louis, Chicago, and Milwaukee.

From "Illinois in 1837," I make the following extracts, in relation to the fires on the prairies, and their origin:

"On the origin of the prairie lands it is difficult to decide; various speculations have arisen on the subject, giving rise to a diversity of opinions. The level surface (according to the ideas of many) was formed by inundations. The whole of the State (Illinois), from a few miles north of the Ohio river, where the prairies commence, affords tolerably conclusive evidence of having been once covered with water, forming, probably, a large lake, similar to Lake Michigan, etc."

"From whatever cause the prairies at first originated, they are undoubtedly perpetuated by the fires that have annually swept over them, from an era probably long anterior to the earliest records of our history."

"It is well known, that in the richest and most dry, level tracts, the aboriginal inhabitants, before they had the use of fire-arms, were in the habit of inclosing their game in circular fires, in order that it might frighten and bewilder the animals, and thus render them an easy prey."

"The Indians and hunters annually set fire to the prairies, in order to dislodge the game; the fire spreads with tremendous rapidity, presenting one of the grandest and most terrible spectacles in nature. The flames rush through the long grass, with a noise like thunder; dense clouds of smoke arise; and the sky itself appears almost on fire, particularly during the night. Travelers then crossing the prairies are sometimes in danger, which they can only escape by setting fire to the grass around, and taking shelter in the burnt part, where the approaching flame will expire for want of fuel. Most melancholy is the aspect of a burnt prairie, presenting a uniform black surface, like a vast plain of charcoal."

Often I have, before now, watched the crackling and roaring fire as it passed, with the mighty winds, over these bright and graceful meadows, for hours in the night, the whole scene one of light, life, and excitement; when suddenly, the combustible matter being all consumed, the flames cease, all is dark, deathly-silent, with the black pall of destruction spread like a universal vail of mourning upon the earth; and, of all spectacles in the world, this is the most perfect exhibition of desolation, and at once realizes to one the fullest sensation of despair imaginable.

Now, to return from this descriptive digression, we will pursue our journey to St. Louis, and thence to Iowa and Minnesota.

At Peru we take passage on board the Illinois river steamboats, which run to St. Louis, a distance of about 311 miles, in twenty to thirty hours; fare $3 to $5.

Immediately along the Illinois river the lands, generally, are low, rich, sometimes wet, and heavily timbered with elm, oak, walnut, linn, pawpaw, locust, sycamore, and many other varieties; valuable for lumber, building, and fencing. This region will be more fully described hereafter in farther remarks upon the counties of the State, when they will be portrayed in alphabetical order.

The principal towns and cities which we shall pass, along the river, on our way to St. Louis, are, Hennepin, Henry, Lacon, Chillicothe, Rome, PEORIA, Pekin, Beardstown, Meredosia, Naples, Columbia, Grafton, and ALTON. These places will all be more minutely described, with the counties in which they are located. Peoria and Alton are flourishing and elegant cities—the former of about 7,000, and the latter some 14,000 population.

The country drained by the Illinois river, and its tributaries, on both sides, presents a greater variety of soil and surface than, perhaps, any other in the state. Its rich alluvial and heavy timbered bottoms; the intervals between these and the highest prairies, combined with these dry undulating meadows, and all within sight of the river at many points—a convenient contiguity of heavy forests, rich grass and corn lands, and dry clover and wheat soils—entitle this district to be reckoned among the very best in the "Sucker State;" and in it there is still considerable government land for sale.

In the opinion of some, this soil and climate are more favorable to the tender varieties of fruit, and the greatest growth of corn; yet, it is contended that Rock and Fox river Countries are better adapted to wheat and flax than that on the Illinois ; with reasonable culture and attention, both are so sure and bountiful, in their products, that after all little or no difference will be perceived; and what little advantage one region may sometimes present over the other, is found really to result much from superior tillage and management. Fruits, flax, grain, cattle, and sheep, in all parts, will do full as well, if not better, than in Western New York and New England, as the climate west is milder, and the seasons longer.

From Peru to Peoria the distance is 77 miles; to Pekin, 10; to Beardstown, 84; to Naples, 26; to Alton, 90; and to St. Louis, 24; in all, 311 miles from St.

Louis to Peru; and 100 more from there to Chicago; and fare the whole distance is $5 to $9.

From St. Louis, Mo., there are regular Steam Packets, up the Mississippi, to Keokuk, in Iowa; to Galena, in Illinois, to Potosi, in Wisconsin; and from Galena and Dubuque there are semi-weekly lines of Steamboats running to St. Pauls and Stillwater, in *Minnesota;* with an occasional small steamer running up the Wisconsin river, for many miles, to the Lumber Region, in good stages of water.

After leaving St. Louis, for a voyage up the Mississippi, the first city we reach is HANNIBAL, in *Missouri*, a place of near 4,000 population, with some fine blocks of buildings, and considerable business; but it palpably feels and shows the blight of the unpaid, compulsory labor system, which prevails in that State; and, as in Kentucky and Virginia, it surely prevents equal growth and enterprise, to what exists in the Free States, on the opposite sides of the great rivers; notwithstanding the Slave States have the advantage, in most instances, in point of climate, soil, and other natural facilities.

Still up about 13 miles is the lovely, neat, and thriving city of QUINCY, on the Illinois side, with a good levee; it is the county-seat of *Adams* county, with a population of over 6,000; with many superb buildings, green parks, shaded walks; and, as its name indicates, an intelligent Yankee community; every thing being done in real down East style, however, with more of life and energy than is found in towns of the same size in New England. Large amounts of Pork are yearly packed here.

The county contains much very excellent land, well watered, and many finely cultivated farms. There is still some very good land here for sale, at government price. Great quantities of corn, and other grain, are raised in this county. Pop. 26,508; dwell. 4,459; farms, 2,294; m. 118.

Next, at some 40 miles above, is WARSAW, well located,

on the river, in *Hancock* county. It has a good landing, is doing considerable business, and surrounded by a good farming country. Corn and Pork are the principal articles of export from this point, and amount to an extensive business. Pop. 14,652; dwell. 2,585; farms, 1,167; man. 43.

Directly opposite to here, in the state of Missouri, are the villages of CHURCHVILLE and ALEXANDRIA, near the mouth of Des Moines river. There is some business done here in Pork packing; but the land lies too low, often inundated; and the same drawback, by which Hannibal suffers, also prevails here.

We now reach the state of *Iowa*, which lies west of the Mississippi.

The first city is KEOKUK, six miles above Warsaw. It is situated in Lee county, on the Mississippi, at the foot of the Lower Rapids, and contains about 4,000 population, though it has but recently commenced growing. It has a good landing and levee. Near here is the mouth of the Des Moines river, up which valley a Canal is being built, and is somewhat advanced.

In his book, of 1848, GEORGE B. SARGENT, Esq., says of Lee county and Keokuk, (from the name of a distinguished chief):

" *Lee* is the southernmost county of the state; it is well watered, and the general quality of the soil is as good as any in Iowa. Keokuk, the most thriving town, is the depot of a large extent of back country, and must eventually make a place of great importance." 'There is a fine opportunity here for creating an available water-power. A Railroad is in contemplation from this thriving town, *via* Fairfield, Oskaloosa, Pella, and Monroe City, to Fort Des Moines. It is proposed, also, to construct a Railroad between Keokuk and Dubuque, through Montrose, West Point, Mount Pleasant, Washington, Iowa City, and Marion, and other towns."

" FORT MADISON, the seat of justice for Lee county, handsomely situated on the Mississippi, about 12 miles above the head of the Rapids [and 20 above Keokuk], is quite an important town, having 1,200 to 1,500 inhabitants. It contains the State Penitentiary."

There is a fine agricultural district, with many thriving villages and cultivated farms, along Des Moines river, with considerable good water-power. There is some government land for sale in this region. Population of Lee county, 18,860; dwellings, 3,252; farms, 1,350; manufactories, 78.

The fare from St. Louis to Keokuk is $2; thence to Davenport and Rock Island, $2; and thence to Galena, $2.

From Keokuk boats proceed with some difficulty, in low stages of water, up the Rapids, 12 miles, to MONTROSE and NAUVOO—the former on the Iowa side, and the latter, in Illinois, and distinguished as the theater of *Mormon* troubles, some years ago; but it has since been purchased by a colony of *French Communists*, or *Icarians*, who now occupy it, under Mons. CABET; and they are said to be a peaceful, intelligent, and industrious people.

It is in Hancock county, of which CARTHAGE is the county-seat, where *Joe Smith* was killed. This is a good county of land, both for crops and grazing. Pop. 14,652; dwellings, 2,585; farms, 1,167; manufactures, 43.

For picturesque scenery and extent of prospect, from the high elevation of the town, which is seen from a great distance in every direction, with its beautifully sloping surface down to the river, which here bends around in an extended crescent, its several channels curving among many luxuriant islands—there are few, if any, positions on that long river, from St. Louis to St. Anthony's, that surpass this; whether we consider the place as viewed from the country around, or the country which it overlooks; and in either case, the enthusiastic admiration of the observer is challenged to the highest degree.

There are three places, in the West, which the writer has had the pleasure of beholding, that are more attractive and picturesque, to the taste of many, than most others; and they are *Madison* (Wisconsin); *Dubuque* (Iowa); and *Nauvoo* (Illinois); while Lake Pepin and St.

Anthony's present scenery scarcely inferior to any location for beauty and variety.

After passing Fort Madison, we reach BURLINGTON, 46 miles above Keokuk, and county-seat of *Des Moines* county. It is, perhaps, the largest city in Iowa, numbering now about 7,000 population; with much wealth, intelligence, and many good buildings. It has a fine steamboat landing. Mr. Sargent says of this county, in 1848, as follows:

"Des Moines was the earliest settled, with the exception of Dubuque, and is at this time the most populous county in the state. The seat of justice and principal town is Burlington, which was formerly the Territorial seat of government. The first legislature that convened in Iowa, met here in the fall of 1837."

Like most of the towns on this mighty river, situated both upon and under the bluffs, this one too overlooks much rich and delightful landscape, with fine improvements. Population of the county, 12,987; dwellings, 1,919; farms, 383; manufactories, 23.

Still 13 miles farther up, on the Illinois side, is the village of OQUAWKA, in *Henderson* county. It is a flourishing town of between 1,000 and 1,500 population. I quote the following, written in 1837:

"Oquawka, or Yellow Banks, is a town recently settled. It is situated on the Mississippi river, about midway between the Keokuk and Rock Island Rapids, and is the principal depot for freight between these points; the town is laid out in two sections on an extensive scale; the soil is sandy, and the surface gently undulating. The site was sold by the original to the present proprietor for $2,000, who last autumn sold one fourth of it for $24,000." There's luck, for you.

We next reach the city of MUSCATINE, in Iowa (formerly Bloomington), county-seat of *Muscatine* county. It is now a city of nearly 5,000 population, doing an immense business, and sustained by an exceedingly fertile and well-cultivated country. No city in Iowa is growing faster than this. There is considerable wealth, and many fine buildings and mills here.

In reaching this place, we passed the mouth of Iowa river in *Louisa* county, containing fine land and timber, with WAPELLO for the seat of justice; a fine little town, beautifully situated on the Iowa river. Population of Louisa county, 4,939; dwellings, 842; farms, 388; manufactories, 18.

Muscatine county is one of the finest in the state. In speaking of this county, Mr. Sargent says:

"This county is situated in one of the great bends of the river, and in point of location has many advantages. Bloomington [now Muscatine], the seat of justice, is situated on the Mississippi; it has an excellent landing for steamboats. Its peculiar situation in the bend of the river gives it the advantages of both a river and inland town. It contains about 1,800 inhabitants; a very extensive business is done here in produce."

People in the interior, and about the state capital, IOWA CITY, come to Muscatine as their natural and most convenient steamboat landing; and emigrants, going into that region of country, will always do well to land there. Population of the county, 5,734; dwellings, 999; farms, 460; manufactories, 19.

Still farther up, thirty miles, is the romantic and flourishing city of DAVENPORT, county-seat of *Scott* county, containing, at this time, about 3,000 population, with fine steam mills, and other general elements of continued growth. Population of Scott county, 5,986; dwellings, 991; farms, 384; manufactories, 19.

Mr. Sargent gives the following of Scott county:

"This is a rich and well-watered county, the Wabsipinecon river bounding it on the north, and the Mississippi flowing along the whole eastern and southern borders, a distance of about 40 miles.

"The lands bordering on the Mississippi are susceptible of cultivation almost to the water's edge, the bluffs rising gradually, and forming the most desirable locations for farming purposes that can be conceived. The beauty of the scenery, the quality of the soil, and the apparent advantages of the situation, induced an early settlement along the banks of the river, where the farms are now numerous and highly improved. In the interior, the land, though mostly prairie, is high, gently rolling, and well adapted to cultivation; and owing to the facilities for procuring all necessary timber from the Mississippi, is rapidly becoming dotted with farms.

"It was in this county that Black Hawk built his village, when the last of the Sacs and Foxes were driven from their homes on Rock river; and from here his warriors started to commence the war of 1832. The treaty, at the close of that war, by which the first land in Iowa was acquired from the Indians, was concluded at Fort Armstrong, by General Scott; and in honor of that celebrated officer, not so much on account of his military achievements as for his agency in effecting this favorable treaty, Scott county received its name. It is one of the smallest counties in the State, not containing over twelve townships of land."

"DAVENPORT, the seat of justice, is situated at the foot of a bluff on the bank of the Mississippi. The scenery in its vicinity is exceedingly picturesque, and long before the country was settled, had been noticed with admiration by passing travelers. Its appearance at that time is thus described in a work published several years ago:

"'At the foot of the Upper Rapids is one of the most picturesque scenes that we recollect to have beheld. On the western side, a series of slopes are seen rising one above another for a considerable distance, until the background is terminated by a chain of beautifully rounded hills, over the whole of which trees are thinly scattered. On the other side of the river is a broad flat plain of rich alluvion, several miles in length, and more than a mile in breadth, and terminated by a range of wooded hills. On this prairie is a small village of the Sac and Fox Indians, composed of rude lodges, scattered carelessly about.

"In front of the landscape, and presenting its most prominent feature, is *Rock Island*, the western shore of which is washed by the main current of the Mississippi, while the eastern side is separated from the main-land by a narrow channel, which is fordable at low water. The southern point of the island is elevated about forty feet above the ordinary level of the river, and is supported by a perpendicular parapet of rock. Here stands Fort Armstrong, a strong and very neat work, garrisoned by two companies of United States troops; and here will be one of the most desirable sites for a town on the Upper Mississippi. Rock river, which enters the Mississippi a few miles below the island, in Illinois, is a rapid stream, which may be easily rendered navigable, and which affords abundant water-power for the propulsion of any kind of machinery. The whole of this region is fruitful, healthful, and agreeable to the eye."

"It is interesting to mark the changes that have taken place since the above description was written. On the 'western side,' with the 'beautifully rounded hills in the background,' now stands Davenport. On the other side, which was then occupied by the Sac and Fox village, is now the flourishing town of Rock Island, in Illinois. Fort Armstrong is abandoned and in ruins. All along the banks of the river are seen the marks of civilization and improvement. But, though the scenery has lost some of its wildness, it retains its original characteristics, and has gained many pleasing features. The towns of Rock Island and Davenport, the old Fort with its deserted block-houses, the Mississippi, winding gracefully above and below, Rock river branching off through the woods, the forest-covered islands, the high, wooded bluffs, and the rich, green prairies of Illinois, form a picture, which, for beauty, variety, and extent, can hardly be surpassed.

"The healthfulness and beauty of the situation, together with the facilities for hunting and fishing in its neighborhood, have made this place the fashionable resort, during the summer months, of large numbers of people, from St. Louis and other Southern cities. It has hitherto been more noted on this account than as a place of trade; but the business of the town is now rapidly on the increase."

"Davenport is the eastern terminus of the contemplated railroad from the Mississippi to the Missouri river. It is 350 miles above St. Louis, and 500 below the Falls of St. Anthony. It contains about 1,000 inhabitants."

"Le Claire is the name of a new town which has lately sprung into existence at the head of the Rapids, about fifteen miles above Davenport. It is situated in a thickly settled part of the county, and bids fair to become a place of considerable importance."

"*Clinton* is a rich and well-watered county of land. In some parts there is a scarcity of timber, which has prevented very extensive settlements being made.

"De Witt, the seat of justice, is a thriving little village, beautifully situated on a high, rolling prairie, about three miles from the Wabsipinecon river."

Population of Clinton county, 2,822; dwellings, 499; farms, 306; manufactories, 10.

Opposite to Davenport, on the Illinois side, is the enterprising and rapidly growing town of ROCK ISLAND, county-seat of *Rock Island* county. It contains a population of between 3,000 and 4,000; who, for intelligence, liberal enterprise, and hospitality, are not surpassed by any people in the West. From its immense, very convenient water-powers, derived from both the Mississippi and Rock rivers, and for its wider surface of level ground between river and bluff, Rock Island possesses importance and business facilities superior to Davenport; though the latter presents more beautiful and striking scenery to arrest the attention of strangers, than the former place.

The rocky foot of the Island is nearly on a line between these towns; and causes a wider body of water than the usual width of the river, giving here the appearance of a small lake in the form of a slightly curved crescent.

The main and navigable channel of the river is on the west side, while that on the east side is narrower, and has been dammed so as to afford a splendid water-power above, and a fine little harbor of still water below, making a most commodious place for building and launching vessels, the bank having a very smooth and gentle slope. The island, which thus divides the river, is one of the most charming and comfortable rural retreats, in the warm summer, that can well be desired; the beautiful groves commingling and interspreading their green branches together, as if with a benevolent design to swing a spacious umbrella or parasol, sufficient for all who might choose to avail themselves of its convenience, in sun or in shower. Many a delightful promenade in the vernal time has the writer of this enjoyed in these sylvan shades, with bird-carols above, leaving palaces and cultivated fields, to be and think amid these quiet midsummer bowers, where all is so still and serene, that Sleep and Rest seem almost to have ordained these groves as their silent sanctuary.

The writer of "Illinois in 1837," thus speaks of this place:

> "Stephenson [now Rock Island] is situated on the Mississippi, opposite the lower end of the Island, and two miles above the mouth of Rock river, and three hundred and thirty above St. Louis. It has twenty or thirty families, and several stores. The fine situation of this place, its natural commercial advantages, and the rapidly increasing population of the fertile country around it, on both sides of the Mississippi, will, no doubt, render it in a short time one of the most considerable towns in this part of Illinois.
>
> "The Island is three miles long and half a mile wide, with limestone rock for its base. *Fort Armstrong* is on its south end. On two sides, the rock is twenty feet perpendicular in hight above the water. A portion of the Island is cultivated."

Since the above was written, Stephenson (now Rock Island) has grown to be a respectable city from its "twenty or thirty families." Since then, too, a smart milling and manufacturing town, called MOLINE, has sprung up, to near a thousand population, at the head of the Island, on the Illinois channel, taking advantage of the large water power; and on Rock river, about the same distance that way, from Rock Island, another town of similar description, named CAMDEN, has been built up, and uses the water-power of that river; so that probably there is not another place in the State, or the West, with so much superior water-power, and so many facilities for using it, as at this point, which must soon render Rock Island the second manufacturing city in the State.

Beside, this high rocky Island, in the river, with steep, high bluffs on both sides, point to this spot as the place where, ere long, the Mississippi will be bridged—and, in fact, the only place where such an undertaking is practicable; and it is already beginning to be talked of with considerable earnestness.

Here, too, is the western or Mississippi terminus of the "Rock Island, La Salle, and Chicago Railroad," upon which the Engineers are already at work. All these things combine to point out Rock Island as likely to become, at no distant day, the second city in Illinois.

While, on the opposite side of the river, the city of Davenport will be likely to maintain a fair comparative growth with her neighbor. Population of the county is 7,000.

One branch of the O'Rielly Telegraph line ends here; running from St. Louis, through Jacksonville, Rushville, Quincy, and other towns in Illinois, crossing over to Keokuk, in Iowa, and running up the river, through Burlington, Muscatine, Davenport, and crossing the river back again, terminates in Rock Island. Most of the towns throughout the West have good weekly newspapers; while many have daily ones, as Galena, Springfield, Alton, Dubuque, and others.

From Rock Island, we pass Moline, and run over the rapids up the river eighteen miles, to Port Byron, passing several smaller towns, or river-landings. This is the head of the main rapids, but there is a slight rapid or broken current still up to New Albany, some twenty-seven miles, in *Whitesides* co. Pop. 5,361; dwell. 923; f. 404; man. 24.

In time of low water, these rapids retard the speed of boats, and the upsticking rocks render navigation somewhat dangerous, except the boats are carefully guided by experienced pilots. By throwing out oblique wing dams, at various places, many water-powers are obtained. Pop. Carroll co. 4,586; dwell. 814; farms, 482; man. 17.

And now, we will pass Elizabeth on the Iowa side, Savannah, in Carroll county, on the Illinois side, and some other small towns.

When about ninety miles above Rock Island we reach the mouth of *Fevre* river. And about six miles up that river, we come to the rich, thriving, and enterprising city of GALENA, one of the first, in size and business, in Illinois. It is the county-seat of *Jo Daviess* county, and contains about 8,000 population.

This river has its name from an early French trader, *Le Fevre*, and not from fever sickness, as some have supposed.

Jo Daviess is perhaps as rich in minerals as any other county in the entire Mining District. Many men in this county have made handsome fortunes in the lead business. Still, portions of the county are well adapted to farming business, and present many highly cultivated farms, with good buildings. Population, 18,604; dwellings, 3,431; farms, 1,370; manufactories, 279.

Ffteen miles from here, up the Mississippi, after passing Bellvue, we reach Dubuque, the most beautifully located city in Iowa, equal in business to any; and is contested only by Burlington for the largest population. This is the heart and grand depot of the *lead mining* operations for this State; of which large and valuable quantities are annually raised, smelted, and sent off down the river from this place. It is the county-seat of *Dubuque* county. Of this county and city, Mr. Sargent says:

> "This county, which embraces the principal part of the mineral region west of the river, was the earliest settled in the state; a party of French Canadians having established at the site of the present town of Dubuque, about the year 1786, for the purpose of trading with the Indians. The first discovery of lead ore in the West is said to have been made in that vicinity by the wife of an Indian chief."

This is a well-timbered county, but much of the land is too broken for agricultural purposes. There are valuable water-powers on Maquoketa river, some of which are extensively improved. Population of Dubuque county, 10,841; dwellings, 1,952; farms, 755; manufactories, 46.

"Dubuque, the seat of justice, beside being the great mineral depot, is a place of much trade, and supplies a very extensive country with goods. It contains about 3,000 inhabitants, several wholesale stores, and one of the largest hotels in the West. The U. S. Land Office for the Northern District of Iowa, and the office of the Surveyor General of Iowa and Wisconsin, are at this place."

Now the city of Dubuque contains near 7,000 population.

From here we pass up to POTOSI, a busy and growing mining town, on the Wisconsin side, situated in "Snake Hollow," near the mouth of Grant river, in Grant county. It has a good steamboat landing, contains a population of above 2,000—an enterprising people—and is a place of considerable business.

Some ten miles above, in the same county, is the dull and dilapidated village of CASSVILLE. It occupies one of the most sightly and attractive positions to be found on the Mississippi, and has the natural resources to become a wealthy and flourishing town. But it is cursed with the Land-monopoly blight—of eager, miserly speculators, mostly non-residents—like some other towns in Wisconsin.

There are those who prey like vampires upon the prosperity of portions of that young, handsome, and noble state; some from whom we had a right to look for better conduct—who have not only pursued a policy to prevent, on their own part, the growth of some fine towns, but have hindered others; and, to a degree, crippled the influence and efforts of those who, with honorable enterprise, were anxious and striving to promote the advancement of their towns. There are some of this kind of moth and Shylock beings scattered through the West, much to its detriment.

We need the true FREE SOIL and LAND LIMITATION doctrines and measures to be realized and applied in such portions of the West, before it can come up to its full and destined dignity and power in the nation; when it shall be a country of real FREEMEN, who own their own homes, manage their own shops, direct and enjoy their own labors —a great community of FREEHOLDERS.

In the earlier history of this part of the West, the means for traveling over it were far less comfortable and expeditious than at a later period. Then, the stage route from Peoria to Galena was a long and circuitous one, but through an excellent country of land, rich in natural resources for agricultural purposes, being through the counties of Knox, Putnam, Whitesides, Henry, Carroll, and into Jo Daviess.

The tourist, whom I have several times quoted from, traveled over this route in 1833, and gives an account of it. But before starting, he gives a description of Peoria, now a rapidly growing city of some 7,000 population; and for good buildings, streets, shady walks, fences, and other fine improvements, it is scarcely surpassed by any city in the West; while the intelligence, benevolence, and accomplishments of the people would be creditable even to Eastern cities of the same size. Here is an account of the same place eighteen years ago:

"Peoria is situated at the lower end of an expansion of the Illinois river, forming a lake about twenty miles long by one and a half in breadth. It ranks among the earliest French settlements in the country; but, while in other directions large towns of recent foundation spring up, Peoria remains a wretched and ruinous collection of habitations; a spell seems to rest on these early settlements of the French."

Our tourist had just undergone some vexatious trials by stage in a journey from St. Louis, and probably was in no very good humor to appreciate the fair side of many objects at all. There is no finer section of country than that which surrounds Peoria. At this place he took the stage for Galena; and his description of that route, as of the Mineral region, is faithful and entertaining. We overtake him on the fourth day of his journey, and find him discoursing in this wise:

"On the fourth day of our journey north, when we were between Rock and Apple rivers, we traveled over the scene of early Indian devastations, on the outbreak of the late Indian war. The ordinary route lay lower down the country, near the Mississippi; but, on account of the swollen state of the streams, we were obliged to follow a trail, keeping the ridge of the elevated country, and traversing a region which we thought unparalleled by any thing we had previously seen, for the magnificence of its *park scenery*—prairies sprinkled with forests."

Here were some five days consumed in performing a journey (from Peoria to Galena), which is now accomplished in less than two days. And that Indian ravaged country, and park scenery so beautiful in its natural garb, are now subdued by the plow, presenting many cultivated farms and comfortable tenements. Our traveler continues:

"On approaching *Fevre* river and the district of the *Lead mines*, the face of the country began to change its character; the soil became poorer and more stony, broken by limestone knolls; and from the summit of an elevated ridge, called *Pilot Knob*, the eye ranges over a vast plain, stretching from the river to northward and eastward, with the *Platte Mounds*, two most singular natural eminences, heaving up from the level in the far distance.

"Galena, which lies below, is situated on Fevre river, about seven miles from its junction with the Mississippi. It is the main depot for the lead ore, collected in vast quantities from the neighboring country, and transported thence by steamboats to St. Louis. The population of this Mining district is computed to be upward of 10,000."

Now, Galena itself contains nearly that number, and Dubuque alone over half of it; while the whole population of that district must be eight or nine times the number it then contained. Pilot Knob is a high rocky cone, the summit of which is of difficult access, but once attained, the prospects, over both sides of the Mississippi, up and down, which it affords, amply compensates for the toil; it stands in the angle formed by the confluence of the two rivers; the eye here commands a view over many little towns and "diggins," far away in the three states of Iowa, Illinois, and Wisconsin; and from its peculiar location, many times serves as a convenient guide to the pilots navigating those rivers, whence it derives its name.

In those days it was a rare thing to find a steamboat going to Prairie du Chien; and the route was generally performed by stage. Following is Mr. Latrobe's felicitous experience in performing the jaunt. Upon preparing to leave Galena, he says:

"Our next halting place was to be at Prairie du Chien, 75 miles distant to the north; and having stored away our chattels, we were happily extricated from the deep mud of Galena by two strong horses, and began to jolt forward over the plain toward the Platte Mounds, taking our morning meal at a snug farm—doubtless the germ of an incipient city—called by the melodious name of 'Hardscrabble.'"

This place is a "lead diggins," some twelve miles from Galena; and the "farm" at which they breakfasted, was Col. Curtiss's, whose hospitable widow still occupies it, while several of her sons are settled in different states, as preachers of the Gospel. It is now a pleasant, thriving village, called Hazel Green, and is noted for the large quantity of mineral which is annually raised from its mines. He continues:

"Our route led us between the Platte Mounds, which, on nearer approach, we found to consist of two regular moulded hills, connected by a band on which, midway, a small conical mound rises. They all are evidently formed of limestone rock, masses of which start up grotesquely from the surface. Several small rivers rise in their vicinity. Our route was a solitary one, the houses being few and far distant; nor were such common-place adventures as being benighted, wet to the skin, and sleeping in comfortless quarters, at all wanting in our experience."

Those rocky elevations, which crop out from amid the

broad prairies, of which there are in fact three, two being called Platte Mounds, over an hundred feet high, and the other Belmonte Mound; the two former stand about one mile apart, like two huge outposts or bastions; while on a gently sloping ridge, which connects them, and over which the stageroad passes, stands the other, a beautiful center cone, almost as uniform in figure as the half of an orange, of between 60 and 70 feet high, nearly to the summit of which you may drive a horse and buggy, on either side, from where we have a most magnificent and charming view, far as the eye is able to reach in every direction, over bright, waving, flowery prairies, cheerful villages, and among the hills and valleys of the Mississippi, Fevre, Platte, Grant, and Peckatonica rivers, some of which take their rise about these mounds.

> "From the promontory gazed
> The stranger, raptured and amazed."

In earlier times, before Wisconsin became a state, a popular *race-course*, of mile heats, was established around the base of this cone; and perhaps a handsomer track, with fairer opportunities for observation, was never combined on any other ground for the turf-sports. The Territorial Capital was established here at the village of Belmonte; and during the sessions of the legislature, I am told the races were well patronized; as the business and interests of the Territory were few, the business of legislation was not as arduous as in the "Empire State"—where so much of party-business and office-seeking enters into the work of law-makers—those pioneer legislators found more time that could be devoted to amusement; beside, sports of this character were more congenial to the early settlers of that region, who were mostly emigrants from Kentucky and Virginia.

Since the capital was removed to Madison, Belmonte

has not advanced very much, though it presents some pleasant dwellings and fine farms.

I once, at this point, on an evening in the Autumn of 1849, had the opportunity of witnessing, in almost a rapture of amaze and delight, the waving *prairies on fire*, for many miles around. I was driving in a buggy from Platteville to Mineral Point, and reached Belmonte mound just at the coming in of twilight. The evening was one of those bland, mellow seasons, usual in the time of Indian Summer; and on reaching the center mound—which lay rolled up and shrouded in smoke, handsome as an apple-dumpling all steaming from the kettle—and feeling strongly tempted to know and see farther, I drove to near its summit to take a leisure survey of the vast flame-lighted and enchanting panorama flung out so profusely by artist-nature; the moon and stars peered but dimly through the hazy air, adding mystic force to the scenes, in the passing twilight.

Soon the fires began to kindle wider, and rise higher from the long grass; the gentle breeze increased to stronger currents, and soon fanned the small flickering blaze into fierce torrent-flames, which curled up and leaped along in resistless splendor; and like quickly raising the dark curtain from the luminous stage, the scenes before me were suddenly changed, as if by the magician's wand, into one boundless amphitheater, blazing from earth to heaven, and sweeping the horizon round—columns of lurid flames, sportively mounting up to the zenith, and dark clouds of crimson smoke curling away and aloft, till they nearly obscured stars and moon; while the rushing, crashing sounds, like roaring cataracts mingled with distant thunders, were almost deafening; danger, death, glared all around—it screamed for victims—yet, notwithstanding the imminent peril of prairie fires, one is loth—irresolute, almost unable—to withdraw, or seek refuge.

I now thought of the spot on the banks of the bright Kankakee, where, some years ago, two young persons—betrothed lovers—perished in the prairie-flames; their crisped forms, near their horse, being found next day, by a hunter. It is a rich, beautiful prairie—the river murmured along to leeward of them, but the flames outstripped their fleet charger—upon which both were riding—before he could reach the stream—why did they not think—resolve—to set a "back fire," and take refuge on the burned space!

But I am back to the mound; will the remorseless flames leap along the high grass that has grown luxuriantly upon the sides, to the very pinnacle of this cone? Surely, the wind is this way, and my horse is already restive; aye, but I've a match in my pocket, and it is easily lighted. Persons traveling in prairie regions should bear this in mind. But see, that ocean of flame; I *must* look, still again; even my little match has sent a lively current dancing down the leeward slope; and I am admonished to follow it; but, in presence of such scenes, at such an hour, the sensitive mind feels its frailty, and instinctively awards the homage due to the majesty of his Creator, from the creature.

Next morning I again visited this mound, rode over the charred grass-stubble to its top; the scene of so much terrific brilliance but a few hours before! now all was changed; the green-brown carpet was displaced by the black-spread—the ravaging flames had consumed every thing—black destruction sickened the heart in sadness—the keenest, darkest emblem of *desolation* that can be imagined—even the livid, confused glimmer, still almost trembled around the eyes from last night's flames—such as gleaming lights leave upon the optic nerve; *now*, it was painful to contemplate, for a moment, the same expanse, which, a few hours ago, it required an effort to withdraw from its enchanting but fearful sublimity; like the giddy fascination of the serpent which holds its victim in thrall till destruction overwhelms beyond escape, is the charm of such spectacles; it was as if the destroying angel flew abroad, crying in terror-tones, breathing tempests of fire and smoke from his nostrils, that should awe and paralyze; I may not describe—my pen is tame and dark—but would you realize such emotions—experience its force—

"Oh, fly to the prairies, and in wonder gaze,
As o'er the grass sweeps the magnificent blaze;
The earth cannot boast so magnificent a sight—
A continent blazing with oceans of light."

And now we reach Prairie du Chien, county-seat of *Crawford* county, in Wisconsin. It has grown to be a town of several hundred population, doing considerable permanent business—a number of stores, taverns, and some mechanic shops; but, like several other towns, too much of it is owned by a single individual, to allow it to grow very rapidly. So much for the present aspect of the place; and I will now extract a description of it, given by a writer who visited the place in 1838, on a trip to St. Pauls:

"Toward the close of the third day, after quitting Galena, we reached the Wisconsin, a large river, flowing through a deep wooded glen from the eastward. Summer and winter were here contending for the mastery in the foliage of the desiduous forest trees on its steep shores. Its channel forms the direct line of communication, by boats, with the waters of the Nenah, a river of Green Bay, in Lake Michigan—a short portage intervening.

"A ferry-boat conveyed us across the river, here flowing in a rocky, deep, and shady valley. Six miles yet remained to *Fort Crawford*, at Prairie du Chien; and you may imagine our pleasure in the hope of soon gaining quarters, where we might rest, after a seven days' journey, during which we had hardly taken off our clothes.

"At our arrival in Prairie du Chien, from the signs of the season, one might have been inclined to augur badly for the prosecution of our scheme of a farther ascent up the Mississippi, of three hundred miles, to the [St. Anthony's] Falls.'

Now, almost daily, the steamboats run from Galena to Prairie du Chien, in a few hours—some of them destined on a run up the Wisconsin river, to the *Lumber Country;* and others, regular semi-weekly lines, for St. Pauls and other parts of Minnesota; of which boats Captain Smith, and Captains Harris, are popular and well-deserving owners and commanders. Boats run from Galena to St. Pauls in from three to four days.

Beside, the stage route now to Prairie du Chien is far more comfortable and expeditious than it then was; passing by the Platte Mounds and through the pleasant villages of Hazel Green, Platteville, and Lancaster; the latter, county-seat of Grant county, Wisconsin; and over this route we now meet many well-cultivated farms, comfortable buildings, several other small towns, and a hospitable people. He continues:

"The Prairie lies between the Mississippi—which here flows in a broad bed of many channels through a wilderness of islands—and a long precipitous line of bluffs bordering the valley on the east; it forms a beautiful grassy meadow of six miles in length and one or two broad; it is bounded on the south by the Wisconsin. Its name is, I believe, derived from that of an Indian chief.

"On the west, the view is limited by the long line of hights, rising directly from the right bank of the Mississippi river, and only broken by the glens which give outlet to the tributary streams. From any of these hights most singular and extensive views are gained, for ten or twelve miles, of the broad river, crowded by grassy and wooded islands—many of them containing large ponds, frequented by innumerable water-fowl—and of the prairie throughout its whole extent, with the village, the fort, the bluffs, and the fertile farms along the base.

"Prairie du Chien is computed to be 600 miles from St. Louis, by water, 300 from the Falls, and about 180 from Fort Howard, at Green Bay, by way of Fox and Wisconsin rivers. But few Indians, and those of the Menominee tribe, were in the vicinity. In the course of the spring, during the season of floods, a steamboat ascends the stream as far up as the St. Peter's river, to carry government stores to the two forts; and the rest of the year the means of communication are restricted to boats, sledges, and canoes.

"By employing one of these latter class, we now hope to secure the means of proceeding; and with considerable delay and difficulty we contrived to get a number of Canadian boatmen, and a large, roomy birch-bark canoe into our service. Meanwhile, our time passed pleasantly enough in the society of the Colonel commanding the post, with half a dozen other officers."

Following is an account of his voyage up to *St. Anthony's Falls*, and back again, he having set off up the river on the 22d of October, 1833:

"Our purpose this evening was merely to get fairly afloat; and accordingly, after having paddled a few miles, we encamped upon an island in the river, a little below the *Painted Rocks*, with a dry starlight night as a good omen over our heads; lulled by the howling of the Indians, encamped in the vicinity, the barking of dogs, and other sounds which betokened that we had not yet passed out of the bounds of the farms on the prairie. It was computed that, unless prevented by unforeseen accidents, we ought to reach the Falls in six days. The whole of this time was however taken up in advancing as far as *Lake Pepin*, one hundred and seventy miles above the prairie, and nearly four more were necessary for the attainment of our object. To give you the outline of our excursion at once, I will mention, that we paddled forward by day, and nightly sought some snug corner of the forest, either on the main, or in the islands—pitched our tent, raised our fire, cooked supper, sang, conversed, and looked at the stars till we were sleepy, and then betook ourselves to our buffalo-robe couch till dawn."

Some 75 or 80 miles above Prairie du Chien, we reach the beautiful prairie called *Prairie la Crosse*, which was a favorite ground with the Indians for playing ball and other games. It is on the Wisconsin side of the Mississippi; and much of it is good farming land. The route from Prairie du Chien to St. Croix lake passes this prairie. There are already some settlements here, and business is increasing.

Still farther up, and on the west, or Minnesotà side of the river, is *Wapasha Prairie;* this is a splendid prairie, both for beauty and for agricultural purposes, and plenty of timber near by. The river here is bordered by rugged and precipitous rocks, with intervals in the ravines, forming convenient boat landings. Altogether, this is an attractive location.

It is somewhat noted as being the place where, in 1848, the *Winnebago* Indians made a halt, and refused to remove farther to the new grounds assigned them, beyond the Mississippi. So great were their regrets at leaving this beautiful spot, their early hunting and council grounds, and the grave-places of their fathers, that additional forces had to be summoned from the Fort down at Crawford, to compel them to leave according to their treaty.

A short distance above here is one of the places where old Captain CARVER pitched his tent, in early days, when trafficking with the Indians in this region.

Some distance above this is the promising town-site of *Pratt's Landing.* It is located just below the foot of Lake Pepin, and nearly opposite the mouth of Chipaway river; and, in time, will probably become a fine town.

"The whole distance to Lake Pepin, the mighty river flows through a deep valley, of perhaps two miles average breadth, among innumerable islands, and under steep bluffs, which rise frequently on both sides, with precipitous fronts to the hight of five hundred feet. Their lower slopes near the river are mostly clothed in oak forest, and many of the summits terminated by a picturesque pile of highly-colored rock, of eighty feet or upward perpendicular. Above and beyond this great channel, hollowed out in the country for the passage of the *Father of Waters*, the country on both sides seems to be rolling prairie.

"The beauty of the scenery—though only the last coloring of autumn lingered on the forests and prairies—quite took us by surprise; and nothing can be more opposite than the impressions suggested by the scenery of the Mississippi above and the Mississippi below its junction with the Missouri—here a scene of beauty and romance, there a terribly monotonous, turbid, and swollen stream.

"Lake Pepin is, in fact, nothing but a basin of the river, twenty miles long and three broad. It is entirely without islands, and is hemmed in by bold shores abounding with interesting details.

"From the upper end, it took us three days to reach ***Fort Snelling*** at the junction of the St. Peter's river with the Mississippi; the character of the intervening scenery is interesting, but not so much so as lower down. At the point of junction, however, it is truly romantic. Up to our arrival at the last-mentioned Fort, which lies seven miles below the *Falls*, the weather favored us in an unhoped-for degree. During the week that we were the guests of the gentlemen posted there, a few inclement days passed over us, but the weather again held up so as to admit of our return between the 8th of November and the 13th, on which latter day we entered the Prairie du Chien, after an absence of three weeks. But in this interval, much came before us which was highly interesting, and my next shall go a little more into detail."

Here follows a chapter of more particular details of that romantic and perilous trip:

"Our pleasure at the resumption of a life of autumnal adventure, similar to last year's, though under different circumstances and in another region, was considerable.

"I have mentioned, that uncertain as the occurrences of genial weather might now be in this latitude, we had been encouraged to hope that the delicious season, known by the name of the *Indian Summer*, which ordinarily intervenes between the fall of the leaf and the commencement of the severe winter of the north, might yet come to our aid in the prosecution of our excursion. It is true, the north wind blew while we were at Prairie de Chien, sprinkling the hights with sleet, and the air appeared full of the water-fowl pressing to the south—led by Him who teaches them to spread their wings upon the keen blast, and seek a milder climate before the winter come; and though the blackbirds might be observed collecting in vast flights, and then, having received the word to go forth, rise at sunset, and by one common impulse, follow their leaders in one narrow, continuous stream over the forest and prairies in the same direction; and though the gorgeous foliage of the painted forests, with its thousand hues of green, yellow, orange, red, was shaken to the ground—still we were not deceived, but before the lapse of many days we saw the sleet disappear—the wind cease to agitate the river and the forest—the wild-fowl pause

in their passage, and, furling their pinions, alight by myriads among the islands and marshes, and, as though by enchantment, a season settle down upon the earth, which, for its peculiar beauties, might vie with the most poetical and delicious in the circle of the year.

"To what shall we compare the Indian Summer? To the last bright and unexpected flare of a dying taper—to the sudden and short-lived return to consciousness and apparent hope in one stretched upon the bed of death, after the standers-by have deemed him gone—or to the warm, transient, but rosy glow which will often steal over the snows of the distant Alps, after the sun is far below the Jura, and after they have been seen rearing themselves for a while, cold and ghastly white over the horizon?

"During the Indian Summer, the air is calm. Glistening strings of gossamer, woven by the æronaut spider, stream across the landscape—all nearer objects are seen through a dreamy atmosphere filled with a rich golden haze, while the distance melts away in violet and purple. The surface of the river, with its moving flood of silver, reflects all objects and every color with matchless fidelity—the harsher tones of the rocks, of the deep-brown forests, and of the yellow prairies appear so softened—the reflection of their pale tints is so perfect, and such a similarity of color and shade pervades the earth, the air, and the water, that all three seemed blended together. The huge piles of bleached timber which lie stranded in the shallows, or the canoes at a little distance, seem suspended in air. Whenever the silence of the solitude is broken, echoes seem to start from every side. Every distant sound is musical; and as you glide along you might believe you were in a dream. The series of pictures presented by our even advance upon the surface of the river, seen through this medium, and under these circumstances, have left on my mind an impression of beauty which will never be effaced.

"Whether we glided through the islands, with their extensive flats covered with poplar and willow—the first in the series of forest trees which will hereafter cover them—skirted the drowned lands—paddled along the bright sand-bars, with their huge pile of drift timber—rustled along the edge of some bright-yellow field of reeds and wild rice, startling the wild-fowl from their meal—or stemmed the deep and powerful current near the foot of the bluffs, the scene presented to our passing admiration was always glorious and beautiful.

"The steep line of rocky and similarly moulded summits which, commencing with Cap de Tiger, excited our admiration in the earlier part of our course as they rose—a line of hills cut in twain, from the right bank high into the mellowed haze, were pre-eminent for the beauty of their coloring and form, from the bright vermilion-colored lichen which painted the bare rock at the summit, to the strips of open, oak-sprinkled barrens at their feet. The action of water upon the façade of these seemingly castellated hills—groove lying beneath groove, plainly indicated the gradual formation of the broad and majestic channel by which the river had for centuries been seeking to gain the level of the ocean.

"What would you have me describe to you? Sunrise with its pale, clear hues—or sunset with its deepening glories, as we saw it evening after evening filling the broad valley with gold and purple—both were matchlessly beautiful; but the latter was the scene of the greatest enchantment.

"If the days were thus delicious, many of the nights were not the less so, and I have to exercise a species of self-control not to attempt the description of each in detail. I might perhaps venture to fill half a dozen lines upon that which we termed the *Camp of the Peak*, where we lay nestled in a dense forest, overhung by one of the noble summits I have mentioned above; or one of those spent on the islands; or the *Camp of the Bent Bough*, but will at all events postpone them till I see what is in advance, and meanwhile give you a little idea of the people with whom we were associated.

"Our progress for the first few days was far from being what we had expected. The canoe, liable to injury at all times from its extremely fragile nature, being merely a light frame-work, covered with birch bark, and held together by cross splints, and to be broken and snagged by running foul of objects in the shallows, or to be strained by the great weight which it carried, and still more by any accident in its daily conveyance to and from the shore on the backs of the men—stood in need of constant repair.

"Beside, we soon found that most, if not all our *Crapauds*, as these French Canadians are jocularly called, were in league with the boat to keep us as long on the road as possible. First, because they were rogues all. They had been born without consciences and never had had the chance of acquiring them since. Secondly, because they were paid by the day, and we were bound to feed them as long as they were in our service. Thirdly, because they saw that we were honest gentlemen, traveling for amusement and instruction—novices in the arts of the *voyageurs*, and of very different habits from the hard-grinding traders whom they usually served, who portioned out their food to them by the square inch—keeping their wages back, if they did not do their duty. You will own that here was a little too much temptation thrown in the way of men who profess no farther morality than would be of very easy carriage among the savages by whom they were surrounded, and no religion beyond Indian religion.

"Demaret acted as pilot, and plied the stern-paddle, as the boat was his. He had made it with his own hands, and all his life had been a *voyageur*. His qualifications and the natural turn he had for this kind of life were so marked, that we found his very companions used to twit him with having 'been born with a piece of birch bark in his hand.' He looked like no class of human beings I ever saw, and his countenance, which was chiefly marked by the width of his mouth, bore signs of both Spanish and Indian blood. When he sang, he sang like a fox with his tail in a trap.

"Garde-Pied, an old Canadian, was our bowman. Then mention we Guillaume, fat and handsome—the *farcour* of the party, the best singer, and, I believe in fact, the greatest rogue among us, and the one who both set the roguery agoing and sustained it. Alexandre, Rousseau, and Henry, were common-place rogues—that is to say, they would be honest, if other people would be honest too. Pascal, a mulatto, held about the same tenets, though, I recollect, he had a fragment of a conscience; and, in mentioning old Julian, a Neapolitan by birth, who had been taken by the British—incorporated with the Anglo-Swiss regiment de Meuron—seen service in India and subsequently in Canada—where he had been discharged, and had turned Crapaud in his old age—I may say that he was the best, the most sober, and most obliging man in the party, and the only one in whom real confidence could be placed.

"For the rest, they were all men who would dance from night to morning at a Gumbo ball—sing profane or pastoral French songs, hour after hour on the water—drink and smoke—cheat their creditors, live for months in the woods—work like slaves without grumbling when they could not help it—swim like otters—maintain their French gayety of character on most occasions, but grumble incessantly when they had nothing to grumble about. They would feed like so many hungry wolves as long as there was any thing to eat, knowing no medium; and then bear the pinch of hunger with the stoicism of the Indian, with whom most of them had associated from infancy

"They measured their way, not by miles, nor leagues, but by pipes, and would say—such a point is so many pipes distant. They generally sang in their peculiar way for half an hour after a halt, solo and chorus, winding up with an Indian yell, or the exclamation, *Hop! Hop! Sauvons-nous!* and would then continue silently paddling with their short quick stroke, all following the time indicated by the bowman, till the pipe was out, or till they were tired; when at a signal, they would throw their paddles across the boat, give them a roll to clear the blade of the water, and then rest for a few minutes.

"A compartment in the center of the canoe, in which our buffalo robes and mats were commodiously arranged, was our ordinary couch. Here we lay in luxurious ease, reading and chatting hour after hour.

"The first certain light which broke in upon us as to the real character of the strange race with whom we had to do—though the singular conduct which we had remarked in them at the Prairie below, had given us warning—was early on the sixth day, when approaching a lonely trading-house, near the remarkable mountain called *La Montagne qui se trempe a l' eau*, scarce a a hundred miles on our way; when their long faces, shrugs, and significant gestures gave token that something was wrong.

"In effect, we found that this devouring squad had—unaided by us, as we had lived principally on water-fowl—actually, in the course of six days, made away with the whole of the provisions laid in with more than usual liberality for twelve days' consumption! Upward of a hundred pounds of bacon, beside bread, and potatoes, and beans in six days! Think of that! We had, to be sure, noticed that they had brought with them a curiously-shaped iron pot, originally, perhaps, a foot in depth; but which, having had the original bottom burned out, had been furnished by some frontier tinker with a fresh one of such form and dimensions as gave the renovated vessel an added profundity of six or eight inches more. We had observed that this marvelous bowl was always piled up to the very edge with provisions; and that frequently, when it was simmering and bubbling over the fire in the camp, our rogues would stand round shrouding it from our too close observation.

"If one or another of us approached, one or two of the *Crapauds* would turn to us with an air of perfect famine and of the greatest tribulation—and ejaculate, *grand misere!* or, *il fait frait icit!*—giving us to understand, that while we considered our common position as one full of amusement, they deemed it to be one of uncommon trial.

"Moreover, we were sometimes awakened hours after supper, when all had appeared to retire to rest for the night—it might be about one in the morning—by loud talking and joyous sounds, and peeping forth we might see that these unhappy mortals were as brisk as lions; sitting about the fire; passing the joke from one to another—by the help of long sharply-pointed sticks, fishing up meat from the depths of that fathomless pot; and making a very hearty meal, for which, as to our certain knowledge, a hearty supper preceded it, and a no less hearty breakfast followed it at dawn—we had unfortunately no name in our vocabulary. Still, though it might cross our minds that they were a little lavish of the provisions, yet we never dreamed of a famine before we should reach *Fort Snelling*. However, there was now no doubt about it, and it was in vain to murmur; and here at the last trading-post we had still to lay in fresh stock.

"Their songs were very interesting to us, in spite of the horrible French in which they were couched, and the nonsense they contained; as we detected in them many signs of their origin on the plains, and in the vineyards of *La belle France*, though now loaded with allusions to the peculiar scenery, manners, and circumstances of the country to which they had been transplanted. In many there was an air of Arcadian and pastoral simplicity which was almost touching, at the same time that we knew that the singers had no simplicity about them, and that their character was much more that of the wolf than of the sheep. The airs were not unfrequently truly melodious, and all were characteristic, and chimed in well with our position.

"I may elsewhere have given you sundry assurances of the *delights of Indian Encampments* in the forests; from the pleasant ideas that these may have conveyed I would take nothing. They are many and great; and far advanced as the season was, we were yet alive to them for a month to come, even in weather that might be deemed inclement elsewhere. Lest, however, you should accuse me of a disposition to paint every thing *couleur de rose*, and to throw dust both in my own eyes and those of my neighbors—here follows a page of *miseries*. I remember one camp, which we called *Cross Camp*, from the circumstance of all going wrong. It was, I believe, the second in this excursion."

Here our tourist gives a long detailed account of the

many vexations and petty calamities which harassed them in pitching their tent; dressing, cooking, and upsetting their supper; tormented with smoke, wind, and ashes; with many other kindred difficulties, such as burning their fingers and their viands, mislaying articles, etc. While it seems, too, they had not selected the most felicitous place for their supper-room, it being "a confined situation among thickets of towering dry grass and brushwood." Such were some of the incidents which led to the cognomen of *Cross Camp.*

"Jaded and gloomy, while the supper is cooking, you lie down with a book in your hand, say, for example, 'Burton on Melancholy,' which, by-the-by, was the only work, beside a BIBLE, that we had with us. You stretch yourself on your blanket in your corner of the tent, but find that beside lying on an unfortunate slope which makes your heels rise higher than your head, there is under you a stubborn knot of hard wood, which no coaxing of yours can extract, and which nothing but a turn out, or application of the ax, will rid you of."

"But, *n'importe*—the coffee is replaced—the beef-steaks get thoroughly burned on one side—the ducks are pronounced to be cooked because the waistcoat is reduced to a perfect cinder, and because the birds insist upon taking fire. The 'medicine-chest,' as we called our store-box, is brought out, and preparations for a meal seriously attempted. It is soon found that notwithstanding all losses and mischances there are still two things left, appetite and abundance; and though nothing, perhaps, is done with real gastronomic nicety, yet, after a day spent in the open air, every thing has a relish which no sauce could give.

"As you have doubtless experienced, nothing predisposes to complacent good humor so much as a satisfied appetite; and, by the time supper is ended, and the moon has risen, and the bright embers free from smoke are glowing in the wind, you are ready to laugh together at every petty vexation. However, we learned wisdom at the *Cross Camp*, and forthwith hired Rousseau to look to our cooking at his own fire—keeping possession of the coffee-pot alone, and henceforth our *miseries* were very sensibly diminished.

"*La Montagne qui se trémpe à l' eau*, lies about one hundred miles above Prairie du Chien. It is remarkable as being completely surrounded by the waters of the Mississippi. The Indians have a tradition that on a certain day in the year it always sinks a little into the earth.

"We had passed the domains of the *Winnebagoes*, and were now in the country inhabited by the tribe of the *Dacota Indians*, or *Sioux*, one of the most numerous of the present day, inhabiting a wide extent of country between the Missouri and Mississippi.

"Their villages, some of which are very strikingly situated—that on *Prairie à l' Ail*, for instance—were all deserted, as the Indians were now absent on their hunting grounds. Many, however, lingered on the river, and we now saw daily some of them encamped on the banks in their commodious conical skin tents; and the ordinary silence of our encampments was frequently broken by the distant howling of the Indian dogs, or the singing and yelling of the savages.

"*Lake Pepin* lay in our path, soon after the renewal of our stock of provisions; and the passage was looked forward to with curiosity by us, and a species of awe by the Crapauds, as its surface is often agitated by storms, and many are the terrors of a long spit of sand about the center, which juts far into the lake from the westward, under the name of the *Pointe aux Sables*.

"We had been detained nearly a whole day by an accident and the illness of Demaret, a few miles below the southern extremity, where the thermometer of Fahrenheit registered fifteen degrees below the freezing point during the night, while the surface of the river was darkened by a strong north wind; however, we moved forward to a point of yellow sand at the entrance toward evening, and, finding that the old saying, 'sun down, wind down,' was likely to be verified, prepared for the passage during the ensuing night. By degrees the miniature billows with their crests of foam diminished in size, and sunk into their bed, and an hour after sunset the whole surface was as tranquil as a sheet of silver. Under such auspicious circumstances, our men were induced to proceed, and our frail canoe glided over the broad surface for some hours without interruption.

"The ordinary mode of navigation takes you across a bight in the shore, to the foot of the bluffs which bound to the east, and along them as far as the celebrated *Cap à la Fille*, or *Maiden's Rock*, when an attempt is generally made to cross the broadest part of the lake, weather the *Pointe aux Sables*, and get round a rocky headland, which forms the division between the upper and lower portions of Lake Pepin, after which five or six miles bring you to the northern inlet.

"As we neared the base of the Maiden's Rock, a ruddy light showed us that our acquaintances in the barge, with whom we had come in contact more than once during the past week, and who had passed us at our last halting place, had been induced to lie to for the night in the sheltered cove at its foot. A moment's halt was allowed for an exchange of salutations, but in pursuance of our object, we judged it advisable to attempt the *traversée,* as the wind gave notice of again springing up; and proceeding, we left them to their repose, and directed the bow of the canoe toward the dark Cape on the opposite shore. Meanwhile, the sky clouded up; the moon and stars peeped by fits through the fissures in the fleecy clouds, the waves began to rise, and to heave the brittle vessel under us in an unwonted manner, straining her so as to render constant attention to baling necessary.

"However, the energies of the Crapauds, though their leader was disabled by the fever and ague, were excited; and with an occasional yell and cry of encouragement, we perceived that we were making advance. Long, however, as the wind was against us, we saw the dreaded *Pointe aux Sables* gleaming to the leeward; and it was not without thankfulness, that, after upward of an hour's hard struggle and unremitted labor, we weathered the great Cape, and got into calmer water. *Nous sommes sauvés! Nous sommes sauvés! Maintenant la pipe!* said our old bowman, as he threw down his paddle behind the bow, and gave the signal for a short repose.

"The termination of another hour found us stemming the current of the Mississippi again, as it poured into the lake amid poplar islands, on one of which we speedily encamped. I have mentioned that from hence three days were occupied in reaching Fort Snelling. The wind turning more to the southward, gave us an opportunity of rigging and hoisting a blanket as a sail, under shadow and favor of which our Crapauds smoked their pipes in luxurious idleness. For all the wonders and remarkable points on the passage—the entrance of the river St. Croix, La Grange, Pointe des Pins, Bois de Médecine, etc., I must refer you to Schoolcraft, Carver, and other writers on this distant country. We passed more than one permanent village of the Sioux, now all deserted; the houses were made of rude poles covered with pieces of oak bark, and swarmed with fleas, numerous as the dust. In their vicinity were seen the dead bodies of their chiefs, wasting in the air, inclosed in rude wooden cases, elevated upon scaffolds raised eight or ten feet above the surface.

"Many of the Sioux still lingered on the river, and would have perhaps given us more of their presence at our encampments than might have been agreeable, had we halted in their immediate vicinity. On one occasion a large canoe full of Indians came to us just as we had landed, with every disposition to do as they had done before—watch our movements, and wait till we should ask them to partake of our hospitality—but all of a sudden, by common consent, they stole back to their canoe, and slipped down the stream. They had seen Demaret brought on shore, wrapped up in his blankets, and placed before the fire, sick and helpless; and it was probable that the idea of Cholera, from which the Indians on the Mississippi had suffered greatly the preceding year, had occurred to them. A large number were encamped on the opposite side all night, where they whooped and whistled around their tents; but not one could be lured to venture near us. The following day—it was that of our arrival at the Fort—we came upon a very large encampment of the same tribe, stretching along the forested shore, just above a range of beautiful white sandstone acclivities. There may have been thirty or forty lodges; among which we landed, partly from curiosity, and partly to barter for Indian pipes and ornaments, of which my companion was desirous of making a collection.

"We found very few males in the lodges, but squaws, children, and dogs in great numbers, in every hut."

Our traveler here gives a long and sad description of the Indians, their lodges, the "old squaws," and a visit, particularly, to one lodge where were some sick children, with a motley group around them, and all looked to him for medical aid, to the relief of the sick. He finally commences the duties of the doctor:

"On my right sat an old Sioux warrior, in his breech-cloth, moccasins, and dingy blanket. He was, like many of his tribe, finely modeled, and with an agreeable cast of face. To the left was seated a young girl, about ten years old, garbed in the dark blue petticoat commonly worn by her sex, with a blanket over her shoulders. Her neighbor was a male, about the same age. Three aged squaws, including my conductress, filled up the remainder of the space round the small heap of red embers, which, with their white ashes, occupied the center.

"Though all the three females were patterns of ugliness, both in persons and physiognomy, I think that the old squaw who enticed me hither bore away the palm; and there we sat, crowded together with our noses over the little fire. Sufficient light was afforded from the top of the cone, where an aperture was left to give issue to the smoke, and by divers cracks in the skins, to see this; and moreover that the wigwam contained nothing beyond the most ordinary Indian utensils and furniture.

"A most affectionate grunt and shake of the hand passed between the old Sioux, the squaws, and myself, the instant I seated myself; and then, as a matter of course, the small redstone pipe was filled with tobacco and *kinnickkinick*, lighted, and passed round from one to another.

"After a brief silence, followed by a few explanatory words, as I suppose, between the elders of the party, the Indian turned to me, made me a speech, accompanied with appropriate gestures. He pointed to the girl, and then to the boy, both of whom were evidently in poor health, and I was now not slow in ascertaining the purpose of my being brought here—which was neither more nor less than to act the doctor and to cure his family. This, though I am no physicianer, set me perfectly at ease, as we had medicine in plenty in the canoe, at his service, and that of the strongest and most efficacious kind, if properly administered. After listening with becoming gravity, I grunted in the most approved fashion, to signify my perfect intelligence and readiness to do as he desired, and then proceeded to examine my patients. One thing you may depend upon. I resolved, if I could do them no good, not to do the poor creatures any harm.

"During an interval of utter silence I felt the pulses of the two children—opened their mouths and peeped at their tongues, and speedily satisfied myself that they must have the fever and ague, that being the common disease of the season and country. Hereupon, turning to the warrior, I gave a grunt of interrogation, being one which ascends the scale of about half an octave; and followed it by pointing to the children and giving a violent shiver, thereby hazarding my opinion as to the kind of malady by which they were afflicted.

"The general satisfaction which this announcement gave, produced a chorus of sounds such as might proceed from the well-furnished sty of a Pennsylvania farmer on the introduction of a plentiful supply of squashes; and, emboldened by my success, I proceeded forthwith, by aid of a calabash of water and an ordinary degree of assurance, to prescribe and administer sundry harmless pills which I fetched from the canoe, at the rate of two to the girl and three to the boy; and after signifying to the old warrior and his squaws that I had done what I could, but that they must look to the Great Spirit for cure, and giving them a few biscuits, I left them amid a clamor of sounds which doubtless were meant for blessings and as marks of admiration, though they would hardly have been interpreted as such in a civilized country.

"The curiosity of Pourtales and M'Euen to know my adventures, was met by a corresponding air of mystery on my part, such as did credit to my newly acquired Indian title of *The Great Medicine.*

"Our visit terminated, and we proceeded. Toward evening we descried the long looked-for Fort, with its towers and imposing extent of wall crowning the high angular bluff, at whose base the upper branch of the St. Peter's enters the Mississippi; and paddling swiftly up the lower channel, a large triangular island separating the two, we landed and were most hospitably received by the officers on duty. We were forthwith furnished with quarters in the Fort above, while the Crapauds pitched a tent under the shadow of the bluff by the water's edge, got their canoe on shore, and set their enormous pot a boiling forthwith. I believe they never saw the bottom of it, nor suffered it to cool during the whole week of their stay. They did not forget, whenever we visited them, to talk a great deal about *misère!* at the same time that they had nothing to do but what they loved best—eat and sleep. They are a singular race, half Indian, half French, with a dash of the prairie wolf.

"Meanwhile we had been admitted to full participation in the rights of hospitality within the Fort, and were furnished with every needful accommodation. We spread our buffalo skins and blankets in an unoccupied apartment, and slept in quiet; not forgetting however in the course of the evening to ascend one of the bastions, and listen to the roar of the *Great Falls* rising on the night air at a distance of seven miles."

MINNESOTA.

Before entering into the history, boundaries, business, towns, etc., of this young Territory, I leave our traveler to finish his story; when more minute particulars will be furnished:

"The military post at the junction of the St. Peter's river with the main stream, is the most northerly station maintained by the United States in the valley of the Mississippi. The *Military Reservation* on which it lies, purchased by Government from the Sioux, forms a parallelogram of eighteen miles by seven. The *Fortification* has much more pretension both to regularity of design and picturesque situation than any of its fellows along the frontier—the outer wall inclosing a lozenge-shaped area of considerable size, surrounded by the barracks, officers' quarters, and other offices. The magazine and round bastion being at one extremity, and the commander's house at the other nearest the angle of the rock overlooking both rivers. Only three companies were stationed here at the time of our visit. A picturesque octagonal tower stands at the termination of the southern line of wall overlooking the sloping ascent from the St. Peter's. The height of the foundation above the rivers may be upward of one hundred feet. It has an appearance of strength which is hardly confirmed on a nearer survey; and the impression you carry away is, that for the purposes of Indian warfare it is far too strong and important a work, while its position would not avail it much in an attack from regular troops, as the interior is commanded from a rise on the land immediately behind. The idea is farther suggested, that the strong stone wall was rather erected to keep the garrison in, than the enemy out. Though adapted for mounting cannon if needful,

the walls were unprovided with those weapons; and the only piece of ordnance that I detected out of the magazine, was an old churn thrust gallantly through one of the embrasures. We were however far from complaining of the extra expense and taste which the worthy officer whose name it bears had expended on the erection of *Fort Snelling*, as it is in every way an addition to the sublime landscape in which it is situated.

"The view from the angle of the wall at the extreme point, is highly romantic. To your left lies the broad deep valley of the Mississippi, with the opposite hights descending precipitously to the water's edge; and to the right and in front, the St. Peter's, a broad stream, worthy from its size, length of course, and the number of tributaries which it receives, to be called the Western Fork of the Great River itself. It is seen flowing through a comparatively open vale, with swelling hills and intermingling forest and prairie, for many miles above the point of junction. As it approaches the Mississippi, the volume of water divides into two branches; that on the right, pursues the general course of the river above, and enters the Mississippi at an angle of perhaps fifty degrees directly under the walls of the Fort; while the other, keeping to the base of the high prairie lands which rise above it to a notable summit called the *Pilot Knob*, enters the Mississippi lower down. The triangular island thus formed between the rivers lies immediately under the Fort. Its level surface is partially cultivated, but toward the lower extremity thickly covered with wood. Beyond their junction, the united streams are seen gliding at the base of high cliffs into the narrowing valley below. Forests, and these of the most picturesque character, interspersed with strips of prairie, clothe a great portion of the distant view.

"A little cluster of trading houses is situated on the right branch of the St. Peter's, and here and there on the shores, and on the island, you saw the dark conicle tents of the wandering Sioux. A more striking scene we had not met with in the United States, and hardly any that could vie with it for picturesque beauty, even at this unfavorable season. What must it be in spring when the forests put forth their young leaves, and the prairies are clothed in verdure! From the summit of the Pilot Knob, surmounted by the tomb of an Indian Chief, the view is most extended and interesting; comprising both rivers before and after their junction, the Fort in all its details, and a wide stretch of level country to the north and west beyond the Great Falls. The Falls were of course a main object of our curiosity, but for a few days we were prevented from visiting them by very rough and wet weather.

"In the meantime we were daily in the lodges of the Sioux and the Chippewas encamped near the Reservation or near the trading houses."

The Territory of Minnesota, at this time, probably does not contain less than 9,000 to 10,000 population. And the village of St. Pauls, probably has 1,500; Stillwater, 1,200; Crow Wing, 500; St. Anthony, 700; Mendota, 200; St. Croix, 300; there are other smaller towns. It is not claimed that the above are precise statements of the population, but as nearly as can be obtained. In 1849 the population of this territory was 4,780.

Minnesota is rapidly filling up, a large portion being from Maine, the rugged climate of that state somewhat resembling that of the Territory.

St. Pauls is situated on the north bank of the Mississippi, near the head of navigation, 15 miles by water, and 8 miles by land, below the Falls of St. Anthony. The central portion of the town is a level, beautiful plateau, terminating on the river in a precipitous bluff about 80 feet high. The bluff recedes from the river at the upper and lower end of the town, forming two landings.

On the west bank of the Mississippi, and below the mouth of St. Peter's river, is the village of Mendota, formerly St. Peters, and for some time was occupied by the American Fur Company. Its location is favorable to command the trade of the northwestern rivers. This is a delightful country in point of health, scenery, wild fruits; and many parts for farming. There are some fine lakes west and north of this point.

I now resume Mr. Latrobe's narrative:

"In mentioning the details of the landscape at St. Peter's, I have omitted one feature in it, which is peculiar. The upper stratum of the country, in which these rivers have grooved their deep channels, consists of beds of limestone resting upon thick layers of the purest and whitest sand imaginable; and wherever the acclivity is precipitous and the latter are exposed to the air, they form, from their brilliant hue, a remarkable trait of the land scenery.

"A few miles below the Fort, a small subterraneous rivulet comes rippling out of a cavern, called by the Indians the *House of Stone*. The cave may be traced for a very considerable distance into the bowels of the earth, under the limestone, and altogether within the sand bed, and a more beautiful sight than that presented by the snow-white walls, roof, and flooring, with the crystal stream meandering over the floor, I have rarely seen. No mound or tumulus is known to exist in this neighborhood, but there is a most singular mass of sandstone lying on the open Prairie, about twenty-five miles to the southeast of Fort Snelling. It is perfectly isolated, eighty feet high, with a base line of from thirty to forty feet in length. It tapers irregularly, and has an area of about three feet square on the summit as far as can be guessed, as it is inaccessible. It is called the *Standing Stone* by the Indians, and considered as a 'Great Medicine.'

"But the Falls of St. Anthony! The first fine day we turned our faces in the direction of the *Hahamina!* the *Laughing Water*, as the Indian language, rich in the poetry of nature, styles this remote cataract—for cataract it is, despite its insignificant hight, compared with others. Here the Mississippi—after a course of three hundred miles, draining a dreary region, where it would appear that a species of chaos still reigns, and the land and water are not yet fairly separated from each other—commences the second great division of its remaining course of upward of two thousand miles to the ocean.

"The surface of the river at the St. Peter's has been calculated to be elevated 680 feet above the tide-water. Above the Falls, the breadth is between five and six hundred yards, and below, it contracts in a narrow gorge to one third that width, till it reaches the Fork, and forms its junction with the St. Peter's. The long line of the Fall, which is in all its parts more or less interrupted by the fragments of the limestone which fall down as the force of the water undermines them by the removal of the soft sand underneath, is farther interrupted near the left bank by an island covered with trees. A second island stands in the river, in advance of the right hand divison of the Fall, with steep perpendicular sides, and bastion-like angles, resulting from the peculiar geological formation of the district.

"Though I admit that the whole had the appearance of an immense wear, and that the open face of the country for many miles round, can hardly lay claim to picturesque beauty, yet the vast size of the body of water thus seen leaping from a higher to a lower region, rendered the scene truly majestic. It is still the mighty Mississippi!"

The dimensions of the Falls at St. Anthony have been variously stated; but the survey, by the officers at Fort Snelling, gives the following: From the west bank to the island, 634 feet; across the island, 276; the east fall, 300—total width of river, 1,210 feet. The perpendicular fall varies from 25 to 30 feet.

It is said that Father Hennepin gave the name to these falls. Lieutenant Pike, when he explored the river, estimated the fall to be 58 feet in a distance of 260 rods portage; and to the foot of the rapids, a distance of several miles, he states the entire fall to be about 100 feet.

At this point there are nearly a dozen saw-mills; but they are scarcely able to supply the demand for lumber. But the number of mills are increasing every year.

The falls here, like much of the country, has its startling legendary. The Indians tell you, that a young *Dacota* mother, goaded by jealousy—the father of her children having taken another wife—unmoored her canoe above the Great Fall, and seating herself and her children in it, sang her death-song, and went over the foaming acclivity in the face and amid the shrieks of her tribe. And often, the Indian believes—when the nights are calm, and the sky serene, and the dew-drops are hanging motionless on the weeping birch on the island, and the country is vibrating to the murmur of the cataract—that then the misty form of the young mother may be seen moving down the current, while her song is heard mingling its sad notes with the lulling sound of "the Laughing Water!"

The village of St. Anthony is a beautiful site, on the

east bank of the river, at the head of the cataract or opposite to it; and is a flourishing place, and must become a a town of considerable business; as a very good portion of Minnesota, for farming purposes, lies east of this place and St. Pauls, and northeast toward Stillwater.

Some 20 or 30 miles below the Falls of St. Anthony, the river *St. Croix* empties into the Mississippi. At the junction of these rivers there is a thriving and handsome little town growing up, called *Point Douglass.*

This river also expands into a lake, not quite as wide or long as Lake Pepin, while its banks are not as high and steep.

Above, midway toward the head of this lake, on the east side, in Wisconsin, at the mouth of Willow river, is located the promising town of *Buena Vista.* Here the U. S. Government have opened a *Land Office.*

On the opposite side of the lake, a little farther up, is the thriving town of *Stillwater*, in Minnesota. Still higher up, is the village of *St. Croix*, with some other lesser ones. These towns are all growing rapidly, from emigration.

Steamers from Galena generally run up the St. Croix to those towns, then down to the forks again, and head up the river for St. Pauls, Fort Snelling, St. Anthony's, and Mendota; between the two last named towns, the *St. Peter's*, from the west, enters the Mississippi. There is little settlement up this river, as the lands are still mostly in the possession of Indians.

"But we must turn our faces southward, for the Indian Summer is past—the lagging files of the water-fowl are scudding before the wind, and another week may curb the mighty Mississippi with a bridle of ice. Another week, in fact, did so; but ere that, paddle, current, and sail had carried us far on our way south, as you may now hear."

On the evening of the second day our voyageurs reached Lake Pepin, and found it in so much of a storm, they thought it best to lie by on their oars awhile, and view the scenery about Maiden's Rock.

"On the opposite side of the troubled sheet of water in the middle ground, over which the rock impended, the range of western bluffs was seen to incline inland, behind the *Pointe aux Sables*, leaving a wide tract of country, partly forest and partly prairie, between their foot and the shore. A singularly conical and prominent hill rose abruptly from the middle of this plain. Around this detached eminence, which, swathed as it was in the smoke of the burning prairies beyond, seemed like a volcano; the fire had been concentrating itself during the earlier hours of the day, now advancing in one direction till checked by a dense tract of forest or a river, and then rushing on in another one, rolling over the summit or the base of the mountains. At sunset, the flame seemed to have gathered full strength and to have reached a long tract of level grassy prairie nearer the shore, upon which it then swiftly advanced, leaving a black path in its trail."

An interesting Indian legend gives name to "Maiden's Rock," in Lake Pepin. It is a craggy peak in some places, perpendicular in others, and many portions covered with forest trees. There is one high perpendicular precipice, from which, as the Indian story goes, an Indian girl, crossed in love, and named "Dark Day," took the leap, Sappho-like, which alike cures love and ambition; and in the same act which ended her days she perpetuated her memory—she secured an everlasting monument, more lofty and enduring than the Egyptian pyramids; Maiden's Rock lasts with the world.

"The following morning brought no cessation of the gale; and as, from our place of retreat, we could see that the light fresh waters of Lake Pepin were running and boiling like a miniature sea, so that no frail bark like ours could live—we unanimously felt disposed to take the rest and leisure thus given, and remain where we were. Nothing could suit the Crapauds better. It was one day more to their pay—the provision-bag and the whiskey-keg were full—and a rare day they made of it!

"The summit of the perpendicular rock, which terminates the

Cap à la Fille, rises about five hundred feet over the lake, and the leap may be nearly one third of the whole hight. As we looked forth from the summit early in the morning, across the troubled surface of the lake, of which it commands a wide view, a dense column of smoke from the opposite side gave us intimation that the prairies were on fire."

One peculiarity of this lake is, that it has *no islands*, but is a plain, uninterrupted sheet of water, which freezes to a great thickness in the winter; and is the only place in the Mississippi, all the way from the Falls to the Gulf, where we may not at all times see islands in the river. Most of the shores of this lake are high precipitous rocks, yet there are a few instances where they slope gradually to the water.

The lands lying about Lake Pepin, in their general appearance and adaptation to farming purposes, particularly that of Stock raising and Dairy business, are seldom surpassed. The Indian titles will no doubt soon be extinguished, or canceled, and the Indians removed; so that this beautiful region will soon be brought into the market for sale, and undoubtedly will find many purchasers; though, it is more likely that most persons, acquainted with the facts and locations, will see better inducements to buy and settle upon the large, superior tracts of lands in Illinois, Wisconsin, and Iowa, which are coming into market along the many lines of Railroads that are being rapidly built in those states.

"The close of another short day, during the course of which we glided on with the combined force of paddle and current, through the most picturesque division of the whole river, saw us encamping in the forest, near the recent battle ground at the mouth of the Bad Axe river, within thirty miles of Prairie du Chien. We had landed here in ascending, and seen the bones of the poor misguided Indians, who, driven to extremity, perishing with famine, encumbered with their wives and children, hotly pursued by both the regular troops and the militia—here tried to cover the retreat of their families over the deep, broad, island-chequered bosom of the Mississippi. The Warrior, an armed steamboat, which had been sent up the river for the purpose, opposed the passage, and some hundred men, women, and children were shot down—some on the bank—some in the marshes—others in the act of swimming; and we saw proof enough that neither age nor sex had been spared."

"The sympathy I feel for the poor benighted Indian, the child of impulse and passion—cozened, mystified, driven to the wall, and degraded far below his natural degradation, by his communion with those who call themselves Christians, and pride themselves upon superiority of gifts and advantages, rises above the horror excited by the details of their savage cruelty, when their wrath is once excited; and makes me inclined to consider them as the aggrieved party. The Winnebagoes, true to the character of treachery they had long borne, turned their knives and towahawks against their former allies, as soon as they saw that the fortune of the unequal war was against them, and ranged themselves on the side of the whites. After the Battle of the Bad Axe, they traced the old chief Black Hawk to his retreat, and gave him and his sons up to the Government. It is hardly necessary to repeat that the prisoners were kindly treated; the same policy which led the Government to confine the chief for a while, led it afterward to bring him to the great cities of the East—give him his liberty, with his companions—and send him back to his humbled tribe loaded with presents."

"Our encampment in the forests, near the Bad Axe, on the night between the 12th and 13th November, was rendered remarkable by one circumstance.

"The night was calm; the wind, which had been northerly the foregoing day, chopped about early in the morning to the south, and blew with some force with a clear sky. Early, it might be between two and three o'clock, the whole heavens became gradually covered with *falling stars*, increasing in number till the sky had the appearance of being filled with luminous flakes of snow. This *meteoric rain* continued to pour down till the light of the coming day rendered it invisible. Millions must have shone and disappeared during the course of these three or four hours. They appeared to proceed from a point in the heavens, about fourteen degrees to the southeast of the zenith, and thence fell in curved lines to every point of the compass. Whether they remained visible down to the horizon or not, we do not know. There were some in the shower of larger size than the others, but for the greater part, they appeared as stars of the first or second magnitude.

Their course in falling was interrupted, like the luminous flight of the fire fly. This celestial appearance bore precisely the character of the phenomenon recorded, as having been witnessed on the 12th Nov., 1799, by Humboldt and his companions, at Cumana, in South America, where the heavens appeared filled with these *bolides* for four entire hours in the early part of the morning; and they were subsequently discovered to have been visible simultaneously in Labrador, Greenland, and Germany—over a space equal to 921,000 square leagues. Like that, the extent over the earth's surface, on which the meteoric shower which I am more particularly describing was observed, was extraordinarily great. At the same hour that it was visible in our camp, it was seen in equal splendor throughout the whole of the valley of the Mississippi, in all the Atlantic cities, in Canada, and in the middle of the Atlantic; how far farther I am not able to discover."

This phenomenon was noticed by the Indians, and regarded by them as a favorable omen in regard to the winter's hunt, and next year's crops; and led them to a sudden and devout worship of the Great Spirit—to be sure, in their rude way.

"Early on the evening of this day, we returned, blithely singing our *Chanson de retour*, down the river, to the little village of Prairie du Chien, where a knot of wives, daughters, and children, awaited the return of our men; and after a few moments spent by them in the ordinary compliments, kissing, and embraces, we were conducted to the landing of the Fort, and there welcomed as old friends."

Here our tourist recites some grotesque and somewhat exciting scenes which occurred upon paying off the Crapauds—seizure by sheriffs—carousals—their efforts to get employment farther down the river, etc.

"Agreeable as we found our position in the society and at the mess of the officers at Fort Crawford, there were urgent reasons why we should continue our flight to the southward. Even our hosts could not but advise us to contrive the means of escape, unless we made up our minds to accept their offer of winter quarters. There were however, as usual, difficulties in the way. To return by land to St. Louis was neither according to our wish, nor advisable; nor, indeed, did it appear practicable."

It now being late in November, and a dreary time of year, always among the Mississippi and Wisconsin bluffs, though cheering and romantic enough in the warm season, our voyageurs were in a puzzle how to get away, when a little good luck fell upon their lines:

"Just in this moment, most unexpectedly and fortunately for us, a number of barges were seen emerging from the deep glen of the Ouisconsin, and turning up the Mississippi toward the Fort. They were found to contain a body of recruits for the frontier posts of St. Peter's and the Prairie, and for a regiment of dragoons forming near St. Louis. They had made their way thus far from the Atlantic States, by way of Detroit, Lake Huron, Green Bay, Fox river, and over the portage into the Ouisconsin.

"The two barges containing the recruits bound to St. Louis were in command of a young officer, who promptly made us an offer to join company; and the following day, the 17th of November, you may imagine us seated round a pan of charcoal in the stern of one of the boats, and pushing away from the hospitable shore of Prairie du Chien, where we left as warm-hearted a set of fine young fellows, and as stanch and brave an old Colonel as you would wish to see.

"The very night after we quitted the Prairie, the Mississippi began to close, and remained strongly frozen for four entire months; the thermometer at the Fort ranging to 25° below zero of Fahrenheit; and at St. Peter's, the mercury continued frozen for three days consecutively."

"We had fortunately however got the start of the winter, dropped down the current propelled by six oars in each barge; and, when the wind served, by the yet more powerful aid of square sails; and though we had to break our way out of the gathering ice for the two first mornings, yet soon after passing the Mining District, we had no longer to complain of extreme cold.

"I shall not go largely into the details of our descent of six hundred miles to St. Louis, which it took us nine days to effect. Though highly entertaining to us, it would be monotonous in description. The shores of the Mississippi and the character of the channel continued to be interesting, without having an equal claim to be considered as romantic as the upper portion of the river. Towns there were none, and the settlements were few and distant from each other, till we got within a hundred miles or so of the mouth of the Missouri.

"Our encampments—for we still spread our beds every night in the forests—continued to be the scenes of much amusement and enjoyment."

I have already given a pretty full portraiture of the country along the Mississippi, from St. Louis to Prairie du Chien—that region where, in 1833, "towns there were none, and settlements were few and distant from each other." How gratifying is the contrast of the present; now, in 1851, some eighteen years later, we see towns and cities, of from two to eight, and even twelve thousand population, built up every twenty or thirty miles, and well sustained in wealth and progress by a rich and thickly-settled country, of well-cultivated farms. And instead of "making encampments, and spreading beds every night in the forests," the traveler now enjoys a comfortable berth in the daily steampacket; or, is lodged in a pleasant room at some of the high and spacious hotels, found in all the towns and cities above alluded to, along the route.

Minnesota is a new and rapidly improving Territory, lying north of Michigan, Wisconsin, and Iowa, on both sides of the Mississippi river. Its winters are long, with several months of very deep snow, but during the growing season vegetation puts forward with remarkable rapidity and luxuriance; so that, even in that region, considerable pleasant and profitable agricultural operations are carried on, and the numbers of persons engaged in that pursuit are briskly increasing. And notwithstanding its northern position and rigorous climate, emigration, from New England, with some foreigners, is pouring into the territory in such numbers, that it must soon be asking for a place in the Union as a State.

It in fact possesses a more mild and favorable climate and surface of country than the northern portion of New England and New York—the spring and autumn being less liable to destructive frosts there, than in those older northern states.

The city of St. Pauls, situated on the Mississippi, some eight miles below the Falls of St. Anthony, is the seat of the Territorial Government.

St. Anthony's Falls were discovered by Father Hennepin as early as 1680; and the same region was visited by other explorers very soon after. Adventurers, both for discovery and trade in furs with the Indians, visited the Minnesota or Dacota country early in the seventeenth century, and planted trading posts at different points. La Hontan visited this country about that time, beside Marquette and De Soto.

In 1812, Earl Selkirk commenced a Settlement on Red river, near the mouth of Pembina river, several hundred miles northwest of St. Pauls. Some years afterward, another post or town was established further down (northward) the river; but since that time, however, the upper settlement has mostly moved down to the lower one, where there is a flourishing, happy Colony of industrious, hardy, peaceful people.

Until the past year, these Falls have been the head of steamboat navigation on the Mississippi; and that two boats per week, now running between here and the southern country, should have profitable employment, is evidence that a large amount of business is there carried on, and considerable emigration moving into this new northern country. But, during the past year, one or two steamboats have been built *above* the Falls, to run in the river for some hundreds of miles still farther up, establishing a new era in the navigation of the "Father of Waters."

At this point is where the *Selkirk Settlement* do their business on the river, in their annual pilgrimages, to dispose of their peltry and other articles, for such merchandise as they may desire. I have seen several companies of these isolated and romantic people, and found them stout, hardy, liberal, and intelligent persons, indicating good health and ability to endure toil and hardships.

Among the most singular or attractive curiosities in Minnesota, beside the great Falls, are the *caves*, or subterranean lakes and creeks. *Carver's Cave* is one of some note; but it can rarely ever be explored, as the entrance to it is constantly changing and being obstructed by sliding rocks and earth, which frequently fill up the orifice, so that there is no access for several days, till the little stream issuing from it bursts out again, leaving a passage, sometimes, through which a man can enter and explore, though it is a hazardous experiment, not often attempted; yet, within the cave there is a beautiful crystal lake, with shining rock walls and inclosures.

The most remarkable and best known of these Grottos is a few miles farther up the Mississippi, and described as follows, by Mr. Seymour, who explored it; and has presented it in a clearer manner than I can pretend to do:

"On Monday, in company with several gentlemen, who lately arrived in the Territory, I set out to explore *Fountain Cave*, which is found near the bank of the Mississippi, two or three miles above St. Pauls.

"The entrance of the cave is at the bottom of a circular bluff, which, curving around in front of the opening, forms a basin or recess, about forty feet deep, and as many feet in diameter. Descending into this basin, we soon found ourselves in a spacious room, about 150 feet long and 20 wide; arched overhead and forming at the entrance a regular arched gateway, about 25 feet in width and 20 feet high. This room, however, may more properly be divided into two; the division being made by a curvilinear projection of one side of the cave, the front room being about 25 feet wide and 20 feet high, and nearly 100 feet long; the other one varying in hight from twelve in front to eight feet in the rear, arched, like the front room, overhead, and decreasing in width at the farther end. The floor is a horizontal plane of sandstone. Along its center glides a pretty rivulet of transparent water, which is heard flowing through the next room in gentle ripples; and far in the interior, out of sight, is heard the sonnd of a rumbling cascade.

"The whole interior of this cave is composed of pure white sandstone, resembling loaf sugar, which is readily cut with a knife. This cave is probably produced by the action of the water, which has broken through the upper strata of limestone and worn a passage through this sandstone; which constantly crumbles off, and is carried away by the current.

"Having quenched our thirst from the limpid rivulet, and examined many of the names carved by visitors on the walls of the cave, we lighted our candles, and advanced to explore the interior. After reaching the farther end of the second room, the roof became so low that we were obliged to stoop and proceed partly on our hands a short distance, until we entered another room of an elliptical form, with an arched ceiling, and about forty feet long, twenty feet wide, and twelve feet high. Here the rivulet has a fall of about two feet perpendicular., into a small basin which occupies the center of the room. Beyond this room the ceiling is so low that we were obliged to proceed on our hands and knees. The water had worn a channel in the rock several feet deep, leaving a narrow shelf on each side for one to crawl upon, or the channel of water, six inches to four feet deep, for one to wade in. Slipping into the water accidentally, I was obliged to adopt the latter alternative, although the extreme coldness of the water rendered it rather uncomfortable.

"Before reaching this point my companions had all given out and were returning, so that I was obliged to proceed alone. I continued to wade until I reached another low room, about twenty feet wide, where I could hear another waterfall; the water grew deeper as I advanced to the upper end of this room—my candle was becoming quite short—my companions were beyond the reach of my voice—my person was pretty well drenched with water—and prudence seemed to dictate that I should retire, without determining whether I had reached the extremity of the cave. I had proceeded, as near as I could estimate distance in such a tortuous and laborious passage, about sixty rods. By constructing a narrow promenade of plank above the water, in the passage between the second and third room, an easy communication to *Cascade Parlor* might be made for visitors."

"On ascending the high land near the cave we found a large number of *snakes* that had been killed at different times; I counted twenty in one heap, and ten more scattered along the path, within a few rods; there were two species, the bull snake, and striped green snake, both said to be harmless. Some might infer from this that the cave would be a resort for snakes; but no snakes will be found there; the walls, floor, and ceiling, is constituted of solid rock, as white and neat as a lady's parlor; with no soil or crevice for harboring this reptile. It is said there are no rattlesnakes in this country; there is a snake called the blow snake, whose breath is said to be poisonous; but it is probably rare, as I could not find any person who had ever seen one."

"A short distance below the cave there is a little creek that leaps over a succession of cascades, making in all a fall of eighty feet, and, if flowing at the same rate during the season, forming an excellent water-power."

Much speculation has been, and still is carried on, in our country, with the *Carver lands*, located in what is called the "Carver Tract," by the heirs and pretended representatives of Captain JONATHAN CARVER, who claimed that the Indians made him an immense grant of land, on the Mississippi, in return for friendships and services he had rendered them. But Congress has never, to my knowledge, confirmed or recognized this title or claim, though it has often been brought before them. The tract claimed under this pretended grant lay south of St. Anthony's Falls, and east of the Mississippi, one hundred miles each way, mostly in Minnesota, and embracing St. Pauls and the surrounding country. Captain Carver was a native of Connecticut.

At St. Pauls, the capital of the Territory, there are three newspapers published: "*The Minnesota Pioneer*," democratic, by Col. Goodhue; "*The Minnesota Gazette*," whig; and the name of the third I have forgotten. Some efforts are being made to have the *Electric Telegraph* extended to that enterprising Territory, to connect with the Chicago and St. Louis lines, through Galena, Dubuque, and Milwaukee; as commercial business is rapidly increasing to the north, and this speedy means of intelligence is needed in that region.

Having thus glanced at things in Minnesota, we will return, agreeably to promise, and make a survey of the interior of those states, which constitute the principal subjects of this volume, and describe them by counties; and starting from where we left our Minnesota voyagers, Prairie du Chien, we will make a tour of observation, through Wisconsin, of such counties and towns as have not before been described. Still, with all that is harsh about it, and perilous, there is a grandeur and a charm about the Mississippi, that always causes one regrets at leaving it, with a desire soon to return to its banks, islands, and scenery.

WISCONSIN.

From the best authorities, it appears that the earliest visits of white men to the territory that now forms the State of Wisconsin, was in 1654, made by some French Traders, from Montreal to Lake Superior. The first white settlement was made in 1665, by Claude Allouez and others, at Lapointe, on an island of the same name, in the western end of that lake; and a few years before the establishment of the settlement at Puans (Green) Bay. According to the authorities quoted by Bancroft, Schoolcraft, and others, those settlements were made in 1665 and 1669; and in 1673, Father J. Marquette, accompanied by Joliet, went up the Nenah (Fox) river, passed the short portage of a mile or two into the Wisconsin river, then descended it to the Mississippi, which they reached in June of that year. The Legislature have named one of the counties, near that portage, after that adventurer, one of the first, Marquette, who ever saw that mighty stream.

In 1679, La Salle made a voyage up the lakes, in the first vessel ever built above Niagara Falls; he called it the *Griffon;* and he has claimed to be the first white man who ever saw the Mississippi; but this is disputed, as Bancroft declares that H. De Soto was the first European that discovered the "Father of Waters," and crossed it in 1541. The Griffon is said to have been a plain, substantial little schooner, of some sixty tons burden, and carrying five small guns. On the 7th of August, 1679, she sailed from Niagara with thirty-four men, bound for the western lakes, and reached Mackinaw the last of the month; on the 2d of September she sailed again for Green Bay. At that port she was laden with peltries; and on the 18th of the same month, La Salle put her in charge of the pilot and five men, and sent her back again; but they never reached their destination, vessel and crew having perished, which was a severe loss to La Salle, as the vessel and cargo had cost him about 60,000 livres. Still, he and his comrades continued their voyage up the coast of Lake Michigan in canoes to the mouth of Chicago river, where they erected a fort; and shortly afterward Father Hennepin, with others, passed from that river into the O'Plain, then the Illinois, and down that river to the Mississippi.

Wisconsin constituted a portion of New France, under French authority, till 1763, when it was surrendered to Great Britain. In 1783, a settlement was began at Prairie du Chien, by Giard, Autaya, and Dubuque, near the site of the earlier French settlement. In 1819 Governor Cass explored the northern country; during which year the garrisons of Prairie du Chien and St. Peter's were established. In 1823 Major Long explored the same region; and in 1832 an expedition under Schoolcraft passed through the country. In 1836 it was organized under a Territorial government, with the title of Wisconsin Territory.

This was a territory, under one authority or another, from 1787 to 1847, when it became an independent state of the Union, making the twenty-ninth star in that galaxy of political existences, whose light is seen throughout Christendom, and whose influence is felt wherever the breezes have carried paper and powder. In fertility of soil, comfort of climate, and all other natural facilities of successful agricultural operations, Wisconsin is scarcely behind any of her sister states; and perhaps is surpassed by none in the rapidity with which her population has increased during the last eight or ten years, and their intelligence. In 1840 the population was something over 30,000; in 1845 it was about five times that, say 115,000; and in 1850 the census shows it to be 305,528.

I take the following boundary of this state from *Darby's Gazetteer*, of 1845:

"WISCONSIN, Territory of the U. S., if taken *in extenso*, is bounded on the N. by the British territories; by Mississippi river, W.; Illinois, S.; and by Lake Michigan, the northwestern part of the State of Michigan, and Lake Superior, E. In latitude it extends from 42° 30′ to 49° 0′ N., and in longitude from 10° 0′ to 18° 30′ W. of Washington. Measured by the rhombs, the area comes out so near that we may assume 80,000 square miles. This region comprises the northwestern part of the original U. S. domain by the treaty of 1783. From SE. to NW., by a diagonal line, the length falls but little short of 600 miles. The breadth is about 160 miles.

"That portion of Wisconsin, organized and subdivided into counties is bounded E. by Lake Michigan; NW. by Green Bay, Fox, and Wisconsin rivers; W., or rather SW., by Mississippi river; and S. by the State of Illinois. In latitude it extends from 42° 30′ to 45° 20′, and in longitude from 10° 0′ to 14° 5′ W. of Washington. From the SW. angle, on Mississippi river, to the NE. point between Green Bay and Lake Michigan, the length is 280 miles. The breadth varies from near 100 to a mere point; area about 11.500 square miles. The face of the country is rather waving than either hilly or flat, though both extremes exist. It is a territory in a remarkable manner supplied with navigable streams. *Fox* river, flowing into *Green Bay*, and *Wisconsin*, into *Mississippi* river, approach each other so near as to leave but a short *portage* between their channels. The higher branches of Rock river rise in Wisconsin, and flow into the State of Illinois.

"It has a coast of about 200 miles on Lake Michigan, over which flow some small streams, but the shallowness of the water of the lake precludes any harbor admitting vessels of more than very moderate draught. The rivers afford much more extensive navigable facilities than does the lake.

"The town of MADISON, on what is called the *Four Lakes*, is the capital of the Territory. This town is situated at N. latitude 43° 5′, and longitude 12° 12′ W. of Washington, and almost directly S. of the portage between Wisconsin and Fox rivers; distance about 40 miles, and about 140 miles a little N. of NW. from Chicago."

MOUNDS AND EARTHWORKS.—In various portions of the Western States, ancient mounds, embankments, and fortifications are found, which show them clearly to have been the work of a people inhabiting here long before the discovery, by Columbus, of this continent.

By what character of people, or for what purpose, the mounds were made, are inexplicable points, about which as yet, no history that we possess can enlighten us satisfactorily.

In Wisconsin, at the town of AZTALAN, the most singular and remarkable, as well as the most perfect of these earthworks, have been found. In April last I visited them. They form embankments of four to six feet high, inclosing fields of from ten to forty acres; with conical mounds varying in size and hight, from ten to twenty high, and thirty and fifty feet diameter at the base—some inside and others outside of the inclosures. They are located near a small river, on a smooth bank sloping gradually toward the water. I ran around on the embankments examining and measuring them; on the top they were wide enough to admit the driving of a buggy, which is frequently done. On several of them, and around, a thin red haze filled the air, through which the bluffs loomed at a distance, and the *Mounds* appeared dilated to a far greater size than they possessed.

If the reader have read any works on America, he will have been made attentive to these extensive remains—the sole antiquities of this part of the world—as, ever since their existence has become generally known, with the fact, that the Indian tribes of our day, apparently declining in number at the very time of the discovery of the continent, were themselves seated on a soil whose ancient monuments attested its prior possession by a more numerous and more civilized race, they became a favorite theme for the speculation of the theorist and the traveler. It is probable that some were built as tombs, others as watch-towers, or for defense, and perhaps the larger class as rude temples. Most of those *tumili* which have been opened have been found to contain human bones, coarse pottery, rude weapons, or ornaments. But none of the larger have hitherto undergone scrutiny.

There is an artificial Mound situated forty miles west of CHICAGO, which measures four hundred and fifty yards in length, by seventy-five in breadth, and sixty feet in perpendicular hight. Its form is elliptical, with a flat top. Also, at Joliet, on the Canal, is a similar one.

From Mr. LAPHAM's work I take the following:

"The village of Aztalan is situated on the west bank of the Crawfish river, on the United States road leading from Milwaukee to the Mississippi, by way of Madison—distant from Milwaukee about fifty miles, and from Madison thirty. It is very prettily situated, on the sloping bank of the river, immediately above the 'ancient city' from which it derives its name.

"This ancient artificial earthwork, consists of an oblong inclosure, about five hundred and fifty yards in length, and two hundred and seventy-five yards in breadth, lying along the bank of the river. The walls are twenty-three feet wide at the base, and four or five feet high, having (except on the river side) an exterior semicircular enlargement, or buttress, and a corresponding interior recess every twenty-seven yards. In some parts of the wall, and especially in the buttresses, the earth of which it is composed appears to have been mixed with straw, and burned in such manner as to resemble slightly burned brick. There is no evidence that this substance was ever moulded into regular form. Within this inclosure are several remarkable mounds and excavations."

12

In many places very large oak trees are found growing on them, proving their great age.

From different works on the subject, I have given several extracts, descriptive and speculative, upon them. From the supposed resemblance of some of the discoveries at this place to the antiquities of the *Aztecs*, in Mexico, did the town receive its name of Aztalan; and certainly there are some things curious and worthy of note there.

Something of the Climate and winters of Wisconsin may be judged by the following statement of the clearing and opening of the harbor, at Milwaukee, for some ten years past. The freezing up of the harbor, during that time, varied from as early as November 15, to as late as the 1st of December.

In the spring it has opened, some years, as early as the first week in March, and at others not till as late as about the middle of April.

The *township* organization system prevails throughout most of Wisconsin, very similar to that in the State of New York; most of the counties have adopted the system.

No argument is needed to show Monied Men that the West is a more advantageous place to loan their funds than the East—that money can be let at higher interest and oftener turned, and always in active demand on safe securities; for this is all very well known, and is so generally remarked, that it has grown into a proverb. It is because there is much land and little money in the West—the country being new, filled up with recent settlers, who are nearly all engaged in making improvements, which, as yet, yield but small revenue; and real estate rising more rapidly, and money scarcer, proportionately, than at the East; the latter being in greater demand, until larger crops are ready for market. So that those having surplus funds, whether to invest in improvements, or to loan, will readily see that it is to their interest to locate in the West, for the highest profitable operations.

In Central and Western New York real estate increased in value more rapidly—after the opening of the Erie Canal and some of the railroads, bringing the products with speed and cheapness to market—in proportion, than it did at the East. In like manner, and for the same reasons, will property be enhanced in value in the states West of the Lakes, above those on the Atlantic; so ample now are the means of communication between the seaboard and the frontier country.

In conversation, a short time since, with an extensive grain and flour dealer, of a western state, my attention was called more forcibly to the contrast between the time occupied a few years ago and that required at the present day to take a barrel of flour from Wisconsin or Illinois, and return the necessary merchandise. Then, two to four weeks were occupied, each way; now, it only takes some six to ten days; and soon, when the whole line of railroads now commenced shall be completed, only two or three days will be consumed in the passage between New York and Chicago or Milwaukee. And what is better, decided cheapness, too, is attained in this rapid transit. But that is not all, nor even the greatest, advantage resulting to the western settler by this speedy transportation; his chief benefit gained by it, is the increased price secured to him for his products—a price approximating very close to the prices of New York and Philadelphia.

All who know any thing about it, understand very well that the prices at the West depend altogether upon the Eastern market; and the longer the time which transpires between the sale and the date at which the articles reach that market, the wider must be the margin and fluctuations in the prices, and greater must be the hazards and contingencies, all of which the purchasers are bound to take into the account when buying the western commodities; as prices at the time of his buying are liable to fall, at the East, before those products reach their destination. But when the transit is quicker—reduced to two or three days—these chances of decline in prices, all the risks much diminished, and the insurance less, so that the produce speculator can very safely venture to pay prices much nearer the full eastern value.

Under these circumstances, western lands must be greatly enhanced in actual value; increased in a ratio decidedly greater than the eastern lands, when taking into the account the respective prices at which both are now held, the former realizing nearly as high profits as the latter, while the cost of producing is vastly in favor of the western farmer—which proves the wisdom of investing in and improving western real estate, while it may be obtained for low prices; as the astonishing progress making in transit facilities is constantly hastening the time of an equilibrium in land value East and West. And when we consider the wonderful productiveness and easy tillage of western soils, even at the same cost per acre, the profit of the capital invested is nearly or quite as great in the one location as the other. As I have elsewhere said, a reference to the state of things in Eastern and Western New York, incident upon the opening of market facilities through the internal improvements of that state, is a palpable corroboration of the position here taken. But my object is simply to state facts and brief suggestions, while the wise and shrewd will enlarge and practice upon them.

These remarks, in relation to the agricultural capacities of the West, are superfluous to those who have been there and examined them; but it is not for such—it is for those east and south, who have never visited the Prairie country—that I am giving this plain description, that they may have some idea, some appreciation of them; enough, at least, to induce them to go and look for themselves at these vast natural Gardens of the West. In some locations there is one serious drawback, *at present,* to the fullest growth and prosperity of the West; but still, it is limited to particular sections and routes; I allude to *land monopoly* by non-cultivators. Mr. Greeley, in his travels through the West, a few years since, observed these things and commented upon them:

"I have found, not only the best dispositions of prairie and timber, but also the most tasteful improvements on the cross roads and by ways, quite aside from the three or four great roads, leading in different directions from Chicago, which are mainly traveled. These routes are largely cursed with the blight of land speculation and non-resident ownership."

This is true in most parts of the New States; along the great and early thoroughfares large portions of the public lands were bought up by non-residents solely for speculation, as it was believed many emigrants would buy those lands and pay a high price, rather than settle farther away from general communication, even at a lower price; and such has been the case in some instances, but not universally so; for, as is stated above, many settled away on the cross and intermediate tracts; and there is where you will see many of the best farms, and much of the finest improvements in several respects; and particularly so, in those instances where a company of farmers and mechanics have gone in and settled down together, creating at once a pleasant neighborhood.

To those who may prefer to engage in the raising of *sheep,* the West offers no less favorable openings than to the *grain* grower; as experiment has satisfactorily demonstrated that sheep can be successfully reared in Wisconsin and Illinois, of as vigorous growth and valuable clip as in states east of the lakes. The writer of this, while traveling in the West, has examined numbers of flocks,

7

containing from one to five thousand, which would compare favorably in size, health, and fleece, with most that he has seen in the older states. The natural pasturage is peculiarly agreeable to them, and is abundant, where they can range prosperingly, among the swells and slopes of the rolling prairies, reasonable care being required to keep them warm and well fed during the short winters; and in some sections there is occasional trouble from small prairie wolves, yet nothing but what may be easily guarded against by cheap yards for night-time; even in many instances a good dog, with slight training, is an effectual protection, as the wolves always avoid them, or flee at their approach.

It is frequent and exciting fun and amusement to many Western people to chase these animals on horseback, over the vast prairies, for which purpose they carry pistols and lances. The horses very soon learn to understand and enjoy the sport, and even get so well initiated as to voluntarily stamp upon, or jump after them as they overtake them bounding through the grass.

For raising *Horses* and *Cattle*, the country lying between Lake Michigan and the Mississippi, and much of that beyond, is unsurpassed by any in the whole range of the "Old Thirteen." The grass and hay, from our boundless prairies, exceeds in luxuriance and succulent qualities that procured from the choicest meadows of the Genesee, Connecticut, or Susquehanna rivers. And when plowed under, they will surpass in product of corn, potatoes, barley, oats, and strawberries, if not wheat, those "Old Flats."

And to those who have children to rear and educate, the West presents transcendent facilities. There is wide, beautiful space for vigorous exercise, with abundance of fresh air and healthful breezes, all peculiarly favorable to the full, strong development of *physical nature*, which is of paramount importance to growing youth—vastly more essential to primary years than mere book instruction, though seemingly not generally so regarded by parents; and these advantages are enjoyed in *moral* locations, apart, too, from the corrupting, hollow, and noisy influences, so prevalent in large cities and dense communities, which with many is too slightly considered.

The advantages of healthy physical development, under general moral influence, is of vastly more consequence to the earlier years of youthful education, than is the simple proficiency in book erudition; and a proper regard to these things is always well attended to by the wise; though, with no disposition to underrate the worth of a high standard of scientific and literary education, nor with less care in seeking such privileges for youth, as they begin to strengthen and advance to riper years; but they do look to moral and physical education as deserving of the first special attention; and in these respects the bright, fresh regions of the New States—the prairie country—are pre-eminently favored; but they are not, thereby, destitute of the advantages of liberal education; for still, the West is not far behind in the matter of good schools and seminaries of learning; the primary schools and seminaries are found to be of the first order, both in the competency of teachers and the comfort of buildings; this is the case in most of the settled sections, though it is to be regretted there are some exceptions.

And where it is needed—where advanced years have more matured the child's mind—and when *mental tuition* becomes the first and leading object, with parents, who wish the educational efforts of their children directed to the acquisition of higher branches of knowledge, they will find in all of these States, Colleges well endowed, under the control of accomplished and competent professors, with spacious and convenient buildings, occupying pleasant and healthful locations; and in all essentials holding a favorable comparison with similar institutions East.

Another important fact exists in favor of Western institutions; that of *economy*, or pecuniary saving; as the desired tuition can here be obtained at considerable less expense than at the East. In fact, Eastern men, of such limited means that they can ill afford to give their children a liberal education there, may remove West, locate in the vicinity of some college, and there, by judicious management, be really able to educate them handsomely.

Thus, we see that in the West, we clearly possess three decided advantages for educating families; namely, moral security, reduced expense, and better physical development; and certainly these things are worth reflecting upon by those interested; and I give the facts, to be entertained as they see fit—to be appreciated and appropriated when wisdom and utility shall direct. Thus, for less toil a competence is acquired, and for less money an education is obtained. Nothing is truer than the following remarks of a foreigner:

> "You may see men of learning and superior minds in Europe toiling week after week, and year after year, merely to procure for themselves and families the bare food, clothing, and shelter they need; which, in the new world [America] is obtained with but seemingly little exertion."

These remarks will hold equally as true, and the contrast is full as striking, in regard to the old and new states of our country. Thousands struggle on through life, in the older states, for barely the means of existence from year to year; when, by removing westward, and expending the same efforts there, it would procure for them an easy competence, often a fortune.

But in many cases the circumstances under which great numbers of honest, faithful men have to labor, are such that it is next to impossible for them to lay up enough of their earnings to remove their families westward, buy land, and commence improvements, or procure the means of living till their improvements will yield them the necessaries of life. This is particularly true with hundreds of worthy mechanics in large cities. In such cases, it would be wise, good policy, nay, it is the duty of Congress, to grant them 80 or 160 acres of land, free of price, if they will settle on and improve it; their little money would then enable them to do this comfortably, as they have not first to pay it all out for their land, with nothing left to help themselves. Government can make no better investment than to give the wild lands to absolute cultivators.

The proposition of our Federal Government to grant to the patriot KOSSUTH, and his compatriots, a colony, a tract of land, without pay, on which to settle, is creditable to it. They have selected it in Iowa, and call the place New Buda.

It lies in a beautiful region of country, in Decatur county, south of Iowa river, and toward the Des Moines. The land was selected by Governor UJHAZY. Whether Kossuth will still struggle on, or settle down in a colony with his fellow refugees, is not yet known.

Our Government would also do just and wisely for its own interests, to give to every needy, industrious, and orderly man—native or foreigner—land enough for a comfortable home, who would occupy and cultivate it; eighty acres is enough; that amount, well cultivated, would give any prudent family a comfortable living, and yearly add a small sum to the surplus in their coffers. Still, let it be a larger amount, if it prove best. We have domain, lying useless and waste, enough to supply all who would ask for such farms, for many generations; and as all must die, the first would give place to their successors, so that the population should not become so dense, on the whole earth, that there should no longer be space left. Has not the Almighty spread out the bright, fertile earth for man's occupancy, and not to lie untenanted and fruitless? If this be not the case, why has civilization, nay, apparent destiny, been allowed to drive off, to almost extinguish, the aboriginal races, from the rich, boundless tracts which they for centuries occupied, but left uncultivated; simply ranging over them for game and wild fruits.

The first and highest wealth of a nation, and its surest protection, is an industrious, independent agricultural population; and the next is an ingenious, prosperous artizan community, working hand in hand, harmoniously, with the former; and they together soon add a third branch of national wealth; that is, good roads and extensive thoroughfares.

In all of these states and territories, described in this book, there are large quantities of public lands that now, and probably for a long time will, lie waste and useless, which would soon be occupied by industrious yeomen, who would speedily cause them to produce with profitable luxuriance, if the Government would throw them open to the free possession of such persons.

The fine towns that are built up at the river mouths, and the huge steamers and sail-vessels which daily enter them, prove how greatly mistaken the early travelers and writers were, many times, in regard to the depth of water or harbor facilities along the lakes; as in the case above quoted from Darby. True, in some instances, *dredging* at the mouth of rivers has been of great benefit, by removing portions of bars, which had collected by the wash into the channels. I take the following from LAPHAM'S History of Wisconsin:

"The *Territory of Wisconsin*, as established at present, is bounded as follows: Commencing in the middle of Lake Michigan, in north latitude forty-two degrees and thirty minutes; thence north along the middle of the lake, to a point opposite the main channel or entrance of Green Bay; thence through said channel and Green Bay to the mouth of the Menomonee river; thence through the middle of the main channel of said river to that head nearest the Lake of the Desert; thence in a direct line to the middle of said lake; thence to the source of the Montreal river; thence through the middle of the main channel of that river to its mouth; thence with a direct line across Lake Superior to where the Territorial line of the United States last touches said lake northwest; thence along said Territorial line to a point due north of the head waters or source of the Mississippi river, in longitude ninety degrees and two minutes west from Greenwich; thence due south to the Mississippi; thence along the middle or center of the main channel of said river to latitude forty-two degrees and thirty minutes north; thence due east to the place of beginning.

"It therefore embraces all that portion of the United States lying between the State of Michigan on the east, and the Mississippi on the west, which separates it from the (now) State of Iowa; and between the State of Illinois on the south and the British possessions on the north; extending from forty-two and a half to the forty-ninth degree of north latitude, and embracing about ten degrees of longitude."

Of the general growth and face of the country, I also quote from the same work the following general and scientific description:

"Many parts of the country are but thinly peopled, and little communication exists between them and other settlements, so that it is difficult to ascertain what are their extent, population, and improvements. New settlements are commenced almost every day, and soon grow into important places, without any notice being taken of them by the public. Towns and villages spring up so rapidly that one has to 'keep a sharp look out' to be informed even of their names and location, to say nothing about their population, trade, and buildings. The building of a town has, in a great degree, ceased to be a matter of much interest—as much so as an earthquake formerly did in some parts of Missouri.

"The Indians have, by various treaties, ceded to the United States all their lands in Wisconsin, except a portion lying between the west end of Lake Superior and the head waters of the Mississippi. This, therefore, is all that now remains in possession of the original owners—the Indians."

To this statement should be excepted the Settlement of the *Brothertown* Indians, who have a prosperous town on the east side of Lake Winnebago, where they have become civilized and Christianized; they live and do business like the whites, and have a Representative in the State Legislature. The *Oneida* Settlement, too, west of Green Bay, is somewhat advanced in civilization, but more inclined to their native habits than the others.

Although, in none of these States are there any mountains; still Wisconsin, probably, presents higher eminences than either of the others.

"There are no *mountains*, properly speaking, in Wisconsin; the whole being one vast plain, varied only by the river hills, and the gentle swells or undulations of country usually denominated *rolling*. This plain lies at an elevation of from six hundred to fifteen hundred feet above the level of the ocean. The highest lands are those forming the dividing ridge between the waters of Lake Superior and the Mississippi. From this ridge there is a gradual descent toward the south and southwest. This inclination is interrupted in the region of the lower Wisconsin and Neenah rivers, where we find another ridge extending across the Territory, from which proceeds another gently descending slope, drained mostly by the waters of Rock river and its branches. These slopes indicate, and are occasioned by, the dip or inclination of the rocky strata beneath the soil.

"The Wisconsin hills and many of the bluffs along the Mississippi river often attain the hight of three hundred feet above their base; and the Blue Mound was ascertained by Dr. Locke, by barometrical observations, to be one thousand feet above the Wisconsin river at Helena. The surface is farther diversified by the Platte and Sinsinawa Mounds; but these prominent elevations are so rare that they form very marked objects in the landscape, and serve the traveler, in the unsettled portions of the country, as guides by which to direct their course. The country immediately bordering on Lake Superior has a very abrupt descent toward the lake; hence the streams entering that lake are full of rapids and waterfalls, being comparatively worthless for all purposes of navigation, but affording a vast superabundance of water-power, which may at some future time be brought into requisition to manufacture lumber from the immense quantities of pine trees with which this part of the Territory abounds.

"There is another ridge of broken land running from the entrance of Green Bay in a southwesterly direction, forming the *divide* between the waters of Lake Michigan and those running into the Bay and Neenah, and continuing thence through the western part of Washington county, crossing Bark river near the Nagowicka lake, and thence passing in the same general direction, through Walworth county, into the State of Illinois. The irregular and broken appearance of this ridge is probably owing to the soft and easily decomposed limestone rock of which it is composed.

"On our northern border is Lake Superior, the largest body of fresh water in the world, and on the east is Lake Michigan, second only to Lake Superior in magnitude, forming links in the great chain of inland seas by which we are connected with the *lower country* by a navigation as important for all purposes of commerce as the ocean itself. Beside these immense lakes, Wisconsin abounds in those of smaller size, scattered profusely over her whole surface. They are from one to twenty or thirty miles in extent. Many of them are the most beautiful that can be imagined—the water deep and of crystal clearness and purity, surrounded by sloping hills and promontories covered with scattered groves and clumps of trees. Some are of a more picturesque kind, being more rugged in their appearance, with steep, rocky bluffs, crowned with cedar, hemlock, spruce, and other evergreen trees of a similar character.

"Perhaps a small rocky island will vary the scene, covered with a conical mass of vegetation, the low shrubs and bushes being arranged around the margin, and the tall trees in the center. These lakes usually abound in fish of various kinds, affording food for the pioneer settler; and among the pebbles on their shores may occasionally be found fine specimens of *agate*, *carnelian*, and other precious stones.

"In the bays where the water is shallow and but little affected by the winds the wild rice (*Zizania aquatica*) grows in abundance, affording subsistence for the Indian, and attracting innumerable water birds to these lakes. The rice has never been made use of by the settlers in Wisconsin as an article of food, although at some places it affords one of the principal means of support for the red men. It is said to be about equal to oatmeal in its qualities, and resembles it in some degree in taste. The difficulty of collecting it, and its inferior quality, will always prevent its use by white men, except in cases of extreme necessity."

Mr. Lapham here occupies a page in giving a somewhat minute description of the Upper Mississippi, Lake of the Woods, Rainy lake, etc., which is not material, as I have elsewhere given all on that point which is deemed essential to the objects of this work.

Adventurers, or lovers and seekers of romance, will find very much to gratify them, by exploring that region, which they will find handsomely portrayed in the writings of various travelers to that direction.

In regard to the indications of an ancient people having occupied this section of country, I copy still from the same work :

"The rivers running into the Mississippi take their rise in the vicinity of the sources of those running into the lakes, and they often originate in the same lake or swamp, so that the communication from the Mississippi to the lakes is rendered comparatively easy at various points. The greatest depression in the dividing ridge in the Territory is supposed to be at Fort Winnebago, where the Wisconsin river approaches within half a mile of the Neenah, and where, at times of high water, canoes have actually passed across from one stream to the other. Some of the rivers are supplied from the tamarack swamps, from which the water takes a dark color.

"Wisconsin does not fall behind the other portions of the western country in the monuments, or *Mounds*, it affords of the existence of an *ancient people* who once inhabited North America, but of whom nothing is known except what can be gathered from some of the results of their labors. The works at Aztalan, in Jefferson county, are most known and visited, but there are many other localities which are said to equal them in interest and importance. The substance called brick at this place, is evidently burned clay, showing marks of having been mixed with straw, but they were not moulded into regular forms.

"There is a class of ancient *earthworks* in Wisconsin, not before found in any other country, being made to represent quadrupeds, birds, reptiles, and even the human form. These representations are rather rude, and it is often difficult to decide for what species of animal they are intended ; but the effects of time may have modified their appearance very much since they were originally formed. Some have a resemblance to the buffalo, the eagle, or crane, or to the turtle or lizard. One representing the human form, near the Blue Mounds, is, according to R. C. Taylor, Esq., one hundred and twenty feet in length; it lies in an east and west direction, the head toward the west, with the arms and legs extended. The body or trunk is thirty feet in breadth, the head twenty-five, and its elevation above the general surface of the prairie is about six feet. Its conformation is so distinct that there can be no possibility of mistake in assigning it to the human figure. A mound at Prairieville, representing a turtle, is about five feet high; the body is fifty-six feet in length; it represents the animal with its legs extended, and its feet turned backward. It is to be regretted that this interesting mound is now nearly destroyed. The ancient works are found in all parts of the Territory, but are most abundant at Aztalan, on Crawfish river, near the Blue Mounds, along the Wisconsin, the Neenah, and the Pishtaka rivers, and near Lake Winnebago.

"The reader is referred to the 'Notice of Indian Mounds, etc., in Wisconsin,' in Silliman's Journal, vol. 34, p. 88, by R. C. Taylor; and to the 'Description of Ancient Remains in Wisconsin,' by S. Taylor, vol. 44, p. 21, of the same work.

"The mounds are generally scattered about without any apparent order or arrangement, but are occasionally arranged in irregular rows, the animals appearing as if drawn up in a line of march. An instance of this kind is seen near the road seven miles east from the Blue Mounds, in Iowa county. At one place near the Four Lakes (Dane County), it is said that one hundred *tumuli*, of various shapes and dimensions, may be counted—those representing animals being among others that are round or oblong.

"Fragments of *ancient pottery* of a very rude kind are often found in various localities. They were formed by hand, or moulded, as their appearance shows evidently that these vessels were not turned on a potter's wheel. Parts of the rim of vessels, usually ornamented with small notches or figures, are most abundant.

"A mound is said to have been discovered near Cassville, on the Mississippi, which is supposed to represent an animal having a trunk like the elephant, or the now extinct mastodon. Should this prove true, it will show that the people who made these animal earthworks, were cotemporaries with that huge monster, whose bones are still occasionally found; or that they had then but recently emigrated from Asia, and had not lost their knowledge of the elephant."

There is scarcely a county in Wisconsin, Northern Illinois, and some portions of Iowa, where the traveler will not meet some of these curious formations; and though by whom or for whatever purpose they were made, is questionable, there can be no doubt that they are artificial works, and constructed under the suggestions of human designs.

Extensive improvements have taken place in Wisconsin, since Mr. Lapham published his book, and the population has more than doubled in that time; towns of but hundreds have increased to thousands of inhabitants; canals have been dug, railroads laid down, mills and factories erected, and steamboats put afloat on some of the small interior lakes; all of which, with the wide improvement of farms, roads, schoolhouses, churches, begin already to give this new state in many parts much the appearance of older ones.

Running along up the Wisconsin river, lying on its north bank, are the counties of *Crawford*, population 2,400; it is more fully described in another place; *Richland*, population 1,000, watered by Pine river, with RICHMOND, on the Wisconsin, for its county-seat; *Sauk*, population 4,400, watered by Baraboo river, with PRAIRIE DU SAC, on the Wisconsin, for its county-seat; *Portage*, population 1,300, watered by the Wisconsin and some smaller streams, with PLOVER PORTAGE for its county-seat. Still north of these, are other counties, not judicially organized, in the Pinery, with but a sparse population, and but little known except for their rich lumber resources.

Lying along the Wisconsin, on its south bank, are the counties of *Grant*, *Iowa*, *Dane*, and *Columbia*. They are more minutely described in another part of this work.

At the line of Columbia and Portage counties, an elbow

is formed in the river, so that from here, its direction to the source in the *Great Pinery* is nearly north.

The first tier of counties north of the river here named, are very good farming counties, containing much good prairie and other land, with some fine timber, embracing valuable *pineries* among the rest; but farther north still, with the exception of one or two counties, much cannot be said in favor of the country as an agricultural one.

Still, for its splendid *pine forests* and grand *water-powers*, it will always be held in high estimation, and attract a portion of emigration thitherward. What Mr. Lapham says of the north part of Brown county will apply generally to much of the northern part of the State, with some exceptions, where are fine prairies:

"Little is known of the geographical details of the northern part of this county; it abounds in *forests of pine*, and the streams are full of *falls* and *rapids*, affording an abundance of water-power, where this pine is, in large quantities, manufactured into lumber and shingles, which find a ready market at ports on Lake Michigan and other places. The soil is said to be of excellent quality, and is covered with dense forests—no openings or prairies being found of any considerable extent.

"A singular feature in the topography of the country is indicated by the course of the principal streams, which have a general southeasterly direction toward Lake Michigan, except the *Neenah*, which, with Green Bay (an enlarged continuation of it), runs at right angles to this course, and nearly parallel with the general course of the lake. The cause of this feature may be found in a rocky ridge extending along the east side of the Neenah, giving direction to that river, and 'heading' all those that take their rise west of it. This ridge extends southwest quite through the Territory, and from it originates another system of streams running east or southeast into Lake Michigan."

This description will hold in regard to what was originally Brown county, when it extended to the northern bounds of the State; and not to its present limits, which embraces a fine county:

"The *Wisconsin river* is one of the most important in the Territory, especially the lower portion, between the *portage* and the Mississippi, a distance of one hundred and fourteen miles, by the course of the river. At the *portage*, it is four hundred yards wide, and it gradually increases in width to the mouth, where it is six hundred yards wide. In *Richland* county, it has a width of about four hundred and fifty yards. This portion of the river is bordered by high sandstone bluffs, from one hundred and fifty to two hundred feet in hight—constituting a scenery of great beauty and even grandeur. The water is shallow, and there are numerous islands and shifting sand-bars. The current is usually quite rapid. Hence the navigation of the Wisconsin is rather difficult and uncertain; but steamboats, such as usually run on the Upper Mississippi, have ascended to the portage. When the channel is better known to the pilots, it may, however, be navigated in ordinary stages of the water, without much difficulty.

"The *Upper Wisconsin* lies principally in *Portage* county, with its numerous *rapids* and *portages*, affording water-power of great extent, which is used at many places to manufacture pine lumber. Large quantities of lumber are annually sent down this river, and the Mississippi, as far as St. Louis. The *pineries* commence about eighty miles above Fort Winnebago; and here a *railroad* has been constructed (the first in Wisconsin) of two miles in length, to convey logs from the forest to the mills. At the *Dells*, the river runs for eight miles between perpendicular cliffs of rock about three hundred feet high, and only forty across.

"The scenery here is grand and picturesque, resembling the gorge below the Falls of Niagara, and probably produced by the same cause. A small steamboat passed through the Dells, in 1845, being the first attempt to navigate the Upper Wisconsin. Near the Dells is the place where Black Hawk and the Prophet were taken (after their defeat at the battle of the *Bad Axe*) by Dekorra and Chaetar, two Winnebago Indians, who had been employed for that purpose by the Indian agent at Prairie du Chien."

Those counties which lie on the south side, next to the Wisconsin river, are among the very best in the State. The first is Grant county. There is no county in all the West that has a better soil for raising wheat than this; it possesses more of the appearance and peculiarities of the New York wheat-growing lands, in Cayuga county, and the

Genesee country, than any county I have seen in this region. It occupies the southwest corner of Wisconsin, bounded on the north by the Wisconsin river, and on the southwest by the Mississippi. Its extreme length, from north to south, is forty-eight miles, and from east to west, thirty-seven miles; its mean breadth, however, is only twenty-four miles. It has a river coast along the Wisconsin and Mississippi of nearly one hundred miles. The soil in both timber and prairie land is very rich and fertile, yielding all the usual crops, found at the East, in similar latitudes, and with comparatively little effort to the farmer. Population, 16,169; dwellings, 2,861; farms, 707; manufactories, 78.

CASSVILLE is situated on the Mississippi river. It was commenced as early as 1835, but very little permanent improvement was made. The scenery about here is very beautiful. Population, two to three hundred.

POTOSI is considered by many one of the most important places on the Mississippi in the *mineral country*, and destined ere long to be the shipping point for much of the lead trade that finds its way down that river. Population about 2,000.

The *Potosi Republican* is one of the best country papers in the State.

From Dubuque the "O'Rielly Telegraph line" crosses the Mississippi, and passes through this county, with offices at Potosi and Lancaster.

PLATTEVILLE is the largest of the interior towns, situated in the immediate vicinity of extensive mineral diggings. It is on a small branch of the Little Platte river. The village was incorporated in 1841, and has an academy, with a newspaper, and 1,500 population.

LANCASTER, the seat of justice, is a flourishing town, situated near the center of the county. It has a Court-house of brick, and a newspaper published weekly. Population about 500.

Grant river is the largest in the county, and is said to be navigable twelve miles above its mouth, at Potosi. It has numerous small branches, among which are Bois, Pigeon, and Rattlesnake creeks.

In this county is located the most, or all of that large 20,000 acre tract, owned by EARL MURRAY, of Scotland. This possession of such large bodies of land by one man, is a detriment to the prosperity of the county and towns; and has prevented as rapid a settlement as would otherwise have taken place; though I am recently told he is now willing to sell a great portion of it at very low prices; as the high taxes imposed upon non-resident and non-improved lands—very wisely and properly—by the New States, render it unprofitable, in most localities, to hold very large quantities of such unproductive property; though not so when improved.

He has married a very rich heiress, of Livingston county, New York, and has been appointed by the British Government to a diplomatic station in Turkey and Egypt, where he is building a castle for his permanent residence.

The next county up the Wisconsin river is *Iowa*. It is one of the largest and most important counties in the Mineral District. The surface is considerably broken by valleys and ridges, the whole having a slight inclination to the north and south from the great ridge, running east and west about ten miles south of the Wisconsin. This broken character is owing to the soft, easily decomposed limestone, which is readily carried away by disintegrating agents. Population, 9,576; dwellings, 1,846; farms, 507; manufactories, 24.

The famous *Platte* and *Belmonte Mounds* are found in Iowa county; they are composed of silicious limestone, and are visible, when the air is clear, about thirty miles.

The Indian name is *Eu-ne-she-te-no*—the two mountains. The views from the top of these mounds are highly interesting. Gen. WM. R. SMITH, of Mineral Point, describes them as follows:

"An ocean of prairie surrounds the gazer, whose vision is not limited to less than thirty or forty miles. This great sea of verdure is interspersed with delightful, varying undulations, like the vast waves of the ocean, and every here and there sinking into the hollows, or cresting the swells, appear spots of wood, large groves, small groups of trees, as if planted by the hand of art, for ornamenting this naturally splendid scene. Over this extended view, in all directions, are scattered the farms of the settlers, with their luxuriant crops of wheat and oats, whose yellow sheaves, already cut, form a beautiful contrast with the waving green of the Indian corn, and the smooth, dark lines of the potato crop.

Throughout the prairie, the most gorgeous variety of flowers are seen rising above the thickly set grass, which in large and small patches has, here and there, been mowed for hay, all presenting a curiously checkered appearance of the table beneath us. The mineral flower, the tall, bright purple and red feather, the sun flower [rosin weed], the yellow bloom, the golden rod, the several small and beautiful flowers, interspersed with the grass, render the scene indescribably beautiful.

"To the north, the Wisconsin hills are seen bounding the view; to the east, prairie and wood are only limited by the horizon; and the Blue Mounds, on the northeast, form a background and a landmark; to the south, the view over the rolling country extends into the State of Illinois; in the southwest, is seen the Sinsiniwa Mound; the view to the west is only bounded by the Table Mound, and the hills west of the Mississippi, and distant about thirty miles; while to the northwest the high hills through which the 'Father of Waters' breaks his sweeping way, close the view.

"Below us, on the plain, is the little village of BELMONTE, with its bright, painted dwellings; the brown lines in the broad green carpet indicate the roads and tracks over the prairie; the grazing cattle are scattered over the wide surface, looking like dogs or sheep in size; while in the distance are seen wagons of emigrants, and ox teams hauling lead, merchandise, and lumber; the horseman and foot traveler are passing and re-passing; pleasure and traveling carriages are whirling rapidly over the sward, as if the country had been improved for a century past, instead of having been only five years reclaimed from the savages. This picture is not exaggerated—it fails of the original beauty in the attempt to describe that scene which is worth a journey of a thousand miles to contemplate in the calm sunset of a summer day, as I have viewed it from the top of the Platte Mounds."

DODGEVILLE is a smart little village, north of Mineral Point, named in honor of General Dodge. Several lead mines have been opened, and furnaces put in operation here, and the mineral diggings in the neighborhood are valuable.

The county-seat of this county is MINERAL POINT, the name indicating plainly the leading business of the place; which is situated on a high ridge, or rather several ridges, of land, between two small branches of the Pecatonica, containing lead and copper ore; and some zinc and iron are found here. The town and county are being steadily improved, and are growing in population and wealth. The lead and copper are principally hauled in wagons to Galena, thence sent down the Mississippi; though recently some portions of it is hauled to Lake Michigan, and there shipped for the East. Mineral Point contains above 2,000 population; a *Newspaper* is published here; and new as the country is, already there are two *Telegraph* offices opened—one on the "O'Rielly line," and one on "Morse's." One of the U. S. Land Offices, for Wisconsin, is located at this place. There is some Government land for sale in this county.

HELENA is another town of some promise in this county; it is situated on the Wisconsin, near the mouth of Pipe creek. The distinguishing business of this place is the manufacture of shot.

Arena is another growing town, several miles farther up, at the mouth of Blackearth river.

Next east of this is *Dane* county, the most interesting county in the state, both for its natural features and the improvements that have been made within it. It is sometimes denominated the *Four Lakes Country*, from the fact that the chain of charming lakes, so universally noticed and admired by all who see them, are located in Dane county. The county is a very large one, being seven townships east and west, by five north and south, or 42 by 30 miles in extent. It is also very nearly central to the populated and tillable limits of the state; and therefore, is very wisely selected as the one in which is located the Seat of Government, where it will undoubtedly be permanently continued. There is not, in the state, a county which presents higher or as numerous inducements to men of industry, taste, or wealth, to settle within its borders, as this. Mr. Lapham thus speaks of the evil effects of *Land Monopoly* in this fine county:

"As soon as it was known that the CAPITAL of the Territory was established on the point or neck of land between the *Third* and *Fourth Lake*, a rush was made to the Land Office at Milwaukee, and all the lands subject to entry in the vicinity, and for many miles around these lakes, were immediately entered, mostly by those who *did not intend to occupy them* for actual settlement and improvement. Hence the improvement of this county has not been as rapid as some others, where the 'speculators' had not opportunity or inducement to *monopolize all the most valuable lands*. The advantage of having the seat of Government, however, has in some degree made up for this misfortune."

I have previously spoken of the overthronged number of industrial classes in our large Eastern Cities, so much so that but portions of them could have assurance of remunerating employment; and that the best present relief is emigrating to the West, where it can be found. On this subject the *New York Tribune* has the following remarks as concerning the city of New York:

"The grasshopper who, having sung all Summer, and being short of food and shelter in the Autumn, was advised by the ant to dance all Winter, read a lesson to many more than have yet heeded it.

Especially to those unwise and improvident parents who spend hundreds, if not thousands, on the education of their children, yet fail to qualify them for any independent, unfailing mode of earning a livelihood, this apologue addresses itself with great force. To qualify a youth for the profession of lawyer, clergyman, or doctor, may be very well; but no man *is* thus qualified until he has been taught how to earn his livelihood *outside* of such vocation. He is not fitted for unbending and invincible integrity in a profession who has not been armed with the consciousness that he can earn a decent living outside of that profession, for which he will not stand indebted to any man's good opinion.

"'Can't you give me something to do?' is now the anxious inquiry of thousands in our city. Winter is just upon us; Business is contracting on all hands; hundreds, who have for months found employment elsewhere, are weekly flocking into the city, while thousands who have been at work here, but are thrown out by the contractions of Trade and Industry, unite with them in swelling the mournful chorus, 'Pray give us something to do!'

"The labor you know how to perform is not now in demand any where; there is no demand for service of any kind here. Our Labor market is glutted, and cannot be otherwise until Spring. If false education and false pride had no existence—if every one who wants work were capable of doing good work, and precisely that kind of it which is most needed—there would still be much distress here every winter from lack of employment. Europe pours her surplus millions upon our shores; and their first cry is for work! work! Our own country meets this host by another as needy and as willing; for every one who can't get a satisfactory living elsewhere, feels sure that fortune awaits him in the city. So here are not less than fifty thousand human beings, many of them expensively educated for professions; some skillful and ready workers if work were to be had; but all destitute, unemployed, desperate, and threatened with starvation, eagerly pressing the inquiry—'Can't you find me something to do?'"

Upon the wisdom—the duty—of the General Government allowing all industrious persons, who wish, a portion of our wild, uncultivated domain, sufficient for a farm free of price, the same paper continues with well-timed remarks. Those lands are now lying tenantless, useless, when thousands of needy ones ought to be cultivating them, and deriving a pleasant, independent livelihood therefrom; the Government ought to invite occupants and tillers upon those lands, instead of repelling them, as is now the case, by requiring terms which thousands of deserving and needy persons are unable to comply with. Still, such as can buy and move on to those lands, would do well to do so, as quick as possible, and leave an opening for better employment to those who cannot move away:

"Your ranks must be thinned by the drawing off of a large portion of your number into other pursuits—but alas! what pursuits? If it were April instead of November, and you were all qualified to succeed as farmers, the earth around us belongs to those of whom you are not able to buy it; and the unappropriated lands in the Far West are held by the Government for sale, and not for unpurchased allotment to the needy and willing, like you. *These lands ought to solicit your free location and settlement*—that would do great good in time, by drawing off from the cities a class who now stand between you and the work you need; but what can be done for your present relief, we do not know and cannot suggest."

"What we *can* do in the premises is simply that which Dives in the parable could find no one to do for him—we can warn some portion of your brethren that they come not into your torment. We can exhort fond parents to heed the warning given them in your hard fortune, and educate their children so that they may earn a livelihood by their own hands if they are not wanted to minister to the intellectual or commercial wants of their neighbors. We can entreat all who love their neighbors, or even their own children, to unite in establishing the principle that a *Government can have no land to sell while it has a single subject needing land to cultivate and unable to pay a price for it.* And we can exhort all who have wealth to so use it as to give the largest measure of fairly rewarded employment to Useful Labor, and thus contribute to the sensible diminution of human suffering, even without obtaining or seeking the reputation of benevolence. Finally, we can exhort the fortunate and the unfortunate, the wise and the simple, to study intently and patiently the great problem of human misery flowing from want, and devise and concert measures for its peaceful and speedy solution. Were the desire for it but general and earnest, that solution would be found."

A very useful and elaborate pamphlet has been got up and published for circulation, by the enterprising inhabitants of Kane county, descriptive of the topography, geology, resources, and improvements of the county, with its history and statistics. From this I have copied the following, in regard to the county:

"The 43d parallel of north latitude, within a minute fraction, passes through the center of Dane county, in longitude 89° 20', west from Greenwich. The county is bounded on the north by Sauk and Columbia counties; east by Jefferson and Dodge; south by Rock and Green; and west by Iowa. Its altitude above the Atlantic Ocean, at the level of the Fourth Lake, is 788 feet, and above Lake Michigan 210 feet. It is by far the largest of the older settled counties, containing thirty-five townships—1,235 square miles —or 790,400 acres of land.

"The surface, in general, slopes to the east and south—rising gradually from a level on its eastern border, of about 163 feet above Lake Michigan, until the vicinity of the Blue Mounds is reached, near its western limits. These Mounds are the highest points in the state, their summits attaining an elevation of 1,000 feet above the Wisconsin river at Helena. The geological structure of the county is worthy of notice in this connection, since the quality of soil, in a given district, depends almost entirely upon the *wash* it receives from its highlands. A section through Blue Mounds, would show the following result, beginning at the top and descending vertically: Hornstone, 410 feet; Magnesian lime, or lead bearing rock, 169 feet; Saccharoid sandstone, 40 feet; alternations of sand and limestone, 188 feet; Sandstone, 3 feet; Lower limestone, (at the level of the Wisconsin,) 190 feet. It will thus be seen that limestone forms the principal masses of solid rock; but in addition to this, the drift formation which covers the surface is composed, in considerable proportion, of limestone boulders and pebbles. Thus all the elements exist here to form a soil of the best possible description, for agricultural purposes; and accounts for that thorough impregnation of lime, so essential to certain crops."

"The surface of the county generally is rolling—hills and valleys succeeding each other—presenting much such an appearance as we might suppose the ocean would have, if, after being lashed by a tempest, its waters were instantly congealed, and the surface clothed with verdure. The hills are seldom so abrupt that they may not be cultivated even upon their summits; valleys, though well watered, are very rarely marshy. There is not a county in the state containing so large a body of good lands, as Dane. It is doubtful whether there is a single section, not covered by water, which is not capable of profitable cultivation. The soil is composed, for the most part, of the black deposit of decayed vegetation, which for countless ages has flourished in wild luxuriance and rotted upon the surface; of loam, and in a few localities, of clay mixed with sand. The deposit of vegetable mold has uniformly several inches of thickness on the tops and sides of hills; in the valleys it is frequently a number of feet. A soil thus created of impalpable powder formed of the elements of organic matter—'the dust of death'—we need scarcely remark, is adapted to the highest and most profitable purposes of agriculture—yielding crop after crop in rank abundance, without any artificial manuring."

The principal rivers in this county are, the Wisconsin, Catfish, Sugar, and many other smaller creeks and rivulets.

The most attractive feature of this county are its clear *lakes*. Their waters generally originating in deep springs, they are necessarily exceedingly cool and pure.

"The lakes in this county are among the most beautiful objects that imagination can picture, and lend a charm to the scenery such as few, if any, localities can present. There are in all twelve lakes in Dane county; but the principal, and those most attractive, are the *Four Lakes*, lying in the valley of the *Catfish*, and nearly in a row, from northwest to southeast. A brief description of each, is all that space here allows. But they must be seen to be appreciated.

"*First Lake.*—This lake is the lowest of the four. Its longest diameter is three and one eighth miles, by two miles in its shortest; its circumference is nine and a half miles, and it covers five square miles. It is situated nine miles above DUNKIRK FALLS, near the southern line of the county.

"*Second Lake.*—This body of water lies three and a half miles above First Lake. Its length is three and a half miles, and its width about two; and, like the First, has an average depth of about twelve feet.

"*Third Lake* is next above, at a distance of seven eighths of a mile. It is about six and a half miles long, by two broad, occupying an area of six square miles. MADISON, the county-seat and

Capital of the State, is located on the strip of land between it and the next, about one mile across.

"*Fourth Lake.*—This is the uppermost and by far the largest of the Four Lakes. It has a periphery of nineteen and one fourth miles, and covers an area of fifteen and sixty-five hundredths square miles. Its diameter is six miles by nine.

"The water of all these lakes, coming from springs, is cold and clear to a remarkable degree. For the most part, their shores are made of a fine gravel shingle; and their bottoms, which are visible at a great depth, are composed of white sand, interspersed with granite boulders. Their banks, with few exceptions, are bold. A jaunt around them affords almost every variety of scenery—bold escarpments and overhanging cliffs, elevated peaks, and gently sloping shores, with graceful swales or intervals, affording magnificent views of the distant praries and openings; they abound in fish of a great variety, and water-fowls innumerable sport upon the surface. Persons desiring to settle in sightly locations with magnificent views of water and woodland scenery, may find hundreds of unoccupied places of unsurpassed beauty upon and near their margins."

Beside the above, *Lake Wingra* is a very pretty one and deserves notice here, as it adds much to the landscapes seen from several points in the neighborhood. It is about half the size of Second Lake, and lies a short distance southwest from the town, and south of Fourth Lake.

The Catfish river is the outlet of these lakes, and is also the clear, bright channel which, running from the upper to the lower one, connects all these glittering bodies in one brilliant chain, like so many pure pearls strung on silver wires.

The following altitudes and measurements are from the reports of Capt. Cram, who was commissioned by the government to make a topographical survey in the Western Country:

"The Catfish, between the Fourth and Third Lakes, a distance of one mile, has a width of from sixty to one hundred feet, and a depth of three feet, except near the Fourth Lake, where the width is only thirty-five feet, and the depth two. The descent is estimated at a little less than two [five] feet. Between the Third and Second Lakes the descent is but very little; the average width is about three hundred and fifty feet, and the depth varies from one to nine feet; distance, seven eighths of a mile. Between the Second and First Lakes, three and a half miles, there are three slight rapids, having a total descent of about two feet; and the depth of water varies from one to three feet. From the First Lake to *Dunkirk Falls*, nine miles, there is but little fall in the river, the water being usually deep, and about one hundred and thirty feet average width.

"At the Dunkirk Falls there is a rapid, in which the descent is six feet, in a distance of one and one fourth miles, there being no perpendicular fall. The banks are from fifty to sixty feet high, and the valley is much contracted. From this point to *Rock river*, twelve miles, there is a constant succession of rapids—one having seven feet and four inches descent in a distance of about one mile. The whole descent on these rapids (twenty-five in all) was ascertained to be thirty-four and sixty-eight hundredths feet. The Catfish enters Rock river eleven and a half miles below the foot of *Lake Koshkonong*. The whole length of the stream, from the head of the Fourth Lake, is forty miles, twenty-eight of which could be made navigable by the erection of one dam at Dunkirk, not exceeding six feet in hight."

From the census of 1850, it appears that the population of Dane County at that time was nearly 17,000, but is estimated now to be about 19,000.

There is now considerable good land for sale in this county, which may be bought for reasonable prices, though some monopolists still hold on to their uncultivated lands, waiting for unreasonably high prices; but there are other men who, with more public spirit and liberal principles, are ready and offering lands at a moderate profit. As one instance of the latter character, we can refer to the enterprising builder and owner of the *Madison Flouring Mills*, which are unequaled in the West, and unsurpassed in any part of our nation. Mr. Farewell spent much time and money, traveling in Europe, to examine minutely the Flour-making business there in its greatest perfection, and to that has added the best improvements of Yankee ingenuity.

Persons visiting that region of country for the purpose

of buying lands, town property, or establishing machinery, will find it to their profit and pleasure to call upon Mr. Farwell, or Mr. Richardson who will readily supply them with information or lands.

Madison, county-seat of *Dane*, and capital of the state, perhaps, combines and overlooks more charming and diversified scenery, to please the eye of fancy, and promote health and pleasure, than any other town in the West; and in these respects it surpasses any other state capital in the Union. Its bright lakes, fresh groves, and rippling rivulets, its sloping hills, shady vales, and flowery meadow-lawns, are commingled in greater profusion and disposed in more picturesque order than we have ever elsewhere beheld.

At some time in our travels or observations, all of us have met with some location that was at once and indelibly impressed upon the fancy as the paragon of all out-door loveliness and beauty—the place with which all others were compared, and to which they must bear some respectable degree of resemblance, to be esteemed delightful locations. With many persons, Madison is that paragon of landscape scenery. As the brilliant diamond, chased around with changing borders, which sparkles on the swelling vestment of some queenly woman, so this picturesque village, with its varied scenery, sits the coronal gem on the broad and rolling bosom of this rich and blooming state.

Nor is it less noteworthy for its business advantages and healthful position. Situated on elevated ground amid delightful groves and productive lands, well above the cool clear lakes, it must be healthy; while the abundance and convenience of fine streams and water-powers must facilitate a sound and rapid advancement here in agricultural pursuits, and the mechanic arts. There are also several liberal charters for Railroads, connecting Madison with

Milwaukee, Chicago, and the Mississippi river; some of which are already being pushed ahead with energy.

For a more minute description of the ground which this town occupies, I copy the following from the pamphlet before referred to:

"MADISON occupies the isthmus between the Third and Fourth Lakes. It is in the geographical center of the county, and near the center of the basin of the Catfish. The land on which it is located rises abruptly from the shore of the Third Lake about 50 feet, and from thence ascends gradually, going northwest, until the center of the CAPITOL PARK is reached, about 70 feet above the Lakes. From thence, with a little greater slope, it pitches to the northwest, descending gradually until near the Fourth Lake, when it rises with considerable abruptness about 75 feet, and then falls off boldly to the shore of the Fourth Lake—the distance across being about three fourths of a mile. Following the cardinal points, the ground descends every way from the CAPITOL, all the streets from the corners of the square terminating in the lakes, save the western, which slopes gradually about half a mile, and then rises, until at the distance of exactly one mile from the capitol, it attains an elevation of at least 125 feet. This is COLLEGE HILL, the magnificent site of the *University* of the State. Fourth Lake washes the north base of this hill."

Madison is rapidly increasing in the number of its population, its buildings, and other improvements. It has four or five Newspaper establishments; and a Telegraph line connecting with the Lakes and the Mississippi.

The population of Madison is somewhere between two and three thousand; a people who for intelligence, taste, and hospitality, are not surpassed by any community in the state.

The purity of the water, with the healthy central location which it possesses, renders this one of the most favorable and appropriate sites for a *Water-Cure* establishment to be found in the West, which the people are anxious to have instituted among them.

The last of the counties, which lie on the Wisconsin

river, on its south bank, is *Columbia* county.. Few counties, if any, in the state, surpass this for the fertility and feasibility of its lands, being mostly prairie, with fine groves of timber at convenient intervals. It lies mostly on the south and east of Wisconsin river, while one corner of it touches on Neenah river. Population, 9,565; dwellings, 1,855; farms, 988; manufactories, 25.

Fort Winnebago is now the county-seat, it having been recently removed from Columbus, a handsome little village of some 1,000 inhabitants. Fort Winnebago contains about 700 population. It is situated at the *Portage* between Wisconsin and Neenah rivers.

I adopt the following description of this point from Lapham's work:

"The Winnebago *Portage*, between the Wisconsin and Neenah rivers, near Fort Winnebago, in this county, is a point often mentioned by all who speak or write about Wisconsin. At times of flood, the waters of the Wisconsin occasionally cover the marshy ground at this place, to the depth of three feet; and being at such times the highest, the water passes into the Neenah, thus sending portions of its water to the ocean by two different routes. The *Portage Canal Company* have dug a ditch across the portage, about two feet wide and two feet deep. Captain Cram reports, that the length of canal necessary to cross this portage is seven thousand seven hundred and thirty-nine feet; and that the fall from the Wisconsin to the Neenah, in October, 1839, was one foot and fifty-five hundredths. This difference constantly varies, according to the stage of the water in the two streams, but it is believed that it seldom exceeds three feet."

There is a Canal in progress, for steamboat navigation between these two rivers; which is also extended down Neenah river, after it leaves Lake Winnebago, by slack water, to admit boats to pass through to Green Bay. Between the lake and bay there is an immense amount of excellent water-power, which recently is being employed by Eastern Capitalists, who contemplate establishing factories on a large scale, something after the manner of those in New England. I shall note this farther when speaking of the counties through which it passes.

There are several small and handsome lakes in Columbia county, the principal of which are Lake Sarah, Swan and Mud lakes. Swan is a widening of Neenah river.

Wisconsin, Neenah, and Baraboo are the chief rivers which water this county, beside some smaller creeks. Baraboo, like Wisconsin, runs through a great Lumber Country.

Marquette county lies north of the last-named, and south and east of Neenah river. It is noted for its good lands, deep lakes, and fine water-powers. It is much settled with tidy, thrifty farmers, who are doing finely. It contains 8,642 population; dwellings, 1,747; farms, 337; manufactories, 9. There are several fine villages in this county.

Two of the largest lakes are Puckawa and Buffalo, which are seven to ten miles long and one to two wide, being expansions of Neenah river. Green lake is distinguished for its clear water, with the fine lands and beautiful scenery which surround it.

" *Green lake* lies immediately east of Puckawa; eight miles long by two broad; its waters deep and clear. The bottom is covered with white pebbles; and wild rice or other vegetation does not grow upon it, as upon many of the lakes of Wisconsin.

" *Little Green lake* lies four miles south of Green lake, one and a half miles long by a mile wide, with a circumference of about seven miles. The water is said to be very deep. The *Green Bay Republican* says, 'It has been sounded to the depth of more than forty feet, and no bottom found; in many places, at a distance of twenty yards from the shore, the water is from eight to twelve feet deep, and remarkably pure. There is no visible inlet, and but one outlet, which is so inconsiderable, that it is in fact only a mere drain. The scenery around is picturesque and beautiful beyond description. On the north side, for more than a mile in extent, the shore is composed of a beautiful white sandstone, rising in some instances perpendicularly to the hight of probably seventy-five or eighty feet. This stone possesses all the properties of the best grindstones brought into this Territory.' "

MARQUETTE is the county-seat, a pleasantly situated and thriving town.

The principal business town is BERLIN, a thriving village, of over 1,000 population, with a good landing on the river.

Fon du lac county lies east of Marquette, and surrounding the head of Lake Winnebago. There is much good land, timber, and water-power in this county, with some marsh, or low wet lands. It presents many good farms, and several thriving villages. Population, 14,512; dwellings, 2,722; farms, 1,073; manufactories, 16.

FON DU LAC is the county-seat, and is not exceeded by any village in the state for rapid growth and active business. It is situated on a river of the same name, near its entrance into the lake. It contains nearly 3,000 inhabitants. Several steamboats run from this port to various points on Lake Winnebago and Neenah river.

This lake is from 30 to 40 miles long, and about 8 miles wide, and is of very pleasant navigation. The counties which surround it are, Brown, on the north; Calumet, on the east; Fon du lac, on the south, and Winnebago, on the west.

As one passes through it, in the steamers which busily ply upon its surface, he is reminded of *Seneca* lake, in New York, as some of the shore-scenery, in many respects, resembles that; there are many romantic and attractive prospects around its borders. Captain CRAM thus speaks of this lake:

"The Neenah river enters it near the middle, on the western shore, and leaves it at the northwest angle, by two channels, enclosing *Doty's island*, by which it is connected with the *Little Butte des Morts* lake. These channels are known as the Winnebago rapids. The water is hard, and when not violently agitated, is quite pellucid, but becomes turbid during long and severe blows; and has a depth sufficient for the purposes of navigation. On the northern extremity the shore is low, having a narrow sandy beach, for an extent of about eight miles. On the east side the shore presents a remarkable feature for an extent of fifteen miles, in a wall composed of rocks laid together, as if placed there by the hand of art. A similar wall pertains to portions of the western shore, but with less continuity than is observed on the east."

TACHEDA is another handsome and thriving village, located on this lake, and with near 1,000 population; some four miles nearly east of the county-seat. There are some other small towns springing up in this county.

In Fon du lac county is the town of CARESCO, established something on the *Fourier* plan, with some changes necessary to adapt it to this country and people. It is in a flourishing condition, and has a very intelligent and industrious population, with good schools, libraries, lectures, etc.; beside, they take a great number of newspapers and periodicals. It was commenced in May, 1844, with twenty-five persons of various occupations. Mr. Lapham, in 1846, gives the following extracts of a letter from Mr. W. Chase, one of the members, in regard to this experiment. He says:

"We are under the township government, organized similar to the system in New York. Our town was set off and organized last winter, by the Legislature, at which time the Association was also incorporated as a joint-stock company by a charter, which is our constitution. We had a post-office and mail, weekly, within forty days after our commencement; thus far we have obtained all we have asked for.

"We have religious meetings and Sabbath schools, conducted by members of some half a dozen different denominations of Christians, with whom creeds and modes of faith are of minor importance, compared with religion. All are protected, and all is harmony in that department.

"The Phalanx has a title from Government to 1,440 acres of land, on which there is one of the best water-powers in the county, a saw-mill in operation, a grist-mill building, 640 acres under improvement, 400 of which are now seeding to winter wheat; we raised about fifteen hundred bushels the past season, which is sufficient for our next year's bread—have about seventy acres of corn on the ground, which looks well, and other crops in proportion. Our property is entirely unencumbered, the society free from debt, and we have an abundance of cattle, horses, crops, and provisions, for the wants of our present numbers, and physical energy enough to obtain more. Thus, you see, we are tolerably independent, and we intend to remain so, as we admit none as members who have not sufficient physical strength to warrant their not being a burden to the society. We have one dwelling-house nearly finished, in which reside twenty families, with a long hall conducting to the dining-room, where all who are able may dine together."

Winnebago county lies north of the one last described. It contains much good lands, with some marsh, and considerable water-power; and it enjoys some of the benefits of navigation on the lake. There are several lakes in this county. I copy Mr. Lapham's descriptions of the principal ones:

"*Pewaugone lake* is an expansion of Wolf river, about ten miles in length, commencing a short distance above its junction with the Neenah.

"*Great Butte des Morts lake* is an expansion of the Neenah river, four and a half miles above Lake Winnebago; three and a half miles in length, and from one to two miles in breadth.

"*Little Butte des Morts lake* is another expansion of the Neenah, immediately below Winnebago rapids; about four and a half miles long, and one mile wide.

"These two last lakes (Buttes des Morts, or *Hills of the Dead*) are named from hills or mounds said to have been formed of the dead bodies of the Indians slain in some battle, which were thrown into heaps and covered with earth. They are now grown over with grass, and present much the same appearance as the ancient mounds so profusely scattered through the West."

Population of the county, 10,179; dwellings, 1,903; farms, 347; manufactories, 30.

OSHKOSH is the county-seat, a very flourishing town of about 2,000 inhabitants. It is situated at the entrance of

Neenah river into the lake, and is a place of much mechanical business and trade. Neenah is another fine growing town in this county.

Calumet county lies on the east side of Lake Winnebago. In this county is located the *Stockbridge* and *Brothertown Indian* Reservation. They have fine schools and churches; while their shops, farms, fences, buildings, etc., compare favorably with others in the country. They have, for some years, been represented by a member of their own people in the state legislature. In 1846 the population of this county was some 800; it is now 1,800. A high rocky ridge runs north and south through the county, parallel with the lake shore, from the east side of which the Sheboygan and Manitowoc rivers take their rise; and through one or the other of these valleys, a very direct communication with Lake Michigan is now contemplated by the construction of a railroad. The soil in this county is rich, and well covered with timber, of which basswood and elm constitute a large proportion. The rocks found here are limestone, and occasionally sandstone; and there are said to be some indications of coal. The scenery, especially about the lake, is highly beautiful and picturesque. There is a Plankroad through a part of this county, and still much good land for sale at low prices.

MANCHESTER, a growing, pleasant little village, of several hundred population, is the county-seat.

Dodge county is in the interior of the state; and is one of the best for the quality of its soil and other farming resources in the state. The West branch of Rock river takes its rise from Fox lake, in this county; it is generally called the Crawfish creek, which runs through Aztalan. The East, or main branch of Rock river, rises in Fon du lac county, and runs through the whole length of Dodge county, passing through the extensive Winnebago marsh

15

in its course. This county contained about 5,000 population in 1846, and it now has about 20,000 population. It is named in honor of Gen. HENRY DODGE, first Governor of Wisconsin. In description of this county, Mr. Lapham quotes the following from the *Milwaukee Democrat*, of 1843:

"Springs, and spring brooks, are more abundant than in most other portions of Wisconsin. The larger streams are skirted by groves of thick and heavy timber, consisting of oak, sugar, linn, elm, ash, butternut, hickory, and walnut; while the smaller streams run through the choicest tracts of burr oak openings and prairies, interspersed with valuable thickets of pin oaks, which will furnish farmers in their neighborhood with an excellent and plentiful supply of rail timber. Excepting the Winnebago marsh, there is scarcely any land in the whole county (thirty miles square) which cannot be cultivated.

"Several causes have hitherto operated to prevent the settlement of this district. Its inaccessibility from the lake shore, because of the want of roads, may be stated as one cause; while another is to be found in the fact, that one half of this county is in the northern land district, and must be entered at Green Bay, which is even more inaccessible from that region than Milwaukee. Until the present year, so far as public notoriety extended, Dodge county has been left a *terra incognita*. Three years since, Mr. HYLAND opened a wagon road from Watertown to the center of the county, and settled on a small prairie which bears his name, whither he was followed by a sufficient number of industrious farmers to occupy not only the whole of the prairie, but every quarter section adjoining the road opened by this hardy pioneer. About the same time six families moved from Fox lake, ten miles down the Beaver Dam, and made a settlement, to which they gave the name of that stream. This settlement now contains twenty-five or thirty families."

The village of BEAVER DAM is now the largest in the county, containing nearly 1,000 population, with fair prospects of farther growth. DODGE CENTER is a pleasantly situated little town. JUNEAN, a new town, is county-seat, occupying a pleasant and advantageous position.

There is yet some good government land for sale, in this county. Number of dwellings, 3,561; farms, 2,338; manufactories, 30. Hustes, Horicon, Fairfield, and others are thriving towns in this county.

Jefferson is another of the interior counties, through which runs both branches of Rock river and Bark creek, with Koshkanong lake in the southwest corner. There is much heavy timber in this county, with some of the largest trees to be found any where in the state. There are also some rough ridges and large marshes in the county; but very little prairie. There is a Plankroad running through this county from Lake Michigan, designed to be speedily continued through the towns of Milford, Aztalan, Lake Mills, to MADISON. It is now completed to WATERTOWN. Other portions of the county are more rolling. There is much excellent farming land in this county, especially along the rivers; and Rock river valley maintains here the high reputation which it so deservedly has farther south.

The geographical position of this county, lying in the direct route between Milwaukee and the capital, is believed to afford it some advantages; and with all her other advantages and sources of wealth, Jefferson is becoming to be known as one of the principal counties. The inhabitants are industrious, enterprising, and public-spirited; as is evinced by the fact that, in one year, six bridges were built across Rock river and its main branch.

The population of Jefferson county, in 1846, was near 5,000; it is now near 16,000. In this county are found many of those mysterious earthworks, which are described in another place. In this county are several handsome lakes; among which are Rock, Ripley, Cranberry, and some others. The streams furnish ample water-power, much of which is already actively improved with mills and other machinery. Dwellings, 2,933; farms, 1,042; manufactories, 74.

JEFFERSON, the county-seat, is situated on Rock river, a little above the junction of the Crawfish. A dam has been thrown across the river, creating a good water-power, on which is erected mills and machinery. Considerable business is done at this place.

WATERTOWN is the largest town in the county, and is handsomely and well situated on Rock river, near the great bend, and at the foot of Johnson's rapids, where a dam across the river creates one of the most valuable water-privileges in the country. The village is built on both sides of the river, and is one of the most thriving in the interior of the state. Its population now numbers between two and three thousand.

FORT ATKINSON is a thriving village, situated on both sides of Rock river, and immediately below the mouth of Bark river. A temporary fort was erected here during the Black Hawk war; the place is destined to considerable increase.

Waukesha county lies between Jefferson and Milwaukee counties, having been set off of the latter as a new county in 1846. This county contains some of the very best prairie, with a portion of timber, openings, and some marsh. The distinguishing feature of this county is its numerous small lakes, many of which are most beautiful, surrounded with charming scenery. In this particular it is surpassed alone by Dane county, and barely equaled by Marquette county. There are probably over thirty lakes in Waukesha county, many of them skirted with handsome groves.

Muskego is the largest, being nearly four miles long and two broad; its outlet runs into *Pishtaka* river, near Rochester; this is the same river which in Illinois is called Fox.

Maquanago lake is a widening of Pishtaka river, at the flourishing town of Maquanago.

Wissaua, or Gold lake, lies on the road westward from Milwaukee, and empties into Bark river, and is something over a mile in diameter.

Kauchee is a triangular lake, with each of its sides over a mile in extent. A dam across its outlet affords a moderate water-power.

La Belle lake, is so called from the beauty which it and the surrounding scenery presents; it is two and a half miles long, by one and a quarter wide. Its elevation is considerably above Rock river.

Nagowicka lake, is near the same size, and is distinguished by a handsome island in its midst.

Oconomewoc is the most southern of the chain of lakes, ranged along the creek of the same name.

But those which present decidedly the most curious and delightful appearance are the *Nashotah* (*Twin*) *lakes*—two small lakes lying north of Nemahbin lake, near the east line of the town of Summit. The north lake is two hundred and ninety-one feet above Lake Michigan, sixty-seven chains long, thirty-one wide, and has a periphery of two miles. On the east bank of this lake is the Episcopal mission station and their college, recently established. The south lake is seventy-five chains long, twenty-seven wide, and has a periphery of two miles and a quarter. There is a bright little rivulet running from one to the other, through the slight ridge which divides these two lovely lakes. The stageroad from Madision to Milwaukee passes on this ridge, affording the traveler a view of them on the right and left. When the valorous Lilliputian passed over the bridge of the notable Gulliver's nose, his great tearful eyes, no doubt, presented to the dwarf something the appearance of these glistening lakes to the passer-by.

The soil in this immediate vicinity is good, though not of the best quality; while the timber is convenient but light. Still, there are several fine farms and pleasant dwellings on the borders of the *Twin lakes.* Population of this county, 20,000; dwellings, 3,409; farms, 1,743; manufactories, 78. The country between this county and Madison is a delightful one for residences.

The county-seat is WAUKESHA, which contains about 2,400 population. It is a very handsomely improved village, situated on the Pishtaka river, in the border of a rich prairie; and contains many excellent buildings. It has railroad communication with the Lake, at Milwaukee. The stage route from this place to Madison is an unusually pleasant one—through diversified and highly romantic scenery—groves, prairies, lakes, and rippling streamlets, alternating at short distances, with occasional rugged rocky bluffs, which, in this level, gently sloping region, amount almost to little mountains, as you wind along the river valleys at their base. Troy and Springfield are other pleasant towns in this county.

There is still considerable good government land for sale, on this route, on which pleasant and productive farms may be made.

Walworth county lies south of Waukesha, and west of Racine, occupying the elevation which divides the waters that fall east to the lake, and those which empty into Rock river on the west. It is an excellent county of land in which the prairie predominates, though there is a fair share of timber, and plenty of water from both lakes and rivers. This county is highly cultivated by an intelligent and forehanded community of farmers. In 1846, its population numbered some 10,000; which is now nearly doubled, being about 18,000; dwellings, 3,092; farms, 1,980; manufactories, 82.

The county-seat is ELKHORN, situated in the midst of a handsome oak grove, is a pleasant, thriving village, and contains a newspaper printing establishment. There are several other fine towns, as Delavan, Geneva, Troy, etc., in this county.

The principal lakes in this county are Como, Delavan, and Geneva, with many other smaller ones.

The principal streams are Geneva, Honey, and Sugar creeks; very sweet list of names, surely.

Rock county lies west of Walworth, and north of the Illinois line, with Rock river running through it north and south, nearly in the center. Its population in 1846 was about 7,000; it is now above 20,000; dwellings, 3,631; farms, 1,975; manufactories, 126. In quality of soil and other agricultural facilities it is not surpassed by any county in the state; while its water-power is probably equal to any. It embraces some of the best prairies in the state, a large portion of which is prosperously cultivated.

Deer lake, and the south end of Kashkanong, are the chief lakes in this county, with several very small ones.

Rock river and Turtle creek are the main streams in Rock county.

JANESVILLE is the county-seat. It contains 3,500 inhabitants, and is rapidly growing. Rock river affords ample water-power, on which is already built several fine mills, and other machinery. The village occupies both sides of the river; and equals most towns in the state in activity of business. Mr. Lapham thus describes its admirable location in 1846:

"It is situated on a flat, or level, between the river and the foot of the bluffs, which are about one hundred feet high. The court-house is erected on the bluff, giving it a very prominent appearance. Janesville is the point at which much of the trade between the eastern and western portions of the Territory crosses Rock river, and a bridge is now erected for its accommodation. The distance from Janesville to Milwaukee is sixty-five miles, and the same to Racine; giving the citizens a choice of two ports on Lake Michigan, reached in the same distance; it is 13 miles from Beloit, 41 from Madison, 31 from Monroe, and about 80 from Mineral Point."

A Railroad Company is chartered, the stock subscribed, and the work commenced in good earnest, to run a line from Fon du lac to this place; thence, southeast through Walworth county into Illinois, and on to Chicago; which will be speedily constructed. Good building and limestone is quarried here in abundance.

BELOIT is another very beautiful and flourishing village in this county, situated on both sides of Rock river, at the junction of Turtle creek; its population is about 3,000. It is a place of active and increasing business; and is noted for its elegant buildings, and fine wide streets. It has several excellent mills, machine shops, and a prosperous college.

Here, I am told, was erected the first flouring mill in the State. Its water-power is valuable. The town is located on a level plain, but is fast extending on to the bluffs each side of the river. The college is erected on a high and airy bluff, commanding an extensive and varied prospect. In this vicinity may be seen many of those singular and mysterious mounds, which abound in the West. Here, as at most other towns on Rock river, abundance of good stone is quarried, valuable alike for lime and building purposes. This place is noted for its fine churches.

The stock has been subscribed, and arrangements made for having a branch from the Galena and Chicago Railroad built to Beloit, which will be rapidly completed.

There are several other small villages in this county, among which are Fulton, Clinton, Milton, Johnstown, Waterloo, etc.

Green county lies west of Rock, and on the northern line of Illinois. The mineral region extends through most of this county; yet it possesses much good land, timber, and many fine farms. Its population in 1846 was about 5,000; it is now 8,583; dwellings, 1,487; farms, 805; manufactories, 46.

This county is watered by Sugar and Skinner's creeks, and Peckatonica river.

MONROE is the largest town in the county, and is the county-seat. It is a pleasant, thriving little town of some 1,200 inhabitants.

There are several other small towns in the county, as Exeter, Decatur, Jefferson, Brooklyn, etc.

Lafayette county lies west of Green, on the Illinois line. It is in the Mineral District, and is rich in the products of its mines, but does a limited business in agricultural operations. It is a new county set off from the south end of Iowa county. Its population is 11,556; dwellings, 2,079; farms, 399; manufactories, 21.

It is watered by the Peckatonica and Fever rivers.

SHULLSBURG is at present the place of holding the courts, though the county-seat has been removed to the center of the county, where a new town is being built up for its accommodation. Shullsburg is a mining town of some 1,700 population. Large quantities of lead ore are raised here.

There are several other mining towns in this county, the largest of which are Benton, New Diggings, Fayette, Gratiot, and others.

Brown county is located around the head of Green Bay, embracing it on the west, south, and east, and on both sides of Neenah river; it formerly extended a long way to the northwest into the pine region; and was originally a very large county, the old block off of which many fine and flourishing counties have been chipped. Mr. Lapham's work, thus speaks of the dimensions of Brown county:

"It is impossible to estimate the area of this county with any degree of certainty, on account of the territorial line between Wisconsin and Michigan not having been finally established; and for the want of an accurate survey of this part of the Territory.

Brown county was organized by an act of the Legislature of Michigan, passed October 16, 1818, and then included all the country between Lake Michigan and a line drawn due north and south through the middle of the portage between the Neenah and Wisconsin rivers. The counties of Manitowoc, Sheboygan, Calumet, Fond du lac, Marquette, Washington, Dodge, Milwaukee, Jefferson, Racine, Walworth, Rock, and parts of Dane and Portage, have been taken from Brown; and as she is still a large county, it is probable that her limits are destined, ere long, to be farther reduced, before her boundaries are finally established."

And this prediction has become a fact, as the last session of the Wisconsin Legislature constructed five new counties off of Brown, viz: *Door*, *Oconto*, *Outagamie*, *Wapaca*, and *Washara*; *Door* county lying east, and the others west of Green Bay.

Lying north of Sauk is *Adams* county, very thinly populated, and attached to the former for judicial purposes. It is rich in timber and lumbering facilities. The Wisconsin and Lemonwier rivers run through this county, furnishing ample water-power to saw lumber, and good channels for rafting it below to market.

There is much wild adventure and perilous exploits enjoyed by the lumbermen of this region; a class of hardy fellows, who could scarcely live in positions of any less excitement.

That part of Brown county lying between Lake Winnebago and Green Bay, is fast gaining in population and business, from the improvements going on along Neenah river, and the new towns which are springing up at different points, to take the benefits of the vast water-powers there afforded; and the Canal which is being constructed to perfect navigation between those two bodies of water. As this river, and the counties through which it passes, are of much importance, and rapidly becoming more so, I will here transcribe, from the work before quoted, a detailed description of it:

"*The Neenah*, or, as it was formerly called, the Fox river, of Green Bay, is one of the most important rivers in Wisconsin, extending, as it does, nearly half across the Territory, and almost touching at the portage the waters of Wisconsin river, by which navigation may, with a little improvement, be extended across the country from Lake Michigan to the Mississippi. It takes its rise in Lake Sarah, Portage county, and runs in a direction a little south of west (almost directly opposite its general course) for eighteen miles, toward the Wisconsin, as if with the intention of entering that river; but, owing to some unaccountable freak of nature, when within one and a half miles of that stream, makes a sudden turn to the north, and soon assumes its general course toward Green Bay.

"From the portage to Lake Winnebego, through which this river passes, it winds about among extensive marshes covered with tall grass and wild rice. Below the lake there is a succession of rapids, that require an expenditure of about four hundred and fifty thousand dollars to render the river navigable. At the Winnebago Rapids, near Lake Winnebago, there is a descent of seven feet and fifty-four hundredths in a distance of seven thousand seven hundred feet. At the Grand Chute, nine miles above the Grand Kakalin, there is a fall of twenty-nine feet and sixty-eight hundredths, in a distance of eight thousand five hundred and twenty-five feet. At the head of the Chute the bluffs are very steep and high.

"At the Little Chute, three miles above the Grand Kakalin, there is a descent of thirty one feet and twenty-two hundredths, in a distance of nine thousand two hundred feet; and the banks are high and steep near the head of the Chute. At the Grand Kakalin there is a fall of forty-four feet, in a distance of eight thousand six hundred feet. At the Rapide de Croche, four miles below the Grand Kakalin, the fall of the river is only one foot and seventeen hundredths, in a distance of thirteen hundred feet; but the 'crook' is so short, and the current so rapid, and sets so strongly against the southern bank, that a boat would experience great difficulty in passing, and would invariably incur the risk of being forced against the shore before it could turn the elbow or crook.

"The Little Kakalin, and Depere Rapids, are already improved, by the Dam at Depere, of six feet in hight. The whole descent in these rapids is about one hundred and twenty feet; and if we add one foot per mile for the descent of the river between the rapids, we find Lake Winnebago one hundred and sixty feet above Lake

Michigan. Above Lake Winnebago, the descent in the river is probably about half a foot per mile, or sixty-three feet to the portage, making that place, as stated in the table of altitudes, two hundred and twenty-three feet above Lake Michigan. At a place on this river called *Red Banks*, there are numerous ancient artificial mounds on both sides of the river."

The splendid water-powers which these rapids afford are being improved and put to use, for driving factories, by Eastern capitalists.

There is much excellent land in Brown county, and yet much that is of little value for agricultural purposes. There are some heavy forests, and some fine prairies; a good deal for sale, and at low prices.

The present size of this county contains between six or seven thousand inhabitants; dwellings, 1,005; farms, 267; manufactories, 23. The Oneida Indians, who were removed from the State of New York, are settled in this county, west of Green Bay, on Duck creek.

The former county-seat, GREEN BAY, is at the head of that bay on Neenah river. It occupies a very important location, and possesses an excellent harbor. It contains many large and superb buildings, and is a point of considerable commercial transactions. In 1846, its population was said to be about 1,000; now it is something more than double that amount. Near here, and to the west, is FORT HOWARD, a commanding eminence on the west bank of the river. Farther up the Neenah, a short distance, is the handsome village of DEPERE, the new county-seat, possessing a good water-power, at the Depere Rapids.

There are some other smaller towns in this county, which have prospects of farther growth; among them are Lawrence, Kakalin, Navarino, Cooperstown, and others.

There are many important rivers, which have either their rise or mouth in this county. The Kewahnee, the Twin rivers, and some smaller ones, empty into Lake

Michigan. The Peshtego, Oconto, and others, fall into Green Bay. The Manitto, the Pewaugonee, or Wolf river, with others, are branches of the Neenah; the latter being larger than the Neenah itself, and rises in the lumber country. The Manitto, or Devil river, rises near the south line of the county, and running parallel to, and only two or three miles from, Neenah river, for a distance of twenty miles, enters that river near its mouth. This peculiar tendency of several streams and lakes to parallelism, is probably owing to some peculiar arrangement of the strata rock beneath the soil, which is generally limestone. There are many other rivers which are not named here.

An important river north of here, in the pine country, is the Menominee, quite a large river, that enters Green Bay near its middle, and forms part of the boundary of the county as well as state. Its course has been very inaccurately represented on the old maps, and some difficulties have resulted in relation to the boundary between Wisconsin and Michigan, requiring the action of Congress to adjust—showing how important is it for map-makers to preserve accuracy in their work.

There are some small lakes in this county, but not much known; in the northern part of the original county is a lake of some curiosity, of which Lapham says:

"Lake Katakittekon, or 'Lac Vieux Desert,' at the head of the Wisconsin river (and not of the Montreal, as has been supposed,) which it is probable may fall within the county of Brown. The middle of this lake was made a point in the boundary of the Territory. On an island in it, there was an old deserted planting ground of the Indians; hence its name with the French, Lac Vieux Desert. Lake of the Desert, as this is sometimes translated, is an improper name, the country about it being not a desert, but one of great fertility. It occupies a high level above Lakes Superior and Michigan, and abounds in small lakes, which constitute the heads of several large rivers. The Menomonee of Lake Michigan, the Otonagon, and Montreal of Lake Superior, and the Wisconsin and

Chippewa of the Mississippi, all take their rise on the summit in the Katakittekon country."

The following extract from Capt. Cram's report relative to this interesting country, is the only information we have in relation to it:

"The water of these small reservoirs, and of the streams generally, is cold and limpid. Some of the lakes were observed to contain the specled trout, such as are generally met with in high latitudes in the United States. The scenery of these lakes is beautiful, and the land adjacent to them is better than is generally believed by those who have not had an opportunity of personal examination. The country is not mountainous, but may be denominated 'rolling.' The growth of timber is tolerably heavy, consisting of white and yellow pine on the borders of the lakes; in some instances of cedar, fir, hemlock, and tamarack; and a little back of the lakes, of sugar maple, white maple, white and yellow birch, poplar, bass, and hemlock.

"The soil is of a nature to be adapted to the culture of wheat, rye, grass, oats, flax, hemp, and potatoes. In some places the soil is rocky, although no very large masses or ledges of rocks were observed. The manufacture of maple sugar is carried on to a considerable extent by the Indians of this region."

From the north part of Crawford county, the Wisconsin Legislature, at its last session, constructed two new counties, under the names of *Bad Ax* and *La Crosse*, watered respectively by the rivers of the same names, and by Black river. They have very little settlements, as yet; but must come speedily to be important and valuable districts for their vast forests of good pine timber; while they also contain some good farming lands. The young village of PRAIRIE LA CROSSE, in the latter county, is favorably situated on the Mississippi, and is growing rapidly; it is 90 miles above Prairie du Chien.

Still north are other large tracts, organized into counties, known by the names of St. Croix, La Pointe, Chippewa, and Marathon, varying from 600 to 1,000 population.

Of Chippewa Mr. Lapham says

"In superficial extent, this county is estimated at about nine thousand square miles. It embraces the basin of the Chippewa river, one of the largest tributaries of the Mississippi in Wisconsin.

"The Chippewa river (Ojibwa, of the Indians) runs entirely across the Territory, having its rise in the State of Michigan, near the sources of the Wisconsin, Montreal, etc., and running into the Mississippi near the foot of Lake Pepin. It is about five hundred yards wide at its mouth. There are six rapids on the Chippewa. The principal one, called the 'Falls,' is about seventy-five miles above the mouth, and has a descent of twenty-four feet in the distance of half a mile. A very large amount of pine lumber is annually sent down this river. Toward the sources of this stream and its branches there are many fine lakes, some of which have received names. The principal are Lac Courtorielle, Lac Chetac, Lac de Flambeau, Tomahawk Lake, Red Cedar Lake, Rice Lake, etc. The Red Cedar Fork is the main branch of the Chippewa, entering from the west about thirty-six miles above its mouth. About sixty miles below Rice Lake, on this river, according to Schoolcraft, commences a series of rapids over horizontal layers of sandstone rocks, which extend, with short intervals, down the river twenty-four miles. The remainder of the distance (about fifty miles) to the junction, is characterized by deep water, with a strong current; and at the junction is commanding and elevated, affording a fine view of a noble expanse of waters."

Population probably 700.

St. Croix county lies west and north of Chippewa, and east of Lake Pepin; it contains some good farming lands, and extensive pine forests, of the best kind, with abundance of fine water-powers for mills. Population now is nearly 1,000. There are several flourishing young towns in this county, as Buena Vista, St. Croix, and others. St. Croix, Rum, and several other rivers drain this region.

La Pointe county lies north of St. Croix county and Chippewa. It is much the same in general character with the last two described counties. Its population is not far from 700. Mr. Lapham says:

"From the geological character of some portions of this county it is supposed that mines of copper and silver may yet be found, similar to those now known to exist farther East, within the 'upper Peninsula' of Michigan.

"The principal rivers are the Upper Mississippi, Rainy Lake river, the St. Louis river, the Bois Brule (or Burnt Wood), the Mauvais, and the Montreal rivers.

"Rainy Lake river is about one hundred miles long, rapid but navigable, and about four hundred yards in width at its mouth. Through this stream the waters of Rainy Lake pass to the Lake of the Woods; and from thence they flow to Hudson's Bay at the north.

"La Pointe, on Madeline Island, in Lake Superior, is the county-seat. The county extends to the source of the Mississippi, and north to the Lake of the Woods. The settlement at La Pointe is the oldest in the Territory—older even than Green Bay."

Marathon county lies north of Adams, with the Upper Wisconsin running through it; and is least settled of any of the lumber counties. The principal settlement in it is Wausaw, with some 600 inhabitants in and around it for several miles, chiefly engaged in lumbering and sugar making.

The principal Lumbering Stations, in the north, lying mostly on the Upper Wisconsin, are the Big Bull and the Little Bull Falls, Lemonwier, Grand Rapids, and Stephen's Point.

The running of Lumber-rafts over the falls and rapids of these rivers is an event of great interest and excitement to those engaged in that business. It is an operation requiring much skill and dexterity; beside, at best, being attended with great danger; and to watch its progress is a scene of lively and feverish entertainment to the spectator—we love to see it, but are glad when it is over.

The new counties of Wisconsin, alluded to in another place, are *Door*, and Gibralter, on the Lake, county-seat· *Oconto*, Jones' Mill, on Oconto river, county-seat; *Outagamie*, Grand Chute, on Neenah river, county-seat; *Waupacca*, Mukwa, on Wolf river, county-seat; *Wau-*

shara, SACREMENTO, county-seat; *Bad Ax*, SPRINGVILLE, county-seat; and *La Crosse*, LA CROSSE, county-seat.

These, with two or three other new and sparsely settled counties, of course, have as yet but few improvements, and have their public buildings yet to erect, which will make demand for mechanics in those counties. Much of the lands surrounding the county-seats are of good quality, and at present can be bought at low prices; which facts make it an object for a sufficient number of mechanics to locate thereabouts soon, by purchasing lands and lots before they are monopolized by non-improving speculators, who will hold them at high prices.

A reference to the Map will show the location and boundaries of these new counties.

RECAPITULATION.—Total population of the State, 305,538; number of cultivated farms, 22,034; number of manufacturing establishments, 1,273; number of dwellings, 56,281.

IOWA.

On the west bank of the Mississippi, and west of the States of Illinois and Wisconsin, lies the new State of Iowa; it having been admitted into the Union in 1846, as an independent state—the 28th sovereignty of that great Confederacy of political powers, which in many respects is, and in others ought to become, a high and noble example for the emulation of the civilized world; a consummation we anxiously hope for our beloved nation—and that it is not far distant.

Darby gives the following boundaries or limitations to the *Territory:*

"*Iowa*, Territory of the United States. There is some difficulty in giving a descriptive sketch of this Territory, so rapidly approaching its change to that of an independent State of the Union, from our ignorance of the limits which may be assigned to it when erected into a State. We assume, however, as probable, the following boundaries: the State of Missouri S., from the Missouri river to the mouth of Des Moines river, thence up the Mississippi river to the mouth of St. Peter's river, and thence up the latter stream to its great bend, thence in a SSW. direction to the Missouri river, and down the latter to the northwestern angle of the State of Missouri.

"Geographically, the preceding limits embrace a zone from 40° 33' to 45° N. latitude; and in longitude from 13° to 19° W. of Washington; area about 70,000 square miles.

"The part organized into counties and included in the census, lies westward from the Mississippi river, and extending nearly due N. from the Des Moines river, to a little above Prairie du Chien, 190 miles; mean width, 70, and area, 13,300 square miles. The whole space, however, included in the designated boundaries in this article extends from S. to N. 310 miles; mean breadth at least 200 miles, and area 62,000 square miles. The southern part, and about the fourth of the surface, slopes southwardly toward the Missouri river, but the residue declines SE. toward the Mississippi river, and in that direction is drained by the rivers Skunk, Lower Iowa, Wabesipinecon, Great Macoquetois, Penaqua or Turkey river, Upper Iowa, etc."

In his work, published in 1848, Mr. Sargent gives the following account of extinguishments of Indian titles, and their removal from that State:

"Until as late as the year 1832, the whole territory north of the State of Missouri was in undisputed possession of the Indians. By a treaty made in 1830, the Sacs and Foxes, who were then the principal tribes, had ceded to the United States the last of their lands east of the Mississippi river. Their unwillingness to leave the ceded territory in compliance with the treaty, led to the 'Black Hawk War,' which resulted, after several fierce skirmishes, in the total defeat of the Indians at the battle of the Bad Ax, in Wisconsin, on the 2d of August, 1832. In the September following, partly as an indemnity for the expenses of the war, and partly to secure the future safety and tranquillity of the invaded frontier, a strip of country on the west of the Mississippi, extending nearly 300 miles north from Missouri, and about 50 miles in width (now commonly called 'the Black Hawk purchase,') was ceded to the United States; and in June, 1833, the settlement of Iowa by the white man was commenced.

"Farther purchases were made, successively, in the years 1836 and 1837; and in 1842, by a treaty concluded by Governor Chambers, an immense tract of land, containing some fifteen million acres, was purchased of the Sacs and Foxes, for the sum of one million dollars. This tract, known as the 'New Purchase,' now contains some of the finest counties in the State, though a large part of it was occupied by the Indians until October in 1845.

"The Pottawattamies, who inhabited the southwestern corner of the state, and the Winnebagoes, who occupied the 'Neutral

Ground,' a strip of country on the northern borders, have been peaceably removed within the last two years; and the Indian title thus became extinct in the whole country lying within the established limits of the State of Iowa."

The limits of this state, as bounded in their Constitution, are as follows:

"Beginning in the middle of the main channel of the Mississippi river, at a point due east of the middle of the mouth of the main channel of the Des Moines river; thence up the middle of the main channel of the said Des Moines river, to a point on said river where the northern boundary line of the State of Missouri, as established by the Constitution of that State, adopted June 12th, 1820, crosses the said middle of the main channel of the said Des Moines river; thence westwardly, along the said northern boundary line of the State of Missouri, as established at the time aforesaid, until an extension of said line intersects the middle of the main channel of the Missouri river; thence up the middle of the main channel of the said Missouri river, to a point opposite the middle of the main channel of the Big Sioux river, according to Nicolett's map; thence up the main channel of the said Big Sioux river, according to said map until it is intersected by the parallel of forty-three degrees and thirty minutes north latitude; thence east, along said parallel of forty-three degrees and thirty minutes, until said parallel intersects the middle of the main channel of the Mississippi river; thence down the middle of the main channel of said Mississippi river, to the place of beginning."

The climate is a pleasant one, the soil productive, for most crops, as wheat, corn, hemp, flax, potatoes, and fruit. Mr. Sargent thus describes the face of the country, in general, which rather falls short than overrates this fine State:

"Perhaps no part of this vast region combines in itself more of the elements of prosperity than that under consideration. Situated nearly midway between the two great oceans—bounded on two sides by the giant rivers of the continent—and watered by innumerable smaller streams; possessing a fertile soil, inexhaustible mineral resources, a healthful climate, a free constitution, and a hardy and industrious population; uncursed by slavery, and untrammeled by debt; the State of Iowa has commenced its career with prospects of far more than ordinary brilliancy. In extent of territory, it is one of the largest in the Union; and it may safely be prophesied, that it is destined, at no distant day, to rank among the first in point of wealth and political importance.

"The general face of the country is that of a high, rolling prairie, watered by numerous streams, and, on the river-courses, skirted with woodlands. An idea prevails at the East, that the prairies are uniformly level. This is by no means the case. Sometimes, indeed, they are spread out in boundless plains: but the high, or upland prairies, which are much the most beautiful, as well as the best adapted to cultivation—present a series of graceful undulations not unlike the swell of the sea, from which they derive the appellation 'rolling.'"

The seat of government of this State is Iowa City, in Johnson county; a thriving town romantically located on the bluffs of the Iowa river, in a pleasant grove surrounded by magnificent prairies. Mr. Sargent thus speaks in 1848:

"Iowa City, the capital of the State, and the seat of justice of this county, is situated near its center, on the left bank of Iowa river. The settlement and growth of this town have been remarkably rapid. In May, 1839, when the seat of government was located, it was entirely in a state of nature. In less than one year afterward it contained from five to seven hundred inhabitants, and several hotels and shops. It has since increased with equal rapidity, and now contains several churches, a college, academy, and excellent schools. Steamboats frequently ascend the river to this point, and some have gone above in high stages of water. About a mile above the city, are an excellent water-power and extensive mills.

"The passage of the bill to locate the seat of government anew, does not seem to have injured in the least, the prosperity of this city. No one appears to entertain a serious idea that the seat of government will be removed from it, at least, for the next fifty years."

The capitol is a fine edifice; it is built of a beautiful stone, quarried at that place, full of small starry spots and rings, which gives it the name of "birds-eye marble," resembling maple-wood of the same name. It is located on a high, broad eminence which overlooks an extensive and charming prospect in several directions; and at this time contains between two and three thousand population. The Railroad from Dubuque to Keokuk, is to run through this place.

The population of Johnson county in 1847 was 2,900; it is now 4,472; dwellings, 799; farms, 377; manufactories, 19.

Those counties, in this state, lying along the Mississippi, I described on the passage up that river to Minnesota. I will now proceed with the other counties.

There are several projects suggested and considerable effort being made to improve the navigation of Keokuk rapids, so the passage of boats at all times may be more safe and easy.

It is said a company in New York are about to complete arrangements for the construction of a ship canal around the rapids, which will also furnish an immense hydraulic power.

Des Moines River Country.—Iowa is bounded on the south a short distance by this river, which still continues its course through the southern part of the state; and the counties which lie along its banks, on both sides, clear up to Fort Des Moines, generally, present as good agricultural facilities, as enterprising a community, and as rapid growth, as any part of the State. A *Canal* has been commenced, and is making considerable progress, up the valley on the north side of this fine river, which, in high stages of water, light steamboats navigate some distance up. There is also a *Railroad* projected, to be laid up this valley, on the north of the Canal, following a ridge which divides the waters that fall south into the Des Moines, from those which run north and empty into Skunk river. This Road is to cross the Des Moines at Fort Des Moines, and run thence west to the Mississippi at Council Bluff.

The course of the Des Moines is from the northwest to southeast, and of course, cutting the counties through which it passes diagonally; thereby affecting a larger portion of each than if it crossed them at right angles with their sides.

In the southeast angle of the state of Iowa, lies *Lee* county, of which KEOKUK is the principal commercial town on the Mississippi. This county has been described in another part of this book. There are other fine towns in the county.

Van Buren is the next county up the Des Moines river; it contains excellent lands, with plenty of timber and water; it is an old, populous county, and well improved. Population, 12,270; dwellings, 2,069; farms, 998; manufactories, 23.

KEOSAUQUE is the county-seat, situated in the bend of the river; it is a place of much wealth and business. There are other thriving towns in the county; as Farmington, Birmingham, Iowaville, and Philadelphia.

Wapello county lies next above, and is well diversified by prairie, timber, and water; it is thickly settled, and pretty well improved. Population, 8,471; dwellings, 1,416; farms, 828; manufactories, 7.

OTTUMWA is the county-seat, situated on the river, and with a good water-power; it is a flourishing village. There are other thriving towns in the county; as Eddyville, Columbia, and others.

Mahaska county is next above, and is one of the best in the New Purchase. It is diversified with prairie and timber, and is well watered, being the only county on the Des Moines, through which Skunk river passes. Population, 5,989; dwellings, 981; farms, 48; manufactories, 18.

OSKALOOSA is the county-seat, situated on the Skunk. It is a new town, is rapidly growing, and is surrounded by numbers of well cultivated farms. Union Mills and Auburn are among the other towns of this county.

Marion county is the next; and is somewhat more broken than the others, with a larger proportion of timber. Here the banks of the river are steep and rugged, affording coal and iron ore. A colony of Hollanders, under President SCHAULTER, have settled in the northeast corner of this county, and commenced a village with the name of *Pella*. Population of the county is 5,480; dwellings, 930; farms, 342; manufactories, 24.

KNOXVILLE is the county-seat, pleasantly situated on a small stream in the prairie.

Polk county is the next. It contains good land, and is well watered and timbered. Raccoon river drains the western part of the county and empties into the Des Moines. It presents many fine farms and comfortable improvements. Population, 4,515; dwellings, 756; farms, 321; manufactories, 9.

The old village of FORT DES MOINES is the county-seat. It was evacuated by the United States Dragoons in 1846. It is situated on the Des Moines, opposite the mouth of the Raccoon; and at the proposed crossing of the Railroad to Council Bluffs. It is a thriving town.

Dallas and *Boone* are the next two, and the last, counties through which the Des Moines runs, within the surveyed and settled portions of the State. They are but thinly settled, being mostly prairie, though people are continually but slowly locating there.

BOONVILLE, on the Des Moines, is the county-seat of the former; ELDELLE, on the Raccoon, is county-seat of the latter.

Lucas and *Warren* counties lie west and south of Marion, and are attached to it for judicial purposes, being but thinly populated as yet.

There are many new and thinly settled counties in the

southern and western portions of this state, which the writer has not visited; and of which he can give but a slight and general account.

Of these, are Mills, Page, Clark, Ringgold, Decatur, Taylor, Wayne, Appanuse, and Davis, on the Missouri line. They are said to be well watered, but contain little timber. In the northwest and north, are Story, Marshall, Poweshiek, Tama, Benton, Black Hawk, Winneshiek, Allomakee, and some others, which are similarly characterized. Still, many portions of all of them offer handsome inducements for colonies and companies of enterprising farmers and mechanics to locate and make independent pleasant homes for themselves and families.

Buchanan and *Fayette* counties, though but newly organized, possessing only about 1,600 population together, and some 70 cultivated farms; and on account of their excellent land, timber, and water, are receiving rapid acquisitions within their borders.

TRENTON, in Buchanan, is the county-seat; is well situated on the Wabsipinecon river, and is rapidly growing.

Delaware is a new county lying between Buchanan and Dubuque, and presents much the appearance of the mineral lands, being rough and broken, in some parts, though much of it is valuable for farming purposes, with plenty of timber and water, being on the head fountains of the Mokauqueta river. Population, 1,759; dwellings, 338; farms, 141; manufactories, 4.

DELHI is the county-seat, situated on the south fork of the Mokauqueta river, a pleasant town, with fair prospects of continued growth.

Clayton county lies on the Mississippi, north of Dubuque, watered by Turkey river. It is a county of good land and plenty of fine timber. Population, 3,873; dwellings, 728; farms, 200; manufactories, 12.

PRAIRIE LA PORTE, pleasantly situated on the Mississippi, is the county-seat. There are one or two other flourishing towns in this county, as Gernayville, Buena Vista, and Farmersburg, with others.

Jackson county lies on the river south of Dubuque. It contains some excellent farming lands, and some broken mineral lands; is well watered and timbered, and numerously settled, presenting many fine farms. Population, 7,210; dwellings, 1,277; farms, 703; manufactories, 10.

ANDREW is the county-seat, and is a flourishing town, on Mokouqueta river. Bellevue and Charleston, in this county, are situated on the river; there are some other small towns in this county.

Jones county lies west of Jackson, and possesses plenty of timber and water-power, with good land, and surpassed by few counties in the state. Population, 3,007; dwellings, 559; farms, 225; manufactories, 3.

EDINBURG is the county-seat, and is a growing town, in the midst of a fine country. Anamosa is a fine thriving town in this county, on the Wabsipinecon.

Linn county lies west of Jones. Its land is of the best quality, well timbered and watered. Population, 5,444; dwellings, 991; farms, 526; manufactories, 23.

MARION is the county-seat. It is a growing town; and is one of the points on the line of the projected Dubuque and Keokuk Railroad. There are several flourishing towns in this county.

Cedar county lies between Johnson and Scott. It is well timbered and watered, presenting much water-power for machinery; and is pretty well settled. Population, 3,940; dwellings, 686; farms, 358; manufactories, 4.

TIPTON, the county-seat, is situated on a handsome prairie, and enjoys a rapid growth. Rochester is another thriving town in this county.

Iowa county lies west of Johnson; it is a new county, but its fine soil, timber, and water must insure its growth.

Population, 822; dwellings, 143; farms, 70; manufactories, 2.

MARENGO is the county-seat. It is situated in the north part of the county, on Iowa river; with prospects of fair growth and business.

Jasper county lies east of Polk; the land is mostly prairie, but of a good quality and well watered. Monroe City, the new proposed state capital, is in this county, at the junction of two proposed Railroad lines. Population, 1,280; dwellings, 214; farms, 150.

NEWTON, the county-seat, is a beautiful and flourishing town, on a prairie between the branches of Skunk river.

Jefferson lies north of Van Buren; its soil is good, well timbered and watered, with ample water-power, and is thickly settled. Population, 9,904; dwellings, 1,649; farms, 1,067; manufactories, 54.

FAIRFIELD is the county-seat; it is a beautiful and rapidly thriving town; and is one of the points through which the Keokuk and Council Bluff projected Railroad is to pass; and is one of the General Land Offices.

Clinton county lies between Scott and Jackson, on the river. It is a county of excellent land, with fair proportions of timber and prairie; presenting several fine farms. Population, 2,822; dwellings, 499; farms, 306; manufactories, 10.

DEWITT is the county-seat.

Washington county is handsomely diversified by timber and prairie; it has a rolling surface and is well watered by streams, several of which furnish good water-powers, and are profitably improved. In 1847 the population was 3,500; now it is 4,957; dwellings, 856; farms, 428.

The county-seat is WASHINGTON, a thriving town, situated in a fine prairie, near a small branch of Skunk river.

Henry county is one of the best in this part of Iowa. It contains much good prairie, a fair portion of timber, and is watered by Skunk river. The population, in 1847, was 6,700; now it is 8,707; dwellings, 1,545; farms, 947; manufactories, 26.

MOUNT PLEASANT is the county-seat, and is a beautiful, thriving village, healthfully situated in a rolling prairie.

In the western, northern, and southern portions of Iowa, on the farther borders of settlements, where the population is very sparse, but the land and farming facilities very good, there have recently—by the last session of the Iowa Legislature—been many new counties established; and with their fine streams, fresh groves, rich soil, and the low price of land, which that region possesses, it presents many favorable inducements to emigrants; particularly, where they can go in Companies, as the land is yet, most of it, to be bought at Government prices, $1.25 per acre; and persons organizing in Colonies, and locating there, with reasonable industry and prudence, can soon make pleasant and independent homes.

Help one another, and make that the universal motto, and every one will have a vast amount of assistance, with no opponents—each person will have all others for friends, while none will have an enemy. Such will ever be the effect of the Golden Rule, when practiced upon—wherein each kindly and justly regards the rights and welfare of every one—none are opponents, but the mass are continual helpers to the individual.

RECAPITULATION.—Total population of Iowa, 192,214; dwellings, 32,962; farms, 14,805; manufacturing establishments, 482.

RIVERS.—The chief Rivers of this State are, the Mississippi, Des Moines, Iowa, Keosauque, Little Iowa, Iowa, Skunk, Cedar, Wabsipinecon, and some others. Of these, the Des Moines, Iowa, and Cedar, are navigable in high water, to distances varying from 50 to 100 miles up. Most of them have abundance of lime or sand-rock, in their banks and bottoms, with considerable currents, and generally skirted with good timber.

MINERALS.—Lead, iron, zinc, and copper ores, and stone coal, are found in portions of Iowa, in greater or less quantities; but lead is the most abundant.

Mr. Sargent closes his valuable little book, with some suggestions on the advantages to be derived, by the Eastern cities, from a Railroad communication direct between the Atlantic and Mississippi. His remarks are very just, and beginning to be realized. He says:

"In the event of the construction of such an iron highway, the provisions and other productions of the great Valley would reach the principal Atlantic cities in less than four days. Were the proposed Road now in operation, flour, to the extent of three millions of barrels, would be transported on it in the coming year. At the same rates as charged on the Reading Road, produce could be transported on the proposed highway, from the Mississippi river to New York, at less than $14 per ton. On the Upper Mississippi river, a few days past, the highest prices paid for provisions and breadstuffs, from Keokuck to Galena, ranged as follows:

Wheat, best winter	50	cents per bushel.
Corn	15	cents do.
Pork, over 200 lbs.	2	cents per pound.
Beef	2½	cents do.
Venison, haunches	3	cents do.
Flour	$3 50 to $4 00	per barrel.

"Could we open an iron avenue from the East to the West, our Atlantic markets would, at all seasons, be bountifully supplied with the surplus products of the Great West; and in a very few years after its completion, the aggregate tonnage transported on this great thoroughfare would reach the amount of tonnage now annually transported on the Erie Canal.

"Our fellow-citizens of the East should liberally contribute to farther the construction of the proposed great highway."

Railroad communication is now nearly completed between the Atlantic and Mississippi. From New York to Buffalo and Dunkirk there are even two lines; and through part of Pennsylvania and Ohio the iron highway is in operation, with fair prospects of being speedily completed. The western counties of Iowa are best reached by Steamboats running on Missouri river. In ascending the river, the first county reached is *Fremont*, LYNDEN the county-seat. Austen is another fine town. It is a county of good land, both prairie and timber. Pop. 1,244; dwellings, 222; farms, 105. The next is *Mills*, of which I have not learned the county-seat. Above this is *Pottawattomie* county; it embraces much good prairie and timber land, and is well watered by Nishnabottany and Boyer rivers, the former passing south through Mills and Fremont counties. There are many points in this region possessing much interest as connected with Indian Missions, Agencies, and Wars, in which are located Forts Crogan, Calhoun, and old Council Bluffs Agency. Population of Pottawattomie county is 7,900; dwellings, 1,500; farms, 90; manufactories, 6. The county-seat is KANESVILLE, a flourishing village, pleasantly situated on the prairie, at the old site of the Catholic Mission. The towns and counties in this region are being fast filled up with immigrants; and it is said to be a superior wheat and stock raising country; and was formerly the favorite resort of buffalo and deer. It presents an extensive scope of most charming and romantic scenery.

COUNCIL BLUFFS, and the Sub-Agency are in this county; there are good *Ferries* here, across the Missouri and other rivers near by to the westward. This place posses-ses importance from being on the direct line, and the most feasible crossing of the Missouri river, for those great National Improvements, the Pacific Telegraph and Railroad. By reference to the Map, it will be seen that the Great Route from Chicago, on the Lakes, crosses the Mississippi at Rock Island or Galena, the Missouri at Council Bluffs, and thence to the South Pass, or other favorable point.

Above here are the new counties *Harrison* and *Manona*, but thinly settled and attached to Pottawattomie county.

ILLINOIS.

We now return from Minnesota, Wisconsin, and Iowa, to Illinois; and, although I have previously described some portions of it, in a general way; I will now proceed to present its boundaries, topography, and history, with other leading features; such is its counties, towns, population, business, prospects, and such local peculiarities and curiosities as are met with in traveling through the States; and also, such distinct inducements as the different locations hold out to the new comer; that persons of different tastes and desires may see, in the Portraiture here given, its various characteristics, and be able to choose to their liking, without the task of traversing the whole country.

All of the States and Territories here described, are connected with and deeply concerned in the navigation of the Mississippi; and none more so than Illinois; for she has a longer border on that noble river than any other State. Hence, she must take a lively interest in whatever tends to give greater safety or facilities to operations upon its channel.

An important Convention assembled at Burlington, Iowa, on the 23d of October, 1851, to deliberate upon measures for surmounting or removing the obstacles to the easy navigation of the Mississippi, which are caused by the Des Moines and Rock Island Rapids; this Convention was attended by Delegates from Minnesota, Wisconsin, Iowa, Illinois, and Missouri; and their deliberations will, no doubt, result beneficially for the object which caused its meeting. The object is a deserving one, and no doubt will meet a favorable response from Congress.

The first white settlements of the Lake and Mississippi country were the result of the adventurous spirits of the French explorers, among whom the most distinguished were H. de Soto, Fathers Hennepin, La Salle, Marquette, Joliet, and N. Perrat. The first of these was the first discoverer of the Mississippi in 1541; and the latter was the first who made a voyage along the western shore of Lake Michigan in 1670. At an early period Lake Michigan was called Illinois lake; and Chicago river was called Miamis river.

About the year 1670, La Salle, Hennepin, and others, made a voyage from Canada, by the lakes, to the Chicago river, and then down the Illinois river, establishing posts in that region. La Salle, leaving Hennepin in the country, returned to Canada; and in 1673, came again to the Mississippi, and established posts at Cahokia and Kaskaskia; and for many years all of the settlements in this country were understood to be in a prosperous condition.

In 1763, upon the cessation of hostilities between the French and English, the Illinois country was ceded to the British Government. In 1765 Captain Sterling was put in possession of the Illinois territory; he was succeeded by Major Farmer, who in turn was succeeded by Colonel Reed in 1766, in which year Illinois was annexed to Canada by Quebec Parliament. And after an oppressive and unpopular administration of two years, he was displaced by Colonel Wilkins, whose administration was more satisfactory to the people.

During the Revolutionary war, in 1778, General George

R. Clarke made a campaign through the Indian country, subjugating Forts Chartres and Kaskaskia, and other posts on the Mississippi; then returning, he took old Port Vincent, now Vincennes, in Indiana.

This region being a portion of the Northwestern Territory, was principally under the jurisdiction of Virginia, whose legislature, in 1778, organized a large portion of what is now the State of Illinois, into the County of Illinois, and appointed a magistrate over it, to conduct its minor judicial affairs.

In 1803, the Territory of Indiana was constructed, of which Illinois was a portion. In 1809 Illinois was formed into a Territory, and remained till December, 1818, when it became an independent State; from which time it prospered but slowly till after the Indian war.

Some of the battles and massacres which occurred in this state during the war of 1812, and the Black Hawk war, present adventures and scenes of as thrilling interest as any other part of the country.

By various treaties, the different tribes of Indians have ceded all their lands to the whites, and they have enjoyed almost entire freedom from Indian troubles for a long period, except during the Black Hawk war of 1832.

The boundaries of Illinois are as follows, as laid down in Darby's Gazetteer:

"*Illinois* lies between Lake Michigan, the Wabash, Ohio, and Mississippi rivers. It has a boundary on N. latitude, 42° 30′, 210 miles; along Lake Michigan and State of Indiana, Indiana to Wabash river, 216; down the Wabash to the junction with the Ohio, 150; down the Ohio to its junction with the Mississippi, 130; thence up the Mississippi to the northwest angle of the state, 500; having an outline of 1,206 miles.

Area, 58,900 square miles—equal to 35,696,000 acres. Extreme S., N. latitude, 37°. Extreme N., N. latitude, 42° 30′. Greatest length from the junction of Ohio and Mississippi to N. latitude 42°—380 miles; mean width, 150 miles.

"Illinois is the fourth State of the Union, in respect to extent of territory, and the first in point of fertility of soil. Excepting Georgia, it is also the state whose climate and seasons differ most at the north and south extremities. Extending through 5° of latitude, this state embraces the greatest extent N. and S. of any section of the U. S., New York only reaching through 4½, and Georgia about an equal distance. The latter is indebted to the greater inequality of its surface for the superior variety of its climate.

"Illinois is a country of very little inequality of surface, compared with its great extent. The lower or southern part is rolling rather than hilly; and not one eminence in the state, it is probable, would reach 600 feet above the common level.

"In point of soil, Illinois admits a similar classification with Ohio and Indiana; though the former has more rich prairie than the two latter. The state may be considered as rolling in its southern and western, and level in its eastern and northeastern sections.

"It has been determined by repeated experiments that loaded boats of considerable size can pass from the Mississippi through Illinois, into the Canadian sea, and *vice versa*. Very little current is found in the small and very short streams which interlock with the sources of the Illinois, and flow into the southern extremity of Lake Michigan; therefore, the sources of Illinois cannot be much above the surface of that Lake. Fifteen or twenty feet is as much as the data before us will justify; of course, the whole volume of Illinois river, from a point opposite the head of Chicago river, in a distance following the windings of upward of 400 miles, does not fall 60 feet.

"The face of the globe may in vain be examined to find any other spot, except the sources of Orinoco and the Rio Negro, in South America, where natural facility to internal communication by water is equal to that we have this moment surveyed. If we glance an eye over the immense regions thus connected; if we regard the fertility of soil, the multiplicity of product which characterize these regions; and if we combine those advantages afforded by nature with the moral energy of the free and active people which are spreading their increasing millions over its surface, what a vista through the darkness of future time opens! The view is indeed almost too much for the faculties of man. We see arts, science, industry, virtue, and social happiness, already increasing in those countries beyond what the most inflated fancy would have dared to have hoped thirty or forty years ago."

At the time of the late war with Great Britain, loaded boats, with men and munitions, passed out of Lake Michigan, through Chicago river into the O'Plain, thence to the Illinois and Mississippi.

And now, by the Canal, with a single lock-lift, at Bridgeport, four miles from Chicago, an immense commerce is carried on between Lake Michigan and the Southern rivers.

The name which this state bears, early and for a long period, belonged to all the Northwestern Territory. It was derived from the *Illini* or *Illinois*, a tribe of Indians which appear to have possessed the country situated on both banks of the river of that name. They were noted for their hospitality and generosity to strangers, and their bravery and skill in war against their foes. Father Hennepin informs us that the name, in the native language, signifies a full-grown, proper man; and no tribe, certainly, were superior to them, in all noble traits found at all among Indians.

Illinois became a state in 1818, when it framed and adopted its constitution, and was received into the Union as the twenty-second State. The leading peculiarity in the Constitution was to *prohibit slavery*, which had before existed in the Territory.

The population of Illinois in 1820, was 55,211; in 1830, it was 157,455; in 1840, it was 476,183; in 1850, it was 855,884; and in 1851, it is over one million.

Some hints in regard to the course to be pursued by immigrants in the West may not be without benefit to those persons.

Farmers from the Older States, where long cultivation has furnished them with every convenience and luxury, might find it somewhat troublesome to submit to the plainer fare and occasional privations incident upon life in a New Country. But to avoid this, as far as possible, it will be well for the emigrant to make up his mind philosophically in the start, to cheerfully undergo these things, throw aside some of his former habits, forget some of his former easy blessings, and thus be prepared the better to accommodate himself to the new state of things which he is about to experience. I copy the following very truthful delineation of the Western people, with some of their social feelings, from an early Gazetteer of Illinois, by Mr. Peck:

"No emigrant need deceive himself with the notion that he can find a spot that will combine *all* the advantages, and *none* of the disadvantages of the country.

"All positions will present some desirable and superior features—some of the richest and finest inducements—while something objectionable will appear, and some trifle be wanting. Yet, on the whole, almost every spot is more inviting, for numerous reasons, than the positions which have been left in the Older State.

"Let a man and family go into any of the frontier settlements, get a shelter, or even camp out; call on the people to aid him on the start, and in three days' time he will have a comfortable cabin, and become fully identified as a *Settler*. No matter how poor he may be, or how much a stranger; if he makes no apologies, does not show a niggardly spirit by contending about trifles; and especially if he does not begin to dole out complaints about the country, and the manners of the people, and tell them of the difference and superiority of these things in the place whence he came, he will be received with blunt, unaffected hospitality. But if a man begin by affecting superior intelligence and virtue, and catechising the people for their habits of rough simplicity, he may expect to be marked, shunned, and ridiculed with some term of reproach.

"A principal characteristic of the Western population is a real unaffected hospitality—a plain spirit of accommodation—they will make every stranger welcome, if he will accept of it in their way. He must make no complaint, throw out no insinuations, and manifest an equal readiness to be frank and hospitable in return. Enter what house or cabin you may, if it is time of meals, you are invited to share a portion; but you must eat what is set before you, making no invidious comparisons."

Nothing is truer in the West, than the homely phrase,

"the latch-string always hangs out," and every one is welcome to enter, who is willing to receive cheerfully.

Says Mr. Flint, an early pioneer in the West:

"The most affectionate counsel we could give an immigrant, after an acquaintance with all the districts of the Western Country of sixteen years, is that he regard the *salubrity* of a spot selected, as of more importance than *fertility*, or nearness to *market*.

"That he depend for health, on temperance, moderation in all things, a careful conformity in food and dress to circumstances and the climate; and particularly, let him observe a rigid and undeviating abstinence from that murderous western poison, *whiskey*, which may be pronounced the prevalent miasm of the country. Let every immigrant learn the art and provide the materials to make good beer. Let him also, during the season of acclimation, especially in the sultry months, take medicine by way of prevention, twice or thrice, with abstinence from labor a day or two afterward. Let him have a Bible for a constant counselor, and a few good books for instruction and amusement. Let him have the dignity and good sense to train his family religiously and honestly.

"Let him cultivate a garden and choice fruit, as well as a fine orchard. Let him keep bees, for their management unites pleasure and profit. Let him prepare for silk-making on a small and gradual scale. Let him cultivate grapes by way of experiment. Let him banish unreal wants, and learn the master secret of self-possession, and be content with such things as he has, aware that every position in life has advantages and trials. Let him assure himself that if an independent farmer cannot be happy, no man can. Let him magnify his calling, respect himself, envy no one, and raise to the Author of all good constant aspirations of thankfulness as he eats the bread of peace and privacy."

Emigrants to any of the Western States, will do well to heed carefully the above wise suggestions, by one who had long and intimate experience in the West.

As a pleasant little prelude in the general tenor of this work, I will here present one of the happy features which characterize some of the Western prairie homes; and which exhibits some of the lovely but unexpensive embellishments which are made to beam around them by the attention bestowed upon the gardens by the girls, whose healths, beauty, and delights, are greatly enhanced by so doing. It is not uncommon there, nor is it considered a lack of good taste or true refinement, to see blooming girls dressing the flowers, pruning the shrubbery, and culturing the garden; they are all the happier and more charming for it; and the garden is among the objects to which they proudly call the attention of their sweethearts upon their afternoon visits. The following merry extract of a letter from a little Western girl to her brother at the East, will give a finer idea of the subject than any description of mine will convey:

"And now, as I have nothing more very important to write about, let me give you a short chapter on my flower-garden, as I came in a little while ago from dressing it and picking a sisterly boquette for you. Those grand *Lady Slippers* you so much admired last summer, seem to have grown very vain from the many fine compliments you lavished upon them, for they have come out in bran-new dresses, of different hues, 'the gayest of the gay,' all seeming to vie with each other in richness and colors of dress. But just let me introduce them to you in rhymes, along with their neighbors:

The first is Miss Lovelawn, as sweet as a rose,
Her white satin slippers just hiding her toes;
And the next is Miss Pink, so sparkling and free,
With her sister Carnation, as charming as she;
Dahlias, scarlet and purple, crimson and blue,
Bright sisters and cousins of every hue;
Each looking as lovely as lovely can be,
Giving breakfasts and suppers to bird and to bee;
Sweet Violets of purple, yellow and blue,
Which teach the thoughts of modesty ever true—
But this scratch of my pen 's too homely, I ween,
To present them to you as they'd wish to be seen.

And then there are their neighbors, the Morning Glories and Four-o'clocks, at their own fashionable hours, looking as pretty as any; while the humming-birds pay their respects just as graciously to Sweet-Williams, Mullen Pinks, and Marigolds, as to the others; then there stand the Tiger Lilies, too, in their dignity and beauty, nodding gracefully to passers-by; beside the heaps of wild, sweet Prairie Flowers, all casting up their bright little eyes to us as we gaze on them; but I fear you'll begin to get tired of my light nonsense; so, with a kiss and good morning, I'll hasten off to school."

Such is one among the many pleasant features of youthful prairie life, which spring up into shining existence, under the hand of tasteful, independent, cheerful industry.

Another healthful and exhilarating amusement much indulged in by the ladies of the prairie country, is that of riding on horseback; and the skill of many of our feminine equestrians is masterly, and would meet the delighted admiration of the gallant knights even of the chivalric feudal days, or the exacting criticism of Napoleon; and, surely, often does receive the coöperative approval of the joyous knights of their own neighborhood. Sometimes the ladies may be seen in merry adventurous troops, unattended by the masculines, bounding away with wild joy over the green fields, their glittering ringlets, and rich sashes, and gay plumes, waving and flying in the breeze, while the bright mane of their proud steeds is tossed lightly in air over their gracefully curbed necks, as if they verily appreciated the charming burdens they bore away with such spirit and strength, seeming scarcely to touch the ground in their elastic gallop.

It is a proud, a glorious sight, thus to see a beautiful girl sit well and manage dexterously, in proper apparel, a noble horse, as he dashes away over the fields, or through the lawns; a more charming object is seldom looked at. No wonder that Grace Greenwood evinced such glowing poetic inspiration, when she wrote that admirable poem on horseback-riding. Following are several detached lines extracted from her poem on that subject. When the heart is sad, or the spirits flag, she says:

"Then bring me, oh, bring me my gallant young steed,
With his high arched neck, and his nostrils spread wide,
His eye full of fire, and his step full of pride;
As I spring to his back, as I seize the strong rein,
The strength of my spirit returneth again.

* * * * * * *

"On, on speeds my courser, scarce printing the sod,
Scarce crushing a daisy to mark where he trod.
What a wild thought of triumph, that this girlish hand,
Such a steed in the might of his strength may command.

* * * * * *

"What a glorious creature; ah, glance at him now,
As I check him awhile on this green hillock's brow
How he tosses his mane with a shrill joyous neigh
And paws the firm earth in his proud stately play;
Ho, a ditch! shall we pause? no, the bold leap we will dare;
Like a swift winged arrow we rush through the air.

* * * * * * *

"Oh, not all the pleasure that poets may praise,
Not the wildering waltz in the ball-room's blaze
Can the wild thrilling joy exceed
Of a fearless leap on a fiery steed."

From a work entitled, "Illinois in 1837," I make the following extracts in regard to boundaries, face of the country, etc.:

"The Act of Congress admitting this State into the Union prescribes the boundaries as follows: Beginning at the mouth of the Wabash river, thence up the middle of the main channel thereof to the point where a line drawn due north of Vincennes last crosses that stream, thence due north to the northwest corner of the State of Indiana, thence east with the boundary line of the same state to the middle of Lake Michigan, thence due north along the middle of said lake to north latitude 40° 30′, thence west to the middle of the Mississippi river, thence down the middle of the main channel thereof to the mouth of the Ohio river, thence up the latter stream along its northern or right shore to the place of beginning. The outline of the state is in extent about 1,160 miles, the whole of which, except 305 miles, is formed by navigable lakes and rivers.

"As a physical section, Illinois occupies the lower part of that inclined plane of which Lake Michigan and both its shores are the higher sections, and which is extended into and embraces the much greater part of Indiana. Down this plane, in a very nearly southwestern direction, flow the Wabash and its confluents, the Kaskaskia, the Illinois and its confluents, and the Rock and Wisconsin rivers. The lowest section of the plane is also the extreme southern angle of Illinois, at the mouth of the Ohio river, about 340 feet above tide-water, in the Gulf of Mexico. Though the State of Illinois does contain some low hilly sections, as a whole, it may be regarded as a gently inclining plane in the direction of its rivers, as already indicated. Without including minute parts, the extreme arable elevation may be safely stated at 800 feet above tide-water, and the mean hight at 550.

"'In some former period,' observes Mr. Schoolcraft, 'there has been an obstruction in the channel of the Mississippi, at or near Grand Tower, producing a stagnation of the current at an elevation of about 130 feet above the present ordinary water-mark. This appears evident from the general elevation and direction of the hills, which for several hundred miles above are separated by a valley from 20 to 25 miles wide, that deeply embosoms the current of the Mississippi.'

"Wherever these hills exhibit rocky and abrupt fronts, a series of waterlines are distinctly visible, and preserve a remarkable parallelism uniformly presenting their greatest depression toward the sources of the river; and, at Grand Tower, these water-lines are elevated about one hundred feet above the summit of the stratum in which petrifactions of the madrepora and various fossil organic remains are deposited. Here the rocks of dark-colored limestone, which pervade the country to a great extent, by their projections toward each other, indicate that they have, at a remote period, been disunited, if not by some convulsion of nature, by the incessant action of the water upon a secondary formation, and that a passage has been effected through them, giving vent to the stagnant waters on the prairie lands above, and opening for the Mississippi its present channel.

"Next to Louisiana and Delaware, Illinois is the most level State in the Union. A small tract in the southern part of the state is hilly, and the northern portion is also somewhat broken. There are likewise considerable elevations along the Illinois river, and the bluffs of the Mississippi in some places might pass almost for mountains. But by far the greater proportion of the state is either distributed in vast plains, or in barrens, that are gently rolling like the waves of the sea after a storm."

"GRAND PRAIRIE.—The largest prairie in Illinois is denominated the Grand Prairie. Under this general name is embraced the country lying between the waters falling into the Mississippi, and those which enter the Wabash rivers. It does not consist of one vast tract, but is made up of continuous tracts with points of *timber* projecting inward, and long arms of prairie extending between. The southern points of the Grand Prairie are formed in Jackson county, and extend in a northeastern course, varying in width from one to twelve miles through Perry, Washington, Jefferson, Marion, Fayette, Effingham, Coles, Champaign, and Iroquois counties, where it becomes connected with the prairies that project eastward from the Illinois river. A large arm lies in Marion county, between the waters of Crooked creek and the east fork of the Kaskaskia river, where the Vincennes road passes through. This part alone is frequently called the Grand Prairie.

"Much the largest part of the Grand Prairie is gently undulating, rich, and fertile land; but of the southern portion, considerable tracts are flat, and of rather inferior soil. No insurmountable obstacle exists to its future population. No portion of it is more than six or eight miles distant from timber; and coal in abundance is found in most parts. Those who have witnessed the changes produced upon a prairie surface within twenty or thirty years, consider these extensive prairies as offering no serious impediment to the future growth of the state.

"Dr. BECK, in his *Gazetteer of Missouri*, published in 1823, describes the uplands of St. Louis county as generally prairie; but almost all of that tract of country thus described is now covered with a young growth of fine thrifty timber, and it would be difficult to find an acre of prairie in the county. This important change has been produced by keeping the fires out of the prairies.

"The first improvements are usually made on that part of the prairie which adjoins the timber; and thus we may see, at the commencement, a range of farms circumscribing the entire prairie. The burning of the prairies is then stopped through the whole distance of the circuit in the neighborhood of these farms, to prevent injury to the fences and other improvements. This is done by plowing two or three furrows all round the settlement. In a short time the timber springs up spontaneously on all the parts not burned, and the groves and forests commence a gradual encroachment on the adjacent prairies; by-and-by you will see another tier of farms springing up on the outside of the first, and farther out on the prairie; and thus farm succeeds farm, as the timber grows up, until the entire prairie is occupied."

Some of these prairies are so broad, and portions of them so far from timber, that it is rather a laborious task for persons of limited means and small help to commence a farm in their midst. In such cases union of effort, in colonies, will be found advantageous.

In 1836–7 to 1840 Illinois projected extensive and extravagant schemes of Railroads and Canals, much beyond her ability to perfect; consequently, there followed the general smash and confusion of a universal suspension.

She has again entered upon a still more magnificent scheme of Railroad building, extending many important lines through various parts of the State; but now under very different circumstances. She has completed her great Canal—one of the most splendid works in the Union—and it is doing an immense and increasing business, the receipt of tolls this year largely exceeding the receipts for any previous year. Portions of several of her Railroads are also completed, and in successful, profitable operation.

These things have established a sound and healthy confidence, among capitalists, in her resources and facilities, to an extent that Eastern Capitalists now freely invest their surplus funds in her lines, which insures their speedy completion; the productiveness of Agricultural operations being proved ample to furnish them with profitable employment; the State being now numerously settled-up and cultivated by industrious, enterprising farmers, who annually raise millions of produce for export east and south. These facts, with others, afford fair guarantee that suspension will not again take place, as in past times.

And what is here said of Illinois, is also true in regard to Wisconsin and Iowa, to a considerable extent.

To give an idea of the extent and location of projected Railroads in Illinois; some of which are constructed, others under contract for speedy completion, and others still with the stocks subscribed and the works in charge of engineers, who are busily running out the routes.

The *Galena and Chicago Union Railroad* is designed to connect the Mississippi river with Lake Michigan; already some sixty miles of it is in operation, west from Chicago to MARENGO. By December it will be completed to BELVIDERE, Boone county; and in January following, it is to be in operation to ROCKFORD, Winnebago county. At this point it will be intersected by the *Union Rock River Railroad*, from BELOIT and other towns in the Upper Rock river country, in Wisconsin, and to run south down the river. These lines will furnish a favorable medium of transportation for a wide, fertile, Farming region, beside a rich portion of the mineral lands; as the Road will be completed during the year, through FREEPORT, Stephenson county to GALENA, Jo Daviess county. Between CHICAGO and ELGIN, branches switch off to AURORA, ST. CHARLES, and BATAVIA, towns on Fox river. This line and its branches make about 200 miles.

The *Sangamon and Morgan Railroad* commences at NAPLES, on the Illinois river in Scott county, and runs east through JACKSONVILLE in Morgan county, to SPRINGFIELD in Sangamon county, and to be continued still on eastward.

The *Illinois Central Railroad* is the longest and most important line in Illinois; and some five corps of engineers are now engaged in exploring the routes for the main trunk and branches. It is to run through nearly the entire length of the State, from CAIRO in the southern extremity, to CHICAGO on Lake Michigan. It is to have two branches; one, running to GALENA, for the convenience of the northwestern part of the state, lying between the

Mississippi and Illinois rivers; the other running through the northeastern portion of the state, to accommodate that part of the state lying between the Wabash and Illinois rivers.

This line is also to be extended southward, to MOBILE, in Alabama, on the Gulf of Mexico, by the Southern States.

The whole route, as contemplated by Congress, in making the grant of land for its construction, is denominated *The Chicago and Mobile Railroad.* It passes through the center of the State of Illinois by the route already surveyed, and from which there will not be any material deviation by the farther surveys now being made. It will cross the Illinois river at La Salle and Peru; and the Ohio at Cairo. By the conditions of the Charter granted to a Company of capitalists, this road must be constructed to Cairo within the next six years. It will involve an expenditure of between sixteen and twenty millions of dollars. Through the exertion of Judge Douglas, Senator Breese, and others, who are resident in Illinois, an appropriation of alternate sections of the public land along the line of the road was obtained from the General Government, which insures its construction. Its eastern branch will bring into cultivation a body of land in the interior, at present removed from market, containing many miles hitherto unsettled. Such, too, must be the case in the counties along the Wabash river, dividing Illinois from Indiana. The Road must transfer much of the travel and business from the Mississippi to the Central parts of this State, making Illinois the center, in many respects, of the Great Valley, having within its borders the principal artery of communication North and South.

That portion of this long line which lies in Illinois is termed the "State Central Road," from Cairo to Chicago, Galena, and Dubuque.

The title to the act of Congress making the grant of land, reads:

"'An Act granting the right of way and making a grant of land to the States of Illinois, Mississippi, and Alabama, in aid of the construction of a Railroad from Chicago to Mobile,' passed September 20, 1850."

After Congress had made this munificent donation, or rather appropriation, of land, to those States, the Illinois Legislature passed an act, chartering a Company, and transferred to it these lands to construct the Road. Senator Douglas, in a letter in relation to this matter, says:

"This Charter transfers to the Central Railroad Company all the lands which the State of Illinois received from the United States in pursuance of that act of Congress, and imposes upon the Company all the obligations which our State assumed in consideration of that grant of land, which obligations the Company pledged itself by the acceptance of the Charter faithfully to perform.

"The act of Congress grants to the State of Illinois a quantity of land equal the alternate section for six miles on each side of said Road and branches, and at the same time increases the price of the other alternate sections to two dollars and fifty cents per acre, so that the United States would receive for the remaining half of the lands as much as they would for the whole. It was the enhancement of the value of the public lands upon each side of the Road that constituted the inducement to get the grant. It was upon this principle that the measure was successfully vindicated and sustained by its friends. The lands had been in market upon an average of twenty odd years, at one dollar and a quarter per acre, and had failed to find purchasers; not because the lands were not rich and fertile, but in consequence of their remoteness from markets, and the absence of timber. The Railroad would supply both of these deficiencies, and thus render desirable that which was before comparatively valueless."

The third clause of the fifteenth section thus defines the routes which shall be pursued in laying this Road and its branches:

"That said Company shall proceed to locate, survey, and lay out, construct and complete said Road and branches, through the entire length thereof—the main trunk thereof, or central line, to run from the city of Cairo to the southern termination of the Illinois and Michigan Canal, passing not more than five miles from the northeast corner of township twenty-one north, range two east of the third principal meridian; and nowhere departing more than seventeen miles from a straight line between said city of Cairo and said southern termination of said Canal; with a branch running from the last mentioned point, upon the most eligible route to the city of Galena; thence to a point on the Mississippi river, opposite the city of Dubuque, in the State of Iowa; with a branch also diverging from the main track at a point not north of the parallel of thirty-nine and a half degrees north latitude, and running on the most eligible route into the city of Chicago on Lake Michigan."

The Illinois and Wisconsin Railroad, to run southeast from FON DU LAC, head of Lake Winnebago, in Wisconsin, through JANESVILLE, WOOSTOCK, Big Foot Prairie, to CHICAGO, has been located, and considerable of it put under contract for speedy construction.

This is an important route, passing through the upper Rock river valley, and leaving Wisconsin in Walworth county, and entering Illinois in McHenry county; thus lying in a superior agricultural district.

The Green Bay and Chicago Railroad is another important line connecting Illinois and Wisconsin. It will probably follow the Lake-shore route, running through those flourishing and beautiful towns, which have grown up to wealth and elegance with such rapidity in the last few years. By this route the distance will be not far from 160 miles.

Another important *Railroad* to Northern Illinois, is the one projected between CINCINNATI and CHICAGO. Much effort is being put forth to have it pushed forward with energy and rapidity.

A glance at the map, to see the district of country this line must run through, will show its vast use.

The Rock Island and Chicago Railroad is still another

very important line, connecting the Mississippi and Illinois rivers with Lake Michigan. Its western terminus is at ROCK ISLAND; thence to run eastward to the Illinois at PERU and LA SALLE, and thence up the valleys of the Illinois and O'Plain rivers to Chicago, through a rich, well populated country, and many fine thriving towns; it is under contract, the work commenced, and will progress to a speedy completion, bringing Rock Island within some four hours of Peru, and six or seven hours of Chicago.

The Railroads eastward are already in operation to the Indiana State line, and in a few months will be completed to Chicago, which will place that city within 36 to 40 hours of New York.

These Roads, therefore, with its other mediums of communication, must make CHICAGO the center or depot of an immense and constantly increasing commerce and population, second only in importance to one or two Atlantic cities.

The Alton and Terre Haute Railroad is an important line, and is in the hands of those who will push it energetically through. Alton alone has taken over $100,000 of the stock. This line is to connect the Wabash and Mississippi rivers at the places named in the title above.

Northern Cross Railroad.—This is a line to connect QUINCY, on the Mississippi, with CLAYTON, GALESBURG, and other towns in the interior of the State; and there is now a fair prospect of the early completion of the first twenty to thirty miles of the Northern Cross Railroad, from Quincy to Clayton, within the next twelve months. The grading is already in a state of forwardness, and the Directors have recently completed a contract with responsible parties for furnishing the materials and laying down the superstructure. The contract price is $6,493 per mile, and the parties agree to take the bonds of the city of Quincy for $100,000 at par, that being the amount subscribed by the city, in its corporate capacity.

The survey of the *Peoria and Oquawka Railroad* has been made, and the stock being mostly taken, the auspices are favorable for the rapid construction of the Road. It is to connect the Mississippi and Illinois rivers at the places named in their title.

Thus I have given the name, location, and state of progress, of most of the important Roads in the State, the construction of which must speedily enhance the value of wild lands in the West, and lead to their rapid settlement and cultivation.

Considerable effort is being made to have a *Railroad* constructed from CINCINNATI to ST. LOUIS, through the southern part of Illinois, and cross the Central Railroad in that region.

The fine Map which accompanies this work, will show most of the lines of Railroads, though I cannot give them with precision, as it is not yet known through what towns, in all their length, they will pass; but it is the aim of the author to have every thing as correct as circumstances will permit.

Of all the various sports in *hunting and fishing*, of the West, none is more intensely interesting than that of shooting prairie chickens; it is done with a perfect vigor and activity; there is little of the patience and waiting that is required, when lying in wait at the "run ways" for deer; or the wary ambush for taking wild turkeys; or the stealth and slew-wading for geese and ducks; but it is lively walking and expectation, to keep up with the skillful dog, who ranges through the grass to discover, and "set," and "start" the bird, and the quick shooting to take them by couplets, before they are too far flown for your shot to reach. It is a "fast operation," in which the adept, with a well trained dog, where the birds are plenty,

19

will take fifty to an hundred in an afternoon, with very few more than that number of shots. These birds are found in great numbers throughout the Western Prairies generally; though they incline to disappear as cultivation advances; they are rather larger than the pheasant of New York and New England, but somewhat resembling it, and equally luscious for the table. In winter time they are shot from the trees, the cornfields, and isolated haystacks, to which they sometimes resort in that season; but in the spring and summer they are really unfit to eat, and should not be killed, especially in the season of laying and hatching; yet, some inconsiderate and gross minded people will even then destroy them, from no other motive than an idle disposition for destruction. They are the best eating, and the greatest sport is enjoyed in taking them, after about the first of September, when the young chickens are large enough to make a good mark and afford fine dishes.

The grass of the prairies is then waving and high, the flowers bright and fragrant, which perfectly secret the birds, and then it is highly amusing to see the dog bound away in a circuit of from 20 to 50 or 100 rods in pursuit; when he comes up to a covey of the birds he manifests it to his master by suddenly stopping, stretches himself out, lying closer to the ground, his nose pointed straight ahead, and his tail straight back, and as he slowly walks toward them his tail begins to wag gently, the birds squat snugly in the grass so that a person could not see them, but as "setter" leads nearly on to them they rise and sail gracefully away in a horizonly line, a few feet above the grass, not very swiftly, curving a little to the right or left, affording the finest possible opportunity for the hunter to make a couple of shots and take a brace of them.

That sport which comes nearest to the delights of this which I have just described, is a branch of Sir Izak's art;

that of taking the glittering trout from our sparkling brooks of the north; this is a percussion operation; the fly, bearing the hidden hook, dips upon the water, trouty snaps it with his shiny mouth, and the next instant a spring of Izak junior's pole causes it to bid a last farewell to its native home; after passing through various degrees of tuition in the culinary scene-room it takes a wardrobe of butter and flour, with perfume of pepper and salt, passes the fervid ordeal of frying-pan, and soon simmers on a plate beside the sparkling champaign, under the chuckling chin of Burley Buster, or is genteely dissected by the tiny fingers of la Belle, who knows right well how to exert the arts that shall entrap larger troutys into her captive nets, when she thinks it worth her while to angle for them. There is much fine trout fishing in Wisconsin, Iowa, and Minnesota; and although in Illinois they are rarely found, still there is abundance of many other fine varieties of fish, such as bass, pickerel, catfish, buffaloes, redhorse, etc., with occasional sturgeon and eels.

Rock River Country.—No portion of the West is remarked with more favor and admiration than this; and it holds about the same relation that the Genesee country does to the East.

It is situated in the northern part of the state, and watered by Rock river and its branches. It is a fertile agricultural region, combining all the advantages of a rich and fruitful soil, a healthy and temperate climate, a fine river, and clear perennial streams, affording excellent mill-seats, together with many of the most useful and important minerals.

Rock river rises in Wisconsin, about midway between Lake Michigan and the Wisconsin river. Its course in Illinois is about 180 miles in extent. It receives its most important tributary, the Peckatonica, from the lead region, a few miles below the northern boundary of the State.

The Rock River Country may be considered as embracing, not only the parts which border immediately upon that stream, but all those portions of the surrounding territory which contribute directly to the development and employment of the resources of Rock river valley.

In this view may be included the mineral wealth and agricultural advantages of the Peckatonica and its branches, with the Kishwaukee and its branches.

The bottom lands of these streams, usually about a mile and a half wide, are seldom surpassed in fertility. Beside other causes which have combined for centuries to produce the same result, the wash of the bluffs enriches the plain below by its deposit. Like the American Bottom, below the mouth of Illinois river, which has been cultivated for more than a hundred years, the fertility of most of Rock river and Upper Mississippi bottoms is indestructible. On such a soil, under proper cultivation, 100 bushels of corn and 40 bushels of wheat to the acre are raised with facility; when you ascend to the elevated tableland—which is generally characteristic of the bluffs beyond the breaks—gullies formed by springs and drains on the edge of the bluffs, most usually the soil is of the richest kind, high and dry, and fanned, in the warmest days of summer, by breezes of the most refreshing character. These breezes, however, become cold winds in winter, as the traveler can sensibly attest.

There can be no doubt of this region being eminently healthy. The country is supplied bountifully with water from good springs, and the air is equal to that on the mountains in purity. It is even thought that the neighborhood of Rock Island will one day be the resort of rich invalids, and men of leisure from the south, on account of its double charm of salubrity of atmosphere and picturesqueness of scenery. The existence of a copious *white sulphur spring* near Rock Island, of medical virtues equal, perhaps, to the waters of any of the celebrated springs in the United States, gives strength to the idea.

Above all countries, this is the land of flowers. In the season every prairie is an immense flower-garden. In the early stages of spring flowers, the prevalent tint is peach-blow; the next is a deeper red; then succeeds the yellow; and to the latest period of autumn, the prairies exhibit a brilliant golden, scarlet, and blue carpeting, mingled with the green and brown ripened grass.

Sangamon River Country.—The region through which the Sangamon river passes, and its tributaries, is an exceedingly fertile one; of undulating prairies interspersed with springs, brooks, and groves. The inhabitants reside chiefly on the borders of the prairies, next to the timber, where they have made many splendid farms.

This country is one of the best for raising stock in the State; the summer range for cattle is inexhaustible, and the amount of excellent hay that may be made every season from the rich prairies is almost without limit; and horses, cattle, sheep, and hogs, can be raised here with but little trouble and expense, compared with the Eastern States. The mildness of the climate has not unfrequently relieved the owners from all care and expense of feeding them through the winter; though it is generally necessary to feed from the commencement of December until March. It has been frequently remarked that both horses and cattle fatten quite as fast in the spring and summer, on the wild grass of the prairies, as upon the tame pastures of the East. And the richness and flavor of the beef thus fattened has been much esteemed, and generally reckoned of the finest quality by all who have tried it. Illinois beef has no superior in the Atlantic market, and is received with high favor even beyond the ocean.

At the great *World's Fair*, even the beef packed by Wadsworth, Dyer, and Chapin, and others at, and shipped from, Chicago, received much attention and credit; this beef was fattened upon the prairies almost entirely.

Much stock is also raised in the Rock, Fox, O'Plain, and Illinois river countries, as well as in the regions of the Sangamon, and other streams of the State.

But it is to be regretted that Western farmers have not, to a greater extent, and in a better manner, engaged in the Dairy business. There is nowhere a better field, nor one where butter and cheese can be made to greater advantage, or of better quality, than upon the great Western Prairies.

SPRINGFIELD, the Capital of Illinois, is in *Sangamon* county, of which it is also the county-seat. It is very nearly central in the State, being about 197 miles nearly north of its southern angle in the junction of the Mississippi and Ohio rivers; 185 south of the northern boundary of the State; 114 west of the Wabash river, the eastern boundary; and 90 miles east of the Mississippi, the western boundary.

This central position, with its delightful location, pointed to Springfield as a most appropriate place for the permanent location of the State Capital, which it became in 1840, by a previous act of the Legislature. From 1818 up to this time it was located at VANDALIA, a town on the west bank of Kaskaskia river, some 70 miles southeast of Springfield. Previous to that time, the Seat of Government was at KASKASKIÀ, also on the west bank of that river, about 100 miles southwest of Vandalia.

The new locations thus successively selected, at each transit of the Capital, indicates pretty fairly the course of the greatest increase of population in this State—in earlier times, its largest portion of population being in the southern part of the State; but latterly, the northern part is getting much the start.

Springfield is located four miles south of the Sangamon

river, on the borders of a broad and charming prairie—adorned with many rich and finely cultivated farms, and elegant rows and groves of planted trees—stretching away in every direction to the blue line of distant forests. It was laid out about the year 1824; and, for the first eight or ten years, contained little else than a few scattered log-cabins; all its present business, wealth, and importance, dating from about the year 1831. Its pleasant, green squares and lawns, with the accompanying shade trees, add vastly to the beauty and comfort of the place; it contains good schools, and splendid public buildings; its population now reaches five or six thousand.

Sangamon is a county of superior land, which is extensively settled and improved. This county has its charms and inspiration for the poet, as will be seen by the following extract:

"All who have visited this fine tract of country admire the beauty of the landscape which nature has painted in primeval freshness. So delightful a region was early selected by immigrants from New England, New York, and North Carolina: more than 200 families had settled themselves here before it was surveyed. It now constitutes several populous counties, inhabited by thriving farmers.

"'Arcadian vales, with vine-hung bowers,
And grassy nooks, 'neath beechen shade,
Where dance the never-resting hours,
To music of the bright cascade;
Skies softly beautiful, and blue,
As Italy's, with stars as bright;
Flowers rich as morning's sunrise hue,
And gorgeous as the gemm'd midnight.
Land of the West! green Forest-Land,
Thus hath Creation's bounteous hand
Upon thine ample bosom flung
Charms such as were her gift when the gray world was young.'

"The prairies frequently contain fine groves of timber, some of which, from their appearance, have received the name of Elk-heart Grove, Buffalo-heart Grove, etc. These groves are generally elevated above the surrounding prairie, and are most advantageous situations for settlements."

Okau River Country.—Another body of nearly as extensive and productive land lies along the course of the Kaskaskia, or Okau river. This stream has a long course through central and southwestern Illinois—a tract of country diversified with prairie and forest. Many of the streams which empty into the Okau have considerable fall, sufficient for mill-sites. Many portions of the country along this river are thickly settled and well cultivated.

Nearly two thirds of this rich and handsome section of the State is prairie, which some people urge as an objection; but the great abundance of coal and peat to be found in the same region, together with the ease with which timber can be floated down the streams, from where it is more plenty, and the rapidity with which locust, walnut, chestnut, and some other varieties of trees can be made to grow, very greatly diminish the inconvenience of sparse forest growths.

Beside, wire fences are cheap, durable, and answer an admirable purpose.

This matter of *wire fences* is becoming an object of considerable attention in the prairie countries, and has been adopted with success and advantage in several locations. The wire can be galvanized, so as to prevent its rusting; or, a still better mode can be adopted, that of affixing little cups or reservoirs at the joints, or other places in the wire, of different metal than the iron, where a small portion of acid or moisture may be constantly deposited, which will keep up, at all times, a slight galvanic current, and will preserve the wire from decay by oxydation, almost entirely.

But when we consider how much lighter is the inconvenience of this lack of timber, than is the task of chopping, logging, and clearing heavy-timbered lands; and how much more pleasant are smooth fields, free of stumps and trees, than are the opposite, we see that, after all, these prairie farms are the most profitable and pleasant, if selected where water for stock is readily procured.

MILITARY BOUNTY TRACT.—The region generally denominated the Military Bounty Tract, was surveyed during the years 1815 and 1816, and the greater part subsequently appropriated in bounties to the soldiers of the regular army, who served in the late war between the United States and Great Britain. It is situated between the rivers Mississippi and Illinois, and extends from their junction due north by a meridian line, denominated the fourth principal meridian, 169 miles, presenting an irregular, curvilinear triangle, the acute angle of which is at the junction of these two rivers. From this point the two rivers diverge, so as to make a distance of 90 miles between the extreme points of the northern boundary. Half way between the extremes, the width is 64 miles. The base line running due east and west, and commencing just above Quincy, on the Mississippi, and terminating at the Illinois, a little below Beardstown, intersects the fourth principal meridian at right angles above the junction of the Mississippi and Illinois rivers.

The whole tract, according to the public surveys, contains 207 entire townships, of six miles square, and 61 fractional townships—altogether 5,360,000 acres, of which 3,500,000 have been appropriated in military bounties.

This tract of country lies between 38° 54' and 41° 40' of north latitude, and 13° west longitude from Washington City, and bounded on the southwest for 255 miles by the Mississippi river, and for about the same distance on the southeast by the Illinois. Thus do these two great rivers, in their diverging course, with Rock river approximating from the north, form a spacious peninsula, furnishing a border to the bounty lands by a sheet of navigable waters for steamboats more than 500 miles in extent, leaving no part of the tract more than 45 miles, and the greater part not exceeding 20 miles from steamboat navigation.

The water communication now completed between the Mississippi and the lakes, by means of the *Illinois and Chicago Canal*, greatly increases the value of the bounty lands, by affording a choice of markets for their products, either at Chicago, Detroit, Buffalo, New York, Montreal, or Quebec, by way of the Illinois Canal and the Lakes, or by the natural channels of the Rivers south, at St. Louis and New Orleans.

In the interior of the tract, traversing it in various directions, are several rivers and creeks of less consequence, in a commercial point of view, but nevertheless of great utility to the settlements in their vicinity. Of these, Spoon, Henderson, Edwards, and Pope's rivers, and Crooked, Kickapoo or Red Bud, Copperas, Otter, McKee's, McCraney's, Hadley's Mill, and Bear creeks, are the most considerable.

About two thirds of this tract is timbered, and the other third is mostly prairie of good quality. It has become considerably settled, and yearly furnishes considerable amounts of products for export. Corn, wheat, barley, hemp, and potatoes, are the principal productions.

Bottom Lands.—Those alluvial lands, along the rivers, in the Eastern States, called "intervals," are termed Bottom Lands, in the West. Portions of them are overflowed part of the year, during high freshets in the rivers. Most of the Western rivers present more or less of this kind of land.

The most extensive tract, of this description, in this State, is the *American Bottom*, a name it received when it constituted the western boundary of the United States, and which it has retained ever since. It commences at the confluence of the Kaskaskia river with the Mississippi, and extends northwardly to the mouth of the Missouri; being bounded on the east by a chain of bluffs, which in some places are sandy and in others rocky, and which vary from

50 to 200 feet in hight. This bottom is about 80 miles in length, and comprises an area of about 450 square miles, or 288,000 square acres. On the margin of the river is a strip of heavy timber, with a rank undergrowth: this extends from a half to two miles in width, and from thence to the bluffs is generally prairie. No soil can exceed this in fertility, many parts of it having been under cultivation for more than a century without apparent deterioration.

The only objection offered to this tract is its unhealthiness. This arises from the circumstance of the lands directly on the margin of the river being higher than those under the bluffs, where the water, after leaving the former, sets back and forms ponds and *lagoons*, which during the summer stagnate and throw off noxious effluvia. These, however, might, at a trifling expense, be drained by lateral canals communicating with the rivers. The first settlement of this State was commenced upon the tract of land above described, and its uncommon fertility gave emigrants a favorable idea of the whole country. Cultivation has, no doubt, done much to render this region more healthy than it formerly was. It will be recollected that a few years ago, Lotteries were numerously got up in the West, declared for the specious purpose of *Draining the American Bottoms;* but we have never learned that they produced any such beneficial results, although many thousand dollars worth of tickets were sold for years.

I will here notice an error of the old inhabitants, in regard to a philosophical fact in vegetation. They recommended the settlers *not to plant corn* near their dwellings on this tract; as its luxuriant growth prevented the sun from dispelling the bad vapors. This is erroneous doctrine; as luxuriant growths of vegetation absorb or take in the carbon and other gases, deleterious to human health, at the same time they give off oxygen, so essential to the existence of life. It is the gases and vapors arising from *dead* and decaying, ***not live***, vegetables which destroy health. Hence, the unhealthiness of the first ***breaking up*** of a new country—it sends up and scatters to the winds clouds of effluvia from long rotted vegetation of years past, which fresh green vegetation will absorb before it can reach man's lungs.

And much on the same grounds, from similar causes, is a region where much fruit blooms and ripens more healthy than before it existed; these orchards taking in from the air (carbon) what man does not want, and giving off (oxygen) what he does need. If only for their salubrious influence, the early planting and raising of orchards in new countries is highly desirable and profitable. The same results do not follow from the proximity of tall natural forests, as they are so high as to shade off the warming, drying operations of the sun, while their chemical operations are carried on, mostly, in an upper stratum or current of air above the region of man's respiring.

These things or principles are highly worthy the careful and extended considerations of farmers, particularly in new countries.

Timbered Land.—As a whole, Illinois is abundantly supplied with timber; and were it equally distributed through the State, there would be no part wanting. The apparent scarcity of timber, where the prairies predominate, is not so great an obstacle to the settlement as has been supposed. For many of the purposes to which timber is applied, substitutes are found. The rapidity with which the young growth pushes itself forward, without a single effort on the part of man, and the readiness with which the prairies become converted into thickets, and then into a forest, shows that, in another generation, timber will not be wanting in any part of Illinois.

The timber of the bottom lands consists of black and white walnut, ash of several species, hackberry, elm (white and slippery), sugar-maple, honey-locust, buck-eye, catalpa, sycamore, cottonwood, pecan, hickory, mulberry; several oaks—as, over-cup, burr-oak, swamp or water oak, white, red, or Spanish oak; and of the shrubbery are red-bud, papaw, grape-vine, eglantine, dog-wood, spice-bush, hazel, greenbrier, etc. Along the margin of the streams the sycamore and cottonwood often predominate, and attain to an amazing size. The cottonwood is of rapid growth, a light, whitewood, sometimes used for rails, shingles, and scantlings; not lasting, and of no great value. Its dry, light wood is much used in steamboats. It forms the chief proportion of the driftwood that floats down the rivers, and is frequently converted into *planters*, *snags*, and *sawyers*. The sycamore is the buttonwood of New England, is frequently hollow, and in that state procured by the farmers, cut at suitable lengths, cleaned out, and used as depositories for grain. It is the *gum-tree* of the negro plantations. They answer the purpose of large casks. The size of the cavity of some of these trees appears incredible in the ears of a stranger to the luxuriant growth of the West. To say that twenty or thirty men could be comfortably lodged in one, would seem a monstrous fiction to a New Englander, but to those accustomed to this species of tree on the bottoms, it is nothing marvelous.

The uplands are covered with various species of oak, among which is the post-oak, a valuable and lasting timber for posts; white oak, black oak of several varieties, and blackjack, a dwarfish, gnarled looking tree, good for nothing but fuel, for which it is equal to any tree we have; of hickory, both the shagbark and smoothbark, black walnut in some parts, white walnut or butternut, Lynn, cherry, and many of the species produced in the bottoms. The black walnut is much used for building materials, and cabinet work, and sustains a fine polish. The different species of oaks, walnuts, hackberry, and occasionally hickory, are used for fencing.

In some parts of the State the white and yellow poplar prevails. Beginning at the Mississippi, a few miles above the mouth of Muddy river, and extending a line to the mouth of Little Wabash, leaves the poplar range south, interspersed with beach. Near the Ohio, on the low creek bottoms, the cypress is found. No poplar exists on the eastern borders of the State till you arrive near Palestine; while on the opposite shore of the Wabash, in Indiana, the poplar and beach predominate.

Of the noble forests of the West; and of the harsh, stern policy of our people, which is fast extinguishing the Aboriginal races of this continent, Miss Frances Fuller has written the following eloquent and beautiful lines:

"Proud *forests!* ye stately old woods of the West,
In what glorious hues are your aged boughs dress'd!
How bravely ye stand in your gorgeous pride,
Decked out in the robes that old autumn hath dyed;
Yet my heart hath grown sadder while gazing on ye,
And list'ning the voices that sigh from each tree,
For they tell of the *red man*—the child of the Wood—
And his form seems to rise in the dim solitude;
And now when the autumn winds sigh through the trees,
His voice haunts my ear with each swell of the breeze;
I hear his low call, and his step stealing by,
The twang of the bow and the bird's sudden cry—
A thousand wild murmurings tremble in air,
And startle my spirit with thrillings of fear;
Yet I love the wild music for breathing the tone
Of ages gone by, and of races long flown.
Old forests! ye stand in your majesty yet,
Bearing proudly the seal by the Deity set."

Among the fine forests and over the beautiful prairie the Indian was wont in his freedom and simple happiness to chase the deer and trap the fur. But where now is he? He has given place to a race with nobler improvements—yet, his destiny is sad.

Rivers.—No State in the Union is so well supplied, in

all parts, with rivers and streams as Illinois, whèther for navigation mill-power, or the purposes of farming, etc.

A glance at the map will show this fact; the several largest rivers, generally holding one common direction, while innumerable smaller ones fall into them from all directions; so that not a county, or scarcely a town, but is sufficiently supplied with water, both for stock and hydraulics.

For the most part I have copied the description of rivers, from "Illinois in 1837;" as in that work they are detailed with great care.

On the West, the State is bounded by the Mississippi. At *St. Anthony's* the real fall of the Mississippi is between sixteen and seventen feet, of perpendicular descent; yet the descent, as the water breaks over different rapids, is considerably more than that. Though it has not the slightest claim to compare with that of *Niagara* in grandeur, it furnishes an impressive and beautiful spectacle in the loneliness of the desert. The adjoining scenery is of the most striking and romantic character.

Below this point, it is bounded by limestone bluffs, from 100 to 400 feet high; and first begins to exhibit islands, driftwood, and sandbars; its current is slightly broken by the Rock river and Des Moines rapids; which, however, present no considerable obstruction to navigation; and 843 miles from the falls its waters are augmented by the immense stream of the Missouri from the west; the latter has, indeed, the longer course, brings down a greater bulk of water, and gives its own character to the united current; yet it loses its name in the inferior stream. Above their junction, the Mississippi is a clear, placid stream, one mile and a half in width; below, it is turbid, and becomes narrower, deeper, and more rapid.

Between the Missouri and the sea, a distance of 1,220 miles, it receives its principal tributaries, the Ohio from the east, and the Arkansas and Red rivers from the west; and immediately below the mouth of the latter, gives off, in times of flood, a portion of its superfluous waters by the outlet of the Atchafalava.

Below here it discharges a portion of its waters by the Lafourche and Iberville; but the great bulk flows on in the main channel, through the flat tract of New Orleans, reaches the sea at the end of a long projecting tongue of mud, deposited by the river. Near the Gulf of Mexico, it divides into several channels, called *passes*, with bars at their mouths. The water is 12 to 16 feet deep and muddy, and colors those of the Gulf for the distance of several leagues.

The river begins to rise in the early part of March, and continues to increase irregularly to the middle of June, generally overflowing its banks to a greater or less extent, although for some years these have not been inundated. Above the Missouri, the flooded bottoms are from five to eight miles wide, but below that point, they expand by the recession of the river hills from the channel, to a breadth of from 40 to 50 miles. From the mouth of the Ohio, the whole western bank does not offer a single spot eligible for the site of a considerable town; on the eastern side, there are several points where the hills approach the river, and afford good town-sites; but from Memphis to Vicksburg, 365 miles, the whole tract consists of low grounds; and below Baton Rouge, where the line of upland wholly leaves the river, and passes off to the east, there is no place on the river border which is higher than the marshy tract in its rear.

The Mississippi is obstructed by *planters, sawyers*, and *wooden islands*, which are frequently the cause of injury, and even destruction, to the boats which navigate it. Planters are large bodies of trees firmly fixed by their roots in the bottom of the river, one of their ends appearing about one foot above the surface of the water, when at its medium hight.

The principal tributaries of the Mississippi, within the State of Illinois, are Rock, Illinois, Kaskaskia, and Big Muddy Rivers.

At latitude 39° comes in the *Illinois*, from the north, a noble, broad, and navigable stream of 400 yards in width, having a course in the State of about 400 miles, and navigable most of that distance.

Near latitude 38°, some 500 miles below the north line of the State, the *Kaskaskia*, from the east, enters the Mississippi; it is 150 yards wide, is some 300 miles in length, and is navigable about one third of that distance. Cotton and tobacco have been raised on its banks.

Above 40 miles farther down, the *Big Muddy* comes in from the north, discovered and named by the French, *Rivière au Vase ou Vaseux;* it is capable of navigation for small craft some distance, and its banks afford large quantities of coal, together with valuable salines.

In latitude 37° north comes in the splendid *Ohio*, which is the largest eastern tributary of the Mississippi; it constitutes the southern boundary of the State, and from the beauty of the country through which it passes, has been called *La Belle Rivière.*

Cairo is a town at the junction of this river with the Mississippi; and is destined to be a place of great commercial importance, as it is the southern terminus of the Illinois Central Railroad, and place of crossing for the extension to the Gulf of Mexico of the Chicago and Mobile Road. In due time enterprise and art will improve over the apparent disadvantages of nature, and a large, wealthy, commercial city must grow up at the junction of the great Rivers and the Railroad.

Between 41° and 42°, *Rock* river from the north enters the Mississippi; its general course is southwest, and it is navigable some ways up, in some seasons of the year. I have been informed, that one season, some 1,200,000 lbs. of lead was shipped from the Mineral region, down this river, by Captain Gear, who run the first Steamboat up Rock river from the Mississippi.

These are the largest rivers of Illinois that fall into the Mississippi, though there are some smaller ones, as Henderson, Pope, Fevre, etc.

The principal rivers which empty into the Ohio from Illinois are the *Wabash*, *Saline*, and *Cash*. The first of these rise in Indiana, and running down the eastern border of the State enters the Ohio about 200 miles above Cairo; it is near 600 miles in length, and is navigable much of that distance; it presents one considerable rapid a short distance below Vincennes. The principal tributaries of this river are Embarrass, Vermillion, and Little Wabash. The Embarrass rises in Champaign county and vicinity, and is about 150 miles long. The Vermillion rises about Vermillion and Livingston counties, and runs southeast into the Wabash. The Little Wabash rises in Gallatin county, is about 140 miles long, and is navigable some distance for flat boats and rafts.

The shores of the Ohio, from Pittsburg to the mouth of the Wabash, are high rocky bluffs; but below that, low and subject to be overflowed. The estimated elevation of this river at Pittsburg is 678 feet, and that of low water, at its confluence with the Mississippi, 283 feet in 949 miles, the length of the intermediate channel, making an average descent of a little over five inches in a mile. Since the *Louisville* and *Portland Canal* has been completed, steamboats of small draft can descend at all times from Pittsburg to the Mississippi. Flat and keel boats descend the river at all seasons, but in periods of low water with frequent groundings on the sandbars, and the necessity of often unloading to get the boat off.

The inundations, as on the Mississippi, are occasionally sources of disease, and in many cases impediments to improvement. There are, however, some elevated situations which afford good town-sites, and which must become places of considerable importance. It is much to be regretted, that at the confluence of the Ohio and Mississippi there is an extensive recently formed alluvion, which is annually inundated, and which cannot, without immense expense, be made an eligible town-site.

Some 35 or 45 miles below the junction of the Kankakee and O'Plain, Fox river enters the Illinois from the north. Both above and below the mouth of this stream, there is a succession of rapids in the Illinois, with intervals of deep and smooth water. From the mouth of Fox river to the foot of the rapids is nine miles, the descent, in all, eight feet; the rock is soft sandstone mixed with gravel and shelly limestone. Nine miles above Fox river, the grand rapids commence, and extend ten or twelve miles. They are formed by ledges of rocks in the river and rocky islands. The whole descent from the surface of Lake Michigan at Chicago to the foot of the rapids, a distance of ninety-four and a quarter miles, is one hundred and forty-one feet and eighty-seven hundredths.

At the foot of the rapids the Vermillion river enters the Illinois from the south, by a mouth of about fifty yards wide; it is an excellent mill stream, and runs through extensive beds of bituminous coal. Some fine groves, and extensive prairies, and at different points superb mills and factories have been erected.

The *Sangamon* is one of the interior rivers, which empties into the Illinois a short distance below Beardstown, and is one of the chief branches of that river; it is about 180 miles long, of which about 120 miles are navigable for small craft. Spoon river is another large tributary of the Illinois.

There are but slight and few bars or other impediments to the navigation of the Illinois; and an effort is now being made by those interested to have them removed, and to induce Congress to grant some aid to the project.

Minerals.—Lead, coal, salt, iron, zinc, copper, and lime are the principal and most abundant minerals found in Illinois; some of which are numerous and a source of large revenue; though the deeper earth and rock foundations have not generally been thoroughly explored.

Lead is found in the northwestern part of the state in vast quantities. The Indians and French had been long accustomed to procure small quantities of the ore, but it was not until about the year 1822 that the process of separating the metal was begun to be carried on scientifically. Since that time, up to the end of 1835, 70,420,357 pounds of lead have been made here, and upward of 13,000,000 pounds have been smelted in one year; but the business having been overdone, the product has since been much less. In 1833, it was 7,941,792 pounds; in 1834, 7,971,579; and in 1835, only 3,754,290. This statement includes the produce of Wisconsin as well as of Illinois. The rent accruing to government for the same period, is a fraction short of 6,000,000 pounds. Formerly, the government received ten per cent. in lead for rents. Now it is six per cent.

Formerly the Mineral Lands were rented and not in market; but they have since been bought and worked as private property, and the product has been greatly increased thereby.

Iron ore has been found in the southern parts of the state, and is said to exist in considerable quantities also in the north.

Native copper, in large quantities, exists in the northern part of the state, especially at the mouth of Plum creek, and on the Peckatonica. It is also found in small quantities on Muddy river, in Jackson county, and back of Harrisonville, in the bluffs of rivers in Monroe county, to some small extent.

In this connection it may be proper to mention a petrified or fossil curiosity which attracts considerable attention. It is on the banks of the O'Plain, a short distance above its junction with the Kankakee; it is a fossil tree, of a very considerable size. It is a species of *phytolites*, and is embedded in a horizontal position in a stratum of *newer floetz* sandstone, of a gray color and close grain. There are about fifty-one feet of the trunk visible. It is eighteen inches in diameter.

As to the precious metals, some indications appear, and some specimens have been found. Silver is supposed to exist in St. Clair county, two miles from Rock Spring, whence Silver creek derives its name. In the early times the French sunk a shaft here, and tradition tells of large quantities of the precious metal being obtained. In the southern part of the state, several sections of land were reserved from sale, on account of the silver ore they were supposed to contain. Marble of a fine quality is found in Randolph county. Crystalized gypsum has been found in small quantities in St. Clair county. Quartz crystals exist in Gallatin and other counties.

Bituminous coal abounds in this state, and may be found in nearly every county. It is frequently found without excavation, in the ravines and at the points of bluffs. Vast beds of this mineral exist in the bluffs adjacent to the American Bottom.

Several large veins of coal, and apparently exhaustless, have been struck in excavating the Illinois and Michigan Canal. A bed of anthracite coal, it is said, has been discovered on Muddy river in Jackson county.

Muriate of soda, or common salt, has been found in various parts of the state, held in solution in the springs.

The manufacture of salt by boiling and evaporation is carried on in Gallatin county, 12 miles west northwest from Shawneetown; in Jackson county, near Brownsville; and in Vermillion county, near Danville. The springs and land are owned by the State, and the works leased. A coarse freestone, much used in building, is dug from quarries, near Alton, on the Mississippi, where large bodies exist.

Medicinal waters are found in different parts of the state. These are chiefly sulphur springs and chalybeate waters. There is said to be one well in the southern part of the state strongly impregnated with the sulphate of magnesia, or Epsom salts, from which considerable quantities have been made for sale, by simply evaporating the water, in a kettle, over a common fire. There are several sulphur springs in Jefferson county, to which persons resort for health.

Between Ottowa and Peru some fine mineral springs exist, which are supposed to be highly beneficial for medicinal purposes. I have never seen an analysis of their ingredients, and cannot speak more definitely.

Productions of Soil.—All the grains, fruits, and roots of the temperate regions of the earth grow luxuriantly in Illinois; the wheat is of excellent quality, and there is no part of the Western Country where corn is raised with greater ease and abundance. Garden vegetables of all kinds succeed well. No country can exceed this for fruit-bearing shrubs. Wild fruits and berries are in many places abundant, and on some of the prairies the strawberries are remarkably fine.

In most parts of the state, grape-vines, indigenous to the country, are abundant, yielding grapes that might advantageously be made into excellent wine. Foreign vines are susceptible of easy cultivation. Wild vines are found in every variety of soil, interwoven in every thicket in the prairies and barrens, and climbing to the tops of the very highest trees on the bottoms. The French in early times made so much wine as to export some to France; upon which the proper authorities prohibited, about the year 1774, the introduction of wine from Illinois, lest it might injure the sale of that staple article of the kingdom. At Peoria, Peru, and Chicago they do well.

Plums, of various sizes and flavor, grow in great abundance; their color is generally red, and their taste delicious. In some locations, acres of these trees exhibit a surface of the color of rubies, others bright-yellow and blue: the quantities of fruit are prodigious.

Crab-apples are also very prolific, and make fine preserves. Wild cherries are equally productive. The persimmon is a delicious fruit, after the frost has destroyed its astringent properties. The black mulberry grows in most parts, and is used for the feeding of silk-worms with success. They appear to thrive and spin as well as on the Italian mulberry. The cranberry, huckleberry, gooseberry, wild currant, strawberry, and blackberry grow wild and in great profusion. Of nuts, the hickory, butternut, black walnut, and peccan, deserve notice. The last is an oblong, thin-shelled, delicious nut, that grows on a large tree, a species of the hickory. The papaw grows in the bottom and rich-timbered uplands, and produces a large, pulpy, and luscious fruit.

Of domestic fruits, the apple and peach are chiefly cultivated. Pears are tolerably plentiful in some settlements, and quinces are cultivated with success. Apples are easily cultivated, and are very productive of large size.

The cultivated vegetable productions in the field are corn, wheat, oats, barley, buckwheat, potatoes, sweet potatoes, turnips, rye, tobacco, cotton, hemp, flax, the castor-bean, and every other production common to the middle states. Indian corn is a staple production. No farmer can live without it, and hundreds raise little else. This is chiefly owing to the ease with which it is cultivated. Its average yield is fifty bushels to the acre. Oftentimes the product amounts to seventy-five bushels to the acre, and in some instances has exceeded one hundred. Corn is generally planted about the first of May, often earlier.

The sugar beet, ruta baga, and cabbages, are raised with great ease, and of very large yield; while the sweet potato is cultivated by many to considerable profit; the only difficulty being that of preserving the seed through the winter, which is easily done, if understood.

Climate.—The climate of Illinois is such as would be naturally expected from the latitude in which it lies. The thermometer does not range more widely here than in similar parallels east of the Alleghany mountains; nor perhaps as much so as in those districts beyond the influence of the sea-breeze. There is every day a breeze, from some quarter of the broad prairies, almost as refreshing as that from the ocean; the easterly winds, so chilling and so annoying along the Atlantic sea-board are seldom; but breezes from the prairies are annoying to the traveler when the mercury is at zero.

The winter commences in December, and ends in February. Its duration and temperature are variable. The winters generally exhibit a temperature of climate somewhat milder than those of the Atlantic states in the same latitude. Snow rarely falls to the depth of six inches, and as rarely remains more than ten or twelve days. There are, however, occasional short periods of very cold weather; but they seldom continue longer than three or four days at a time. The Mississippi is sometimes frozen over and passed on the ice at St. Louis, and occasionally for several weeks together. The year 1811 was remarkable for the river closing over twice—a circumstance which had not occurred before within the memory of the oldest inhabitant.

During the winter of '49–50, there was nearly three months continuous sleighing in Illinois, Wisconsin, and Iowa; a circumstance which had not occurred before for many years. The writer of this, during that winter, crossed the Mississippi in a sleigh on the ice, at Rock Island, in the first week of January; and he crossed it as far down as Keokuk, on the ice, as late as the first week in March, of the same winter. At Chicago, and along the Canal, the holidays were made the more merry by fine sleigh-riding, which is very unusual in that region. Still, the winters in these States are on the average much milder and more favorable to stock than in similar latitudes at the East.

The summers are warm, though during the sultry months the intensity of heat is modified by a free course everywhere to genial breezes, constantly giving to the atmosphere a refreshing elasticity. During this season, the appearance of the country is gay and beautiful, being clothed with grass, foliage, and flowers, of endless hues and fragrance.

Of all the seasons of the year, the autumn is the most delightful. The heat of the summer is over by the middle of August; and from that time till December, there is almost one continuous succession of bright, clear, delightful sunny days, flecked with fitful clouds. Nothing can exceed the beauty of summer and autumn in this country, where, on one hand, we have the expansive prairie strewed with flowers still growing; and on the other, the forests which skirt it, presenting all the varieties of color incident to the fading foliage of a thousand different trees.

About the middle of October or beginning of November, the Indian Summer commences, and continues from fifteen to twenty days. During this time, the weather is bland but languid, the atmosphere is smoky, and the sun and moon give a mellowed light, and are sometimes almost totally obscured. It is generally supposed that this is caused by the burning of the withered grass and herbs on the extensive prairies of the north and west, which also accounts for its increased duration as we proceed westward. The softened lights, the serene breezes, and the mystic haziness, which envelops every thing, and seems to place all objects at an unusual remoteness from the observer, during the, not sad, but pensive season of Indian Summer, is like the approach of a good man's last days, as he looks toward the grave, after a useful and upright life, ripened into usefulness; and through the mystic clouds of death the sun is but dimly seen; yet, his brightness beyond is no less certain, to this good man's anticipations—he sees his heavenly reward garnered in mansions where thieves steal not, as is faintly and imperfectly emblemmed by the bountiful harvest which is now stored in the granaries of the faithful husbandman, for winter's need.

"I saw an aged man upon his bier:
His hair was thin and white, and on his brow
A record of the cares of many a year—
Cares that were ended and forgotten now—
And there was sadness round and faces bowed,
And women's tears fell fast and children wailed aloud.

"Why weep ye so for him, who having run
The bound of man's appointed years, at last,
Life's blessings all enjoyed, life's labors all done,
Serenely to his final rest has passed,
While the soft memory of his virtues yet
Lingers, like twilight hues, when the bright sun is set?"

Persons who have not lived in Illinois, to know by personal observation, may judge something of the climate and seasons in that region, from the following statement:

For the last fifteen years, in Central Illinois, peach trees have blossomed, at different dates in the several years, from the 25th of March to the 20th of April. Strawberries blossomed about the same time. Apple trees put forth leaves from the 1st to the 20th of April; they blossom from the 10th of April to the 3d of May, and meet with no after frosts.

Prairies began to be green and furnish pasture from the 10th of March to the 15th of April. Forests put forth leaves, half size, from the 5th of April to the 10th of May; full size from the 22d of April to the 14th of May.

Last frosts in spring, from as early as the 16th of April to as late as the 7th of May.

During the same period, the earliest frost of autumn was about the 17th of September, and some years it did not appear till as late as the 23d of October; and from year to year alternating between those dates. So that the seasons are uniformly long enough to ripen the large Mississippi corn, which requires three to four weeks more time than the varieties of corn usually grown in New York and New England. On the rich prairies and river bottoms, this corn often grows to the hight of 13 to 15 feet, with three ears to the stalk; frequently yielding from 70 to 100 bushels per acre. From 30 to 70 bushels of oats; 20 to 40 bushels of wheat; and 300 to 600 bushels of potatoes per acre are obtained.

From the latitude of the mouth of Rock river, down to the latitude of the mouth of Illinois river, the climate, in blandness and freedom from frost, is as favorable as at New York or Long Island; and the more delicate or tender fruits may be raised as successfully, and of as good flavors, if the same care and labor is put forth to procure the best varieties, and then in culturing them. Melons, peas, raddishes, and squashes, come forward as early, and of as good quality, as those raised on Long Island or the Jersey shore.

The following statements of population, etc., in the counties are taken mostly from the United States census returns of 1850:

Alexander is the most southern county in the State, and comprises the peninsula between the Mississippi and Ohio rivers; in which Cairo and Unity are situated; it is well timbered, the soil fertile but low, and parts of it subject to inundation; and is watered by Cash river, a small stream emptying into the Ohio. Population, 2,484; dwellings, 455; farms, 202; manufactories, 8.

Its county-seat is THEBES, situated on the east bank of the Mississippi. In this county, near this ancient city, is a circular lake, called *Horseshoe* lake from its shape.

Adams county, and QUINCY, its county-seat, were described in the Mississippi tour; it is a superior county of land, and QUINCY, one of the finest cities in the State; population between six and seven thousand. Population of county, 26,508; dwellings, 4,459; farms, 2,294; manufactories, 118. Ashton, Fairfield, Columbus, and Liberty, are among the other towns of this county.

Bond county is watered by Kaskaskia river and its branches; the surface is gently undulating, with a due proportion of prairie and timbered land; some coal is found in this county along the banks of Shoal creek. Population, 6,144; dwellings, 1,070; farms, 665; manufactories, 17.

GREENVILLE, a pleasant and thriving town, located on the east fork of Shoal creek, is the county-seat.

Boone county lies on the north line of the State, and is watered by the Kishwaukee, Piscasaw, Peckatonica, and other smaller streams. The soil is of the best quality, undulating, and divided between prairies and timber; and in general agricultural resources, is scarcely inferior to any county in the State. Population, 7,626; dwellings, 1,352; farms, 897; manufactories, 17.

BELVIDERE, the county-seat, is a pleasant town, situated

on the Kishwaukee; it is a flourishing town of over two thousand population, and is on the line of Railroad from Chicago to Galena, which is to be completed to this place during the present winter. In one edge of this town is a large *mound;* the cemetery of *Big Thunder*, an Indian Chief, is on this mound; he died near the close of the Black Hawk war; and was placed on a grass and weed mat, in a sitting posture, stayed up with sticks, wrapped in his blanket, with his knife, hatchet, etc., at his side; he was also supplied with tobacco and provisions to sustain him on his trip to the Spirit Land; a frame-work of poles, covered with grass and earth, was built over him. It was near this village that Mrs. Towner so heroically destroyed three Indans, who assailed her log cabin, in the absence of her husband. There are several other small towns here, as Amesville, Amazon, Cleveland, and Cherry Valley.

Bureau is a new county, lying on the west bank of the Illinois, with Bureau creek running through it. It contains much excellent prairie, with a fair share of good timber. Population, 8,413; dwellings, 1,464; farms, 741; manufactories, 20.

Princeton, the county-seat, is a pleasant town, located in the midst of a fine prairie, with some groves in the vicinity, and near Bureau and Indian Creeks. Lamoile, located in the borders of a fine grove, is a pleasant town.

Brown county is an excellent one, lying on the west bank of the Illinois river; it is well watered by McKee creek and smaller streams; it contains fine groves and prairie lands, much of which is well cultivated. Population, 7,198; dwellings, 1,353; farms, 818; manufacts., 73.

Mount Sterling, a pleasant and flourishing village, situated in the border of a beautiful grove, is the county-seat. Chambersburg, Milton, New York, Richmond, with some others, are the principal villages of this county.

Calhoun county occupies the most southern part of the

Military Bounty tract, and is a long narrow piece of land lying between the Mississippi and Illinois rivers, where considerable tracts are subject to inundation, and in the interior are bluffs, ravines, and sink holes; still there are some tracts of good land, and the bottoms furnish excellent range for stock; cattle, beef, pork, corn, honey, and beeswax are its exports; coal in large bodies is found on the Mississippi. Population, 3,231; dwellings, 600; farms, 205; shops, 5.

HARDIN, the county-seat, is a smart town, and advantageously located on the west bank of the Illinois river. Gilead and Gilford were, respectively, the county-seat at earlier dates; and are well situated for prosperity and business on the Illinois.

Cass county is the smallest in the State, except Wabash; it lies on the east side of the Illinois, and south of the Sangamon river; the land is of the best quality, fairly divided into prairie and timber. Population, 7,253; dwellings, 1,169; farms, 606; manufactories, 26.

BEARDSTOWN, the county-seat, is situated on the Illinois, and is a pleasant, flourishing town. There are some other thriving towns in this county, as Verginia and Bath.

Champaign county is watered by the head streams of Sangamon, Kaskaskia, and Big Vermillion rivers; and contains large prairies, bordered by fine groves of good timber, with a rich soil. Population, 2,649; dwellings, 480; farms, 273; shops, 6.

URBANNA is the county-seat, situated on the Salt fork of the Vermillion, and is a prosperous village. This county has some other towns of considerable growth, as Van Buren, Union, and Sidney.

Cook county, and CHICAGO, are described in the lake and canal districts. Persons going to that region for the purpose of buying land, or dealing in produce, will do well to call upon MR. CHARLES R. STARKWATHER, of Chicago; Mr.

S. has had a long and extensive acquaintance in the West, is a gentlemanly, reliable business man, and is largely connected with such business. Population of Cook county, 43,385; dwellings, 7,674; farms, 1,857; manufactories, 227. Other towns are Wheeling and Gross Point.

Cumberland county is located west of Clarke, and is watered by the Embarrass and its branches; it is a small, new county, and contains considerable prairie, with some timber. Population, 3,720; dwellings, 634; farms, 326; shops, 5.

GREENUP is the county-seat, a young and growing town, well situated on the Embarrass river. Woodbury is another town in this county.

Clarke county is situated on the Wabash, opposite to Terre Haute, Indiana; it is watered by the north fork of the Embarrass, and contains both prairie and timbered land, of good soil. Population, 9,532; dwellings, 1,621; farms, 636; manufactories, 14.

DARWIN, county-seat, is a flourishing town on the Wabash. Marshall, on the National Road, was formerly the county-seat. Martinsville, Livingston, Melrose, etc., are other towns.

Clay county is a small one, on the Little Wabash; its land is of a good quality, and divided between timber and prairie. Population, 4,289; dwellings, 715; farms, 237; manufactories, 6.

MAYSVILLE, county-seat, is situated on the border of Twelvemile Prairie, near the Little Wabash. Louisville and other towns are in the county.

Clinton county is watered by the Kaskaskia river, Shoal and Sugar creeks; its land is good prairie and timber. Population, 5,139; dwellings, 947; farms, 628; manufactories, 8.

CARLYSLE, the county-seat, is situated on the west bank of the Kaskaskia, and is a thriving town.

Coles county lies in the eastern part of the state, and is watered by the Embarrass, and head waters of the Kaskaskia, which in some places afford good mill-sites; the land is rolling, divided between prairie and timber. Population, 9,335; dwellings, 1,571; farms, 996; shops, 6.

CHARLESTON is the county-seat, handsomely situated on Grand Prairie, near the Embarrass river.

Christian county is one of the new counties, and is watered by the south fork of Sangamon river; it contains much fine prairie and some good timber. Population, 3,202; dwellings, 555; farms, 434; manufactories, 12.

TAYLORVILLE is the county-seat, situated on the river. Bethany, Stonington, Sylvan Grove, and Mount Auburn, are other fine towns in this county.

Crawford county lies on the Wabash river, and contains a large proportion of good prairie land; its streams are the branches of the Wabash and Embarrass. Population, 7,135; dwellings, 1,192; farms, 542; shops, 8.

PALESTINE, situated on a fine prairie, is the county-seat. There are other thriving towns in the county, as Robinson, Hutsonville, and York, the latter on the Wabash.

Carroll county, and SAVANNAH, were noticed in the tour up the Mississippi. Population, 4,586; dwellings, 814; farms, 482; manufactories, 17.

Edgar county lies on the Wabash, and contains portions of prairie and timber of good quality, with considerable good cultivation. Population, 10,692; dwellings, 1,702; farms, 1,175; manufactories, 38.

PARIS, the county-seat, is advantageously situated on a fine prairie, and surrounded by good farms. Other towns are Bloomfield, Ono, Grandview, and Florence.

Edwards county lies on the Little Wabash, and is farther watered by the Bon Pas; the soil is mostly high and rolling prairie, with some timber. Population, 3,524; dwellings, 595; farms, 329; manufactories, 7.

ALBION, the county-seat, occupies a healthy and handsome position on a high prairie.

Effingham county is situated on the Little Wabash, and embraces considerable good land, generally very level. Population, 3,799; dwellings, 712; farms, 391; shops, 6.

EWINGTON, the county-seat, is advantageously situated on the National Road. Freemantown is another village in this county.

De Kalb is a long county, lying in the north part of the state, and west of Kane; it is watered by branches of the Kishwaukee and Fox rivers; its soil consists of the best kind of prairie, with some good timber, and a rolling surface, which presents many fine farms.

SYCAMORE, the county-seat, is a pleasant town on the prairie, near a clear brook, making altogether a delightful location. The other towns of the county are Genoa, Syracuse, and Little Rock.

Dupage county, with its county-seat NAPERVILLE, are described in the Canal Route. Population, 9,290; dwellings, 1,568; farms, 960; manufactories, 18. Other towns in the county are Brush Hill and Cottage Hill.

De Witt is a new county, and lies on the head streams of the Sangamon river; about equally divided between timber and prairie of good quality. Population, 5,002; dwellings, 881; farms, 482; manufactories, 18.

The county-seat is DE WITT, situated pleasantly on a prairie. The other towns are Clinton, Franklin, Waynesville, Marion, and Mount Pleasant.

Fayette county was one of the large counties, and has been divided into several; it is watered by the Kaskaskia and branches; portions of it are subject to inundations; it contains both good timber and prairie. Population, 8,075; dwellings, 1,431; farms, 826; manufactories, 4.

VANDALIA, formerly capital of the state, situated on the

Kaskaskia, is the county-seat. There are some other smaller towns in the county.

Franklin county is one of the southern counties of the state, on the Big Muddy river, and branches of Saline creek; it is heavily timbered, with but small prairies; portions of the county are subject to inundations. Population, 5,681; dwellings, 971; farms, 577; shops, 6.

BENTON is the county-seat, situated on the Big Muddy. Frankfort was previously county-seat.

Fulton is a very wealthy county, and occupies a portion of the Bounty Tract, west of Illinois river; the land is of a good quality, about equally divided between timber and prairie, and is watered by Spoon river and Apple creek; it contains many thriving villages and superior farms, as Fairview, Bernadotte, Farmington, Liverpool, Canton, Utica, and others. Population, 22,508; dwellings, 3,811; farms, 1,942; manufactories, 104.

LEWISTON, the county-seat, is a growing town, situated in the midst of good timber, west of Illinois river. Fulton is one of the most thriving counties in the state, having a triangular form, its longest side lying along Illinois river.

Gallatin county is located in the southeast corner of the state, at the junction of the Wabash with the Ohio; it contains a large proportion of timbered land, which is particularly valuable on account of its contiguity to the *salt springs:* these are situated on Saline creek, about 20 miles above its junction with the Ohio river. The principal spring was formerly possessed by the Indians, who called it the "Great Salt Spring:" and it appears that they had been long acquainted with the method of making salt. Large fragments of earthen-ware are continually found near the works, both on and under the surface of the earth. They have on them the impression of basket or wicker work. These Salines furnish quantities of salt for home consumption, but little for exportation.

In a treaty between the United States, and the Delaware, Shawanee, Pottawattomee, Eel River, Weea, Kickapoo, and Piankasaw Indians, at FORT WAYNE, on the 7th of June, 1803, this Saline was ceded to the United States, with a quantity of land, not exceeding four miles, surrounding it; in consideration of which, the United States engaged to deliver annually to the said Indians a quantity of salt not exceeding 150 bushels, to be divided among the several tribes in such a manner as the General Council of Chiefs should determine. For a number of years it was possessed by the United States, with a reservation of 161 sections of land in the vicinity, the whole of which were ceded in 1818 to the State of Illinois, by whom it was leased to different individuals for about 10,000 dollars per annum. The works are situated on section 20, township 9, south range 8, east of the third principal meridian. Saline river is navigable to the works, and the surplus salt is thus shipped to Southern markets.

This part of Illinois is well adapted to the growth of stock; large amounts of horses, beef, pork, cattle, lumber, and tobacco, are sent out of the county. Population, 5,448; dwellings, 1,000; farms, 570; manufactories, 17.

The seat of justice is EQUALITY, on the east side of Saline creek. It is situated in the midst of the salt manufactories, fourteen miles northeast from Shawneetown, which is the principal commercial depot in the southern part of Illinois, and is situated on the west bank of the Ohio, some miles below the mouth of the Wabash; and it will be recollected that Shawneetown is distinguished with the history of the Illinois State Bank.

Greene county is located on the east bank of the Illinois, and is watered by Apple and Macoupin creeks; it contains a large proportion of timber, with small undulating prairies, constituting beautiful landscapes. Population, 12,429; dwellings, 2,024; farms, 1,155; manufactories, 27.

Carrolton is the county-seat, situated in the midst of a fine prairie, and is a flourishing town. There are several other fine towns in the county, as Albany, Bluffdale, Fayette, Greenfield, Newton, Kane, Whitehall, and others.

Grundy, a new county, with Morris its county-seat, are described in the Canal district.

Hamilton county is watered by Little Wabash river and Saline creek ; and contains both timber and prairie. Population, 6,362 ; dwellings, 1,058 ; farms, 417 ; shops, 6.

McLeansboro is the county-seat, and situated in the edge of timber and prairie, on the high ground at the head waters of the Saline.

Hancock county, and Carthage, are described in the Mississippi tour. Population, 14,652 ; dwellings, 2,585 ; farms, 1,167 ; manufactories, 43.

Henry county was laid off from Knox, and is watered by Rock and Green rivers ; its lands are good, consisting of fair portions of prairie and grove ; and presents many fine farms. Population, 3,807 ; dwellings, 772 ; farms, 281.

Cambridge, the county-seat, is situated in a pleasant prairie. Geneseo, Andover, Richmond, Oxford, Lagrange, and others, are the principal towns.

Henderson is a new county, lying on the Mississippi, and in the Bounty Tract ; it is watered by Henderson river, and several creeks ; the land is of good quality, both prairie and timber. Population, 4,612 ; dwellings, 805 ; farms, 420 ; manufactories, 27.

Oquawka, the county-seat, is situated on the Mississippi, and is a place of considerable business ; Henderson, Benton, Warren, and other towns are in this county.

Hardin county is a new one, taken off from Pope, and located in the southeast part of the State, on the Ohio ; its lands are fair, both prairie and timber ; and is drained by Saline river.

The *Cave in Rock* is well known to all navigators of the

Ohio river; it is situated on the bank of the west river, about 30 miles below the mouth of the Wabash. It is a large cave, supposed by the Indians to be the habitation of the Great Spirit.

The following description of this cave is given by Thaddeus M. Harris, an English tourist, who visited it in the spring of 1803:

"For about three or four miles before you come to this place, you are presented with a scene truly romantic. On the Illinois side of the river, you see large ponderous rocks piled one upon another, of different colors, shapes, and sizes. Some appear to have gone through the hands of the most skillful artist; some represent the ruins of ancient edifices; others thrown promiscuously in and out of the river, as if nature intended to show us with what ease she could handle those mountains of solid rock. In some places you see purling streams winding their course down their rugged front; while in others, the rocks project so far, that they seem almost disposed to leave their doubtful situations. After a short relief from this scene, you come to a second, which is something similar to the first; and here, with strict scrutiny, you can discover the cave. Before its mouth stands a delightful grove of cypress trees, arranged immediately on the bank of the river. They have a fine appearance, and add much to the cheerfulness of the place.

"The mouth of the cave is but a few feet above the ordinary level of the river, and is formed by a semicircular arch of about 80 feet at its base, and 25 feet in hight, the top projecting considerably over, forming a regular concave. From the entrance to the extremity, which is about 180 feet, it has a regular and gradual ascent. On either side is a solid bench of rock; the arch coming to a point about the middle of the cave, where you discover an opening sufficiently large to receive the body of a man, through which comes a small stream of fine water, made use of by those who visit this place. From this hole a second cave is discovered, whose dimensions, form, etc., are not known. The rock is of limestone. The sides of the cave are covered with inscriptions, names of persons, dates, etc. Part of the trees have been cut down, and the entrance into the cave exposed to view."

In 1797, this cave was the place of resort and security to *Mason*, a notorious robber, and his gang, who were accustomed to plunder and murder the crews of boats, while descending the Ohio; and has been a place of concealment, resorted to by thieves and robbers, even at a much more recent period, as the pioneers in that region, and unfortunate boatmen on the river, often attest to their loss. Population of Hardin county, 2,887; dwellings, 2,585; farms, 1,167.

Elizabeth is the county-seat, a flourishing village on the Ohio. There are some other towns in this county, as Twitchelburg, Illinois Furnace, and Rockincave. The Tennessee river enters the Ohio opposite this county. The general aspect of the river shores, through most of this section of country, presents many curious objects to the eye of the traveler.

Iroquois county is located on the east border of the State; it is watered by Iroquois river, and several creeks; the land is mostly good prairie, with some timber and sand ridges. Population, 4,149; dwellings, 718; farms, 387.

Montgomery is the county-seat, pleasantly situated on the south bank of the Iroquois. Among the other towns, are Milford and Iroquois City.

Jackson county is in the southern part of the State, on the Mississippi; it is watered by the Big Muddy river; the surface of the county is mostly timbered, though it contains many prairies. Muddy river, running through the interior of the county, is navigable for a considerable distance, and affords to the inhabitants every facility for exporting their surplus produce. On this stream there is a *saline*, or salt spring, where considerable quantities of salt are manufactured. A large body of excellent coal exists on this stream. The bed is said to be inexhaustible.

The *Fountain Bluff*, frequently called the "Big Hill," in the southwest corner of the county, is a singularly formed eminence, on the Mississippi, eight miles above the mouth of the Big Muddy. It is of an oval shape, six miles in circumference, and with an elevation of 300 feet. The western side is on the river, and the top is broken, full of sink holes, with shrubs and scattering trees. The north side is nearly perpendicular rock, but the south side is sloping, and ends in a fine rich tract of soil, covered with farms. East is an extensive and low bottom, with lakes and swamps. Fine springs of limpid water gush out from the foot of this bluff on all sides. Population, 5,862; dwellings, 1,038; farms, 604; manufactories, 23.

MURPHRYSBORO is the county-seat, situated on the Big Muddy, a thriving town; Brownville was formerly the county-seat; Vergennes and Liberty are other towns of this county.

Jasper county lies on the Embarrass, and is also watered by some other streams; it contains fertile tracts of prairie and timber, with some wet lands. Population, 3,220; dwellings, 588; farms, 283.

NEWTON, situated on the Embarrass, is the county-seat; Ste. Marie and Rosehill are two other villages in this county.

Jefferson county contains a large proportion of prairie, and lies about half way between the Mississippi and Wabash; it is watered by Big Muddy and Little Wabash. Population, 8,109; dwellings, 1,368; farms, 470; manufactories, 2.

MOUNT VERNON, the county-seat, is situated on a small stream in the edge of a fine prairie, and is a pleasant, thriving village.

Jo Daviess, and GALENA, are described in the Mineral region. Population, 18,604. Persons visiting Galena, or this county, for the purpose of buying lands, or lots, or speculating in lead, will do well to call on Mr. WILLIAM HEMPSTEAD, a gentleman of long experience in this region, and an excellent, reliable business man; having his office in Galena.

In prospecting and sinking shafts for the lead mineral, or *galena*—which is the most proper name—after penetrating the earth from 40 to 70 and even 100 feet, the miner sometimes finds himself in caverns, of different dimensions, from the size of a small room to that of several rods in extent. Sometimes he strikes a crevice, which affords space barely sufficient to crowd the body through, and this passage often leads to a cavern.

Many of these subterranean apartments present scenes of curious and brilliant splendor; from the various *crystalizations* found in them; with various representations of carbonate of lime. *Calcareous spar*, in great diversity and beauty of form, is found in considerable quantities, in some of the richest mineral-bearing of these caves or grottos. Sometimes it is found in the form of *stalactites*, suspended from the roof and sides, in the shape of leaves, vines, fingers, icicles, and birds; and generally of the purest white, with a velvety surface, though often more angular and sparkling, like broken glass or smalt; and some of it is clear and porous like coarse snow glistening in the sun. Another sort is more properly called *stalagmites;* this is found on the bottoms of the caves, where the impregnated or carbonated water has dripped through and fallen to the ground, and becomes crystalized in the shape of small animals, birds, vegetables, and other objects; it is generally pure, sparkling white, but often becomes a *calcareous* alabaster, variegated beautifully by different coloring matters, which become incorporated into it from the earth.

The most extensive, as well as most elegant and various specimens, which I have ever seen, were procured from the rich caves discovered by Mr. Levins, of Dubuque. It is worth the trouble of a short journey to examine his large cabinet of these beautiful cavern jewels.

In some of the caves, more particularly in the vicinity of the copper mines, the *sulphates* of *lime* are found in different forms, such as opaque *plaster* and ***gypsum;*** and sometimes in handsome transparent and crystalized forms, as *selenites* and *alabastrites;* which are generally of a pure sparkling white; but other specimens are of diversified hues, like the stalagmites, and other carbonated varieties.

The richest and most abundant lead mineral is generally found in caves, beneath an earth whose drippings are fruitful with these beautiful spars; it is generally a clay or marl soil, in which *alluminum* constitutes a large ingredient, and where soap-clay is found in abundance, of curiously diversified colors. To many persons this soap-clay is quite a curiosity. In some cases this clay is known to extract grease from silk and linen cloths. It can be easily cut or modeled into various forms and images, and hardens when dried—but slakes into fragments, when exposed to outside air.

Johnson county is the middle one of three counties, the the other two being Pope and Hardin—which, in the southern part of the State, reach from the Ohio to the Mississippi; it is watered by Cash and Cedar creeks; it contains but little prairie, and much timber, though generally level land. Population, 4,103; dwellings, 718; farms, 301; manufactories, 4.

VIENNA, the county-seat, is a pleasant little village, on Cash creek.

Jersey is a new county, lying on the Mississippi and Illinois rivers, at the mouth of the latter; it is watered by Macoupin and other creeks; it contains prairie and timber of good quality. Population, 7,354; dwellings, 1,222; farms, 645; manufactories, 44.

PERRYSVILLE is the county-seat, situated on a small creek in the prairie.

Kane county is one of the best populated and cultivated counties in the state, situated in the northern part, with Fox river running through its entire length, from north to south; furnishing numerous water-powers, and abundance of good limestone; its soil is generally of the best kind of rolling prairies, sprinkled over with handsome groves and strips of timber. Population, 16,703; dwellings, 2,828; farms, 1,015; manufactories, 49.

GENEVA, the county-seat, is a beautiful and busy little village on Fox river. Aurora, St. Charles, Elgin, Batavia, and Dundee, are other villages on Fox river, in this county, with from 1,000 to 4,000 inhabitants; they contain various excellent mills and other machinery. These towns are much settled with people from New York.

Knox county is in the Bounty Tract, and watered by Spoon river; it is a good county of land with prairie and timber. Population, 13,279; dwellings, 2,193; farms, 619; manufactories, 100.

KNOXVILLE, county-seat, occupies an elevated position on Haw creek. At Galesburg is Knox College, an institution of a useful and high order; Trenton, Abigton, and other villages are in this county.

Kendall is a new county, with Fox river running diagonally through it from northeast to southwest; it is a splendid prairie county. Population, 7,730; dwellings, 1,258; farms, 659.

YORKVILLE, the county-seat, is situated on Fox river. The other thriving towns are Oswego, Newark, Bristol, Lisbon, and Penfield.

La Salle county lies on both sides of the Illinois river; and for agricultural purposes compares favorably with any in the state; but like many other parts of the state it is deficient in timber; still, this is much supplied by abundant coal beds. For a long time this county embraced what is now Grundy and Kendall counties. Although I have before given a partial description of this county, the following items will be none the less acceptable to the reader.

Starved Rock, situated in the left bank of the Illinois, some six or eight miles below Ottowa, and which attracts attention, is a perpendicular mass of lime and sandstone, washed by the river, and elevated 150 feet above it. Its perpendicular sides, rising from the river, are inaccessible. It is connected with a chain of hights that extend up the stream, by a narrow ledge, the only ascent to which is by a winding and precipitous path. The diameter of the top of the rock is about 100 feet; it is covered with a soil of some depth, which has produced a growth of young trees; with the bare rocks cropping out in some places. The advantages which it affords as an impregnable retreat, induced a band of Illinois Indians, seeking refuge from the fury of the Potawattomies, with whom they were at war, to intrench themselves here. They repulsed all the assaults of their besiegers, and would have remained masters of their high tower, but for the impossibility of obtaining supplies of water. They had secured provisions, but their only resource for the former was by letting down vessels with bark ropes to the river. Their enemies stationed themselves in canoes at the base of the cliffs, and cut off the ropes as fast as they were let down. The consequence of this was the entire extirpation of the band. Many years afterward, their bones were whitening on the summit.

An intrenchment, corresponding to the edge of the precipice, is distinctly visible; and fragments of antique pottery, and other curious remains of the vanished race, are strewn around. From this elevated point, the Illinois river may be traced as it winds through deep and solitary forests or outspread plains, until it disappears from the vision in the distance. In the opposite direction, a prairie stretches out and blends with the horizon, encompassing a most beautiful and romantic range.

On Indian creek, in the northern part of the county, a

most horrible tragedy was enacted, at the commencement of the Indian war of 1832. On the 20th of May, of that year, fifteen persons belonging to the families of Messrs. Hall, Daviess, and Pettigrew, were massacred by the Indians. Two young ladies, Misses Halls, were taken prisoners and afterward redeemed, and two young lads made their escape. The bodies of men, women, and children, were shockingly mutilated, the houses of the settlers burned, their furniture destroyed, and their cattle killed—all in daylight, and within twenty miles of a large force of the militia. This was done by the Indians under *Black Hawk*, near what is now known as the village of Lamoile, a pleasant location. A portion of that band were exterminated during the same season by the combined forces of United States troops and Illinois militia, and the remainder dispersed over the prairies west of the Mississippi.

Persons visiting La Salle county, for the purpose of buying lands or village lots, will do well to call upon John L. Coates, Esq., at Peru, or D. L. Hough, Esq., at La Salle; both reliable business men, and well acquainted with that part of the country.

Lawrence county is located in the eastern part of the State, on the Wabash; it is watered by the Embarrass, and contains a fair proportion of prairie and timber, with some bad sink holes and swamps, called "Devil's Holes." Vincennes, in Indiana, is opposite this county. Population, 6,121; dwellings, 1,057; farms, 656; manufactories, 26.

Lawrenceville, situated pleasantly on the Embarrass, is the county-seat, and a thriving town.

Near by, and a little above Starved Rock, is another overhanging ledge of precipitous rocks, called *Lover's Leap;* it is so called from the fact, as the Indian legend goes, that a young squaw, of the besieging tribe, loved and was affianced to a young brave of the besieged party. She being more intensely interested in the desire and matters of her own heart, than with the contest of the tribe, had devised the means of her wild lord's escape, and they fled together. But they were not permitted long to enjoy the success of her devoted stratagem, for their flight was very soon discovered, and they were hotly pursued, until they took refuge in an apparently concealed crevice of an eminence some mile or two above where the Illinois were confined; but the lovers finding themselves discovered, and unable to elude their pursuers, at once mutually resolved, rather than be captured, separated, and tortured, that they would die together, that their spirits might take flight in company to the more peaceful hunting grounds in the land of spirits; and in this resolute purpose they embraced, gazed in sad, firm earnestness up to the moon and stars, at the forests, and the rushing stream below, and into each others' eyes, then encircled, arm in arm, they made the plunge which dashed them, crushed and broken, down the craggy steep, where the river drank their blood and swallowed their mangled forms.

And ever afterward, in the misty moonlight, the Indians could see the pale corpses of that pair hovering around the precipice, and hear faint, sad moanings, and then more exulting shouts and songs.

In this connection, the following lines from a poem by HOSMER, will be read with interest:

"There is a place—a lonely place,
Deep in the forest green and old;
And oaken giants interlace
Their boughs above the fruitful mold.

"Though fled have many weary suns
Since rose wild yell and cry of fear;
Its bowers the roving Indian shuns
When belted for the chase of deer."

"Linked with the fair enchanting place
Sad legend of the past he knows,
And with a deeply troubled face
Wild, watchful looks around he throws."

* * * *

"Wa-noo-sha was a chieftain's child,
And sweetest flower of womanhood,
That ever grew untaught and wild
Within the green-roof'd mossy wood.

"A suitor, hated by her sire,
Had seen, till night's chill gloom was gone,
And moon had tipped the hills with fire,
Love's torch in her bark lodge burn on."

It is a custom in the courtships of some Indian tribes for the young chief to light a torch and place it in the wigwam where his love sleeps; and if she allow it to burn on, till all is consumed, he understands that his suit is favorable and accepted; but otherwise, if she rise and extinguish it.

Near this place, rising up in the alluvial plain, on the opposite side of the river, is another curious formation, some 100 feet high, called *Buffalo Rock.* On one end and side it is grassy and accessible for cattle to depasture; but the upper end and right bank are nearly perpendicular craggy rocks setting into the river. It used to be a practice with the Indians to find or drive herds of buffaloes into this promontory, and then rush with fires and other frightening devices after them till they were forced in scores to plunge over the beetling precipice, to destruction, and were thus secured by the Indians.

Livingston county is watered by the Vermillion of the Illinois; which furnishes good water-power and coal beds, lime quarries and sandstone; it contains good prairie, with some fine tracts of timber, among which are maple and walnut. Population, 1,552; dwellings, 261; farms, 185.

PONTIAC is the county-seat, a thriving village on the Vermillion. There are some other smaller towns in the county.

Lake county, with WAUKEGAN, the county-seat, was partly described with the other counties on the Lake. In this county are several handsome small lakes, as Pistakee, Lake Zurich, and others. On the borders of the latter is a fine, smart little village of the same name. Population, 14,226; dwellings, 2,455; farms, 1,595; manufactories, 43.

Lee is a new county, lying on Rock river, and contains much very excellent prairie, with some timber; the river furnishes some water-powers in this county. Population, 5,292; dwellings, 905; farms, 478; manufactories, 12. The Stageroad, from Peru to Galena, crosses Rock river, at Dixon.

In the southeastern part of Lee county are two pleasant and valuable groves, with fine settlements of good farmers in and around them; one is known as Malugin's Grove; and the other, as *Shab-be-na's* Grove; it is so called from an Indian Chief of that name, who was friendly to the whites, and rendered good and timely service to them, in time of the Black Hawk war, by keeping a watch on the stealth and advance of the Indians, and giving the inhabitants warning of their movements, which, in some instances, saved the whites from massacre.

Shabbena lives in this grove; which, with a tract of prairie adjoining it, was reserved and donated to him by the Government; much of which, however, some graceless villains in that region have contrived to swindle him out of, and apparently with impunity. He is now very old, and is a man of noble nature, sagacity, and peaceful dispositions; and is justly deserving similar honors as are paid to white heroes who have protected or rendered service to their kind in times of conflict and danger.

On the Stageroad from Aurora to Dixon are some fine farms, beside several small and growing villages, among which are Pawpaw, Little Rock, Johnson's Grove, Inlet, and some others. And from Dixon to Galena the Stage-route is through Buffalo Grove, Elhorn and Cherry Groves, and several others, all pleasant and desirable locations.

DIXON is the county-seat, and is handsomely situated on Rock river. Lee Center is a pleasant little village, on a fine prairie, nearly central in the county.

Logan county is situated on Sangamon river, and contains a large amount of prairie, with some timber and swamp. Population, 5,128; dwellings, 835; farms, 476; manufactories, 14.

POSTVILLE, the county-seat, is handsomely situated in a bend of the Sangamon.

Marshall county is a new one, and lies on both sides of the Illinois, and contains both prairie and timber, with some bottom land; it is watered by Sand and Crow creeks. Population, 5,180; dwellings, 1,132; farms, 464; manufactories, 11.

LACON, on the Illinois, is the county-seat; it is a place of considerable business, and, like most of the towns on that river, is advancing briskly.

Mason county is a new one, lying on the east side of the Illinois, and north of Sangamon river; it has considerable prairie, with some timber and marsh. Population, 5,921; dwellings, 1,041; farms, 727; manufactories, 3.

BATH is the county-seat, pleasantly situated on a prairie. Havanna is a shipping town, on the Illinois, for most of this county.

Massac is one of the new counties, in a bend of the Ohio river, opposite the mouth of the Tennessee; it is heavily timbered with some sloughs. Population, 4,092; dwellings, 704; farms, 385; manufactories, 11.

METROPOLIS is the county-seat, situated on the Ohio river.

Menard county is located on Sangamon river, and embraces prairie and timber of good quality. Population,

6,349; dwellings, 1,035; farms, 706; manufactories, 38.

PETERSBURG is the county-seat, pleasantly situated on the Sangamon.

Macoupin county lies north of Madison, and is watered by Macoupin river, its tributaries, and Otter creek; it is a good county of land, mostly prairie, and settled by a worthy class of farmers. Population, 12,355; dwellings, 2,137; farms, 1,183; manufactories, 24.

CARLINVILLE is the county-seat, situated on a pleasant prairie near the river. There are other fine villages in this county.

Marion county lies about half way between the Wabash and Mississippi; and is watered by the Embarrass and other smaller streams; it is part of Grand Prairie. Population, 6,720; dwellings, 1,132; farms, 827; manufactories, 9.

SALEM, the county-seat, is a pleasant village on the borders of Grand Prairie, at the head of Crooked creek.

Macdonough county occupies a portion of the Bounty Tract, and about midway between the Illinois and Mississippi; it is watered by Crooked creek; the soil is mostly a rich prairie. Population, 7,616; dwellings, 1,262; farms, 843; manufactories, 19.

MACOMB, the county-seat, is pleasantly situated on a fertile prairie; Macdonough College, a valuable institution, is located here.

McHenry county is on the north line of the State, embracing both fine prairie and good timber; it is watered by Fox river and branches of Kishwaukee. Crystal lake is in this county, with a pleasant town of the same name in its vicinity. There are many fine farms and beautiful prospects in this county, with pleasant groves and prairies, and small villages. Population, 14,979; dwellings, 2,650; farms, 1,950; manufactories, 17.

Woodstock is the county-seat, situated in a pleasant grove, near a small brook. McHenry, formerly the county-seat, is situated on a small mill creek which empties into Fox river.

McLean county lies east of Tazewell, and is watered by the Sangamon river and some other streams; the soil is good, divided between prairie and forest; good coal and building stone are found in different parts of the county. Population, 10,163; dwellings, 1,851; farms, 916; manufactories, 3.

Bloomington, the county-seat, is beautifully located on a fine prairie, at the head of a small stream.

Mercer county occupies a northern portion of the Bounty Tract, on the Mississippi, and is watered by Edwards, Pope, and Henderson rivers; the soil is of a good quality, with plenty of timber. Population, 5,246; dwellings, 892; farms, 517.

Millersburg, situated on Edwards river, is the county-seat. Keithsburg, on the Mississippi, is the chief business town. New Boston was formerly the county-seat.

Monroe county is in the southwest part of the State, on the Mississippi; the interior is watered by several small streams; a portion of the county is level and fertile, and another portion is hilly and broken. Population, 7,679; dwellings, 1,421; farms, 874; manufactories, 33.

Waterloo, the county-seat, is situated in prairie and grove, on elevated ground, and is a pleasant, growing village.

Macon county is situated on the north fork of the Sangamon, and is also watered by some branches of the Kaskaskia; the land is mostly prairie, of a good quality, with some timber; and some portions rather wet. Population, 3,988; dwellings, 693; farms, 487; manufactories, 17.

Decatur is the county-seat, a thriving village on the Sangamon. Clinton and Franklin are thrifty, promising towns in this county.

Madison county is one of the best and most important in the State; situated on the Mississippi, opposite the mouth of the Missouri. This county, both on account of its soil and situation, possesses great advantages. Part of it lies in the American Bottom. It extends from the mouth of the Kaskaskia river to Alton, a few miles above the mouth of the Missouri; above this, the bank is high, watered by fine springs, and contains building stone and coal of the best quality. The interior of the county is generally elevated and undulating.

On the banks of the Mississippi, below Alton, it is low and wet, and in many places marshy. No soil, however, can exceed it in fertility. Upon ascending the bluff which bounds this Bottom upon the east, there is a district of country which continues eastward to the Kaskaskia river, and is called the Table-Land. This is also very fertile. The banks of the streams which run through the interior of this county are generally well-wooded, leaving between them prairies of considerable size. Wheat, corn, beef, pork, horses, cattle, and almost every production of Illinois, are raised in this county, and find a ready market at Alton.

Monk Hill, situated on the American Bottom, is eight miles northeasterly from St. Louis. The circumference at the base is about 600 yards, and its hight about 90 feet. On the south side, about half way down, is a broad step or apron, about 15 feet wide. This hill, or mound, was the residence, for several years, of the monks of the order of La Trappe. Their monastery was originally situated in the district of Perché, in France, in one of the most lonely spots that could be chosen. They fled from the commotions of that kingdom to America, lived for a time in Kentucky, and came to Illinois in 1806 or 1807, and settled on this mound. Population, 20,436; dwellings, 3,490; farms, 1,367; manufactories, 182.

EDWARDSVILLE is the county-seat, and is well and pleasantly situated east of the river, amid a finely improved farming country.

But ALTON is the chief town; and, in fact, the largest place on the Mississippi, above St. Louis, and has fair prospects of becoming a saucy rival to that city. It already contains twelve to fourteen thousand population, and is rapidly increasing. *Shurtleff College*, and other institutions of learning, are located here, of a high character.

The *Alton Telegraph* gives the following as the receipts of lumber at that port since the opening of navigation to the 1st October:

Plank, Joists, and Scantling, ft., ... 5,800,000
Shingles, ... 4,470,000
Lath, ... 3,063,000

Moultrie county is one of the new counties, lying on the head waters of the Kaskaskia and Sangamon rivers; containing portions of timber and prairies, of good quality. Population, 3,234; dwellings, 554; farms, 304; manufactories, 11.

AUBURN, the county-seat, is pleasantly situated on a small stream, near the borders of a prairie. Julian and Livingston are other towns in this county.

Montgomery county is located between Bond and Sangamon, and is watered by Sangamon river, with Macoupin, Shoal, and other creeks; it contains much prairie, with some timber. Population, 6,270; dwellings, 1,051; farms, 811; manufactories, 17.

HILLSBORO, the county-seat, is a thriving village, situated on elevated ground, near Shoal creek. Zanesville and Douglass are other towns in this county.

Morgan county is located on the east bank of the Illinois, and is one of the most thickly populated and highly cultivated counties in the state, with good land and improvements; it is watered by Apple, Mauvaiseterre, and Sandy creeks; the *Morgan and Sangamon Railroad*, which commences at Naples, on the Illinois, in Scott county, runs eastward through Jacksonville, in Morgan county, to Springfield, in Sangamon county. Population, 16,164; dwellings, 2,661; farms, 1,574; manufactories, 89.

JACKSONVILLE, the county-seat, is one of the most elegant and finished towns in the state, beautifully located in the edge of a pleasant prairie, near a small creek. The *Illinois State College*, an excellent and flourishing institution, is located here, on a delightful eminence; there are also other institutions of education in this place.

Ogle county lies on Rock river, and is one of the finest in the state; it contains a large amount of excellent rolling prairie, with a fair share of timber, and is watered by some small streams running into the river; there is an excellent seminary at Mount Morris, in this county. Population, 10,020; dwellings, 1,678; farms, 1,058; manufactories, 30.

OREGON CITY, a thriving village on Rock river, is the county-seat. Grand de Tour, a flourishing town, doing considerable manufacturing business, is situated on Rock river in this county.

The towns in this county are noted for the manufacture of farming implements.

The following description of Oregon City and Ogle county was given some years ago in the *New York Star:*

"This place of course (as well as others on Rock river) is in its very infancy; but a more lovely site for an important town could not have been selected, and soon the noise and clamor of manufactures and extensive traffic will give it life and animation. The bluff, which follows the river until it reaches the town, leaves it and falls back for a mile, forming the half of a circle, and meets it again just below in picturesque grandeur. The situation of Oregon City itself has forcibly reminded me of Palermo, the capital of Sicily, surrounded on the land side by a chain of mountains, forming a complete amphitheater, which has been poetically called the '*Conco l'Ora*,' or Golden Shell. The banks of Rock river are not so high as those in the Sicilian landscape; but, contrasted with the wide expanse of country around, are quite as effective, and more rich in fertile charms. The swelling of the prairies, gemmed with wild flowers of every hue, the stately forest, and valleys interspersed with shady groves on the opposite side of the river surrounding Hyde Park, from which we started the wild and bounding deer in great numbers, form features rarely to be met with in a single glance of the eye, either in this or any other country; and amid all these beauties,

" 'The river nobly foams and flows,
The charm of this enchanted ground,
And all its thousand turns disclose
Some fresher beauty varying round.'

"This fairy-land was the scene of human slaughter during the war of 1832 and '33, with the Sac and Fox Indians and the United States, conducted by the celebrated chief Black Hawk and the Prophet, who, after their capture, ceded the country east of the Mississippi to the United States, including the Rock river from its mouth, or nearly so, to the dividing line between Illinois and Wisconsin territory. Above this are scattered along the western shore of the river a line of mounds, more ancient than even the wild and fabulous traditions of the Indians. A hardy class of New England settlers are now tilling these extensive plains. The Indian gardens are now grown up with tall rank weeds, and the war-cry is only heard beyond the Mississippi. The last of the savages left in May, 1836. Since I have seen this fair field, this noble river, I am no longer surprised that the Indian, whose eloquence is the poetry of nature, clung with such tenacity to this country, so passing lovely in itself, and containing their homes and the sepulchers of their dead warriors."

Peoria county is located on the west side of the Illinois. I have before described this section, in the trip down Illinois river; it has a central position on the east line of the Bounty Tract; it has valuable coal mines. Population, 17,547; dwellings, 3,036; farms, 1,191; manufactories, 134.

The following farther description is taken from a communication in the *Peoria Register* of 1837:

" Peoria is well divided into prairie and timber land, of about equal quantities of each. To have a correct idea of the form, beauty, and peculiar adaptation of our prairies to farming purposes, the reader will recollect that five streams of no inconsiderable magnitude water this county, all of which, with the exception of French creek, run a southerly direction into the Illinois river. Snatchwine ('Elbow') passes through the northeast part of the county; Kickapoo, with its east, north, and west forks, through the center; and Lamarche and Copperas creeks through the west. Spoon river runs along near the northern border, and French creek has a westward course through the north part of the county. All of these streams are bordered by timber from one to two miles wide (save the interval bottoms), the prairies occupying the balance of the space between, and descending in delightful slopes toward the timber, from the dividing ridge in the center. Thus, it will be seen at a glance that the whole county is admirably divided into alternate tracts of timber and prairie land. No county in the state has more facilities for speedily enriching the industrious farmer than Peoria."

PEORIA, the county-seat, is situated on the river at the foot of the lake, and is one of the most beautiful towns in all the West.

Perry county is a small one, situated on the Beaucoup creek, east of Randolph county; it is also watered by branches of the Big Muddy; it is a good county of land, and pretty well cultivated. Population, 5,278; dwellings, 967; farms, 638; manufactories, 7.

PICKNEYVILLE, the county-seat, is located on the Beaucoup, in the border of a prairie, and is a pleasant, thriving village.

Pyatt county is situated on the Upper Sangamon, and west of Champaign county; it is a new county, and contains good land, both prairie and timber. Population, 1,606; dwellings, 157; farms, 163; manufactories, 2.

MONTECELLO, the county-seat, is pleasantly situated on the Sangamon.

Pike county is located in the southern part of the Bounty Tract, and contains much timber with some prairie; it is watered by Beaucoup and Little Muddy creeks;

its lands are good, both prairie and timber, and well cultivated. Population, 18,819; dwellings, 3,152; farms, 1,382; manufactories, 37.

Pittsfield, the county-seat, is located on a high, pleasant prairie, in the borders of fine timber. There are many other fine villages in this county.

Pope county is located in the southeastern part of the state on the Ohio; it is watered by Bay, Lusk, and Grand Peirre creeks; its soil is rather sandy, composed of both timber and prairie. Population, 3,975; dwellings, 747; farms, 504; manufactories, 12.

Golconda is the county-seat, situated on the Ohio, a short distance below good quarries of building stone.

Pulaski county is a new one, situated in the southern part of the state, between Cash creek and the Ohio; it contains considerable timber, with some fine bottom lands. Population, 2,265; dwellings, 418; farms, 266; manu factories, 18.

Caledonia is the county-seat, located on the Ohio river, and is a place of some business. Napoleon is a village in this county.

Putnam county, lying on the Illinois, mostly in the great bend, contains much excellent prairie, with a fair proportion of good timber; it is watered by Bureau, Crow, and Sandy creeks. Population, 3,924; dwellings, 636; farms, 317; manufactories, 26.

Hennepin is the county-seat, situated on the east bank of the Illinois, occupying a high and pleasant position, and is a place of considerable business.

An early account of Putnam county was given in the *Hennepin Journal*, as follows:

"Almost every county in the state has had its topography and history published to the world, in some of the public journals of the day; while of ours, which is one of the most important in the northern part of the state, there has been nothing said; and at a distance, there are few who have heard that there is such a county in the state as Putnam. And in order to obviate this, and let the readers of the Journal at a distance know something of this region, and its progress of improvement, we will attempt a brief account of the history and topography of Putnam county.

"Putnam county was organized in the year 1831, but did not increase rapidly in population until after the termination of the Black Hawk war in 1832 and '33. But after the conclusion of hostilities, and when security was restored to the settler, immigrants came in from every quarter of the Union, and spread over the country in every direction like a flood, so that nearly every grove of timber soon found an inhabitant of a very different stamp from the native red man, who, but a short time since, was lord of the grove and the prairie, and who roamed over these fair plains unmolested, having none to dispute his right to the soil, or disturb him in his scenes of pleasure at his wigwam, and enjoyments of the chase.

"We have no hesitation in saying that Putnam county possesses agricultural and commercial advantages equal to those of any county in the state, and that it has as beautiful a surface and as rich a soil, with as good a supply of timber, as is found anywhere in the West. The land being dry and rolling, is pleasant and easy to cultivate, and yields to the industrious farmer an abundant reward for his labor, producing every thing incident to the climate in the greatest profusion, and with an ease to the cultivator that would appear almost incredible to the people of the states farther east, who are accustomed to a hard and sterile soil, when compared with ours.

"The inhabitants of this county are enterprising and intelligent, having emigrated mainly from Ohio, New York, and New England; and coming here with their accustomed habits of industry, they soon succeed in subduing these fertile prairies to a state of high cultivation."

Randolph county lies on the Mississippi, and is located on both sides of the Kaskaskia, and contains much timbered land with little prairie; the surface is undulating and hilly in places. Population, 11,070; dwellings, 2,046; farms, 1,100; manufactories, 36.

The following description of old *Fort Chartres* is taken from "Illinois in 1837:"

"In the northwestern part of the county are the ruins of Fort Chartres, a large stone fortification, erected by the French while in possession of Illinois. It is situated half a mile from the Mississippi, and three miles from *Prairie du Rocher*.

"It was originally built by the French in 1720, to defend themselves against the Spaniards, who were then taking possession of the country on the Mississippi. It was rebuilt in 1756. The circumstances, character, form, and history of this fort, are interesting, as it is intimately connected with the early history of this country. Once it was a most formidable piece of masonry, the materials of which were brought from the bluffs, three or four miles distant. It was originally an irregular quadrangle, the exterior sides of which were 490 feet in circumference. Within the walls were the commandant's and commissary's houses, a magazine for stores, barracks, powder-magazine, bake-house, guard-house, and prison.

"This prodigious military work is now a heap of ruins. Many of the hewn stones have been removed by the people to Kaskaskia. A slough from the Mississippi approached and undermined the wall on one side in 1772. Over the whole fort is a considerable growth of trees, and most of its walls and buildings have fallen down, and lie in one promiscuous ruin."

Chester, the county-seat, is well located on the east bank of the Mississippi, some miles below the mouth of the Kaskaskia; and is a place of large commercial business; Kaskaskia the early capital of the territory was formerly the county-seat.

Prairie du Rocher is an ancient French village, in the northwest part of the county, on the American Bottom, near the rocky bluffs, from which it derives its name, and 14 miles northwest of Kaskaskia. It is in a low, unhealthy situation, along a small creek of the same name, which rises in the bluffs, passes across the American Bottom, and enters the Mississippi. The houses are built in the French style, the streets very narrow, and the inhabitants preserve more of the simplicity of character and habits peculiar to early times, than in any other village in Illinois.

Rock Island county, with its county-seat, ROCK ISLAND, were described in the Mississippi tour. Population, 6,937; dwellings, 1,246; farms, 585; manufactories, 21. Among the other business, there is considerable boat building done here.

Richland is one of the new counties, situated between Lawrence and Clay counties; it contains a large portion of prairie, and is well watered by Fox and Bonpas creeks. Population, 4,012; dwellings, 704; farms, 204; manufactories, 3.

OLNEY is the county-seat, a pleasant little village situated on a small stream in the edge of a prairie.

Saline is a new county, lying west of Gallatin, and is generally timbered; it is watered by Saline and other creeks. Population, 5,588; dwellings, 961; farms, 678; manufactories, 11.

RALEIGH is the county-seat, situated on a branch of Saline creek, on a pleasant elevation.

Sangamon is one of the most thrifty counties in the State, and is thickly settled; it is diversified with prairie and timber; and is watered by the Sangamon and its branches. Population, 19,228; dwellings, 3,173; farms, 1,578; manufactories, 92.

SPRINGFIELD, the State Capital, is also the county-seat; and is located in a beautiful prairie, sprinkled about with fine groves. This place has enjoyed a rapid growth, and is becoming improved and ornamented with much elegance. The Railroad from Illinois river passes through Springfield, and runs on east some eight miles to Rochester, ultimately to be continued to the Wabash. Although a new place, Springfield already numbers several thousand population, and is the depot for a large amount of business, sustained by a rich and enterprising country.

The following extract of a letter, dated Springfield, March 2, 1837, contains matter that will be interesting to many early residents as well as new immigrants, in this region:

"Our Far West is improving rapidly, astonishingly. It is five years since I visited it, and the changes within that period are like the work of enchantment. Flourishing towns have grown up, farms have been opened, and comfortable dwellings, fine barns and all appurtenances, steam-mills and manufacturing establishments erected, in a country in which the hardy pioneer had at that time sprinkled a few log cabins. The conception of Coleridge may be realized sooner than he anticipated; 'The possible destiny of the *United States of America*, as a nation of a hundred millions of freemen—stretching from the Atlantic to the Pacific, living under the laws of Alfred, and speaking the language of Shakspeare and Milton, is an august conception—why should we not wish to see it realized?' On the subject of internal improvements the young giant of the West is making herculean efforts. A bill passed the Legislature, a few days since, appropriating eight millions of dollars for Railroads, Canals, etc.; works which, when completed, will cost twenty millions.

"On Monday last another bill was passed, transferring the Seat of Government from Vandalia in Fayette county to this place—Springfield—which is in the fertile district of Sangamon county; and, as near as may be, the geographical center of the State, and soon will be the center of population. There will be but one more session at Vandalia.

"The State of Illinois has probably the finest body of fertile land of any State in the Union, and the opportunities for speculation are numerous. Property will continue to advance; admirable farms and town-lots may be purchased with a certainty of realizing large profits. The country here is beautiful—equal in native attractions, though not in classic recollections, to the scenes I visited and admired in Italy. The vale of Arno is not more beautiful than the valley of Sangamon, with its lovely groves, murmuring brooks, and flowery meads—

"'Oh Italy, sweet clime of song, where oft
The bard hath sung thy beauties, matchless deemed,
Thou hast a rival in this Western Land!'"

Scott is a small, new county, on the east bank of the Illinois, with considerable timber; it is watered by the

Mauvaisterre and Plume creeks. Population, 7,914; dwellings, 1,300; farms, 712; manufactories, 54.

NAPLES is the principal commercial town, situated on the Illinois, and is a place of considerable business. It is the western terminus of the Sangamon Railroad.

WINCHESTER, nearly in the center of the county, is a fine and thriving town, and is the county-seat.

Schuyler county is located on the west bank of the Illinois; it is an excellent county of land, conveniently divided between timber and prairie; and well watered by Crooked and Sugar creeks; it is settled with thrifty farmers, and presents many thriving villages. Population, 10,573; dwellings, 1,783; farms, 624; manufactories, 52.

RUSHVILLE, a handsome, flourishing village, is the county-seat; it occupies a pleasant location on the borders of a fertile prairie, skirted by fine timber, at the head of a small stream. Huntsville is another flourishing village in this county.

Shelby is a prairie county, with some timber, and located well up on the Kaskaskia river, and watered by its head branches. Population, 7,807; dwellings, 1,411; farms, 834; manufactories, 7.

SHELBYVILLE, the county-seat, occupies an elevated and pleasant situation on the Kaskaskia. In this county are several fine towns and groves.

Stark county is located on Spoon river, north of Peoria; it contains fair proportions of prairie and timber; and is watered by Spoon creek and branches. Population, 3,710; dwellings, 594; farms, 343; manufactories, 23.

TOULON, the county-seat, is situated on the border of a prairie, near the head of a small stream; and is a pleasant, healthy place.

St. Clair county is located between the Mississippi and Kaskaskia rivers; it is composed of prairie and timber, and portions of it hilly, with a portion of the American Bottom lying in one corner of it; it is watered by Richland and Silver creeks. This county lies opposite St. Louis, and supplies that city with large amounts of excellent coal, and great quantities of agricultural produce. Population, 20,181; dwellings, 3,727; farms, 1,961; manufactories, 62.

Bellville, the county-seat, is a fine flourishing town, occupying a pleasant and elevated position on a fertile prairie, some 12 miles east of Illinois Town, which is on the Mississippi. At Lebanon, in this county, is McKendrie College, a valuable institution. Cahokia, an early French post, is in this county.

In regard to the coal operations of this county, the *Chicago Democrat*, in October, 1851, makes the following announcement:

"This Company was organized some three or four years since. Its object is to furnish the market of St. Louis with a supply of coal from the bluffs on the Illinois side of the Mississippi, some ten miles from the city. Ex-Governor Casey and Judge Scates are among the principal stockholders of the Company. Colonel O'Fallon and Dr. Barrett, of St. Louis, are also interested in it. A town had been laid off on the Company's lands at the foot of the bluffs, to which the name of Caseyville has been given. The Company have constructed a Railroad from the river at Illinois Town, opposite St. Louis, to the bluff. They have fifty coal cars, each capable of holding one hundred tons. The road was built at a cost of $120,000. It is thought an arrangement will be perfected with some of the roads projected across the State, to terminate at Illinois Town, to unite with this road, and in view of such probability, it has been built in a most substantial manner. On the 22d September a train passed over the road for the first time, on which occasion a number of invited guests visited Caseyville, and partook of a free dinner."

Stephenson county lies between Jo Daviess and Winnebago counties, on the northern line of the State; it contains the best of prairie and timber lands, in due proportions, and is thickly settled and much cultivated; a portion of the Mineral district extends into this county; it is watered by the Peckatonica, and other smaller streams. Population, 11,666; dwellings, 1,950; farms, 1,179; manufactories, 75.

FREEPORT, the county-seat, is a very thriving village, near the junction of Yellow creek with the Peckatonica; it is bordered in different directions by prairies and groves; the Chicago and Galena Railroad route passes through this town, and will be in operation to here early next year.

Situated on the borders of both farming and mineral lands, as it does, Freeport must continue to have much growth; and like the county the town contains an enterprising population.

Tazewell is a new and excellent prairie county, on the east of Illinois river; it contains a fair share of timber, and is watered by Mackinaw and other creeks; it is thickly settled and well cultivated. Population, 12,052; dwellings, 1,991; farms, 1,110; manufactories, 76.

TREMONT, the county-seat, is pleasantly situated on a beautiful elevated prairie, and is a place of considerable trade. Pekin, on the river, is the principal commercial town of the county.

Union county is located in the southern part of the State, on the Mississippi, below the Big Muddy river. To the northwest of this county is the *Grand Tower*.

JONESBORO, is the county-seat, and pleasantly located in the skirts of a fine grove of timber, with fair prospects of some growth. Population of the county is 7,615; dwellings, 1,289; farms, 810; manufactories, 21.

Vermillion is a county of good land, on the eastern line of the state, and is thickly populated; it contains fair proportions of prairie and timber land, of good quality; and is watered by the Big and Little Vermillion rivers, with a branch of Saline creek, from which salt is manufactured. Population, 11,492; dwellings, 1,985; farms, 1,269; manufactories, 15.

DANVILLE, the county-seat, is a beautiful and flourishing village, of large business and fine prospects; it is situated on the Big Vermillion, between two small streams emptying into it; its position is on a sandy elevation, with prairie on one side and timber on the other. It lies due south of Chicago, about 130 miles on the stageroad to Vincennes, on the Wabash. This town with the county are considered among the best on the east border of the state.

Wabash is the smallest county in the state, situated on the west bank of the Wabash, and opposite White river, in Indiana, and the Rapids and Coffee Islands in the Wabash; the land is prairie and timber, and cultivated by a pretty thick population of thriving farmers; it is watered on the west line by Bonpas creek. Population, 4,690; dwellings, 808; farms, 533; manufactories, 9.

MOUNT CARMEL, the county-seat, is situated on the Wabash below the Rapids, and is a place of increasing business. Centreville and Armstrong are other towns in this county.

Warren county lies east of Henderson, and in the western part of the Bounty Tract; it consists of the best of land, both prairie and timber; it is watered by Henderson river, and some smaller streams. Good coal and limestone are found here. Population, 8,170; dwellings, 1,401; farms, 956; manufactories, 42.

MONMOUTH, the county-seat, is pleasantly located on a fertile prairie, and is a thriving village, near the head of Cedar creek.

Washington county is located on the south of Kaskaskia river, and is watered by Elk, Big Beaucoup, and Crooked creeks; it contains much fine prairie with a fair share of good timber, and is pretty well settled and cultivated; Grand Prairie runs into the north side of this county. Population, 6,953; dwellings, 1,288; farms, 829; manufactories, 9.

NASHVILLE, the county-seat, is pleasantly located on a rich prairie, near the head of a small stream, and is a flourishing village. Okau, Beaucoup, and Elkhorn are other towns in this county.

Wayne county contains much timber, with some good prairie; it is watered by the Little Wabash, Elm, and Skillet creeks; and is pretty well populated with good farmers. Population, 6,825; dwellings, 1,209; farms, 492; manufactories, 6.

FAIRFIELD, the county-seat, is a pleasant village, situated on the borders of a fertile prairie, and is doing a thriving business.

White county is located on the west bank of the Wabash, with the Little Wabash running through it from north to south; the land is mostly timbered, with some scattering prairies, which are much cultivated. Population, 8,925; dwellings, 1,537; farms, 1,101; manufactories, 22.

CARMI, the county-seat, is a pleasant town situated on the Little Wabash.

Whitesides county lies on both sides of Rock river, and is otherwise watered by Elkhorn and Rock creeks. It contains much good prairie and a fair share of timber. Population, 5,361; dwellings, 923; farms, 404; manufactories, 24.

STERLING is the new county-seat; it is handsomely situated on the banks of Rock river, mostly surrounded by a beautiful prairie; the noted Merredosia slough is in this county. Lynden was formerly the county-seat; Como, Albany, Union Grove, Fulton, and Prophetstown, are other towns of this county.

Will county, and JOLIET, are described in the Canal

district. People visiting this county to purchase lands, will find it to their interest to call on Mr. A. J. MATHEWSON, at *Lockport*, a surveyor and engineer, possessing extensive knowledge of the West.

Winnebago is located on both sides of Rock river, and is one of the best counties in the State; its prairies are rich, and much cultivated; they are interspersed by pleasant groves of timber; it is among the best portions of the celebrated "Rock River Country;" and in no part of its course does that river present a handsomer appearance than in this county; at Rockford it affords an excellent water-power, which is well improved; while its banks furnish abundance of good building and limestone; the Kishwaukee, on the east, and Peckatonica, on the west, are two rivers which empty into Rock river in this county; and near the mouth of the former are elevated prairies which command some of the finest views in the State. Population, 11,773; dwellings, 1,979; farms, 919, manufactories, 14.

The fertile prairies of the West seem to be as inspiring to poets, as they are attractive to the soil-tiller. The following beautiful "Hymn from the Prairies," was written by Mr. J. CLEMENT, last summer, while on a tour through Illinois and Wisconsin:

"I've felt thy presence, O my God!
In gorges deep, amid the roar
Of torrents, shooting far abroad,
And shaking earth's firm, rocky floor.

"I've felt thy presence on the hights
Of hills, sky-cleaving and sublime,
Where thoughts are bred for angel flights,
And near to heaven the soul may climb.

"I've felt thy presence 'mid the swell
Of billows leaping to the sky;
While Fancy, shocked at Furies' yell,
Rolled Death's black waves before the eye.

"But gorges deep and mountains grand,
And e'en the Fury-ridden sea,
No more than this broad *Prairie-land*
The presence, Lord, bespeak of thee.

"The hand that smoothed these boundless plains,
And fashioned all their charms, is Thine;
And e'en the silence here that reigns,
Is eloquent of power divine.

"This holy hush at noontide hour,
Amid this sea-like field of bloom,
Steals o'er me with a soothing power,
Like whispers from a Hope-lit tomb.

"Amid thy solemn fields below,
Permit me, Lord, to often rove,
And daily make me humbler grow,
Till fit for holier fields above."

Rockford, the county-seat, is one of the most beautiful and prosperous villages on Rock river; it does a large, active business, and contains many fine buildings and mills; it is connected with Chicago by a Telegraph line which passes through the towns on the Railroad route; the Chicago and Galena Railroad is to be completed to this place during the coming winter. The prairie fires, in the West, are much noted, and truly magnificent spectacles. Roscoe, Rockton, Newburg, and Harrison, are other towns in this county.

Williamson is a new county, located in the southern part of the State; composed of portions of prairie and timber; it is watered by the head streams of Saline and Big Muddy rivers. Population, 7,216; dwellings, 1,195; farms, 752; manufactories, 10.

Marion, the county-seat, is pleasantly located on the borders of grove and prairie. Bainbridge and Sarahville are other towns in this county.

Woodford is a new county, situated on the east bank of Peoria lake and Illinois river; it consists of much prairie and little timber, but of good quality of soil; it is watered by branches of Mackinaw and Crow creeks. Population, 4,416; dwellings, 747; farms, 506; manufactories, 14.

Metamora, the county-seat, is located on a pleasant and fertile prairie. Woodford and Blackpartridge are other towns in the county.

Recapitulation.—Total population, 851,470; whole number of dwellings, 146,544; whole number of farms, 76,208; whole number of manufacturing establishments, producing annually five hundred dollars or upward, 3,099.

North and South.—The northern portion of the State is less rough than the southern, though it is rolling and contains more prairie, with the richest bottom and alluvial lands, and most favorable for corn; the south has more marsh and timber, but the north presents more smooth prairie and isolated groves, which thus exhibits more beauty to the eye of the spectator.

Here a beautiful scene lies spread out before the eye; it is one of nature's portraits, most in harmony with Omniscient Love, who ordained it for man's comfort; frigid and infidel, indeed, must be the being whose mind could not admire and harmonize with it; small hillocks, with vales between, rolled away successively; the Earth looks a luxuriant, almost voluptuous form, arrayed in glorious robes, tinted and green, whose fruitful bosom is ever ready to yield fruition and vital sustenance to all who trustingly nestle there; such was the charming picture displayed before the zealous, active toiler, as it undulated before him, with soft swells and valley-dimples, almost breathing with life, as its rich, glowing, verdure-robes waved in the breeze, gently rising and falling like the maternal bosom when agitated by emotions of affection; and then the whole face cheered into brighter gladness by the Sun's ardent kisses, as he imprinted them while the fitful passing clouds removed their mystic veil from the enamored features; and all this is fruitful harmony in obedience to the laws of the Author-love, so long as constancy cultivates and sincerity sanctifies.

Yet, storms will pass; uniform tranquility remains not with Earth, with man; for life is everywhere, and so change; transgression has stalked forth, and so confusion;

after agitation, though, comes rest, and deeper joy; for revolution, excitement, intensifies feeling, and contrast hightens appreciation. The sun shines brighter after the sable cloud-storm, and the landscape sparkles brighter under the starry rain-drops just sprinkled over it.

Then, O man, learn cheerfully alike to endure stormy agitations and welcome fervent sun-kisses; for there is no fructification on earth without both.

The kernel, casually scattered by the way-side, or in temporary stealth planted beneath the shade-bush, will still reproduce, even under only fitful glimpses of sun-love, through clouding-boughs, and watered only by the dew-tears violently shaken down by the ruthless blast; but, how much more bountiful and gratifying is the fruit gathered from the permanency of enlightened culture. The wild vine that climbs, at random, the craggy oak will bear fruit; yet how far sweeter and enduring is the cluster gathered from the vine which is vitalized by the same sun-kisses, but led by the legitimate and intelligent hand along the clean trellis ordained to its use.

In no place have I ever beheld the *Thunder Storm* exhibit so much terrific grandeur, so much of the Mighty One's oratory, as while traversing one of the vast prairies of the West.

Once in the summer of '48, I had set out on foot to travel westward over one of those green, undulating prairies, between Rock river and the Mineral district, in the afternoon. I had been stepping on some hour or two, over the light swells and gentle slopes, when the storm came buzzing and bellowing portentously after me; directly I turned to look at the approaching storm, when soon an indescribably grand conflict, or agitation of the elements, was presented, where lightnings, thunders, rain, and wind, seemed to be contending for the mastery, in their startling displays. Thunder-bursts held you in awe, flashes of lightning would make you start and shrink; gusts of wind whirled you in the high grass; and rain torrents drenched you to the skin: yet, suffering and dreading all, you felt no power or will to escape—there was no retreat, no refuge—the jarring sounds vibrated on every hand, torrents and blaze poured around in every direction, the muscles, alike with volition, seemed paralyzed—two sensations alone took possession of you, awe and admiration; which, anon, as you looked aloft into the dread concave, were resolved into that of heart-homage for Him who holdeth the storms in His hand. The herds which grazed upon these luxuriant meadows ran, in confused fright, down the vales to the groves; the crane and wild-bird flew, screaming with fear, to the forests for shelter. All was one boundless scene of rushing dread. The expanded prairie carpeted in deep green below; above, the dark blue clouds, with their pendant folds, were ranged along, one after another, (like the lower edges of curtains in the theater's dome,) as you gazed toward the east, the nearest being darkest, then an interval of hesitating light falling between, then another cloud-sheet was swinging, and so on in a series of some half a dozen, till at the farther end of the arched-way greater light appeared, much as if you looked for miles through a vast tunnel, with occasional openings for light from above. While I was gazing, absorbed, upon this already gorgeous spectacle, the fury of the storm had abated, the black upper clouds were mostly dispersed, and as a brighter sky poured its floods of light into this magnificent amphitheater, its splendor and beauty were hightened beyond all description, and presented a panorama to the rapt beholder which unmistakably proclaimed that only by the Almighty could it have been swung out before the world: and presently the Author's signature was dashed across it in the bright BOW which clasped the whole.

Not often can such scenes be witnessed; a single view, a moment's study, of such a master-piece would be worth months of examination in the old artistic pantheons of Italy, to the ingenious and enthusiastic votary of line and color; but my description is only a feeble picture of the original scene.

The *pitiless* storm which raged *in mercy* over the frantic head of Lear presented only the sable, frowning features of a night-storm, while to that which overwhelmed the prairie traveler were flung out all the glories of the day-god's bright drapery and glittering sheen.

Though it lacked a few hours of night, when I *experienced* the above storm, still, in the following graphic description, by Dr. R. W. Griswold, of similar storms, I can read the deep soul-poetry of such exhibitions of nature in her mighty freedom:

"The summer sun has sunk to rest
Below the green-clad hills,
And through the skies, careering fast,
The storm-cloud rides upon the blast,
And now the rain distills!
The flash we see, the peal we hear,
Till pains the ear.
It is the voice of the Storm-King
Riding upon the lightning's wing,
Leading his bannered hosts across the darkened sky,
And drenching with his floods the sterile lands and dry.

"The wild beasts to their covers fly,
The night-birds flee from heaven,
The dense black clouds that veil the sky,
Darkening the vast expanse on high,
By streaming fires are riven.
Again the tempest's thunder tone,
The sounds from forests overthrown,
Like trumpets blown
Deep in the bosom of the storm,
Proclaim his presence in its form,
Who doth the scepter of the concave hold.
Who freed the winds, and the vast clouds unrolled."

Of the evils of Land-monopoly—the accumulation of large, too large tracts of land in the ownership of a single person or of a corporation—at the West, as elsewhere, I have repeatedly spoken, and here again remark upon it. I speak thus often of it, because, wherever we move, every step we take, almost, we meet it; we see its injurious effects upon community; it is not only detrimental to communities and neighborhoods, but it is largely detrimental to the best progress and prosperity of the Nation, by retarding the settlement and population of the frontier and exposed borders of the New States, and by hindering useful and comfortable improvements among the few settlers in those locations—extensive and non-resident owners neither laboring and improving themselves, nor selling the large tracts at fair prices to those who would do it—such as making roads, sustaining schools, churches, and town operations.

There is a very just policy that might be pursued by Congress, to abate this evil, and greatly subserve both the the national and personal interests of the West, as well as East.

Let the Government allow to every person who will go on and improve—become an actual occupant—the free right to 80 or 160 acres of the wild lands—give him, without price, a suitable quantity for a comfortable farm—and at the same time prohibit any person from buying or possessing any more than that amount; or cease altogether the traffic in public lands, and dispose of them only by gift to actual settlers. By pursuing such a course, Government would encourage the speedier filling up our vast domain, now lying waste and useless, with an industrious and enterprising population of agriculturists and mechanics, who would speedily make roads, farms, fill schools and churches, bring up the treasures of the earth; and these, singly or combined, are a nation's greatest wealth, and its surest protection.

Where a man's HOME is, there is his deepest interest—

there his deepest treasure is—when he has a spot on *terra firma* that is his own, and his home is located there, he at once feels that he has more than a passing interest in the peace and prosperity of the nation, that his welfare and the welfare of the nation are identical; and as he will strive, endure, toil, every thing, for Home, so then would he do the same for the country; in defending the nation he defends his home; and what soldier-wages or camp-pleasures can make a man risk, suffer, and combat to the extent and with the devotion that his love of Home will?

HOME! four sweet letters; what other word, in the whole vocabulary of our language, expresses so much that is lovely; around what other little name do so many endearments, such sweet associations, cluster; what other single short syllable embraces in its significance all that is desirable in society or worth toiling for on earth? In its full development are life, love, and joy; and which are all combined nowhere but in Home.

Then, if we would have a happy, holy, and loyal community, let us establish and secure as many independent, self home-owning citizens as possible in the nation—permanent operators upon their own premises—and reduce as far as we may the number of the birds of passage, who to-day are here, but to-morrow are somewhere else. And though worthy people oftentimes, unsettled persons cannot be relied upon to the full extent, by government or society, in all emergencies, as can those who own permanent homes, and live upon them. Hence Government will advance its greatest welfare by doing what it can to induce the full settlement of Western lands.

In one of his letters from Europe, HORACE GREELEY thus speaks of the love of country and home with the American:

"But I must not linger. The order to embark is given; our good ship Baltic is ready; another hour, and I shall have left England and this Continent, probably for ever. With a fervent good-bye to the friends I leave on this side of the Atlantic, I turn my steps gladly and proudly toward my own loved Western home—toward the land wherein man enjoys larger opportunities than elsewhere to develop the better and the worse aspects of his nature, and where evil and good have a freer course, a wider arena for their inevitable struggles, than is allowed them among the fetters and cast-iron forms of this rigid and wrinkled Old World. Doubtless those struggles will long be arduous and trying; doubtless, the dictates of duty will there often bear sternly away from the halcyon bowers of popularity; doubtless, he who would be singly and wholly right must there encounter ordeals as severe as those which here try the souls of the would-be champions of progress and liberty.

"But political freedom, such as white men enjoy in the United States, and the mass do not enjoy in Europe, not even in Britain, is a basis for confident and well-grounded hope; the running stream, though turbid, tends ever to self-purification; the obstructed, stagnant pool grows daily more dank and loathsome. Believing most firmly in the ultimate and perfect triumph of good over evil, I rejoice in the existence and diffusion of that liberty which, while it intensifies the contest, accelerates the consummation. Neither blind to her errors nor a panderer to her vices, I rejoice to feel that every hour henceforth till I see her shores must lessen the distance which divides me from my country, whose advantages and blessings this four months' absence has taught me to apprecate more clearly and to prize more deeply than before. With a glow of unwonted rapture I see our stately vessel's prow turned toward the setting sun, and strive to realize that only some ten days separate me from those I know and love best on earth.

"Hark! the last gun announces that the mail-boat has left us, and that we are fairly afloat on our ocean journey; the shores of Europe recede from our vision; the watery waste is all around us; and now, with God above and death below, our gallant bark and her clustered company together brave the dangers of the mighty deep. May Infinite Mercy watch over our onward path and bring us safely to our several homes; for to die away from home and kindred seems one of the saddest calamities that could befall me. This mortal tenement would rest uneasily in an ocean shroud; this spirit reluctantly resign that tenement to the chill and pitiless brine; these eyes close regretfully on the stranger skies and bleak inhospitalities of the sullen and stormy main. No! let me see once more the scenes so well remembered and beloved; let me grasp, if but once again, the hand of friendship, and hear the thrilling accents of proved affection, and when sooner or later the hour of mortal agony shall come, let my last gaze be fixed on eyes that will not forget me when I am gone, and let my ashes repose in that congenial soil which, however I may there be esteemed or hated, is still

"'My own green land forever.'"

In these Prairie regions the farming work is generally done more expeditiously than in the East; a larger proportion of it being performed by labor-saving machines in the former than the latter locations.

The plowing, or breaking up prairie, is generally done with from four to six yoke of oxen, or horse-team of equal strength, drawing plows which turn a furrow of from 30 to 40 inches wide, and in some instances even wider; plowing two, three, and sometimes four acres a day with one plow. These, as well as the small plows, are made of sheet steel, and polished on emery wheels, so that they are light and slip through the soil very smoothly. Generally, therefore, plowing is done in the West much more expeditiously than at the East.

Corn is cultivated mostly with a cultivator, and very little time is spent with the hoe, so that this branch of work is done up rapidly.

Wheat and other fine grains are, to a considerable extent, beginning to be put in with a drill, by which both time and seed are saved, and greater certainty of crop secured. The drills mostly used and approved at the West, are those invented by Piersons and by Gatling; and there are others, preferred by some farmers.

The grain is almost wholly cut by harvesting machines. Those most in use are McCormick's, Hussey's, Danforth's, Haine's, Cook's, Seymour and Morgan's, and some others. It is said that Hussey's and McCormick's have proved to be superior; they were tested at the World's Fair.

Mowing machines are also beginning to be much used to cut the hay on the large prairie-meadows; and they are found to serve an admirable purpose. There are already a number of these machines in the field that work well, among which are Scoville's, Danforth's, McCormick's, and others.

Then there are a great number of thrashers, some of which thrash in the field, and others at the yard and in the barn.

In cases where immigrants lack the necessary means and help, within themselves, to make a full and easy commencement at the West, or to secure, on the start, the privileges of society around their new homes, it would be a judicious and convenient plan, for numbers of farmers, mechanics, and others to join their forces and settle down together, in some place well selected for health and natural advantages, in the shape of *a colony*—with or without all interests in common, as shall be most agreeable to all concerned—where they may help one another, in the heavier portions of their work, and "join teams to break up," as one man, generally, cannot afford to own four to six yokes of oxen, a team sufficient for the first plowing the rich heavy prairies. Going in colonies or companies, this way, not only renders business lighter, but furnishes at once the pleasures of society, which are not enjoyed in the early sparse settlements of a new country.

The following announcement in the *New York Tribune*, last summer, is an instance of this manner of operation:

"A movement is being made in this city for the organization of a company to form a new settlement on the public lands of the West. The scheme is to take up a township of Government land, six miles square, *by means of a fund* accumulated by individual subscriptions. The number required will be about 100, each of whom is to be allowed to subscribe for 160 acres, or less, and a village lot of three or four acres. The period required to complete the organization of the company and the purchase of the land will not probably extend beyond April or May next.

"The proportion of artizans required for each department of industry to organize and commence the settlement of a single township and village, is estimated to be nearly as follows:

"Agriculturists, 50; Bakers, 2; Barber, 1; Blacksmiths, 4; Bookseller and Stationer, 1; Boot and Shoemakers, 6; Brickmakers, 8; Bricklayers, 4; Butcher, 1; Cabinetmakers, 4; Cooper, 1; Millers, 2; General Merchants, 2; Grocers, 2; Hardware and Tinshop, 1; House Carpenters and Joiners, 20; Limeburners, 2; Laborers, 10; Masons, 10; Printers (Newspaper), 2; Painters, 2; Physician, 1; Saddle and Harnessmakers, 4; Sawmill Hands, 8; Tailors, 4; Wagon and Carriagemakers, 8; all of whom are supposed to be employers and journeymen."

Whether the proportion into which the various branches of laborers are above distributed is correct, I am not prepared to say positively; at least, the number of farmers there set down is full small enough; for the number of mechanics stated could do more work in their lines than that number of farmers would require; but perhaps that would be no objection, as mechanics could do some agricultural labor, as well for their health as profit; and every shopkeeper ought to own a piece of land, more or less, on which he would find it pleasant to devote some portion of his time.

Such companies should look out to have established among them good liberal schools, and well supplied reading rooms, where they might have access to books and papers, during their leisure hours.

MISCELLANEOUS.

The Exemption and Collection Laws of these three Western States, are all very liberal; and, in that respect, are an advance upon the Eastern States; still, men pay their debts full as promptly in the former as the latter region.

Homestead Exemption.—In the State of *Illinois*, the amount exempted from forced sale for debt is $1,000; either a house and lot in town, or a farm and appurtenances. In *Wisconsin*, the amount is a farm of 40 acres, with buildings, etc.; or a town lot of one-fourth acre, with the buildings on it. In *Iowa*, a town lot or farm, not to exceed in either case the value of $500. The exemption is valid only while the debtor or family live on the premises; and an exception is made in favor of Mechanics' liens, and of mortgages voluntarily signed.

Personal Property Exemption.—In Illinois, necessary wearing apparel; bedsteads and bedding for family; necessary stoves and cooking utensils; and $15 worth of other furniture; two sheep and fleeces, or equal amount of wool purchased, to each member of family; one cow and calf; necessary food for family and stock for three months; working implements in the house; and $60 worth of other property, suited to wants or wishes of debtor; and the rights of burial, etc. In Wisconsin, books, pictures, and rights of burial; all necessary wearing apparel, with household furniture worth $200; two cows; ten swine; span of horses, or one horse and yoke of oxen; ten sheep and wool from same, in fleece or fabrics; food for family and stock one year; wagon or cart and sleigh; plow, drag, and other tackle for team of $50 worth. In Iowa, Bible, school books, and library of $100 value; one cow and calf; one horse, or yoke of oxen; twelve sheep and their wool, in fleece or fabrics; five swine; the flax in the possession of the family, or the fabrics made from it; necessary beds and bedding; one hundred yards of cloth made up by the family; all spinning wheels and looms kept for use; stove and pipe, with other furniture to amount of $50; mechanics' tools necessary for use; and the necessary books and instruments for lawyers and doctors to practice their professions. In the case of claim of Mechanics' liens, suits must be prosecuted within six months in Illinois, and within one year in Wisconsin and Iowa.

Qualifications of Voters.—In Illinois, all white male citizens, of the age of 21 years, who have resided in the State six months next preceding the election. In Wisconsin, all white male citizens, 21 years of age, who have resided in the State one year next preceding the election. In Iowa, all white male citizens, of the age of 21 years, who have resided in the State one year, and 20 days in the county next preceding the election.

Religious Societies.—Most of the ordinary religious denominations are thoroughly established in these States; and nearly all of them have flourishing Colleges in different locations. And such institutions are as generally attended to and liberally sustained, in proportion to population and ability, in the West as at the East.

I cannot say which sect is most numerous; but the Presbyterians, Baptists, Methodists, Episcopalians, Catholics, and Universalists all have churches in most of the towns and settlements. There are also flourishing societies of the New Jerusalem Church or Swedenborgians, in Chicago, Peoria, and some other towns. There also some Quakers and Friends in some of the towns; and in many of the cities and towns Jews and Mormons are to be found. In Illinois, the Rev. Dr. Whitehouse, of New York, has recently been appointed Bishop over the Episcopal churches.

And here I will repeat the suggestion to Emigrants, that it is eminently desirable that they should all, whenever able to do so, take into the New States all the improved stock, good seeds, and scions for fruit, and shrubbery and grove trees; and this, too, in preference to taking much furniture or tools and farming implements; as all of those can be obtained of the best quality and at cheap rates in the Western cities and villages.

Good breeds of cattle, horses, sheep, hogs, and poultry, with choice fruits are much needed, and in lively demand.

THE HIGHER ASPECTS AND PROMISES OF THE WEST.

As an interesting ornament to the more plain and statistical aspects of my rustic picture, I here insert an elegant sketch from the pen of my early and esteemed friend, JOHN E. WHEELER, Esq., one of the purest and ablest writers of the West; his philosophy is pure and elevated, and his religion humane and spiritual. For years the leading Editor of the *Gem of the Prairie*, and the *Chicago Daily Tribune*, his spirit's genius raised those papers to an elevation of usefulness and popularity unsurpassed, if not unequaled, by any other journal west of the Lakes.

He has alluded to the West, in her characteristics of inspiration to Human Improvement and upon the Artist. Surely, no portion of our Continent—of any continent—is richer in natural scenes, to challenge the enthusiastic efforts of the pen, pencil, and chisel, than that portion drained by the Mississippi from St. Anthony's to St. Louis, bordered on the east by the majestic Lakes, and on the west by the boundless Missouri plains. Here the aspiring Artist, of whatever branch, may find glowing and splendid originals, from which to make more living copies than can be obtained from the master-pieces in ancient and rusty pantheons of the Old World; where the early masters excelled, in *their times and sphere.* But there is no good reason why Art should not progress and mount up to greater excellence, on a newer, wider soil—in a more propitious, freer clime—as has Science, and Government, and Religion: have not all these improved, to a higher and more glorious standard, in the New World? And why should the Painter or Sculptor still bend in an agony of ambition to simply copy the excellence of Europe's *faded* masters? Indeed, Excelsior has seized America's poet-pen; let it also feather her chisel and pencil for higher flights.

The free, fresh, and boundless spirit and face of the West, should be courted to dictate a style and inspire a taste above and beyond the samples of earlier and ruder ages; then will our Artists, as do our Politicians, surpass their predecessors. In this connection Mr. Wheeler furnishes the following, at my request:

"We remember, some year or two since, to have read a discourse, by Rev. Dr. Bushnell, the subject of which was, in substance, 'The Barbarian Tendencies of Society at the West;' and on this view of the subject the reverend gentleman predicated an appeal to Christianity and Benevolence to put forth the necessary efforts to save this Garden of the Union from a relapse into barbarism. This tendency, he supposed, grew out of the disruption of social, religious, and political ties in the case of those seeking homes in the West—the jarring and heterogeneous character of the social elements, drawn as they are from all quarters of the world—and the unbridled license resulting from the well known disregard, in new communities, of the various restraints by which men are moulded and held in check in the older States.

"After our first surprise was over at the idea of a tendency to 'barbarism' in any portion of our country, especially the great and glorious West, we were, on second thought, obliged to confess that there was a sort of half truth in it. We know, from a study of the whole course of human history, that no real progress in the elevation and refinement of the race can be made while it is migratory or nomadic. Man, like a tree, must plant the roots of his institutions deep in the soil, before they can lift themselves in beauty and majesty toward heaven. And, of course, all disordered states of society, just in the degree they approach the migratory character, are unfavorable to advancement in any direction.

"We understand, from long-continued observation, the evils incident to the unsettled character of society at the West; and we are also aware, from the same course of observation, that Dr. Bushnell took a one-sided and very partial view of the subject. The evils which he enumerates are, in the very nature of things, temporary; while the vast good which is to grow out of the fusion of races upon the great theater of the Mississippi Valley, is incalculable. Consider the character of immigrants who have settled in, and are still crowding in an unbroken human tide to that magnificent region; surely they are many removes from 'barbarism,' and we see no reason why a mere change of location should transform them from civilized to barbarous men. The predominant element is, of course, the Anglo-Saxon, and, to a large extent, of the Puritan stock—the most orderly, self-governing race in existence. They are not the broken down, inefficient members of the communities from which they come; but, as a general thing, the most intelligent and energetic among them. They carry within themselves, wherever they go, all of the elements of an orderly, well-governed State, and of polished communities. It is true that multitudes of foreigners, less favorably developed, constitute a large portion of the people of the West; but the intelligent and the cultivated are sufficiently numerous to give a tone to public sentiment and manners, and a right direction to public affairs.

"Throughout Illinois, Wisconsin, and Iowa, of which this volume principally treats, whole neighborhoods, and even clusters of counties, are found which exhibit all the intelligence and refinement of any portion of the Eastern States. They are foremost in all works tending toward material progress; religion is honored, and its institutions liberally sustained; and a special zeal is manifested in the advancement of general education; and in matters of taste—an appreciation of those little refinements that add a charm to social intercourse, and throw a grace around the externals of life—they might, in frequent instances, serve as models to those who have always lived in the midst of such associations.

"The reverend gentleman to whom we have referred, while he has seen and pointed out some of the evils inseparable from the unsettled state of society at the West, has, it seems to us, strangely overlooked one of its strikingly hopeful phases—we mean the almost absolute freedom of mind which is there enjoyed. There is in this a good, calculable by no ordinary mode of computation.

"Freedom is indispensable to the development of human character, whether in the individual man or in the more complex man composed of a community or a state. If we would put ourselves in a position favorable to the attainment of some great good, we must, by a law of eternal necessity, at the same time subject ourselves to the liability of falling into its opposite evil. Between these two opposing powers is the only proper theater of wholesome discipline. Never were a people placed in so favorable a position, in this respect, as those of the West. The danger which they incur is only temporary, while the good which is to result from the struggle will be as enduring as the soul itself.

"Freedom, as we have said, is absolutely essential, whatever risks may be incurred by its exercise. Without it a community must be either stationary, if that be possible, or in a state of retrogradation. *With* it, we see what has been and is to be achieved by the people of the West. Their energies and aspirations seem to be expanding into correspondence with the noble features of the country which they inhabit. Nowhere else do we see such simultaneousness of conception and execution. Without irreverence, it may almost be said, they speak, and it is done. Nowhere else is there such an arena for the free exercise of Thought in canvassing all questions—nowhere else such complete toleration of the most variant forms of opinion. And, we may confidently add, that nowhere else in this great confederacy of States, is there such hope for the future in respect to all that can dignify and elevate the race. In the broad valley of the Father of Waters this young but great Republic can stretch its free limbs, and give as full and beneficent play to its heart and intellect as is now enjoyed by the winds which career over its broad rolling plains, and the majestic streams which course as the life-blood of the land for thousands of miles through its bosom.

"The vast material resources of this region are treated of at large in preceding pages. These are necessary as the foundation of a true social edifice, and no other portion of the world presents them in so great profusion. We have seen also that they are being developed and applied to the noblest uses on the most magnificent scale. Young as society is there at present, in the more thickly settled portions of the country it will compare favorably with the better aspects of society in the oldest and most flourishing States. What, then, may we not predict for the future? We feel confident that society in the West, just so soon as the material basis shall be sufficiently consolidated, will flower into such beautiful and harmonious proportions as the world never witnessed before. Intelligence will be as widely diffused as the sunlight. The rather free manners which now prevail will be softened by time and culture to a noble, graceful courtesy, and the whole community be brought up to the standard which we now see exhibited here and there in individuals. Religion, purified from sectarian narrowness by the tolerant strife of manifold opinion, will, by its attractiveness and power, win all hearts but those of the hopelessly incorrigible. Need we say that, when all this shall come to pass, Art will here find its chosen home, as the highest expression of all that is beautiful and harmonious in the heart and mind of the people? Will not numerous shrines then be reared to the Beautiful—that heavenly vesture which hovers over and sanctifies all noble uses—and the pen of the Poet, the pencil of the Painter, and the chisel of the Sculptor, vie with each other in 'bodying forth' her highest ideals, as vouchsafed to the most harmonious souls? We believe so. All will come in good time. The political empire of the West over this Union will ere long be undoubted and universally acknowledged. It is consoling to think that its sway will be as beneficent as the vastness of its power and manifold wealth for all the uses of man."

Names of States.—Most of the States are known by other appellatives than the incorporate ones; as the "Empire State," the "Key-stone State," the "Buck-eye State," etc. The more Western States also have their provincial *sobriquets;* Michigan is the "Wolvarine State," from its great number of small mischievous prairie wolves; the Indianians are called "Hooshers," from a little incident which occurred with some of the earlier settlers, and is, in fact, a contraction of the phrase, "Who is here?" Wisconsin is called the "Badger State," from the numbers of that little animal found there, and seldom seen in other parts of the Mississippi country. Iowa is called the "Hawk-eye State," from the great number of hawks and buzzards formerly found in that region, as some say; while others contend, an illustrious Indian chief of that name was once a terror to voyageurs to its borders. The Illinoians are called "Suckers," from the customs of the early settlers, who were in the habit, in spring-time, of going up to the mines to labor; and in the fall, at the approach of Jack Frost, returning to the warmer south; thus, running *up* in the spring, and *down* in the fall, which is the natural habit of the fish known as ***suckers***. Illinois is also called the "Prairie State," from its immense superior prairies. The Missourians are called "Pukes," from the great amount of sickness which used to be suffered on its rivers.

Routes of Travel.—For the information and convenience of travelers and emigrants, I give the following description of some of the principal mediums of conveyance, from the Atlantic seaboard, for reaching the Great Lakes and the Mississippi; and cross routes to the Ohio and the Missouri rivers. I am not able to give all of the lines of travel; but have given those most traveled and the most popular.

From New York, Boston, and other Atlantic towns, Passengers and Freight are conveyed to Buffalo and Dunkirk by various lines of Railroads, Riverboats, and Canals; the New York and Erie, and the Hudson River, and Albany and Buffalo Railroads, being the principal and favorite routes.

From Buffalo and Dunkirk regular lines of first class Steamers run daily to Cleveland, fare $1 to $3; to Monroe, Toledo, and Detroit, fare $2 to $4; to places on St. Clair lake and river, and to Mackinaw, fare $5 to $7; and to all ports on the Western Shore of Lake Michigan, fare $4 to $8. Time of running from Monroe, Toledo, and Detroit, one to two days; to Mackinaw, three to four days; and to Milwaukee and Chicago, four to six days.

From Chicago and other ports along Lake Michigan, boats leave weekly for Green Bay. From Mackinaw and Saut Ste. Marie's a boat leaves every week for different ports on Lake Superior, to the copper and lead regions, and fur trading posts.

From Detroit, Monroe, and Toledo, daily trains of Railroad cars leave for the head of Lake Michigan, near Chicago, whence boats or stages convey passengers to that city, and other places on the Lake, and into Illinois, Indiana, Wisconsin, and Iowa.

From Sandusky, on Lake Erie, the conveyance to Cincinnati is by Railroad; distance, 218 miles; time, 12 to 16 hours; fare, $6.50 and less in second class cars.

From Manhattan and Toledo to Evansville, on the Ohio river, by Canal, 467 miles.

From Cleveland to Cincinnati the conveyance is by Railroad, via Columbus; distance, about 255 miles; fare, $7.50; second class, less. There is also a Canal between these places.

From Erie, the conveyance to the Ohio, at Beaver, is by Canal; distance about 140 miles; then a short distance by Steamboat up the river to Pittsburg.

From Philadelphia and Baltimore, to Pittsburg and Wheeling, by different routes—Railroads, Steamboats, and Coaches on National road—varying in distance, from 390 to upward of 400 miles; time, 36 to 40 hours; fare, $10 and $11. Also, a route by Railroad and Canal, about 390 miles; time, 3 to 5 days; best for transportation of emigrants and goods, as it is much cheaper.

From Pittsburg down the Ohio to Mississippi river are several lines of Steamboats. To New Orleans, distance, 2,000 miles; time, 12 days; fare, $12. To St. Louis, distance, 1,200 miles; time, 4 to 6 days; fare, $8 to $10. To Cairo, distance about 1,000 miles; time, 3 to 5 days; fare, $6 to $8. To Cincinnati, distance about 500 miles; time, 2 to 4 days; fare, $4 to $6. To Portsmouth, distance, 370 miles; fare, $3 to $4. To Wheeling, distance 100 miles; fare, $1 50.

From Cincinnati to Madison, 90 miles; fare, $1 50. To Louisville, about 150 miles; fare, $1 50 to $2. From

Madison to Indianapolis, by Railroad, 86 miles; fare, $2 50.

The conveyances carry passengers from New York to Chicago and Milwaukee, at prices varying from $14 to $20.

The two Railroads from Lake Erie to Chicago are, the "Michigan Southern and Northern Indiana Railroad," leaving Lake Erie at both Toledo and Monroe, running through southern Michigan and northern Indiana to Chicago, 246 miles; and the "Michigan Central Railroad," leaving the Lake at Detroit, and running through central Michigan to Chicago, 280 miles.

Over all the principal thoroughfares of the Western States, Frink, Walker, & Co., run daily lines of Stages, leading from the chief towns and cities on the Lakes and Rivers. And on the cross routes and roads, leading to smaller towns and newer settlements, they run semi-weekly and weekly lines.

MR. THOMPSON'S LETTERS.

THE following are extracts of letters, written in June and July last; in copying from these letters I have omitted what was not of general interest:

"Before leaving CHICAGO, I must say a word of its present aspect. The changes wrought there within a few years are more marked than in any other place that I have yet revisited. New hotels of the largest class, and kept in the best manner, new docks, new pavements, long rows of stores substantially built and wearing a showy front, bear witness to a rapid growth and an increasing business. Standing at the head of Lake Navigation, and connected by Canal with navigable waters to the Gulf of Mexico, it must rapidly increase in wealth and trade; and when the projected lines of Railroads and Plankroads are completed, it must become the Commercial center of the Northwest. The business men of the city are mostly young and enterprising Yankees, who are determined here to carve out a fortune for themselves. There is also at Chicago some admixture of the southern element, together with a fair quota of foreign characteristics; but eastern emigration has mainly given character to the place.

"Churches and church edifices have shared in the generous spirit of improvement. Six years ago I found the First Presbyterian Church worshiping in a sort of deserted warehouse which had been tinkered up in various ways to answer that purpose. The Second Church, at that time, occupied a small frame building facing the public square. Now, the First Church, under the pastoral care of Rev. Mr. CURTIS, have erected a commodious and substantial edifice of brick fronting the square.

"The Second Church have exchanged their wooden box for a massive and elegant building of stone, of Gothic architecture, with stained windows and a semi-cathedral air. The material of this building was brought from a quarry south of the city on the line of the Canal, and affords an interesting study to the geologist. Its aspect is peculiar on account of the oozing of bitumen through the pores of the stone, which, blending with the limestone and the silex, gives a variety of colors from the lightest gray to the deepest black; it is said to become hardened by exposure. The building is about 120 feet in length by 80 in breadth, but some thirty feet of the length are included in a lecture-room, Sabbath-school rooms, etc. The audience-room will accommodate about 1,200 persons. The entire cost of the building and ground was a little more than $40,000."

This rock is called by the people of that region, "Tar Granite," and is procured in large quantities near the city, of the finest quality.

"A Congregational church has recently been formed in Chicago, on the west side of the river, in part by a secession from the Third Presbyterian Church, provoked by the arbitrary proceedings of the Presbytery toward that church, while those proceedings in turn were called forth by the extreme action of the church on the subject of slavery. I regret that I had no opportunity to confer with the brethren immediately concerned in this movement, but was obliged to get all my information either at second-hand, or from sources liable to prejudice. A strong movement for a Congregational church upon the proper basis, while it might be resolutely opposed, could not fail to attract to itself some important influences at Chicago, and to become a center of influence for a wide region. There is an element in the place and in the region that demands such an organization, and that would develop itself powerfully under the proper man. But the movement should not be controversial or sectarian, and much less should it be simply or mainly *reformatory* in the humanitarian sense. It is to be hoped that Congregationalists will labor earnestly and practically through the individual pulpit, through a free press, through the ballot-box as citizens; and above all, through the power of personal holiness, giving weight and force to every effort at reform. Perhaps the movement at Chicago, though occasioned by unpropitious circumstances, may result in a permanent organization, such as I have characterized; a church formed not upon some abstract proposition in morals, but upon the broad, free principles of the Gospel, and animated more with the kindly spirit of Christ than with a zeal for specific reforms. Its power in such reforms will depend not upon the stringency of its resolves, but upon the depth and earnestness of its piety. I hope it will not be a mere family quarrel. In saying these things I speak not so much with personal references as from general principles, knowing that with regard to this new church I am much in the dark.

"Chicago, with all its improvements, its activity, and its wealth, can never vie with Cleveland *as a place of residence*. It is situated on a dead level, where water does not know which way to run. Its broad streets are almost wholly destitute of trees. Its soil is miry beyond endurance, though a system of drainage lately introduced has rendered a three foot cellar a practicable thing. The surrounding country is a vast prairie, now under good cultivation, but too uniform to please the eye. A few miles out of town is what is called by a figure of speech *a Summit*, where the waters divide for the lakes and the Mississippi; this way seeking the Atlantic by the river St. Lawrence, and that way by the Gulf of Mexico; flowing like the benevolent impulses of the heart to embrace a continent, and to mingle in the warm gulf stream of an ever-circling beneficence. Yet uninviting as Chicago is, to the tourist, and with few exceptions to the resident, it is and will be a place of business, the thoroughfare of emigration, the entrepot of western commerce. This will make it wealthy, prosperous, and great."

Mr. T. must have been rather limited in his examination, not to have seen the large number of streets with their two sides shaded with rows of fine trees on both sides of the river.

Mr. Thompson was greatly annoyed by the failure of conveyances to perform their trips, as advertised; but, from my own experience of several years in the West, I can say that punctuality is their general rule, and that these delays are only the exceptions, and are deserving of the censure here applied; especially on the Canal and Illinois river general promptitude is observed: but here is Mr. T.'s own narrative:

"I observe that Dr. Bacon in his letter from Lyons, which I have just read, says that in his calculations of distances he did not make 'sufficient allowance for the uncertainties of French lines of conveyance,' and accordingly was disappointed in his plans. If Mr. Pilatte should visit the West, he might reciprocate the compliment as to the uncertainties of American lines of conveyance, for it would puzzle the shrewdest Yankee to make any calculations based upon the advertisements of Steamboats on these Western waters. For a boat to lie at her wharf hours after the time set for starting, and by innumerable stops to prolong her trip a day or two beyond the promised time, is an event of common occurrence. Western people take it as a matter of course, and it is impossible to get vexed at such a delay—if it were even worth while to get vexed at any thing—when every body about you is as unconcerned and phlegmatic as if time had not been divided into periods of six working days, each of which has its appropriate duties. Indeed *time* does not yet seem to enter as an element into Western thought. It answers about as well to do a thing next week as this; to wait a day or two for a boat, as to meet it at the hour appointed; and so on through all the details of life.

"This is a great country, and it is a great ways to any where, and there is no use of being in a hurry. The very magnitude of the distances to be overcome, instead of exciting to diligence, punctuality, and speed, rather begets a loaferish habit, which becomes a characteristic of society. But the increase of population, the demands of commerce, and especially the construction of railroads, will soon correct this habit, and restore the pendulum to its proper place in the affairs of men.

"I observe that some of the St. Louis papers are ridiculing the idea of a pendulum for rendering visible the rotation of the earth. I cannot but think, however, that any contrivance that should make the earth's motion a palpable fact to the Western mind, would have a salutary moral effect upon the people of 'this country.' The immensity of these western prairies, the sluggishness of many western rivers, and the absence of all tidal influences, tend greatly against any practical belief of the Copernican system. In fact you can see on the same plain just where the sun rises and where he sets, while the great prairie lies still with its quiet bosom upheaved to receive his beams. If any philosopher in mechanism could set the prairies whirling before the astonished natives, things would jog on here a little faster. Not that I would have life always busy, always hurried—I am too thankful for a temporary relief for that—but the habit of punctuality and regularity is very desirable even in the earliest stages of society. I find it hard to shake off my Eastern system for the laxity of the West. But I fear you will think I have already done this, if I prolong this dissertation on time instead of setting out upon my travels.

"The immediate occasion of these thoughts (alas how have such occasions since multiplied !) was the derangement of my whole plan at Chicago. Reaching that place at an early hour on Friday morning, I said to myself, 'Less than 300 miles to Jacksonville, by canal, steamboat, and railroad, we shall surely finish that by Saturday night.' So off I posted to the packet office to take passage for the 8 o'clock line 'through in 20 hours,' which would leave only 160 miles by steamboat, with a whole day before us. But, behold, the steamboat does not connect with the morning line of packets, and it is just as well to remain at Chicago till evening. So the idea of reaching Jacksonville for the Sabbath is abandoned. However, by taking the evening packet at 5 o'clock, 'through in 20 hours,' we shall reach La Salle, the head of steamboat navigation on the Illinois, by 1 P. M., on Saturday; then as Peoria is but 60 miles down the river, a steamboat going with the current will surely carry us there by early evening, so that we can pass the Sabbath with dear old New England friends, and in the midst of Sabbath-schools and churches. Not quite so fast; but we will take our journey in regular order. At 5 o'clock we are on board the packet, but the steam-tug which is to take us up the Chicago river to the first canal lock, has been detained, and it is almost 7 before we are fairly under way; but never mind, '20 hours' will allow some margin, and we shall have time enough.

"This Canal, by-the-way, as originally projected, was intended to be a ship canal, uniting Lake Michigan with the Illinois river, and so with the Mississippi. It was partly constructed with reference to that idea, and had the plan been carried out, the whole lockage would have been downward from Chicago, carrying the water of the lake into the river, and thus keeping the channel of the Illinois always full. This would have given immense facilities for trade, and would have brought to Chicago, and *via* Chicago for New York, much of the produce of the interior, which now goes down the Mississippi and up the Ohio, or by way of New Orleans and the Gulf. Steamboating without transhipment from St. Louis to Chicago, would contribute greatly to the trade of both cities. But the failure of all the gigantic plans of Internal Improvement in Illinois, and the heavy incumbrance of State debt, led to the completing of this as a Canal of ordinary width and depth, under the management of three Trustees who act in behalf of the stockholders and of the State. The work is well constructed, and the business is beginning to pay a good interest on the capital invested.

"The packet boats are regulated with a due regard to neatness and comfort, and excepting the inconvenience of being suspended, by lot, for the night somewhere in a double tier of hammocks, swung up three deep, and the still greater inconvenience of having no fit place for the morning's ablutions, a day upon one of them can be very well endured. The Railroad, however, now fast progressing, will soon draw off all mere business and pleasure travel, and leave the canal to the transportation of freight and emigrants. Nothing so strikingly illustrates the progress of our country as the facility with which one great internal improvement is set aside for another that offers better facilities for travel. The canal upon which millions have been expended gives place to the railroad at a cost of yet other millions; the tow-path makes way for the iron track. What comes next? Let flying machines be invented, that shall combine certainty and safety of transportation with a greatly increased speed, and the rails of many a road will be left to rust in the ground.

"Canal traveling gives good opportunities for the study of character and for usefulness to one's fellow-passengers. What with books, pen and paper, conversation and discussions, the evening and the subsequent day were whiled away very pleasantly. I was gratified with the general regard for propriety and morality which was shown by travelers brought into such close contact. There was little swearing and little drinking; and whoever indulged in any sort of intoxicating beverage, felt called upon to apologize for the act, by saying to his neighbors, that the water of the country did not agree with him, and that he took ale or brandy as a preventive of cholera. How essentially have the habits of society in this particular been changed by the temperance reformation! A stranger drinking liquors at a public table is apt to find himself alone, and to feel obliged to plead some special excuse. Much, however, remains to be done."

Here Mr. T. narrates a series of conversations, usual on a long tour in a boat's cabin, upon various topics, as Reforms, Religion, and Politics.

"A long digression this! yes; and a long jaunt we have had, twenty-three hours, but here we are at La Salle.

"It was now about five P. M., and as the probability was that the steamboat would not reach Peoria, some sixty miles distant, till the dawn of the Sabbath, we went on shore and rested the seventh day according to the commandment. It was curious to notice how our decision to remain affected the minds of our passengers. Some, I think, were influenced by it to do the same; and others, to whom it seemed a novelty, evidently respected our feelings and course in the matter. It led to some interesting conversation about the Sabbath, and I aimed to give the impression that Christians do not keep the day from constraint, from mere scruples of conscience, or in a legal spirit, but from a hearty interest in the great object of the institution, and for the benefit it brings to themselves and others. I am thus particular on this point, because I see that Sabbath-breaking is the almost universal habit of travelers; and at the West the temptations to this are very strong. This I felt. I might have made a plausible argument for trespassing a *little* upon holy time. La Salle was represented to us as a cheerless place, without a church and without society. My invalid companion needed the comforts of a good home, such as would be found with friends at Peoria, and we should reach that place perhaps by day-break. By staying at La Salle we might be detained two days. But I would not feel justified in leaving Albany or Stonington on Saturday evening to reach New York at day-break on the Sabbath; and what is not right at the East is not right at the West. To be sure, to keep the Sabbath when traveling at the West costs money, and time, and comfort, and requires that one should be singular. But have we not learned to obey God implicitly, and to the full, and leave the results with Him? If we have not learned this, we know nothing of the obedience of His children.

"Now came a series of agreeable disappointments. First, we found at La Salle an excellent hotel. The cordial welcome given us by the host and ladies of the house, made us feel quite at home. As soon as my calling was surmised, a claim was put in for preaching on the Sabbath. I sallied forth into the town to see what arrangements could be made for hearing or preaching the Gospel. And here occurred my next surprise. I found I was not in a heathen country, as it had been represented. To be sure, I saw evidence enough of the presence of evil; for in a walk of ten minutes I counted as many groggeries, a billiard saloon, and other appurtenances of vice. But on inquiring at one or two stores, I ascertained that there were Christians in the place; that a house of worship was then erecting for a Congregational Church about to be organized, and that a Baptist brother was transiently preaching to the people.

"A greater surprise, however, awaited me on returning to supper; for who should seat themselves at the table, by my side, but

Rev. Dr. Blagden, of Boston, President Wheeler, of Burlington, Vt., a brother to Dr. B., and a worthy Presbyterian elder from Mississippi, all on their way from St. Louis to Chicago. This gave fine promise for Christian society and the means of grace. It was presently ascertained that Rev. Dr. Hough, formerly Professor at Middlebury College, resided in the place with a son who is Canal Collector, and through him arrangements were made for the morrow's services.

"For the accommodation of the Irish population, there is a Catholic church at this point, and a Cathedral of considerable dimensions is nearly completed, on one of the best sites in the town. This building will answer the uses of both La Salle and Peru, two miles below, and as a number of laborers will soon be employed here on the line of the Central Railroad, it is likely to be well filled for a time. But I doubt whether so large a permanent investment at a point where the Irish population must be somewhat transient, is good policy for the Catholics.

"Our Sabbath at La Salle proved to be a most pleasant one. In the morning we assembled for social worship in a parlor of the hotel; thence we went to the house of God in company; there Dr. Wheeler preached in the morning, Dr. Blagden in the afternoon, and your Correspondent in the evening; and the day was closed with social worship at the hotel.

"'An' is it engineers yees are?' said Patrick, as we walked out to survey the line of the railroad near La Salle; 'sure its ourselves would like the work; wees very poor here.' 'No, Patrick, we're not engineers, but we hope you'll get the work and have the road done before we come this way again.' 'I thought the gentlemen looked like engineers.'" T. .

"In leaving La Salle, I must not omit to mention a terrific storm of wind, accompanied with thunder, lightning, and rain, which passed over us there on Saturday evening. Never before did I realize the wild grandeur of the elements when let loose for their Titan sports, The wide reach of prairie around us gave to the wind a sweep and a power that the steadfast piles of brick in the great city entirely forbid. It seemed to gather force from its freedom, and to accumulate strength in proportion to the area that it traversed. The house shook to its foundations, and to our inexperienced ears each new blast, as it came howling over the prairie-sea, forboded its overthrow. And then the thunder! I have heard the thunder roll along the narrow gorges of the mountains, reverberating with a thousand echoes as it shook the everlasting hills; I have stood on the bare and ragged summit of Mount Washington, as the flaming bolts dashed against the rocks at my feet, while the monarch of the hills was wrapped in clouds that poured upon his head hailstones and coals of fire; but never did my soul quiver with awe as on that night when earth and sky were commingled in one sheet of flame, and the thunder leaped through the vast unbroken expanse of ether. No echo was there, no artificial multiplier of sound, but *sound* itself, as if the hemisphere were a mighty bell of harshest metal, within whose circumference we were inclosed, while ponderous bolts were hurled against it till the din and roar of ten thousand gongs clanging louder and hoarser was concentrated upon our ears. 'Then the earth shook and trembled,' for Jehovah 'bowed the heavens and came down.'

"The poet has described the effect of a night-storm among the mountains of Switzerland:

"'The sky is changed! and such a change! O Night,
And Storm, and Darkness, ye are wondrous strong,
Yet lovely in your strength, as is the light
Of a dark eye in woman! Far along,
From peak to peak, the rattling crags among,
Leaps the live thunder! not from one lone cloud,
But every mountain now hath found a tongue;
And Jura answers, through her misty shroud,
Back to the joyous Alps, who call to her aloud!

"'And this is in the night—most glorious night!
Thou wast not sent for slumber! let me be
A sharer in thy fierce and far delight—
A portion of the tempest and of thee!
How the lit lake shines—a phosphoric sea—
And the big rain comes dancing to the earth!
And now again 'tis black—and now, the glee
Of the loud hills shakes with its mountain mirth
As if they did rejoice o'er a young earthquake's birth.

"This description was more than realized in that the majestic tread of the thunder across the plain, far surpassed its quick leaping among the mountains. No hill, no forest, no city broke its sound, but it poured down from heaven to earth, and resounded from earth to heaven, till it swelled into a continuous roar, augmented by successive peals that seemed never to die away. Now, far as the eye could reach the prairie shone like a 'phosphoric sea;' again it lay enwrapped in an impenetrable gloom. Our thoughts were not the transcendental sentimentalism of the poet;

our wishes were not for a soul-absorption into Nature, but we thought of Him who, amid these terrific displays of His power, guards the sparrow nestling with its young, and numbers the hairs of our heads. The Lord was nigh in His awful majesty, yet were we not afraid! Though the wind blew and the floods came, the house that shook above our heads fell not, for it was founded upon a rock. Be thou my soul established on the Rock of Ages, when the floods of divine wrath shall be poured out upon the ungodly, and—

"'Thunder and darkness, fire and storm,
Lead on the dreadful DAY.'"

The River Floods, an event of great sublimity, and characteristic of the West, occurring annually, are here forcibly described. Memorable and destructive floods occurred on the Mississippi and Illinois rivers, in 1832 and 1846:

"Observing some warehouses surrounded with water, from which boats were taking in their freight, we concluded that the owners had hit upon this expedient for the convenience of those engaged in transportation; but we were presently informed that in ordinary stages of the water these warehouses stood high and dry upon the levee, and that what seemed to be the bed of a wide, flowing river, was usually a 'bottom'—the name given to a low tract of land, meadow or timbered, on the margin of a river, and intervening between its channel and the bluffs or high grounds denoting its ancient bed. Some of these warehouses were surrounded with water to the depth of ten or twelve feet. Indeed I was assured that at one time the water rose fourteen feet in twenty-four hours, and some 3,000 sacks of grain, stored in a new warehouse built quite above the old high-water mark, were destroyed in a single night.

"As we proceeded down the river we saw on every hand the desolations of the flood. In nearly every river-town the street fronting the river was overflowed, and stores and dwellings were submerged to the depth of ten or twenty feet. In some places large and cultivated farms were entirely under water; the stock, crops, fences, every thing destroyed. The loss falls most severely on the poor woodmen, who occupy log-cabins on the river bottoms, and earn their living by supplying the boats with wood; the whole winter's work of many has been swept away in an hour, while they and their families have been obliged to leave their huts and flee for refuge to the bluffs at a distance often of several miles. At some points the river is expanded from an average width of half a mile to the breadth of eight or ten miles from bluff to bluff. We saw several cabins and houses of which the roofs only were above the water. But I have since seen so much greater desolations on the Mississippi, that these seem almost of no account.

"A western steamboat is at first sight a novelty to one familiar only with eastern models. The boats on the western waters are very slightly built—mere shells of pine, shallow, long, narrow, flat-bottomed, open and flaring on all sides, just as represented in Banvard's panorama. There is no cabin either below the deck or upon it."

Most of the boats have good cabins and well-furnished saloons, both for ladies and gentlemen, beside state-rooms.

"The engines are placed immediately on the lower deck, two huge furnaces flaming upon you as you enter the boat, and giving you rather uncomfortable hints of a choice between fire and water in making your exit from the world.

"Huge flaming brands and coals are dropping continually upon the thinnest possible sheathing of sheet-iron, in many places worn through to the plank; heated pipes on which you cannot bear your hand are in immediate contact with boards as dry as tinder, and perhaps already charred; goods, you know not how inflammable, are strown promiscuously around the boilers, while huge piles of dry pine wood, waiting to be consumed, are crowded in the vicinity of the fires. But not every traveler has the habit that I confess to of prying into every thing about him, and therefore few probably enjoy the peculiar sensation of sailing on the rim of a volcano. However, there is nothing like getting used to it, and I learned to sleep quite soundly.

"The cabin is up stairs, and extends nearly the whole length of the deck, over which it is perched upon sundry posts that seem too frail for a summer's breeze; this is divided into a long, narrow saloon, from stem to stern, and a row of state-rooms on either hand. An apartment for ladies is curtained off at one extremity, while the main saloon is used for meals, conversation, promenading, card-playing, and whatsoever one may list. The kitchen, pantry, bar, etc., are all contiguous to the saloon; with every convenience for 'life above stairs,' so that passengers may spend days in and around this saloon without knowing any thing of the deck life below. Some of the state-rooms that open both into the saloon and upon the guard are very airy and pleasant. If, however, there is any deficiency in regard to neatness and comfort, it is in this department of the boat. We took passage in the *Prairie State*, one of the best boats on the river. The furniture was neat, and the table excellent—always excepting the preponderance of grease in western cookery. But the ideas of civilization exhibited in the state-rooms reminded me of Dr. Bushnell's discourse on Barbarism as the first danger of the West, a sermon that contained some of the truest of his paradoxes. In a cozy chat with the captain, I found him a clever, polite, and attentive gentleman.

"The scenery of the Illinois river is rather low and monotonous, but sufficiently picturesque to arrest the eye of a stranger. It savored of the romantic to sail at times through the woods—the water spreading indefinitely among the trees—and in the middle of the stream to bring up at the second story of a house that seemed to say, 'For freight or passage apply within.'

"Peoria is the most beautiful town on the river. Situated on rising ground, a broad plateau extending back from the bluff, it has escaped the almost universal inundation. Indeed, the river here expands into a broad, deep lake, that embosoms the rising flood. This lake is a most beautiful feature in the natural scenery of the town, and is as useful as it is beautiful, supplying the inhabitants with ample stores of fish, and in winter with an abundance of the purest ice. It is often frozen to such a thickness that heavy teams and droves of cattle can pass securely over it. A substantial drawbridge connects the town with the opposite shore. The town is neatly laid out in rectangular blocks, the streets being wide and well graded. A public square has been reserved near the present center. The place wears quite a New England aspect; its schools and churches are prosperous, and its society is good. Back of the town extends one of the finest rolling prairies in the State; this region already furnishes to Peoria its supplies and much of its business, which is destined to increase as plankroads and like improvements shall bring the producer nearer to the market I am struck with the sagacity shown in selecting the sites of many of these Western towns, of which La Salle and Peoria are examples. May 'the children of light' be equally sagacious in choosing their points of action and influence for Christ!

"Traveling on these western waters throws one into all sorts of society, and affords a fine opportunity for the study of human nature. I found a number of emigrants, Irish and German, on the deck, occupying sundry extempore bunks, and living on their own bread and cheese.

"These emigrants have a hard life of it. Poor fare and exposure to the elements, on the open deck of the boat, often engender disease among them, and break up families before they reach their destined home. There should be an active missionary agency on all the rivers of the West. The deck-hands need such an influence, for they have no Sabbath, and are fearfully addicted to profaneness and intemperance. Their manner of life begets a recklessness of death and of all solemn and sacred things. 'A man overboard,' no unusual event on boats nowhere guarded by a rail, or a death by cholera, now becoming frequent, make these men callous rather than thoughtful, and render life and death alike cheap in their estimate.

"The freedom of the western character, and the independence of the western mind, united with the native love of argumentation in the Anglo-American race, render it easy to engage men in discussion, to while away the listless hours of steamboat traveling."

Here a long theological discussion was had among the passengers, to while the time pleasantly and excitingly away.

"From Naples to Jacksonville the ride is by railroad, about twenty-five miles over a rolling prairie, the name given to those vast tracts of land, level or undulating, which in their natural state are entirely destitute of trees, and crowned with a rich growth of grass. Jacksonville is located in the heart of such a region, with no streams or timber, except here and there a grove, with no rocks or stones, and hardly an approximation to a hill. It looks not like an oasis in the desert, but like a finely cut medallion set upon a bosom of the richest satin. As I drew near, I availed myself of the kind offices of a genteel colored man, who pointed out the various public buildings. When he showed me the College, he assured me that the President was 'a very intelligent gentleman,' an opinion which I have had ample means of confirming. It is well for a college when its President is not only respected in the world of science and of letters, but, like the illustrious Dwight, is known and esteemed and loved by all classes in the community in which he lives.

"The first view of the prairies reminds one of the truthful and eloquent description of our own BRYANT:

"'Lo! they stretch
In airy undulations, far away,
As if the Ocean, in his gentler swell,
Stood still, with all his rounded billows fixed,
And motionless forever. Motionless?
No—they are all unchained again. The clouds
Sweep over with their shadows, and, beneath,
The surface rolls and fluctuates to the eye;
Dark hollows seem to glide along and chase
The sunny ridges. * * * *
Man hath no part in all this glorious work;
The hand that built the firmament hath heaved
And smoothed these verdant swells, and sown their slopes
With herbage, planted them with island groves,
And hedged them round with forests. Fitting floor
For this magnificent temple of the sky—
With flowers whose glory and whose multitude
Rival the constellations! The great heavens
Seem to stoop down upon the scene in love—
A nearer vault, and of a tenderer blue,
Than that which bends above the eastern hills.'

"The descent from the poetic to the practical would be far too tame; so I will close.

"Dear me! how long it takes this letter-writer to come at any thing. He has been five or six weeks, already, in getting to our town.

"Have patience, reader, and always remember that this is a great country, and letter-writing, at least to him who perpetrates it, a great bore. T."

"The Earl of Carlisle, [formerly Lord MORPETH,] in his 'Travels in America,' speaks of the place whose name is the subject of this communication in the following terms: 'At Jacksonville, in Illinois, I was told a large colony of Yorkshiremen were settled, and I was the more easily induced to believe it, as it seemed to me about the most thriving and best cultivated neighborhood I had seen.' I know nothing of the nationality of the first actual settlers of Jacksonville; but the tradition of the place is, that the township was entered and named by a company of reckless adventurers, who, having halted at this locality, on an exploring tour, held here a drunken revel, and under this excitement agreed to enter the lands around them and to found a city, which, in honor of the then

President, they named Jacksonville, solemnizing the christening by breaking and pouring out a bottle of spirits. For awhile the place partook of the character of its founders ; but being an inland settlement, it did not afford the same facilities for the growth of wickedness as do the river towns.

"Of this early character of the place no trace remains at present but its name and this tradition. Lord Morpeth would hardly claim for his countrymen such an agency in founding a community as has now been described; but, considering the beauties of the place, it was a handsome compliment, while lecturing before a Yorkshire Lyceum, to attribute the thrift and comeliness of Jacksonville to a colony of Yorkshiremen. If the appearance of the town ten years ago warranted such an encomium from an intelligent stranger, I shall not be thought extravagant in pronouncing it the Paradise of the West, where, amid the luxuriant growth of the fruits of the earth flourish with a scarce less vigorous growth all good social, educational, and religious institutions.

"But the praise of its present prosperity is due not to the farming skill of Yorkshiremen, or the mere agricultural thrift of any class of settlers, but mainly to the influence of a colony of young men who went there years ago not for farms or merchandize, but for the cause of education and religion. This has made the place a center of knowledge, of piety, and of benevolence, for a region destined to be as populous as it is fertile and inviting. Upon this very field there have been conflicts and sacrifices for Christ and his Gospel kindred to those of the foreign missionary work, and that not in a remote period, but within the memory and in the persons of some who are now among the active men of the community. But the day of sacrifice is over—that of reward has already come; the conflict is ended and the triumph secure.

"The men who planted the institutions of Jacksonville had been thoroughly trained in schools of academic and theological learning at the East, and put themselves thoroughly under the school of Christ amid the privations and toils of a new society at the West. The result shows the wisdom of looking very early in the history of a community, toward permanent institutions that shall mould that community and give it its life and power for generations. I rejoice in the work of tract and book distribution now so thoroughly organized over our country; I wish it were even ten times more active and efficient; I see its necessity, its adaptation, and its general usefulness. But I bless God that the energies of His people are not wholly absorbed in efforts for *to-day;* that some, as wise master builders, are engaged in laying foundations for generations to come; nay, foundations that ere this generation shall pass away —such is the growth of society at the West—shall sustain stable and beautiful superstructures, built for Time.—But I anticipate.

"At first sight of Jacksonville, you wonder how the spot ever came to be chosen for the location of a town. It looks like a village made to order at the East, with neat houses—some wood, some brick—some cottage-shaped, and others more ambitious, with gardens filled with flowers and shrubbery, with wide and cleanly streets adorned with shade trees, with a pleasant public square inclosed with a plain white fence, and graced (except that the rickety building has no grace about it) with the court-house and public offices, with schools and academies, with churches, and a college, all clustering about the village center, while well-tilled farms stretch along the borders on every side—it looks, I say, like a model New England village made to order, with such improvements as old villages that have grown up gradually do not admit of, and transported hither by some magic machinery and set down in the midst of the prairie, for picturesque effect, or as a wholesale speculation in city lots.

"Now that the village is there, you see that it is pretty, and seemly, and convenient; that there was need of it, and that it is likely to prosper, in a moderate way, as a place of business; and when you have heard the forementioned tradition, you understand how there happens to be a village in this precise meridian at all; but when you inquire farther for the propriety of the location, you see no river, no hills, no forests, no streams, nothing in short that should have led to the selection of this particular section of the vast prairie as the site of a town, rather than any other within twenty miles of it. A more careful study, however, of the features of the country shows that it was a lucky accident that hit upon this location; for while there is nothing in or about Jacksonville that can aspire to the name of a hill, the adjacent country is rolling and exhibits sundry mounds, not Indian, but natural, that swell in some instances to the hight of forty or fifty feet! While there are no forests, there are sundry beautiful groves, that vary the scenery and also furnish a partial supply of lumber; and, in the absence of a mill-stream, the low, sluggish, muddy, ever devious Movestar, winds itself all about the town. This name, by the way, is a corruption of the French *Mauvaise Terre* (bad country), which for some unknown reason was given to the creek by French explorers at its mouth, where it empties into the Illinois.

"But never was there a more decided misnomer. Bad land, forsooth! Let the New England farmer who has spent half his life in gathering the stones and grubbing the stumps out of a five acre lot, and the other half in trying to make lean, jaundiced corn grow in the two inches of soil, come out and look upon these corn-fields of hundreds of acres, where the rich black loam is turned up by the plow to the depth of two feet, where is never seen a stick or a stone, where the hoe is never used, but weeds are plowed up by driving the team between the rows, and where, as the season advances, one may ride on horseback through acres of corn without once seeing over the tops of the gigantic stalks, and where in harvest time the wondrous cutting-machine, drawn by horses, like the old scythe-armed chariot of Roman warfare, as it forces its mighty swath through the toppling grain, mocks at the puny efforts of the sickle, and the hot and weary day's work of a man.

"To one who has not looked upon these immense fields, waving for the harvest, it is impossible to convey any adequate idea of the richness of the *cereal* products of this region. Here may be realized the statement of the vast wealth of Job in lands, and corn, and stock. In the immediate vicinity of Jacksonville is one farm containing *seven thousand* acres, under cultivation, with thousands of sheep and oxen, and ten thousands of *ephahs* of corn. The proprietor finds it no easy matter to ride over his vast domain, and to superintend the management of its every part.

"A prairie farm is always conducted on a magnificent scale. The fences, if there are any, do not cut it up in little acre patches, but divide it into stately squares ranging from forty-acre lots to half a 'section.' This I found to the sorrow of my aching feet upon going one day to see some buffaloes kept for improving stock. I was told that I would find them 'just down at the lower end of the field,' in reaching which I had to walk full half a mile or more. The sight of such a farm on a rolling prairie, partly in grass, partly in corn, partly in grain and garden vegetables, as the sun chases over it the cloudy shadows, and the light breeze waves the distant grove, to a lover of the beautiful is perfectly enchanting.

"But it is not in cereals alone that these prairies are productive. Fruits come to great perfection in this soil and climate. Peaches are very abundant, and the choicest varieties of apples may be introduced by grafting. It is so easy, however, to raise the one great staple, corn, that orchards have been comparatively neglected; indeed they have hardly had time to come to perfection. I had no thought of detracting from the merits of 'this country'—to use the current western phrase—when I spoke dubi ously of my prospects for the strawberry season, in taking leave of the Erie Railroad. But on the very morning of my arrival I was regaled with finely flavored strawberries swimming in lucious cream; and I found this delicious fruit to be everywhere a common article of the table. It is a gross idea of some Eastern people that the inhabitants of the West live entirely upon pork and corn, in some parts of the West the living is coarse enough; but in such villages as I am now describing, the family table is spread with all the comforts and delicacies of the East—excepting of course sea-food, which can be had only in pickle or in jars hermetically sealed.

"And then the living is *cheap*, even in the choicer articles of food. Think of fine, fat, spring chickens for $1 or $1 50 per *dozen;* of quails (partridges) and pigeons in abundance; of eggs at three or four cents a dozen; of beef at six or eight cents a pound; of a turkey weighing nineteen pounds for *fifty cents;* and of flour at $3 or $4 a barrel. A man can live like a prince in Jacksonville for what would barely suffice to pay his house-rent in New York.

"And yet how many mechanics and clerks are ekeing out a scanty subsistence in New York upon a precarious income of from $500 to $1,500, when for the first named sum they might live comfortably in such a western village, and possibly lay up money besides. Many, especially mechanics, could find ready employment in such places at good wages. If, however, *too* many should crowd at once into the same place, competition would ensue, and with it would come many of the evils of city life. Indeed I almost hesitate to let out the secret of this western paradise, and I surely dread to have its Arcadian repose disturbed by the puffing of the locomotive with an express train from New York.

"The great railroads will essentially modify the main features of western life; will equalize prices by finding a market for produce, and by bringing in more abundantly goods from abroad; will introduce more of the city element into business, and will make adventurers and speculators still more abundant. In due time these prairies will be attached to the suburbs of New York; the great West will be but a day's ride into the country; and its inhabitants will be sending to New York for their flour and garden sauce.

"The churches contribute to all objects of Christian benevolence. There are also in the village several societies—some formed exclusively of ladies—for aiding the cause of missions and the cause of education. From this source relief is afforded to indigent students in the college, and female teachers are educated for the common schools of the State; the daughters of ministers and of farmers, accustomed to hard fare and hard work, and familiar with western society, are thus qualified for the office of instruction, and these in general prove to be more efficient and adaptative teachers than those sent from the East. The money expended upon Jacksonville is already yielding a good return. Here the Portuguese exiles have found a home, with a congenial climate, warm Christian sympathy, and steady employment and support. They are mostly doing well; and with a little Yankee thrift and tidiness might do far better.

"The Charitable Institutions of the State are located at this point. Asylums for the *Deaf and Dumb*, the *Insane*, and the *Blind*, occupy relatively three sides of a quadrangle around the village, each about a mile from its center. The first of these has about one hundred inmates, and is under excellent regulation.

"The institution is sustained wholly by State-tax. Its inmates appeared cheerful and bright, as the deaf and dumb always do. In general they are quick learners, and enjoy the acquisition of knowledge. While I stood by and witnessed their devotions at morning prayer in the chapel, I was so struck with the expressiveness of signs or symbols for religious uses, that I almost became upon the spot a convert to Dr. Bushnell's theory of language. It was affecting to hear the unintelligent, mechanical utterance of sounds by some who had once used the organs of speech, but who, with the loss of hearing, had ceased also to speak. The Asylum for the Insane is not yet in operation. The noble building, like that for the deaf and dumb, occupies a little rise of ground, and is visible at a great distance. From the cupola of either you have an extensive prospect of the prairie sea, diversified with island groves. The Institution for the Blind is in successful operation, but the building designed for it is not yet completed.

"The Methodists have erected at Jacksonville a large Female Seminary, a product of their centenary fund. There is also another Female Academy in the place, of a high order, and of long standing, under the auspices of Congregationalists and Presbyterians. In addition to this, there is a sort of Free Academy, and a good supply of schools of every grade. But to me the chief object of interest, both historically and prospectively, was *Illinois College*. For years I had been familiar with the toils and struggles of the men engaged in founding and rearing that institution, and it was with no common emotion that I looked upon the work of their hands. The site selected for the college is the most beautiful in all the region, and perhaps is not equalled in the State. Upon a rise of ground, skirted with a luxuriant grove, far away from the miasma of rivers, the bustle of commerce, and the wrangle of politics, is this seat of learning and religion, which was itself modeled in the main after Yale College.

"I was more disturbed than disappointed at finding the college buildings so unsightly and so illy adapted to the present wants of the institution. The main building, which is the primitive chapel pieced out, is so low in the stories and so cramped in all its dimensions, that one has to stoop in order to enter it or to get up the steep and narrow stairway; the recitation rooms are poorly finished, and the whole structure looks old and crazy. It was built with poor brick and in dear times. The *people of Jacksonville* should replace it by one more worthy of their present prosperity; they should not suffer such an eye-sore to mar the most lovely spot in their town. Let them send a committee to Beloit to see the building that the citizens of that infant place have erected for *their* College, and then go to work at once with a subscription paper for their own.

"The College is now well manned both in the number and the quality of its instructors. There is need, however, of a Professor of Rhetoric, to impart a polish and finish to the strong, rough materials of the western mind.

"To pass from the intellectual to the physical, I saw at Jacksonville a striking connection between these two, in the *hedge* recently introduced by Mr. Turner, formerly Professor in the College. It would puzzle the 'cutest Yankee to guess out the connection between hedges and common schools; but here they must rise or fall together. Years ago, Professor T. attempted to introduce into Illinois the New England system of Common Schools. But he soon found that the farmers, who had located their farms along the borders of the prairies, near the timber, in order to build their fences with ease, were too widely scattered to be formed into school districts after the New England fashion. Before this could be done, some method must be devised of *fencing the prairies*, so that settlements could be made in the centers. Mr. T. experimented with various shrubs for hedging, but without success, until he made trial of the *Osage orange;* this grows rapidly, endures the winter, and is covered with thorns. It has become universally popular, and already stretches across the prairies for hundreds of miles. Now it is practicable to plant a village in the very heart of a prairie, with farms stretching outward to its borders; and in these compact settlements schools and churches can be sustained. So much for the union of natural and moral husbandry. *Apropos* of shrubbery, I may mention that every shade tree in Jacksonville, of which there are hundreds, was set out within the memory of inhabitants not yet gray.

"I have now said enough of Jacksonville for one letter, and yet the half is not yet told. But I must hasten on to the Mississippi.

"In conclusion I will give only one additional evidence of progress in this region. Fifteen years ago, about the time of the *Alton riot*, the College commencements were held under the restraint of a mob, upon the watch lest any allusion should be made to Liberty. Now, a graduate of Illinois College, an intelligent lawyer residing in Jacksonville, has just been elected to Congress as a known free-soiler. T."

Some pages back is given a description, by Mr. T., of a flood in the Illinois river; and here follows his account of a flood in the Mississippi; the fearful grandeur of these occurrences cannot be appreciated without witnessing them:

"It was worth no little inconvenience and disappointment in other respects, to see the Mississippi at its flood, and especially the flood of this year's June. The water has been higher in some former years; at St. Louis it was yet some eighteen inches below the highest mark on the flood monument; but the annual rise of the Missouri had not taken place, and this flood came chiefly from the Upper Mississippi and its tributaries. In Iowa there was a more general rising of the streams than has been known since its settlement by white men.

"To conceive rightly of the appearance of this flood, one must form a conception of the bottoms that flank the Mississippi on either side. These bottoms resemble what at the East is called a marsh, except that when the river is low they are not wet and miry like our marshes, and they are commonly more or less covered with a heavy growth of timber. The bottoms of the Mississippi are not uniform; sometimes they occur on both sides of the river, sometimes only on one, while there is a high bluff or bank on the other; not unfrequently they reach back to a distance of eight or ten miles and even farther, being bounded by an elevation or bluff, which may have been the ancient bank of the river. In ordinary stages of the water these bottoms are so far drained by absorption and evaporation, that they may be brought under cultivation, and the temptation to this is strong, on account of the richness of the alluvial deposits. Hence in spite of past floods the soil of the bottom is broken up by the plow, and the seed sown in hope of exemption from another rise. These bottoms, however, are more apt to be occupied by the poorer class of people, who earn their living by cutting wood for the boats, and who are content to live in a rude cabin surrounded by a little garden patch.

A rise of a few inches in the level of the river suffices to overflow the bottoms, and sometimes, as during the present summer, they are covered with water for an area of many miles, and to the depth, perhaps, of several feet. Such a rise is of course highly destructive to property, and sometimes to life. Wood, grain, and cattle are swept away; crops are destroyed; fences and other improvements are demolished; houses made untenantable, and their occupants obliged to flee for safety to the higher ground in the rear. The damage done by such a flood, spreading over thousands of miles and continuing for many weeks, can be computed only by millions of dollars. I heard of one individual who lost by this flood 1,500 cords of wood (worth from $3,000 to $4,000) and 3,000 sacks of grain.

"The aspect of the river during the flood is at once majestic and picturesque. Well does it then deserve the name Father of Waters. You behold a strong, swift current, in or near the accustomed bed of the stream, running perhaps seven miles an hour, and sometimes forcing for itself a new channel, while on either hand the water spreads out among the trees as far as the eye can reach, giving the impression of a sail through a deluged grove. The many islands of the river, some of them beautifully wooded, highten the picturesque effect, and contribute to this illusion. In one instance, through an opening in the woods, I saw the bottom overspread to an extent that the eye could not measure—the bluffs seemed as remote as does the Long Island shore in passing up the Sound to New Haven—but here and there fragments of fences, a haypole, or the roof of a barn were seen jutting up as melancholy monuments of the general ruin.

"Some of the towns on the river have suffered severely from the inundation of their lower streets; but others, such as Alton,

Quincy, and Keokuk, which are built mainly upon the bluffs, have escaped. Alexandria, at the mouth of the Des Moines river, appeared to have been the heaviest sufferer; nearly if not every house being more or less inundated, and the inhabitants having deserted the town almost *en masse.* I was told by a fellow-traveler that the ferry-boat which usually runs about half a mile across the mouth of the river, was obliged to sail *eight miles* across the bottom to make a landing.

"Think now of the volume of water requisite to raise the Mississippi a few inches only, when these immense bottoms are overflowed, especially to raise it, as was one day noted, at the rate of an inch an hour, or two feet in the twenty-four! I never before had such an impression of the power of water as an agent in geological changes; nothing can resist such a flood. There is much in the geological features of this region to indicate the agency of far mightier floods in years or ages gone. Perhaps, as has been suggested, the great lakes once emptied through this channel to the sea. Lake Michigan seems now on the map to be turned upside down, and the almost dead level at Chicago favors the idea that it once emptied itself southward. In digging a well at Jacksonville there was found, twenty-five feet below the surface, a solitary piece of Lake Superior copper. How came it there? Or whence came the marine shells that strew the bank of the Mississippi near New Boston?

"For a considerable distance above St. Louis, the banks of the Mississippi are comparatively level, excepting the bluffs of Alton and Quincy; but above the rapids, the bluffs become a more frequent feature of the scenery, and when cultivated or covered with shrubbery, are exceedingly beautiful. The entrance of Fevre river, especially, presents commanding bluffs, rising in a conical form, to which the name of *mounds* is given, and which serve as way-marks to the traveler. Opposite Dubuque I noticed several artificial mounds, usually supposed to be the burial places of the Indians.

"As I here gazed at sunset upon the bluff of castellated rock, its green summit crowned with these sepulchral knolls, arranged with the precision and order of a camp, and then looked down upon its solemn shadow in the still stream below, I seemed to stand within the halls of a departed race, where wild mirth and revelry; the war-whoop and the battle dance broke on my ear, till suddenly there came a rush of many feet, a whirlwind, and a cloud, and mirth and dance and battle song were hushed in death.

"'Are they here?—
The dead of other days?—and did the dust
Of these fair solitudes once stir with life
And burn with passion? Let the mighty mounds
That overlook the rivers, or that rise
In the dim forest, crowded with old oaks,
Answer. A race that long has passed away,
Built them; a disciplined and populous race
Heaped, with long toil, the earth, while yet the Greek
Was hewing the Pentilicus to forms
Of symmetry, and rearing on its rock
The glittering Parthenon. * * *
* * * * The red man came—
The roaming hunter-tribes, warlike and fierce,
And the mound-builders vanished from the earth.
The solitude of centuries untold
Has settled where they dwelt. * * *
Thus change the forms of being. Thus arise
Races of living things, glorious in strength,
And perish, as the quickening breath of God
Fills them, or is withdrawn. The red man, too,
Has left the blooming wilds he ranged so long,
And, nearer to the Rocky Mountains, sought
A wider hunting-ground.'—BRYANT.

T."

"A day spent at KEOKUK was not lost nor regretted, for it gave me an opportunity of seeing one of the most promising young cities of the West, in the first impulse of its growth and prosperity. Keokuk is finely situated in the southeastern extremity of Iowa, at the foot of the Mississippi rapids, where it must always be a principal depot of trade between the river and the interior. Having one broad street on the river slope, the main body of the town is built back upon the bluff, whence is enjoyed a fine prospect of the river and its bends above and below. A few years since this place was the rendezvous of gamblers, horse-thieves, and all sorts of miscreants. Its very name was a terror, and the lives of immigrants and strangers were never secure there for a single night. But the owners of the soil, and others who saw the fitness of the place for trade, entered into a combination to oust these nefarious characters, and now all trace of them is gone, except here and there a gambling-saloon, which you will see undisguised in almost every Mississippi town. Religious influences came in to aid this reform, and the result is that the whole character of the place is changed, and it offers the highest inducements to settlers. To be sure, its growth has been somewhat impeded by the Half-Breed difficulties, and dispute about titles (the Half-breeds to whom this land was ceded, having sold their interest over and over again, and thus created a variety of claimants); but notwithstanding this, its natural advantages and the enterprise of its business men have put it quite in the foreground as a commercial town.

"At present the Presbyterian Church is without a pastor, but Rev. Mr. Williams, who is engaged in teaching, supplies its pulpit very acceptably. Mr. W. is building a fine stone mansion, after the plan of Downing's *octagon*, in connection with which he will have a Seminary for young ladies, of the highest order. I found an excellent teacher from the Ladies' Society of Boston, engaged here in a prosperous school, herself and her labors being held in much esteem.

"There is a grant of forty acres of valuable land in this place for the use of a Congregational church, whenever one shall be established; but the time for a second church does not yet seem to have arrived.

"It was interesting to observe how the trade of this region is setting toward New York. While Keokuk is increasing its trade with the interior by plankroads, it is looking forward to the completion of railroad enterprises that shall bring it within a few days of this metropolis. The same is true generally of Iowa, Wisconsin, and Illinois. An intelligent merchant was one day commenting, in my hearing, on the foolish and suicidal subserviency of the St. Louis press to the slaveholding interest. I rejoined, that I supposed St. Louis was sure of her Western trade, and was bidding for the Southern. 'Not so,' said he; 'it is exactly the reverse. She is sure of some southern trade, but we are only waiting for railroads to be completed that we may deal with New York.' There is some moral here for New York merchants.

"The geology of Keokuk is interesting. There is a rich quarry near by, where *geodes* and *trilobites* are found in abundance, and of remarkable beauty.

"Montrose is a small town about twelve miles north of Keokuk. The approach to it by land is very beautiful. From a bluff about two miles distant, you see cultivated farms and a neat village spread out in the bottom at your feet, the river winding gracefully around, while on the opposite bluff glitters the huge marble temple of Nauvoo, where the Icarian CABET is now trying his Socialist experiment with four hundred families, that live apart, but have all things in common. I allude to this place merely to speak of the worthy and self-denying labors of Rev. Mr. Beaman, the home missionary stationed here, who traverses a circuit of fifteen or twenty miles, and sustains ten preaching stations.

"FORT MADISON.—This town is somewhat of a rival to Keokuk, though its natural advantages are inferior, on account of the rapids, which at low water are impassable by the larger boats. It has the air of a substantial, well-built town, whose inhabitants are pretty independent of the rest of the world. The State Penitentiary is located here, to which a criminal convicted of murder was conducted as we were passing up the river. Thus crime everywhere obtrudes itself, and deforms the most lovely scenes of nature and the happiest abodes of men.

"BURLINGTON.—A fair and thriving city is Burlington, with its long levee bustling with busy life, and its substantial stores and fine churches of brick and stone. It does not grow now so rapidly as heretofore, partly because of the removal of the Seat of Government to IOWA CITY, and partly on account of a reputation for unhealthiness, which has been greatly exaggerated. Yet it increases with a steady and healthy growth. The society of the place is hospitable, intelligent, and refined; and in religious privileges Burlington is not surpassed by any western town. Its ministers, of all denominations, are able and efficient men, and its newspaper press is quite above the average. I heard here an excellent discourse from Rev. Mr. Salter, pastor of the Congregational Church, in improvement of the then desolating flood. One could not but remark how serious a detriment to the quiet, the good order, and the good morals of the place, is the desecration of the Sabbath by the arrival and departure of steamboats. The shrill whistle startles the whole town; all is bustle at the hotels, while the levee is thronged with laborers awaiting to receive or send off freight. No wonder that western pastors are grieved when, in the midst of all this tumult, some minister or other Christian brother from the East lands from the boat, or takes his passage to economize time.

"DAVENPORT.—This town boasts of a finer location than almost any other on the Mississippi. Here the bluff assumes a sort of Highland beauty, cultivated however to a degree of which the barricades of the Hudson will not admit. Davenport is a healthy location, and partly on this account has been selected as the site of Iowa College. This institution has opened under good auspices. A small but neat building has been erected for its use, on a summit in the rear of the town. The location is central as regards the river boundary of Iowa, but as the state fills up it may require to be removed to the interior, and away from the temptations of a river town, with its usual incidents of gambling houses and strolling circuses and theaters, which are here transported by steamboat from place to place. This should be well considered before much money is invested in college buildings, and especially in view of the proximity into which Davenport will soon be brought by railroad to Illinois and Knox, and to Beloit Colleges. Beautiful as is the present location of the College, and eligible just now in all respects as is the town that has adopted this infant institution, I must doubt whether it should here become a fixture. These, however, are mere passing observations, thrown out in entire friendliness, as hints to those more competent to judge.

"Bellevue is rightly named, seated as it is upon a bend of the river, where it commands a view for miles of its broad rolling flood. Like Keokuk, once a nest of thieves and gamblers, now purified and reviving under happier influences. How destructive is vice to prosperity, and to society itself! Religion is the conservator of both."

"DUBUQUE.—I felt at home in Dubuque, especially when I found myself in the comfortable abode and amid the warm fraternal greetings of 'Our Iowa Correspondent.' How sweetly this queen city, with its wide, rectangular, well-shaded streets, lies spread out upon its broad plateau, much as New Haven lies between east and west rocks; but New Haven can never boast of such a verdure as here clothes alike bluff and plateau. And then the river, here a mile in width, rolling so majestically, flanked on its other shore with tall and verdant bluffs, and studded with islands of richest green! How gorgeous that sunset view, varying with every tint of sky, and water, and meadow, and woodland, as I reclined upon the bluff, (I should call this a hill, but that nomenclature is foreign to the West,) and for a moment forgot that there was aught in the world save beauty and love, the love of nature, the love of God, the love of Christian brethren, here made one!

"I was surprised to find in these remote parts a fine, commodious brick church, with a neat white steeple, pretty green blinds, an organ, a lecture-room, and every appurtenance for the comfort of the congregation. This was built mainly through the personal exertions of Rev. Mr. Holbrook, who came here as a home missionary to a then insignificant settlement, and has seen spring up around him a city that can subscribe its hundreds of thousands to railroads and other public improvements. In ten years its population has increased from 1,300 to 3,710; but that of Burlington has increased from 1,300 to 5,102."

The population of these cities is understated; they each contain not far from 7,000 inhabitants, and are rapidly growing; one, sustained by a rich mineral region, and the other by a farming country:

"Here, as in many western towns, are the foundations of a huge Catholic cathedral, yet to be; and the bishop has here fixed his seat. A Fourth of July procession of the united Sabbath schools of Galena and Dubuque—a row of happy children a mile in length—that chanced to cross his path, must have suggested to him that he has work to do. Our Bishop HOLBROOK can well afford to laugh, where once he might have feared.

"The mining resources of Dubuque and its vicinity, in marble and coal, and in lead and other metals, are very extensive, and must be productive of vast wealth. Iowa is destined to become a rich State; for, beside a most fertile soil, it has treasures within the earth, unmeasured and perhaps inexhaustible. Emigration is setting largely toward this State the present season, and the emigrants are generally of the better class. I asked several why they did not go into Missouri, where the land and climate are equally good. The uniform reply was, that they would not live in a slave State. An intelligent man from the interior of Iowa, on the Missouri line, told me that he could buy cleared farms in Missouri for a very slight advance on *government prices;* while farms in no better condition, on the Iowa side of the line, would command from *ten* to *fifteen* dollars an acre! There is the economy of slavery. I found some emigrating from Missouri into Iowa for that very cause. I was surprised at the quantity of household furniture and farming utensils brought up the Mississippi by every boat.

"A true pioneer crossed my path. He had lived in Iowa since its first settlement, but now the inhabitants were getting too thick for him there. They had towns and fences, and 'lawing and jawing,' and he was going West. He had been up to the head waters of the Missouri, and had secured a quiet spot among the Indians of Nebraska.

"What a field does Iowa open to the emigrant, and what a field to the Christian! With 50,914 square miles, or 32,584,960 acres of rich land, and yet greater riches in the bowels of the earth; with schools, academies, churches, and a college, springing into vigorous life, Iowa must yet become one of the chief States of the Union. As yet, only its Mississippi border can be said to be inhabited; but, in ten years, its population has increased from 43,111 to 192,247, a gain of nearly 150,000. This increase will hereafter be much more rapid.

"'I hear
The sound of that advancing multitude
Which soon shall fill these deserts. From the ground
Comes up the laugh of children, the soft voice
Of maidens; and the sweet and solemn hymn
Of Sabbath worshipers. The low of herds
Blends with the rustling of the heavy grain
Over the dark-brown furrows.'

"One thing already gives everywhere the sign of civilized life—the Telegraph wire stretching from post to post along all the routes of travel, and having a station in almost every town. It seemed like the nervous system of the nation, conveying, quick as thought, the least sensation from extremity to head, the least volition from head to extremity. Like the great sympathetic nerve, too, it has its ganglions, where nervous action is concentrated to be farther distributed along the lines of feeling. Or, like a vast arterial system, it carries the pulsations of the heart to the farthest extremity; and by these wires stretched across the Mississippi, I could hear the sharp, quick beating of the great heart of New York. Hugh Miller's beautiful conception of the telegraph music, as he stood waiting for a railroad train, chimes in with my feelings as I gazed upon the wires beyond the Father of Waters.

"'There blew a breeze from the west, just strong enough, though it scarce waved the withered grass on the slopes below, to set the wires of the electric telegraph a-vibrating overhead, and they rung sonorous and clear in the quiet of the morning, like the strings of some gigantic musical instrument. How many thousand passengers must have hurried along the rails during the last twelvemonth, their ears so filled by the grinding noises of the wheels and the snortings of the engine, as never to have discovered that each stretch from post to post of the wires that accompanies them throughout their journey, forms a great Æolian harp, full, when the wind blows, of all rich tones, from those of the murmurs of myriads of bees collecting honey-dew among the leaves of a forest, to those of the howlings of the night-hurricane amid the open turrets and deserted corridors of some haunted castle. I bethought me—as the train, half enveloped in smoke and steam, came rushing up, with shriek and groan, and the melody above, wild, yet singularly pleasing, was lost in the din—of Wordsworth's fine lines on 'the voice of tendency,' and found that they had become suddenly linked in my mind with a new association:

"'The mighty stream of TENDENCY
Utters, for elevation of our thought,
A clear, sonorous voice, inaudible
To the vast multitude, whose doom it is
To throng the clamorous highways of the world.'

"One more sheaf to be gathered from the prairies and groves of Illinois and Wisconsin, and I shall lay aside the sickle. T."

"It was with feelings of regret that I bade adieu to the Mississippi, whose company I had kept for seven days. I had sailed on the bosom of a flood that was everywhere asserting its dominion over the works of man, submerging alike the graves of a departed race and the habitations of living men, and bearing down the puny barriers that had been reared to arrest its progress. I had traced its desolating march through dense forest shades, over well-tilled meadows, and along busy streets, and had received an idea of power—silent, majestic, irresistible—never before attained. Yet with this power there was beauty, as when amid the lengthening shadows of bluff and island, in the calm hour of setting day, I was paddled across the flood in a little skiff, and laved my hands in the ripple of the oarsman which alone disturbed its surface. The rude worshipers of the Nile and the Ganges, in the adoration of their monarch rivers, reveal a sentiment of the grand and beautiful, which, alas, they know not how to follow up to its highest development in a spiritual and a personal God!

"For days, too, I had sailed along the borders of mighty States, the growing empires of the New World; and above the sepulchral remains of creations preparatory to our own, on the deep alluvium which for thousands of years has been depositing over the rocky graves of the *mammalia* and the *crustacea* of by-gone ages, above the tombs also of the human mound-builders of a modern era, I had seen springing up, in full growth and vigor, the towns and cities of that energetic and all-diffusive race that conceives itself to be fulfilling the mission of man's exalted destiny. I had seen everywhere the flood of emigration rolling like the Mississippi, and, unchecked by the natural flood, rolling on over it, as the Missouri pours its red rushing tide across the bosom of the Father of Waters. I was loth to leave a river that so expresses the powerful and the beautiful, and that links together the almost infinite Past, the eager Present, and the boundless Future.

"And, before I leave it, I will put in yet another plea for the freights of sin and of living death that it bears evermore upon its bosom. 'Sin and living death' on every boat that plies its waters, on every raft that floats down with its current. An intelligent English traveler makes this observation upon a class that he encountered in a western tour:

"'The reckless notions and habits of the vagrant pioneers of the West, evinced as these are by the practice of gambling, drinking, and licentiousness, by an habitual disregard of the Sabbath, and by more constant swearing than I ever heard anywhere else, fearfully disfigure that great valley of the Mississippi, destined inevitably, at no distant day, to be the preponderating section of the entire Union.'

"What is here affirmed of a class of pioneers is fearfully true of portions of the boatmen and raftsmen of the Mississippi. I took occasion to mingle with these men for the sake of studying their character and mode of life, and of ascertaining if there was any feasible way of doing them good. The deck hands on the steamboats are commonly Irish or Americans of the lowest class, interspersed with negroes. Their dress and fare are coarse, their sleeping bunks miserably furnished, and their whole physical condition is exceedingly uncomfortable. As many of these boats consume several days in their regular trips, in the course of which they often stop for wood, and at every town land or take in freight, they usually have two sets of hands, who work and rest alternately at intervals of four hours. The resting intervals are spent in sleeping, lounging, smoking, drinking, swearing, and carousing, and the habits of profaneness and intemperance grow fearfully upon men who have no companions out of this depraved circle, and no means of excitement but the bottle and the vulgar story or song. On some boats, too, they are treated as mere brutes.

"Since few boats on the Mississippi lie by upon the Sabbath, these hands have no opportunity of attending public worship or of coming under any religious influence. They are deprived, too, in a great measure of the humanizing influence of the family. I never saw men who seemed so hardened; never before had I heard or even conceived of such profaneness as fell from their lips. They do not open their mouths without an oath—and such oaths!—they are the vomiting forth of the Abyss. These men seemed to be impervious to any religious impression. Death by drowning, or by cholera, is a frequent occurrence on the Mississippi—two such cases came under my immediate knowledge—yet death produces no solemnity in such minds. I saw no point at which they could be successfully approached. But shall they be utterly abandoned? Is there no way of reaching them? Might not missionaries travel with these boats continually with a view to the religious benefit of their crews? For such a work men of peculiar tact are needed, but, doubtless, the men can be found if the churches will employ them in the work.

The *lumbermen* who in the spring of the year crowd the Mississippi with their rafts are mostly Americans, rough, hardy men, who spend the winter in the pine regions of Wisconsin and the upper Mississippi, and in the spring float down the product of their winter's toil to the St. Louis market. They then return to the 'pinery' by steamboat and stage, with plenty of money, and ripe for all manner of vicious indulgence. Some of them are men of intelligence, and have had their education in the Common-schools and Sabbath-schools at the East; such a one I fell in with, but found him ready to drink, swear, and gamble, like the rest, though with a general air of restraint. These men have much of the free and easy air of sailors; they lead a lawless, plundering life, for the lumber they cut is not their own, but felled from Government lands, and many were the curses and threats heaped upon the United States Marshal, whose advent to the pinery was expected; at times they work hard, and again they are idle and listless, and while away time in games of chance; they encounter hardships and drink 'for health;' their money comes in the lump and melts rapidly away under the warm impulses of sensual passion; they are reckless and improvident. Now cannot these men be reached? They could be if some Nelson could be found to go to their encampments. Those to whom I suggested it, entertained favorably the idea of a circulating library of historical and other useful books, and I doubt not some would welcome the discreet and intelligent missionary. Let Christians remember these men.

"GALENA.—By an unfortunate transposition of letters Galena is located on the maps upon *Fever*, instead of *Fevre*, river (the latter being a proper name), and thus has gone forth a rumor of the unhealthiness of the place. The river on whose rocky shelf this town is built, is here more properly an arm of the Mississippi setting up between lofty bluffs, around whose base it winds with most picturesque effect. The town lies very much like Norwich, Conn.; the streets rise one above another, and the communication between them is by flights of steps, so that the houses on the higher streets are perched like an eagle's eyrie, overlooking the rest and commanding an extensive prospect. No sooner do you step on shore from the steamer than you see the signs of thrift and enterprise, and in the huge piles of pig lead you see also the great resource and stimulus of all this in the mines in which the region here abounds. The town wears a pleasant, lively air, and as it suns itself on a bright morning among the verdant hills, looks altogether coquettish. Pleasant churches meet the eye on the first ledge or steppe above the levee, and private residences wearing the aspect of neatness and comfort, and sometimes of luxury—which the munificent hospitality of their inmates enabled me to verify—adorn each successive hight.

"In the number of its gambling and drinking saloons Galena betrays the influence of a foreign mining population; yet after all these are not so numerous as at first they appear to a stranger, who meets them all at once along the river front by which he enters the city. The dominant influences in the place are moral and even religious. In view of the rapid growth and the prospective increase of Galena, it is gratifying to find the ground so well occupied by active and efficient churches and an able ministry. Galena is already straitened between its hills, and land on the main business street begins to command New York prices per foot. When the Central Railroad shall have its terminus there, its business and its population must increase five-fold; then, perhaps, the lower town will be abandoned, as a place of residence, and churches and dwellings will adjourn *en masse* to the beautiful table-land on the summit of the bluff.

"From Galena I rode out to the Sinsinawa mound—the site of the Roman Catholic College, the corner-stone of which was laid with so much pomp and noise (including that of cannon), on a certain memorable Sabbath, a few years ago. This mound is situated some twelve miles northwest of Galena, toward the Mississippi, and offers a most beautiful site for a college, or any other public institution, for which a healthful location and an extensive and varied rural prospect are desirable. I found here a most indifferent building, four stories high, quite roughly finished, and having hardly a pupil within its walls. The reason of this destitution is that Protestant enterprise has established upon the neighboring mound, at Plattville, that rivals this in beauty, a Seminary of the highest order, which absorbs the youth of the country.

"Eastward from Galena, by stage, one crosses those immense prairies of northern Illinois, which have been aptly compared to seas—where the horizon of many miles circumference, shuts down upon a dead plain, whose surface is not disturbed by one undulation or shadowed by a single tree. You have a feeling of desolation in the midst even of harvests that might feed the world. This region is destined to sustain an immense population, when the building of railroads and the liquidation of State debts shall invite the emigrant to settle on its fertile plains. And all the resources of northern Illinois must be poured into the lap of New York. The State is nearly eight times as large as Massachusetts, and containing 35,459,200 acres of rich black loam. But oh, the mud, deep, black, adhesive, which that same soil makes under rain! through what sloughs we waded, (*slews* they call them; think of John Bunyan's *slew* of despond!) sometimes knee deep, in the darkness of the night, as we slowly dragged on toward the Rock River country. That country, the Paradise of Wisconsin, I shall best describe, as it struck me on coming to it *from* the eastward some years ago.

"Immediately on leaving Milwaukee, you pass through a belt of woodland, and in a few hours reach the far-famed oak openings, though these are already disappearing before the march of civilization, which keeps out the autumnal fires. Picture to yourself a park laid out with royal magnificence, as verdant as the most carefully kept inclosure, covering hundreds and thousands of acres, extending for miles around you, planted with sturdy oaks with the order of a well-set orchard, having no underbrush to intercept your progress, and no fences to prohibit you from trespass, where you can walk or ride in almost any direction over the rich green sward, and where the farmer can drive his plow among the trees almost without clearing, and 'break up' a most luxuriant soil; and after reveling amid these works of nature so far surpassing those of art, imagine that you break forth upon an extended prairie, a plain, or gently undulating surface, bright with the ever varying hues of flowers, upon which for miles you do not see a tree, or fence, or stone, but where the luxuriant grass invites the cattle to the marshes on its border, while flocks of sheep are cropping the sweet herbage in its center—where the ripening wheat over hundreds of acres waves its golden locks in pledge of a nation's sustenance, the unaided soil often yielding 25 or 30 bushels to the acre, with but half the labor of cultivation in New England; and having traversed such a field, as I did, twelve miles broad, strike a sparkling river, whose banks will soon vie in fertility, and even in neat and thriving villages, with those of the Connecticut, and beyond which prairie and opening still stretch onward to the Father of Waters; this will give you a picture of a State as rich and fair as the sun visits in all the West.

"The scenery of the Rock river corresponds more nearly with that of Massachusetts and Western New York than any other in the Western country. The long-extended bluffs, of various hight, resemble the hilly banks of a New England stream, the bottom of the river is pebbly and the water clear and bright, and the banks are well covered with groves. And then you have what New England nowhere affords, the prairie, the beautiful prairie, not so vast as to be overpoweringly dull and tame, but large enough to be novel and wonderful to eastern eyes. The difference between the make of Wisconsin and Illinois is given, in the fact that in Wisconsin the prairies are named, and in Illinois the groves.

"In the southern border of Wisconsin, just across the line of Illinois, on the bank of the Rock river, stands BELOIT, a town of some fifteen hundred inhabitants [nearer three thousand], and the seat of a College which is sustained in part by the College Society. I hardly knew the town when I alighted from the stage, so greatly has it changed in six years. It spreads along both sides of the river, and is laid out with much taste. When I was here in 1845, I went up on the highest bluff upon the eastern bank to examine some Indian mounds and to enjoy the view of the rolling prairie stretching southward into Illinois. This bluff was then talked of as a site for a college, and Rev. Mr. Squier, of Geneva, had just been on the ground and had made liberal proposals for the endowment of such an institution. (Thanks to the kind nursing of that gentleman during that trip, I am now alive to write this letter, having greeted him as a professor in his adopted College.) Now upon that same bluff, sheltered by its lofty grove, and beside the undisturbed mounds of other days, stands a College edifice of more imposing architecture and of better adaptation to the wants of such an institution than any college building I have seen in the West. This edifice, substantially built of brick, is about a hundred feet long by forty in depth, four stories high, with lofty ceilings, spacious and well ventilated rooms for recitations and lectures, and several good dormitories in the fourth story. This is intended for the main college building, to be hereafter flanked with corresponding wings. It was erected by the citizens of Beloit at a cost of about $12,000.

"Beloit College is already in vigorous operation. The decorum of the students, and the general order of the institution are worthy of all praise.

"The ride from Beloit to Janesville in a buggy by night, along the lately flooded bank of the river, through deep sloughs and over bridgeless creeks, was somewhat perilous, and on reaching Janesville, a stage-driver congratulated us that we had got safely through a ditch that he avoided by day by a circuit of three miles! One collocation of incidents interested me greatly. Soon after leaving Beloit at sunset, we came upon an encampment of emigrant wagons near some Indian mounds; there were the tombs of the old savage occupants of this rich soil, there were the eager travelers from the Old World coming to find a home in the New, there stretched the telegraph wire, the symbol of a far-reaching civilization, and yonder loomed the college which should mould these raw materials and shape them into a cultivated religious society.

"JANESVILLE is already a town of considerable trade, one of those inland river towns that every State requires as a central depot. It has now one of the best hotels in the State and many fine stores. The ride from Janesville through Rock, Walworth, and Milwaukee counties, though it exhibited the riches of the country—'as good land as ever lay out doors'—was any thing but comfortable to a spare body already jolted by two days' staging. That Troy marsh and the corduroy make one ache for the completion of plankroads.

"Of MILWAUKEE what shall I say, now that it is brought within three days of us and is familiar to every one; a city that in ten years has increased from 1,700 to 20,000, and whose growth as the great lake outlet of Wisconsin has only begun. It is by one-half a German city, with German signs, German churches, German concerts, German gardens, every thing German. Indeed the German language is almost a *sine qua non* for a business or professional man. The city lies beautifully upon a half-moon harbor of Lake Michigan, and encompasses the Milwaukee and Menomenee rivers. Its peculiar cream-colored brick gives to its buildings a very unique and lively appearance. I brought away a brick as a specimen, being careful to carry it in my trunk and not in my 'hat.'

"Determined to avoid the inconveniences of the overland route by Michigan, we took passage in the Hudson, around the lakes, and were favored with three days of calm and beautiful weather. Gorgeous was the setting and rising of the sun in the clear latitude of Mackinaw and in the broad bosom of Lake Michigan. The boat was crowded to excess, so that the tables had to be set three or four times for each meal, and many had no place to lay their heads. But captain, steward, waiters, all were polite and attentive, doing their utmost to relieve the crowd. The scramble for meals was quite a contrast to what Lord Morpeth describes as a usual characteristic of American dinners:

"'Who that has seen, can ever forget the slow and melancholy silence of the couples who walk arm-in-arm to the tables of the great hotels, or of the unsocial groups who gather around the greasy meals of the steamboats, lap up the five minutes' meal, come like shadows, so depart?' There was no slow and melancholy silence in that three days' voyage; but the constant din and strife of hungry men, women, and children.

"A pleasant Sabbath at Cleveland, a calm moonlight sail to Dunkirk, a day of grateful repose at Binghamton, and we were once more amid the din and heat and strifes and labors of New York.

T."

Repeatedly, in this book, are the vast magnificent Prairies described, by different pens, so universally do they elicit the enthusiastic admiration of all who behold them. And the "gorgeous rising and setting of the sun at Mackinaw," are also objects of delighted wonder to all who witness them.

NEWSPAPERS IN THE WEST.

The following is a list of the Newspapers published in the States treated of in this book, so far as I have been able to obtain them; the statement is principally obtained from the Census Reports to the General Government, and presents, probably, all papers that were in existence when the Census was taken by the Marshal. I have added to the list some papers which were recently started, within my own knowledge, not reported in the official list:

PAPERS AND PERIODICALS IN WISCONSIN.

NAME OF PAPER.	CHARACTER.	TOWN.	COUNTY.
Green Bay Advocate, wky.,	Dem.,	Green Bay,	Brown.
River Times,	do.	Fort Winnebago,	Columbia.
Patriot,	Neutl.,	Prairie du Chien,	Crawford.
Wisconsin Express,	Whig,	Madison,	Dane.
do. Statesman,	do.	do.	do.
do. Argus,	Dem.,	do.	do.
do. Democrat,	do.	do.	do.
Education Journal, mthy,	Educa.	do.	do.
Journal, wky.,	Dem.,	Fon du Lac,	Fon du Lac.
Fountain City,	do.	do.	do.
Union,	Lite'y,	Monroe,	Green.
Herald,	Whig,	Lancaster,	Grant.
Republican,	Dem.,	Potosi,	do.
State Register,	do.	Watertown,	Jefferson.
Chronicle,	Whig,	do.	do.
Kenosha Democrat,	Dem.,	Kenosha,	Kenosha.
do. Telegraph,	F. Soil,	do.	do.
do. American,	Whig,	do.	do.

NAME OF PAPER.	CHARACTER.	TOWN.	COUNTY.
Daily Wisconsin,	Dem.,	Milwaukee,	Milwaukee.
Tri-Weekly do.	do.	do.	do.
Weekly do.	do.	do.	do.
Daily Sentinel,	Whig,	do.	do.
Tri-Weekly do.	do	do.	do.
Weekly do.	do.	do.	do.
Free Democrat,	F. Soil,	do.	do.
Tri-Weekly do.	do.	do.	do.
Weekly do.	do.	do.	do.
Wisconsin Banner,	Dem.,	do.	do
Tri-Weekly do.	do.	do.	do.
Weekly do.	do.	do.	do.
Taglicher Volksfreund, daily,	do.	do.	do.
do. do. wky.,	do.	do.	do.
Commercial Advertiser, daily,	do.	do.	do.
do. do. tri-wky.,	do.	do.	do.
do. do. wky.,	do.	do.	do.
Daily Journal,	Whig,	do.	do.
Weekly do.	do.	do.	do.
Commercial Advertiser,	Whig,	Racine,	Racine.
Racine Advocate,	Dem.,	do.	do.
Old Oaken Bucket,	Temp.,	do.	do.
Democraten,	Dem.,	do.	do.
Wisconsin Farmer, mthy.,	Ag'l,	do.	do.
Beloit Journal, wky.,	Whig,	Beloit,	Rock.
Janesville Gazette,	do.	Janesville,	do.
County Badger,	Dem.,	do.	do.
Standard,	Whig,	Prarie du Sac,	Sauk.
Mercury,	do.	Sheboygan,	Sheboygan.
Democrat,	Dem.,	do.	do.
News,	do.	do.	do.
St. Croix Inquirer,	Whig,	Willow River,	St. Croix.
Blade,	Dem.,	Ozaukee,	Washing'n.
Democrat,	do.	Oshkosh,	Winnebago.
Telegraph,	Whig,	do.	do.
Tribune,	do.	Mineral Point,	Iowa.
Western Star,	F. Soil,	Elkhorn,	Walworth.
Democrat,	Dem.,	Waukesha,	Waukesha.

In Lafayette, Manitowoc, Richland, Adams, and Portage counties, there are weekly Newspapers published, the names of which are not known to me.

PAPERS AND PERIODICALS IN ILLINOIS.

NAME OF PAPER.	CHARACTER.	TOWN.	COUNTY.
Quincy Whig, wky.,	Whig,	Quincy,	Adams.
Wochenblatt,	Dem.,	do.	do.
People's Journal, daily,	Indep.,	do.	do.
do. do. wky.,	do.	do.	do.
Herald and Argus,	Dem.,	do.	do.
Western Legal Obs., mthy.,	Legal,	do.	do.
do. Temp. Magazine,	Temp.,	do.	do.
Cairo Delta, wky.,	Neut.,	Cairo,	Alexander.
Greenville Journal,	Fam'y,	Greenville,	Bond.
West'n Fountain, semi-mthy.,	Temp.,	do.	do.
do. Evangelist, mthy.,	Bapt.,	Rockwell,	do.
Primitive Preacher, quart'y,	do.	do.	do.
Prairie Democrat, wky.,	Dem.,	——	Brown.
Bureau Advocate,	F. Soil,	Princeton,	Bureau.
Gazette,	Whig,	Beardstown,	Cass.
Tribune,	do.	Mt. Carroll,	Carroll.
State Democrat,	Dem.,	Marshall,	Clarke.
Illinois Globe,	do.	Charleston,	Coles.
Courier,	Whig,	do.	do.
Daily Democrat,	Dem.,	Chicago,	Cook.
Tri-Weekly do.	do.	do.	do.
Weekly do.	do.	do.	do.
Daily Tribune,	F. Soil,	do.	do.
Weekly do.	do.	do.	do.
Gem of the Prairie,	Lite'y,	do.	do.
Daily Journal,	Whig,	do.	do.
Tri-Weekly do.	do.	do.	do.
Weekly do.	do.	do.	do.
Daily Com. Advertiser.	do.	do.	do.
Weekly do. do.	do.	do.	do.
Daily Argus.	Dem.,	do.	do.
Weekly do.	do.	do.	do.
Western Citizen, wky.,	Indep.,	do.	do.
Prairie Herald,	Pres.,	do.	do.
Watchman of the Prairie,	Bapt.,	do.	do.
New Covenant,	Univ.,	do.	do.
Eclectic Review, mthy.,	Educa.,	do	do.
Prairie Farmer, mthy.,	Agric.,	do.	do.
Commercial Register, wky.,	Adv.,	do.	do.

NAME OF PAPER.	CHARACTER.	TOWN.	COUNTY.
Medical Journal, semi-mthy.,	Med.,	Chicago,	Cook.
Homœopathic Jour. mthy.,	do.	do.	do.
Norwegian Paper, wky.,	——	do.	do.
German Paper,	——	do.	do.
Du Page Recorder,	Dem.,	Naperville,	Du Page.
Plaindealer,	do.	do.	do.
Prairie Beacon,	Whig,	Paris,	Edgar.
Fayette Yeoman,	——	Vandalia,	Fayette.
Standard,	Dem.,	Benton,	Franklin.
Register,	Neut.,	Lewiston,	Fulton.
Republican,	Whig,	do.	do.
Illinois Advocate,	Dem.,	Shawneetown,	Gallatin.
Grundy Yeoman,	Whig,	Morris,	Grundy.
Gazette,	do.	Carrollton,	Greene.
County Banner,	Dem.,	do.	do.
Warsaw Signal,	Whig,	Warsaw,	Hancock.
Hancock Patriot,	Dem.,	Carthage,	do.
Spectator,	Lite'y,	Oquawka,	Henderson.
Prairie State,	do.	Jerseyville,	Jersey.
N. W. Gazette, daily,	Whig,	Galena,	Jo Daviess.
Weekly and Tri-Weekly do.	do.	do.	do.
Jeffersonian, daily,	Dem.,	do.	do.
Weekly do.	do.	do.	do.
County Democrat,	do.	St. Charles,	Kane.
Aurora Beacon,	Indep.,	Aurora,	do.
Western Mercury,	do.	Geneva,	do.
Journal, wky.,	Neut.,	Knoxville,	Knox.
News-Letter,	do.	Galesburg,	do,
N. W. Gazetteer,	do.	do.	do.
Chronicle,	Dem.,	Waukegan,	Lake.
Gazette,	Whig,	do.	do.
Constitutionalist,	do.	Ottawa,	La Salle.
Free Trader,	Dem.,	do	do.
La Salle Co. Democrat,	do.	Peru	do.
Telegraph,	Whig,	La Salle,	do.
Banner,	do,	Lawrenceville,	Lawrence.
Madison Record,	Neut.,	Edwardsville,	Madison.
Telegraph and Review,	Whig,	Alton,	do.
Illinois Gazette,	do.	Lacon,	Marshall.
Herald,	Dem.,	do.	do.
Metropolitan,	do.	Metropolis City,	Massac.

NAME OF PAPER.	CHARACTER.	TOWN.	COUNTY.
Metropolis Register,	Whig,	Metropolis City,	Massac.
Western Whig,	do.	Bloomington,	McLean.
Patriot,	do.	Waterloo,	Monroe.
Yeoman Prairie Land,	do.	Millersburg,	Mercer.
Morgan Journal,	do.	Jacksonville,	Morgan.
do. do. tri-wky.,	do.	do.	do.
Gazette, wky.,	do.	Mount Morris,	Ogle.
Democratic Press,	Dem.,	Peoria,	Peoria.
Republican,	Whig,	do.	do.
Peoria Motto, mthy.,	Relig.,	do.	do.
Free Press, wky.,	Whig,	Pittsfield,	Pike.
The Union,	Dem.,	do.	do.
Spartan Freeman,	F. Soil,	Sparta,	Randolph.
do. Register,	Dem.,	do.	do.
Chester Herald,	Neut.,	Chester,	do.
Republican,	Dem.,	Olney,	Richland.
Advertiser,	Whig.,	Rock Island,	R. Island.
Daily Journal,	do.	Springfield,	Sangamon.
Tri-Weekly do.	do.	do.	do.
Weekly do.	do.	do.	do.
Daily State Register,	Dem.,	do.	do.
Weekly do.	do.	do.	do.
State Organ, wky.,	Temp.,	do.	do.
Liberia Advocate, mthy.,	Col.,	do.	do.
Observer, wky.,	Dem.,	Naples,	Scott.
Prairie Telegraph,	Neut.,	Rushville,	Schuyler.
Advocate,	Dem.,	Belleville,	St. Clair.
Zeitung,	do.	do.	do.
Illinois Republican,	Whig,	do.	do.
Illinois Advocate,	M. Ep.,	Lebanon,	do.
Freeport Journal,	Whig,	Freeport,	Stephenson.
Prairie Democrat,	Dem.,	do.	do.
Tazewell Mirror,	Whig,	Pekin,	Tazewell.
Illinois Reveille,	Dem.,	do.	do.
do. Herald,	do.	Danville,	Vermillion.
do. Citizen,	Whig,	do.	do.
Gazette,	Dem.,	Jonesboro',	Union.
Register,	Whig,	Mount Carmel,	Wabash.
Monmouth Atlas,	Indep.,	Monmouth,	Warren.
Telegraph,	F. Soil,	Lockport,	Will.
Signal,	Dem.,	Joliet,	do.

NAME OF PAPER.	CHARACTER.	TOWN.	COUNTY,
True Democrat,	Whig,	Joliet,	Will.
Forum,	do.	Rockford,	Winnebago.

The above list does not embrace all the Papers in the State, as the names of some of them have not been obtained.

PAPERS AND PERIODICALS IN IOWA

NAME OF PAPER.	CHARACTER.	TOWN.	COUNTY.
Tipton Times, wky.,	Lite'y,	Tipton,	Cedar.
Hawkeye,	Whig,	Burlington,	Des Moines.
State Register,	Dem.,	do.	do.
Telegraph,	do.	do.	do.
do. tri-wkly.,	do.	do.	do.
Miners' Express, wky.,	do.	Dubuque,	Dubuque
Tribune,	Whig,	do.	do.
Telegraph,	do.	do.	do.
Norwesliche Dem.,	Dem.,	do.	do.
Iowa Observer,	Whig,	Mount Pleasant,	Henry.
True Democrat,	F. Soil,	do.	do.
Western Evangelist, mthy.,	Relig.,	do.	do.
do. Democrat, wky.,	Dem.,	Andrew,	Jackson.
Iowa Sentinel,	do.	Fairfield,	Jefferson.
Fairfield Ledger,	Whig,	do.	do.
Iowa Republican,	do.	Iowa City,	Johnson.
Capital Reporter,	Dem.,	do.	do.
Iowa Statesman,	——	Fort Madison,	Lee.
Keokuk Despatch,	Dem.,	Keokuk,	do.
Whig and Register,	Whig,	do.	do.
Louisa County Times,	Indep.,	Wapello,	Louisa.
Herald, wky.,	Whig,	Oskaloosa,	Mahaska.
Democratic Inquirer,	Dem.,	Muscatine,	Muscatine.
Muscatine Journal,	Whig,	do.	do.
Iowa Star,	Dem.,	Des Moines,	Polk.
Des Moines Gazette,	Whig,	do.	do.
Frontier Guardian,	do.	Kanesville,	Pottawat'e.
Gazette,	do.	Davenport,	Scott.
Banner,	Dem.,	do.	do.
Jeffersonian,	do.	Keosauque,	Van Buren.
Des Moines Republican,	do.	Ottumwa,	Wapello.
do. Courier,	Whig,	do.	do.

CONCLUSION.

Thus have I given a general portraiture of the natural features, scenery, waters, prairies, forests, mounds, soil, etc., with a brief history of the country; with an account of the growth, prospects, resources, internal improvements, the counties, towns and cities, the population, education, business, etc. of the States embraced in the work. And if it shall prove tolerably satisfactory to readers, or be of service to them, in the light for which it is intended, the writer will have gained his object.

The achievements are numerous, in this country, of art and industry over the great and impassable impediments to navigation and transit, which in many locations the grand, bold features of nature interpose; and among them are, the two passages for boats and vessels from Lake Ontario to Lake Erie, an elevation of between one and two hundred feet, overcome by means of lift-locks in the Erie Canal at Lockport, on the south of Niagara river, and the Welland Canal on the north; the span of that great river by a Wire Bridge; the passage of the fall in the Ohio river by means of a Canal at Louisville, Kentucky; and the passage between Lake Michigan and the Mississippi river, by Canal and locks.

And then the great works of a similar character which are contemplated and underway, are—the Canal at Sault Ste. Marie's, for passing from Lake Huron to Lake Superior, to be laid before Congress this winter, and highly deserving its attention. The improvement, by Canals and otherwise, of the navigation between Green Bay and the

Wisconsin river, designed to connect the Great Lakes and the Mississippi at the north, as the Illinois Canal does farther South.

In regard to this work, Governor DOTY, of Wisconsin, writes me as follows:

"Contracts are let for the improvement of all of the rapids between Green Bay and this place (Menasha); and the lands granted by the United States to the State of Wisconsin are deemed sufficient to complete the work. Two dams and locks are finished, which give Steamboat navigation to Kaukauna, twenty miles. From thence a Plankroad has been constructed ten miles to this place, which is situated at the outlet of Winnebago Lake. From this town a line of Steamboats ply around Winnebago Lake, and up Neenah (or Fox) and Wolf rivers, say one hundred miles each. The first is ascended to Wauonah (or Wisconsin Portage), where the Canal and lock are completed, by which they can pass into the Wisconsin river. This stream is now navigable for boats of 150 tons; but being filled with sand bars, it is to be improved by dredging. It is now, however, as good a stream to navigate as the Upper Mississippi. The whole work is expected to be finished in two years or less; but the route for travel or freight is now an excellent one, and the cheapest between Lake Michigan and the Mississippi in the north.

"Respectfully, yours,

"JAMES DUANE DOTY."

Individuals who are well acquainted with the States and regions named, or have traveled much through them, may not meet with much in this book which they do not already know; still if their visits have not been recent, the progress and improvements of the Great West must have greatly outstripped their knowledge.

The list of newspapers of the different States appended to this work will, doubtless, be found serviceable both to emigrants and business men at the East for reference.

Persons who contemplate visiting the West for location, business, or pleasure, may find this volume useful to them; and it is therefore thrown out to the public, with a hope that it may not prove 'a blind guide to the blind.'

Correction.—Through a mistake of some kind the description of Lawrence County has become mixed up with that of La Salle County, on page 260, which confuses the matter, without this explanation.

THE END.

CATALOGUE
OF
MAPS, CHARTS, BOOKS, ETC.,
PUBLISHED BY
J. H. COLTON,
NO. 86 CEDAR-STREET, NEW YORK.

Illustrated and Embellished Steel-Plate

MAP OF THE WORLD,

On Mercator's Projection, exhibiting the recent Arctic and Antarctic Discoveries and Explorations, &c. &c. 6 sheets. Size, 80 by 60 inches.

Price, mounted, $10 00.

This splendid and highly-finished map is the largest and most accurate work of the kind ever published. It exhibits a full *resumé* of all geographical knowledge, and shows at one view, not only the world as it *now* is, in all its natural and political relations, but also the progress of discovery from the earliest ages. In its compilation, every facility has been rendered by the liberality of our own government in furnishing published and private maps and documents; and also by the governments of Europe, especially those of France and England, whose rich stores of geographical works have elicited much, that until the present publication has been as a sealed letter. As a work of art, it excels all its predecessors, and is as ornamental as useful. It is beautifully colored, and mounted in the handsomest style.

MAP OF THE WORLD,

On Mercator's Projection, exhibiting the recent Arctic and Antarctic Discoveries and Explorations, &c. &c. 2 sheets. Size, 44 by 36 inches.

Price, mounted, $3 00.

This work is reduced from the large map, and contains all the more important features of that publication. It has been constructed with especial reference to commercial utility; the ports, lines of travel, interior trading towns and posts, &c., being accurately laid down. An important feature in this map is the transposition of the continents so as to give America a central position, and exhibit the Atlantic and Pacific oceans in their entirety. The map is engraved on steel, highly embellished, and mounted in the best style. As a medium sized map, it contains much more than the usual amount of information.

MAP OF THE WORLD,

On Mercator's projection, &c. 1 sheet. Size, 28 by 22 inches. Price, mounted, $1 50.

This is a beautifully got up map, and, from the closeness of its information, contains as much as the generality of maps twice its size. It is well adapted for the use of those who do not require the detail of topography, which is the peculiar feature in the larger maps. As a companion to the student of general history it is, perhaps, preferable to any other, as it is compact and easy of reference. The progress of discovery, from the times of Columbus to the present day, is fully exhibited; and especial care has been taken to show distinctly the recent explorations in the Arctic and Antarctic regions.

MISSIONARY MAP OF THE WORLD,

On a hemispherical projection, each hemisphere being six feet in diameter, and both printed on one piece of cloth at one impression. Size, 160 by 80 inches. Price, $10 00.

This map presents to the eye, at one view, the moral and religious condition of the world, and the efforts that are now making for its evangelization. It is so colored, that all the principal religions of the world, with the countries in which they prevail, and their relation, position, and extent are distinguished at once, together with the principal stations of the various missionary societies in our own and other countries. It is so finished, being on cloth, that it may be easily folded and conveyed from place to place, and suspended in any large room. It is especially recommended for the lecture-room, Sunday-school, &c., and should be possessed by every congregation.

MAP OF NORTH AND SOUTH AMERICA,

With an enlarged plan of the Isthmus of Panama, showing the line of the railroad from Chagres to Panama; also tables of distances from the principal ports of the United States to all parts of the world, &c. 1 sheet. Size, 32 by 25 inches. Price, mounted, $1 50.

MAP OF NORTH AMERICA,

Compiled from the latest authorities. 1 sheet. Size, 29 by 26 inches.

Price, mounted, $1 25; in cases, $0 75.

TOPOGRAPHICAL MAP OF THE WEST INDIES,

With the adjacent coasts: compiled from the latest authorities. 1 sheet. Size, 32 by 25 inches. Price, mounted, $1 50; in cases, $0 75.

MAP OF SOUTH AMERICA,

Carefully compiled from the latest maps and charts and other geographical publications. 2 sheets. Size, 44 by 31 inches. Price, mounted, $4 00.

This is the largest and best map of South America ever issued in this country, and the only one available for commercial purposes. It is also an excellent school map.

MAP OF SOUTH AMERICA,

Compiled from the latest authorities, and accompanied with statistical tables of the area, population, &c., of the several states. 1 sheet. Size, 32 by 25 inches. Price, mounted, $1 50.

MAP OF EUROPE,

Carefully compiled from the latest maps and charts, and other geographical publications. 4 sheets. Size, 58 by 44 inches. Price, mounted, $5 00.

The best map of Europe extant, exhibiting the topography and political condition of that continent with great accuracy. It is an excellent map for schools as well as for the merchant's office.

MAP OF EUROPE,

Compiled from the latest authorities, &c., with statistical tables exhibiting the area, population, form of government, religion, &c., of each state. 1 sheet. Size, 32 by 25 inches. Price, mounted, $1 50.

MAP OF ASIA,

Carefully compiled from the latest maps and charts and other geographical publications. 4 sheets. Size 58 by 44 inches. Price, mounted, $5 00

This map is the largest and most accurate ever issued in America and contains all the most recent determinations in British India, &c

It is indispensably necessary to merchants trading with China, India, &c., and must be especially valuable at the present time, when our connection with those countries is daily becoming more intimate. Nor is it less valuable for seminaries of learning.

MAP OF ASIA,

Compiled from the most recent authorities, together with statistical tables of the area, population, &c., of each state. 1 sheet. Size, 32 by 25 inches.
Price, mounted, $1 50.

MAP OF AFRICA,

Carefully compiled from the latest maps and charts, and other geographical publications. 4 sheets. Size, 58 by 44 inches. Price, mounted, $5 00.

The largest and most accurate map of Africa ever published in the United States. It exhibits the most recent discoveries of travellers—the new political divisions on the north and west coasts and in Southern Africa, &c., &c. As an office or school map it has no superior.

MAP OF AFRICA,

Compiled from the latest authorities, and accompanied with statistical tables of the area, population, &c., of each state. 1 sheet. Size, 32 by 25 inches.
Price, mounted, $1 50.

MAP OF THE UNITED STATES,

THE BRITISH PROVINCES, MEXICO, AND THE WEST INDIES,

Showing the country from the Atlantic to the Pacific ocean. 4 sheets. Size, 62 by 55 inches.
Price, $5 00.

Extraordinary exertions have been employed to make this map perfectly reliable and authentic in all respects. It is the only large map that exhibits the United States in its full extent. Being engraved on steel, and handsomely mounted, it forms not only a useful, but highly ornamental addition to the office, library, or hall. All the railroads, canals, and post-roads, with distances from place to place, are accurately laid down. To make the map more generally useful, the publisher has appended to it a map of Central America and the Isthmus of Panama, and also a map of North and South America conjointly. It deserves to take precedence of all maps heretofore published in this country.

MAP OF THE UNITED STATES,

THE BRITISH PROVINCES, MEXICO, THE WEST INDIES, AND CENTRAL AMERICA, WITH PARTS OF NEW GRENADA AND VENEZUELA,

Exhibiting the country from the Atlantic to the Pacific, and from 50° N. lat. to the Isthmus of Panama and the Oronoco river. 2 sheets. Size, 45 by 36 inches. Price, mounted, $2 50; in cases, $1 50.

The vast extent of country embraced in this map, and the importance of the territories portrayed, render it one of the most useful to the merchant and all others connected with or interested in the onward progress of the United States. It is peculiarly adapted to the present times, showing, as it does, the whole sphere of American steam navigation on both sides of the continent, and giving the best delineations extant of our new territories on the Pacific. All the railroads and canals are laid down with accuracy. There is also appended to the map a diagram of the Atlantic ocean, in reference to steam communication between Europe and America; and a detailed plan of the Isthmus of Panama, showing the proposed lines of inter-oceanic intercourse. The map is engraved on steel and highly embellished.

MAP OF THE UNITED STATES,

THE BRITISH PROVINCES, WITH PARTS OF MEXICO AND THE WEST INDIES.

4 sheets. Size, 48 by 38 inches. Price, mounted, $2 00.

This is a good map of the settled portion of the United States, &c., and contains all the railroads, canals, and post-roads, &c., with the distances from place to place.

MAP OF THE STATE OF NEW YORK,

WITH PARTS OF THE ADJACENT COUNTRY,

Embracing plans of the principal cities and some of the larger villages. By David H. Burr. 6 sheets. Size, 60 by 50 inches. Price, mounted, $4 00.

This is the largest and best map of the state in the market, and exhibits accurately all the county and township lines; all internal improvements, and the position of cities, villages, &c. A new edition, embracing all the alterations made by the state legislature, is issued as early as possible after the close of each session annually, so that the public may rely on its completeness at the date of issue.

MAP OF THE STATES OF NEW ENGLAND AND N. YORK,

With parts of Pennsylvania, New Jersey, the Canadas, &c., showing the railroads, canals, and stage-roads, with distances from place to place. 1 sheet. Size, 30 by 23 inches. Price, mounted, $1 25.

This is an exceedingly minute and correct map, having been compiled with great care and a strict adherence to actual survey.

MAP OF THE COUNTRY 33 MILES AROUND THE CITY OF NEW YORK.

Compiled from the maps of the United States' Coast Survey and other authorities. 1 sheet. Size, 29 by 26 inches.
Price, mounted, $1 50; in cases, $0 75.

MAP OF LONG ISLAND,

With the environs of the city of New York and the southern part of Connecticut. By J. Calvin Smith. 4 sheets. Size, 60 by 42 inches.
Price, mounted, $3 00.

TRAVELER'S MAP OF LONG ISLAND.

Price, in cases, $0 38.

A neat pocket map for duck-shooters and other sportsmen.

MAP OF THE CITY AND COUNTY OF NEW YORK,

Brooklyn, Williamsburg, Jersey City, and the adjacent waters. 3 sheets. Size, 56 by 32 inches.
Price, mounted, $3 00.

The Commissioners' Survey is the basis of this map. The improvements have been accurately laid down: and to make the work more valuable, maps of the vicinity of New York, of the Hudson river, and of the cities of Boston and Philadelphia, have been appended. No exertion has been spared to keep the work up with the progress of the city and neighborhood. The exceedingly low price at which it is issued ought to secure to it a large circulation.

MAP OF THE CITY OF NEW YORK,

Together with Brooklyn, Williamsburg, Greenpoint, Jersey City, Hoboken, &c., exhibiting a plan of the port of New York, with its islands, sandbanks, rocks, and the soundings in feet. 1 sheet. Size, 32 by 26 inches. Price, mounted, $1 50; in cases, $0 75.

MAP OF THE CITY OF BROOKLYN,

As laid out by commissioners and confirmed by acts of the Legislature of the State of New York, made from actual survey—the farm-lines and names of original owners being accurately drawn from authentic sources. Containing also a map of the village of Williamsburg and part of the city of New York, &c., &c. 2 sheets. Size, 48 by 36 inches. Price, mounted, $4 00.

SECTIONAL MAP OF THE STATE OF ILLINOIS,

Compiled from the United States' surveys. Also exhibiting the internal improvements; distances between towns, villages, and post-offices; outlines of prairies, woodlands, marshes, and lands donated by the General Government for the purposes of internal improvements. By J. M. Peck, John Messenger, and A. J. Mathewson. 2 sheets. Size, 43 by 32 inches. Price, mounted, $2 50; in cases, $1 50.

The largest, most accurate, and only reliable map of Illinois extant.

MAP OF THE STATE OF INDIANA,

Compiled from the United States' Surveys by S. D. King. Exhibiting the sections and fractional sections, situation and boundaries of counties, the location of cities, villages, and post-offices—canals, railroads, and other internal improvements, &c., &c. 6 sheets. Size, 66 by 48 inches. Price, mounted, $6 00.

The only large and accurate map of Indiana ever issued, and one that every land-owner and speculator will find indispensably necessary to a full understanding of the topography of the country, and the improvements which have been completed, and those which are now in progress. It is handsomely engraved and embellished.

MAP OF THE STATE OF INDIANA,

Compiled from the United States' surveys. Exhibiting the sections and fractional sections, situation and boundaries of counties, the location of cities, villages, and post-offices—canals, railroads, and other internal improvements, &c., &c. 2 sheets. Size, 43 by 32 inches. (In progress.) Price, mounted, $3 00.

This map is a reduction from the large work, and contains equally with that important publication all the essential features of the state and the improvements that have been effected. It is suitable for an office or house map.

A NEW MAP OF INDIANA,

Reduced from the large map. Exhibiting the boundaries of counties; township surveys; location of cities, towns, villages, and post-offices—canals, railroads, and other internal improvements, &c. 1 sheet. Size, 15 by 12 inches. (In progress.) Price, in cases, $0 38.

MAP OF MICHIGAN,

Map of the surveyed part of the State of Michigan. By John Farmer. 1 sheet. Size, 35 by 25 inches.
Price, mounted, $2 00; in cases, $1 50.

MAP OF THE WESTERN STATES,

Viz.: Ohio, Michigan, Indiana, Illinois, Missouri, Iowa, and Wisconsin, and the Territory of Minesota, showing the township lines of the United States' Surveys, location of cities, towns, villages, post-hamlets—canals, railroads, and stage-roads. By J. Calvin Smith. 1 sheet. Size, 28 by 24 inches.
Price, mounted, $1 25.

MAP OF FRANCE, BELGIUM,

And the adjacent countries. Compiled from the latest authorities, and exhibiting the railroads and canals. 1 sheet. Size, 32 by 25 inches.
Price, mounted, $1 50.

STREAM OF TIME,

Or Chart of Universal History. From the original German of Strauss. Revised and continued by R. S. Fisher, M. D. Size, 43 by 32 inches. Price, mounted, $2 50.

An invaluable companion to every student of History.

THE FAMILY AND SCHOOL MONITOR,

An Educational Chart. By James Henry, Jr. 2 sheets. Size, 42 by 32 inches. Price, mounted, $1 50.

In this chart, the fundamental maxims on Education—physical, moral, and intellectual—are presented in such a manner as to fix the attention and impress the memory. It cannot fail to be eminently useful; indeed, we believe the public will regard it as indispensable to every family and school in our country.

PORTRAITS OF THE PRESIDENTS,

And Declaration of Independence. 1 sheet. Size, 42 by 31 inches. Price, mounted, $1 50

NEW MAP OF CENTRAL AMERICA,

From the most recent and authentic sources; showing the lines of communication between the Atlantic and Pacific oceans. One sheet. Price, in cases, $0 50.

MOUNTAINS AND RIVERS.

A combined view of the principal mountains and rivers in the world, with tables showing their relative heights and lengths. 1 sheet. Size, 32 by 25 inches. Price, mounted, $1 50.

A CHART OF NATIONAL FLAGS,

Each represented in its appropriate colors. 1 sheet. Size, 28 by 22 inches. Price, mounted, $1 50.

AN ILLUSTRATED MAP OF HUMAN LIFE,

Deduced from passages of Sacred Writ. 1 sheet. Size, 25 by 20 inches. Price, mounted, $0 75.

MAP OF PALESTINE,

From the latest authorities: chiefly from the maps and drawings of Robinson & Smith, with corrections and additions furnished by the Rev. Dr. E. Robinson, and with plans of Jerusalem and of the journeyings of the Israelites. 4 sheets. Size, 80 by 62 inches.

Price, mounted, $6 00.

This large and elegant map of the Holy Land is intended for the Sunday-school and Lecture-room. It is boldly executed, and lettered in large type, which may be read at a great distance. Both the ancient and modern names of places are given.

MAP OF PALESTINE,

From the latest authorities: chiefly from the maps and drawings of Robinson & Smith, with corrections and additions furnished by the Rev. Dr. E. Robinson. 2 sheets. Size, 43 by 32 inches.

Price, mounted, $2 50.

This map is elegantly engraved on steel, and is peculiarly adapted to family use and the use of theological students. It contains every place noted on the larger map, the only difference being in the scale on which it is drawn. While the large map is well suited for a school or lecture-room, this is more convenient for family use and private study. Plans of Jerusalem and the vicinity of Jerusalem are attached. The religious and secular press throughout the country has expressed a decided preference for this map of Professor Robinson over all others that have ever been issued.

MAP OF EGYPT,

The Peninsula of Mount Sinai, Arabia Petræa, with the southern part of Palestine. Compiled from the latest authorities. Showing the journeyings of the children of Israel from Egypt to the Holy Land. 1 sheet. Size, 32 by 25 inches. Price, mounted, $1 50.

An excellent aid to the Bible student.

NEW TESTAMENT MAP.

A map of the countries mentioned in the New Testament and of the travels of the Apostles—with ancient and modern names, from the most authentic sources. 1 sheet. Size, 32 by 25 inches. Price, mounted, $1 25.

"Its size, finish, distinctness, fullness, and accuracy, make it very elegant and useful. Sabbath-school teachers and private Christians, as well as theological students, may esteem and use it with great advantage. * * * I own and value." *Samuel H. Cox, D. D.*

"On a scale neither too large to be unwieldy, nor yet too small to be accurate, it presents at a single view, with great distinctness, the scenes of the striking events of the New Testament, and cannot fail to give to those events a greater clearness, and by presenting so plainly their localities to throw over them new interest. * * * * * It seems to have been drawn in accordance with the best authorities."
Erskine Mason, D. D.

"Valuable for accuracy, beauty, and cheapness. Having both the ancient and modern names of places, and being of portable size, it would appear happily adapted for the use of Sabbath-school teachers."
William R. Williams, D. D.

"I have been much pleased with the apparent accuracy, and the beautiful execution of a map of the countries mentioned in the New Testament, published by Mr. Colton, and think it adapted to be useful."
Stephen H. Tyng, D. D.

GUIDE-BOOK THROUGH THE UNITED STATES, &c.

Travelers' and Tourists' Guide-Book through the United States of America and the Canadas. Containing the routes and distances on all the great lines of travel by railroads, canals, stage-roads, and steamboats, together with descriptions of the several states, and the principal cities, towns, and villages, in each—accompanied with a large and accurate map. Price, $1 25.

ROUTE-BOOK THROUGH THE UNITED STATES, &c.

Travelers' and Tourists' Route-Book through the United States of America and the Canadas. Containing the routes and distances on all the great lines of travel by railroads, stage-roads, canals, rivers, and lakes, &c.—accompanied with a large and accurate map. Price, $1 00.

MAP OF THE UNITED STATES,

The Canadas, &c., showing the railroads, canals, and stage-roads, with the distances from place to place. Size, 28 by 32 inches. Price, in cases, $0 63.

MAP OF THE UNITED STATES,

The British Provinces, &c. Size, 24 by 20 inches. Price, in cases, $0 38.

MAP OF THE UNITED STATES,

The British Provinces, Mexico, and Central America, showing the routes of the U. S. Mail Steam-ships to California and Oregon, with a plan of the "Gold Region," &c. Size, 32 by 25 inches. Price, in sheets, $0 25; in cases, $0 38.

GUIDE-BOOK

THROUGH THE NEW ENGLAND AND MIDDLE STATES.

Traveler's and Tourist's Guide-Book through the New England and Middle States, and the Canadas. Containing the routes and distances on all the great lines of travel by railroads, canals, stage-roads, and steamboats, together with descriptions of the several states, and the principal cities, towns, and villages in each—accompanied with a large and accurate map. Price, $0 75.

MAP OF NEW YORK,

With parts of the adjoining States and Canada, showing the railroads, canals, and stage-roads, with distances from place to place. Price, in cases, $0 38.

MAP OF THE NEW ENGLAND STATES,

Showing the railroads, canals, and stage-roads, with distances from place to place. Price, in cases, $0 38.

THE WESTERN TOURIST,

And Emigrant's Guide through the states of Ohio, Michigan, Indiana, Illinois, Missouri, Iowa, and Wisconsin, and the territories of Minesota, Missouri, and Nebraska, being an accurate and concise description of each state and territory; and containing the routes and distances on the great lines of travel—accompanied with a large and minute map, exhibiting the township lines of the United States' surveys, the boundaries of counties, and the position of cities, villages, and settlements, &c. Price, $0 75.

THE BOOK OF THE WORLD;

Being an account of all Republics, Empires, Kingdoms, and Nations, in reference to their geography, statistics, commerce, &c., together with a brief historical outline of their rise, progress, and present condition, &c., &c. By Richard S. Fisher, M. D. In two volumes, pp. 632–727. (Illustrated with maps and charts.)

Price, $5 00.

OPINIONS.

"I have looked over the work with a good deal of interest. It appears to me to be a very useful publication. It brings down the geographical and statistical information of the various countries of the world to a much later period than any other work that has come under my observation, and will not only be useful to the student, but to every man desirous of obtaining the latest and most authentic information."
Millard Fillmore, Vice Pres. of U. S.

"The work appears to me a very excellent one, and a very valuable contribution to American literature." *Charles Anthon, LL. D.*

"I have examined it sufficiently to perceive that it contains an immense amount of interesting and useful information."
Robert C. Winthrop, M. C.

"It deserves a place in that indispensable department of every private, and especially of every school library—the department of books of reference." *Henry Barnard, Sup. Com. Schools in Conn.*

"I have been fully satisfied with the fulness and extent of the information its ample pages present in answer to every inquiry—embracing topography, physical geography, climate, products, mineral resources, commerce, and history." *S. W. Seton, Agt. Pub. Sch. Soc. N. Y.*

"It appears to me to contain a more full and accurate exhibition of the world, in its geographical, commercial, and statistical aspects, than any work with which I am acquainted."
Rev. R. R. Gurley, Chaplain U. S. Senate.

"As a book of reference it is of great value, and contains more in the same space than any work of a similar character I have yet seen. * * * * I have great pleasure in recommending this book to all persons who desire to possess a work of reference touching the great interests of all nations."

Abbott Lawrence, U. S. Minister to England.

"The work, as a whole, may be said to constitute a library within itself. There is no point, scarcely, in art, science, literature, economy, or history, at all appropriate to the subjects treated upon, which, on reference to the work, will not be found fully elucidated; and the aim of the author seems to have been to condense into as small a space as possible the entire circle of human knowledge."

Hunt's Merchants' Magazine.

"No work of a similar character, or on so magnificent a scale, has been issued from the American press since the volumes of the veteran Morse. * * * * The author has omitted nothing that could at all add to the perfection of his work." *Democratic Review.*

"We feel assured that the learned compiler of these volumes has spared no investigation and care to exhibit the world as it now is, and we can very confidently recommend the result of his labors. Such a work was especially needed." *National Intelligencer.*

"It is written in a style at once easy, perspicuous, and energetic."

Independent, N. Y.

"We feel satisfied that the greatest labor and pains-taking must have been expended, to have brought together such an amount of valuable information." *N. Y. Journal of Commerce.*

"Editors and politicians, especially, have great use for such a work. They have constant occasion to appeal to just such statistics as these volumes embody, to illustrate and enforce their arguments or explode the sophistries of dogmatists." *National Era.*

"The 'Book of the World,' embodying as it does a vast and varied amount of information, drawn from all available authentic sources, possesses great intrinsic value, and must prove useful to all classes of American readers." *Texas Wesleyan Banner.*

A CHRONOLOGICAL VIEW OF THE WORLD,

Exhibiting the leading events of Universal History; the origin and progress of the arts and sciences, &c.; collected chiefly from the article "Chronology" in the new Edinburgh Encyclopedia, edited by Sir David Brewster, LL. D., F. R. S., &c.; with an enlarged view of important events, particularly in regard to American History, and a continuation to the present time, by Daniel Haskell, A. M., American Editor of McCulloch's Universal Gazetteer, &c. 12mo. pp. 267.

Price, $0 75.

COLTON'S OUTLINE MAPS,

ADAPTED TO THE USE OF

PRIMARY, GRAMMAR, AND HIGH SCHOOLS.

This new and valuable Series of Outline Maps comprises—

A Map of the World, in two hemispheres, each 80 inches in diameter, and separately mounted.

A Map of the United States, 80 by 62 inches.

A Map of Europe, 80 by 62 inches, on the same plan with that of the United States, will complete the series

THE MAPS OF THE WORLD

Are nearly *quadruple* the size of any others now in use, and exhibit the different portions of the Earth's surface in bold and vivid outline, which makes them sufficiently distinct to be plainly seen and studied from the most distant parts of the largest school-room. They exhibit the physical features of the World, and also give an accurate view of its political divisions, showing the relative size of each, with their natural and conventional boundaries. In the corners of each map there are diagrams which exhibit the elements of physical geography, as the *parallels*, *meridians*, *zones*, and *climates*—the latter by isothermal lines. There are also appended two separate hemispheres, exhibiting the Atlantic and Pacific Oceans complete, &c., forming in all *eight* different diagrams, illustrative of the primary elements of the science. These appendices will greatly assist the teacher in his elucidations, and make tangible to the scholar the basis of geographical mechanism.

THE MAP OF THE UNITED STATES

Exhibits the entire territory of the Union from the Atlantic to the Pacific Oceans, and also the greater portion of the British Possessions in the North, and the whole of Mexico and Central America, with part of the West Indies, in the South. It has also appended to it a MAP OF THE NEW-ENGLAND STATES, on a larger scale. The physical and political geography of this interesting region is minutely detailed. The localities of the cities, and important towns, ports, and harbors are denoted by points, and the map generally has been constructed on the most approved principles, under the supervision and advice of several competent and experienced teachers.

The Price of these Maps is $5 each

COLTON'S UNIFORM SERIES

OF

TOWNSHIP MAPS

OF THE SEVERAL

STATES OF THE UNION.

Compiled from the U. S. Surveys and other Sources.

These Maps are compiled from the original U. S. surveys, and other authentic and reliable sources. The size of each is 29×32 inches. They contain all the internal improvements, as railroads, canals, and post-roads; the location of mines and mineral lands; the names of all cities, towns, villages, post-offices, and settlements; the county and township lines; and all other information usually sought for on maps—each map forming in itself a complete reflex of the condition of the State it represents. The following States of the series have been completed:—

MAINE,	OHIO,
N. HAMP. & VT.	WISCONSIN,
MASS., R. I. & CONN.	IOWA,
NEW YORK,	MISSOURI,

VIRGINIA, MARYLAND, & DELAWARE.

Similar maps of the other States and Territories will be issued at an early period; and when the whole series is finished, it is intended that it shall form a splendid

NATIONAL ATLAS OF THE UNITED STATES,

which, in point of scale, accuracy of information, embellishment, and general finish, will be superior to any like publication that has ever issued from the press of either Europe or America.

The price of each map, when handsomely mounted, colored, and varnished, is $1 50; and when put up in portable cases, $0 75.

MAP OF THE REPUBLIC OF MEXICO,

Compiled from official and other authentic sources: to which is appended a corner map of the States of Central America. 1 sheet. Size, 42 by 32 inches. Price, mounted, $2 00; in cases, $1 50.

MAP OF THE COUNTRY 12 MILES AROUND THE CITY OF NEW YORK,

With the names of property-holders, &c., from an entirely new and accurate survey. By J. C. Sidney. 2 sheets. Size, 40 by 40 inches. Price, mounted or in cases, $3 00.

WESTERN PORTRAITURE;

And Emigrants' Guide: a Description of Wisconsin, Illinois, and Iowa, with Remarks on Minnesota and other Territories. By Daniel S. Curtiss. In 1 vol. 12mo. pp. 360, (illustrated with a township map.) Price, $1 00.

Actual observation and great experience are the bases of this work; and in language and incident it has much to interest. It treats of the "Great West," its scenery, its wild sports, its institutions and its characteristics, material and economic. In that portion devoted to statistical illustration, the topography of sections and the adaptation of localities to particular branches of industry occupy a large space: the geology, soil, climate, powers and productions of each are considered, and their allied interests, their respective values and destinies, and their present conditions, are accurately described.

MAP OF NEW ENGLAND,

Or the Eastern States: together with portions of the State of New York and of the British Provinces adjacent thereto. 4 sheets. Size, 64 by 57 inches. (In progress.)

MAP OF THE PROVINCES OF NEW BRUNSWICK, NOVA SCOTIA, AND PRINCE EDWARD'S ISLAND,

And parts of the country adjacent thereto. 1 sheet. Size, 32 by 29 inches. (In progress.) Price, mounted, $1 50; in cases, $0 75.

STATISTICAL MAP OF THE STATE OF NEW YORK,

Comprising all the principal statistics of each county—agricultural, manufacturing, commercial, &c. By R. S. Fisher, M. D., author of the "Book of the World," &c. 1 sheet. Size, 32 by 26 inches. Price, $0 25.

Useful to all classes of our citizens, and indispensable for the information of parties engaged in the construction of railroads and other internal improvements, speculators in land, and persons designing to settle in any part of the State. All the material interests of the country are plainly indicated in figures on the face of the map, or in the tables which accompany it.

THE SEVENTH CENSUS OF THE UNITED STATES

Of America, compiled from official sources. By Richard S. Fisher, M. D., author of the "Book of the World," &c. Pamphlet of 72 pages, accompanied with a map. Price, $0 25.

This pamphlet contains a vast fund of information. useful to the legislator, merchant, speculator, and editor. Not only the results of the late census, but the aggregates of each former census, are accurately exhibited.

CORDOVA'S MAP OF TEXAS,

Compiled from new and original surveys. 4 sheets. Size, 36 by 34 inches.

Price, mounted, $5 00; in cases, $3 00.

This is the only reliable map of Texas, and being on a large scale, exhibits minutely and with distinctness the natural features of the State and its several political divisions. The following government officers certify to its accuracy and completeness.

"We have no hesitation in saying that no map could surpass this in accuracy and fidelity." DAVID S. KAUFMAN, THOS. J. RUSK, S. PILSBURY, SAM. HOUSTON.

"I certify to the correctness of this map, it being the only one extant that is truly correct." JOHN C. HAYS.

Besides his own publications, J. H. C. has constantly on hand a large assortment of Atlases and Foreign Maps.

Mounting in all its forms carefully executed for the trade public institutions, &c.

www.ingramcontent.com/pod-product-compliance
Lightning Source LLC
LaVergne TN
LVHW010142110826
845151LV00002B/399

* 9 7 8 1 4 2 5 5 3 8 8 3 5 *